藤崎　竜

A reader gave me the red stamp I've used above.

Thank you!!

I'll use it here and there.

Ryu Fujisaki

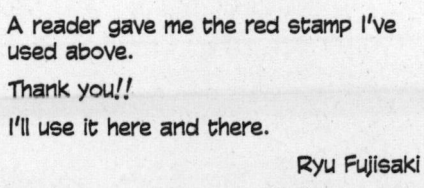

Ryu Fujisaki's *Worlds* came in second place for the prestigious 40th Tezuka Award. His *Psycho +, Wāqwāq* and *Hoshin Engi* have all run in *Weekly Shonen Jump* magazine, and several are available on DVD in Japan and elsewhere. His combination of science fiction, literature and Chinese history made *Hoshin Engi* a mix of genres that truly showcases his amazing art and imagination.

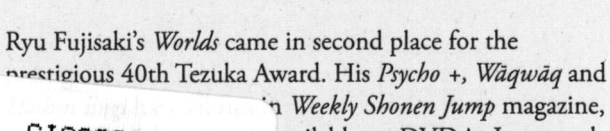

HOSHIN ENGI VOL. 15
The SHONEN JUMP Manga Edition

STORY AND ART BY RYU FUJISAKI
Based on the novel *Hoshin Engi*, translated by Tsutomu Ano,
published by Kodansha Bunko

Translation & Adaptation/Tomo Kimura
Touch-up Art & Lettering/HudsonYards
Design/Matt Hinrichs
Editor/Jonathan Tarbox

VP, Production/Alvin Lu
VP, Publishing Licensing/Rika Inouye
VP, Sales & Product Marketing/Gonzalo Ferreyra
VP, Creative/Linda Espinosa
Publisher/Hyoe Narita

Printed in the U.S.A.

Published by VIZ Media, LLC
P.O. Box 77010
San Francisco, CA 94107

SHONEN JUMP Manga Edition
10 9 8 7 6 5 4 3 2 1
First printing, October 2009

www.viz.com

THE WORLD'S MOST POPULAR MANGA
www.shonenjump.com

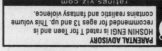

HOSHIN ENGI

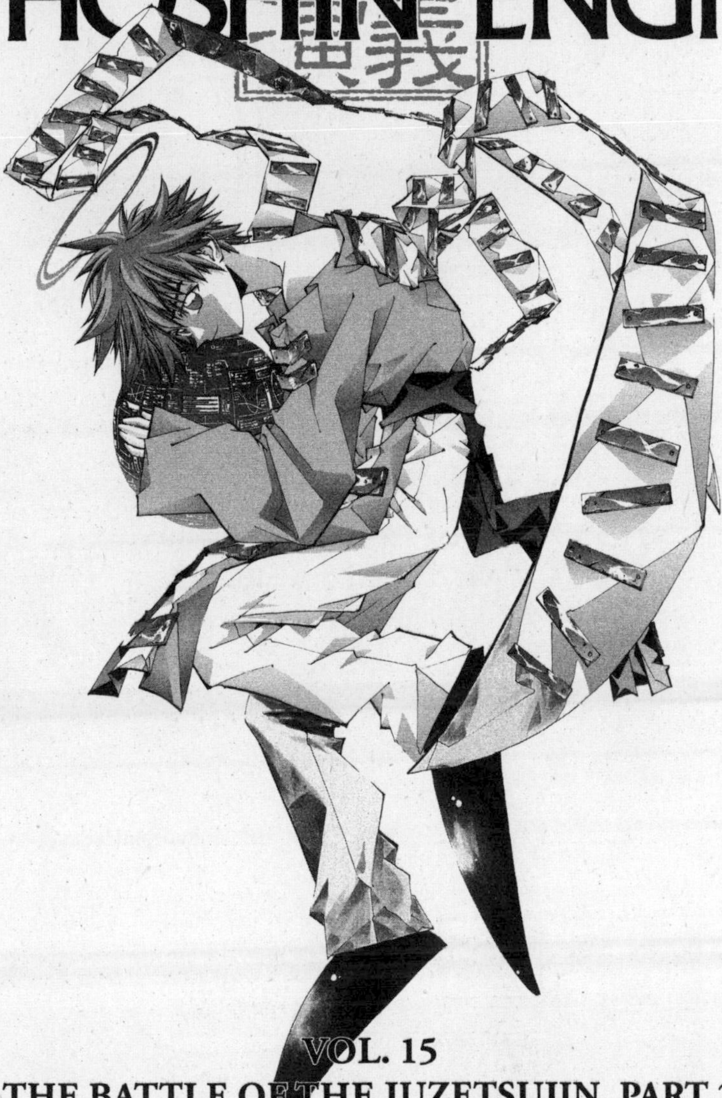

VOL. 15
THE BATTLE OF THE JUZETSUJIN, PART 2
STORY AND ART BY RYU FUJISAKI

THE CHARACTERS

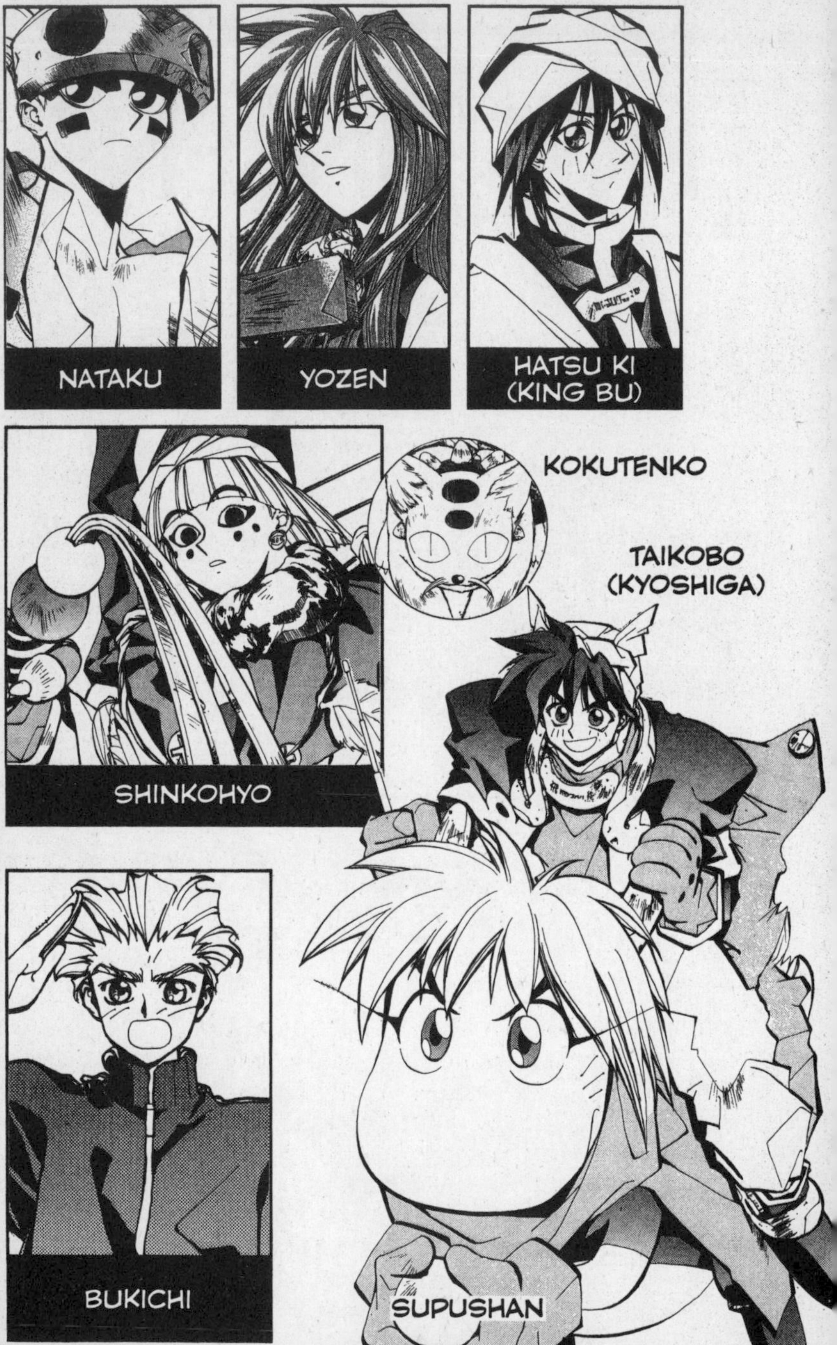
HATSU KI
(KING BU)
YOZEN
NATAKU
KOKUTENKO
TAIKOBO
(KYOSHIGA)
SHINKOHYO
SUPUSHAN
BUKICHI

KING CHU

BUNCHU

DAKKI

OTENKUN

The Story Thus Far

Ancient China, over 3,000 years ago. It is the era of the Yin Dynasty.

After King Chu, the emperor, married the beautiful Dakki, the good king was no longer himself, and became an unmanly and foolish ruler. Dakki, a *Sennyo* with a wicked heart, took control of Yin and the country fell into chaos.

To save the human world, the Hoshin Project was put into action. The project will seal evil Sennin and Doshi into the Shinkai, and cause Seihakuko Sho Ki to set up a new dynasty to replace Yin. Taikobo, who was chosen to execute this project, acts to install Sho Ki's heir Hatsu Ki as the next king. Seiki declares itself the state of Zhou, appoints Taikobo as gunshi, and continues advancing towards Yin. However, due to Bunchu's resurrection and the Kingo Juttenkun joining battle, they are forced to engage in a bitterly fought struggle. Otenkun seals Gyokutei Shinjin, one of the 12 elite Sennin of Kongrong, and the all-out war between Kongrong and Kingo begins!!

VOL. 15
THE BATTLE OF THE JUZETSUJIN, PART 2

CONTENTS

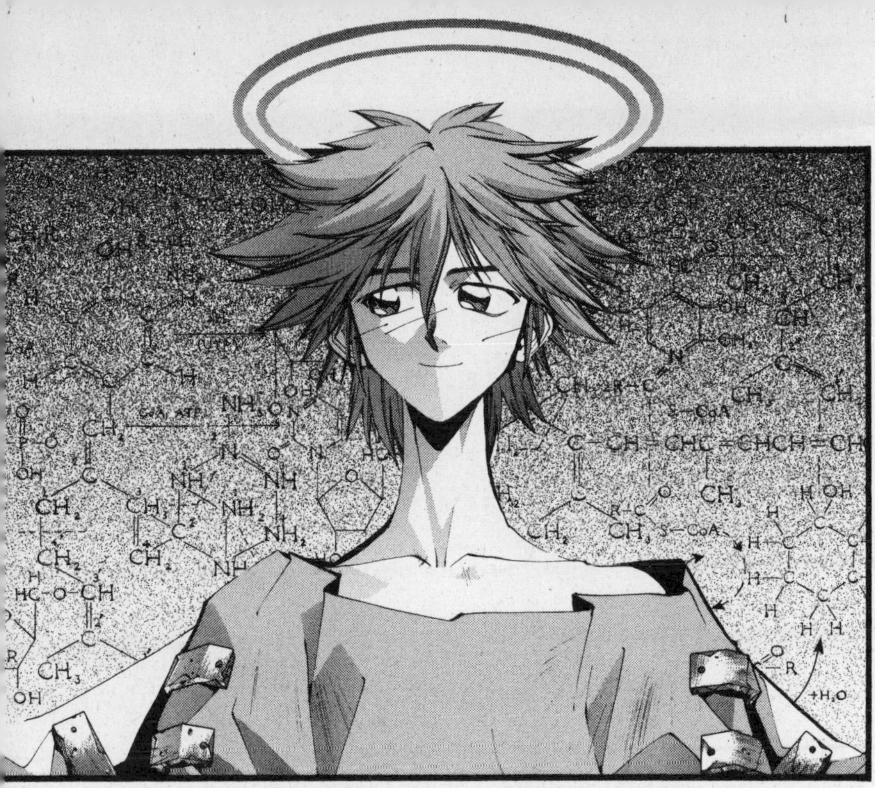

Chapter 125

THE BATTLE OF THE JUZETSUJIN "KANPYOJIN" QUANTUM FORCE

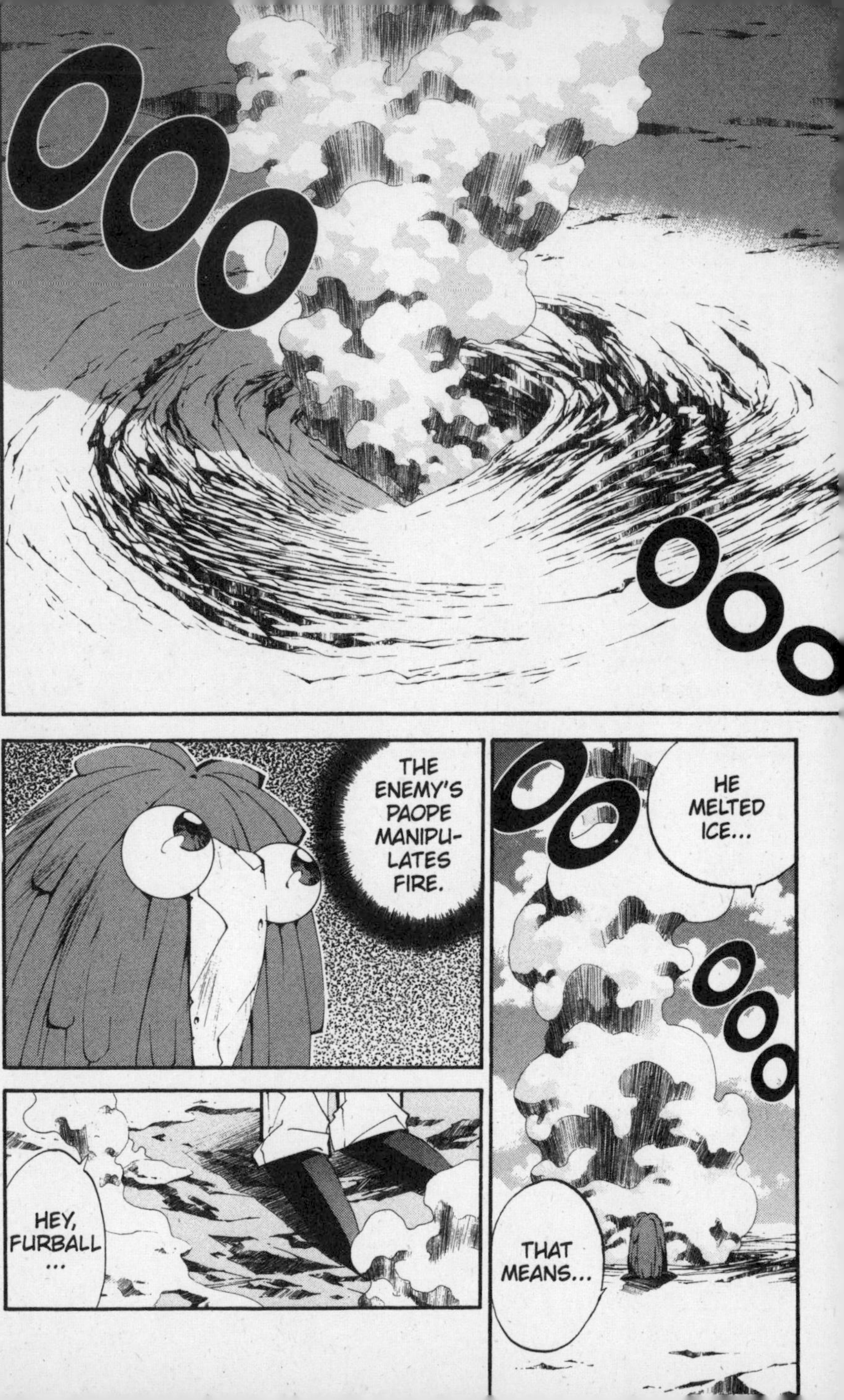
OOO
OOOO
OO
HE MELTED ICE...
OOOO
THAT MEANS...
THE ENEMY'S PAOPE MANIPU-LATES FIRE.
HEY, FURBALL...

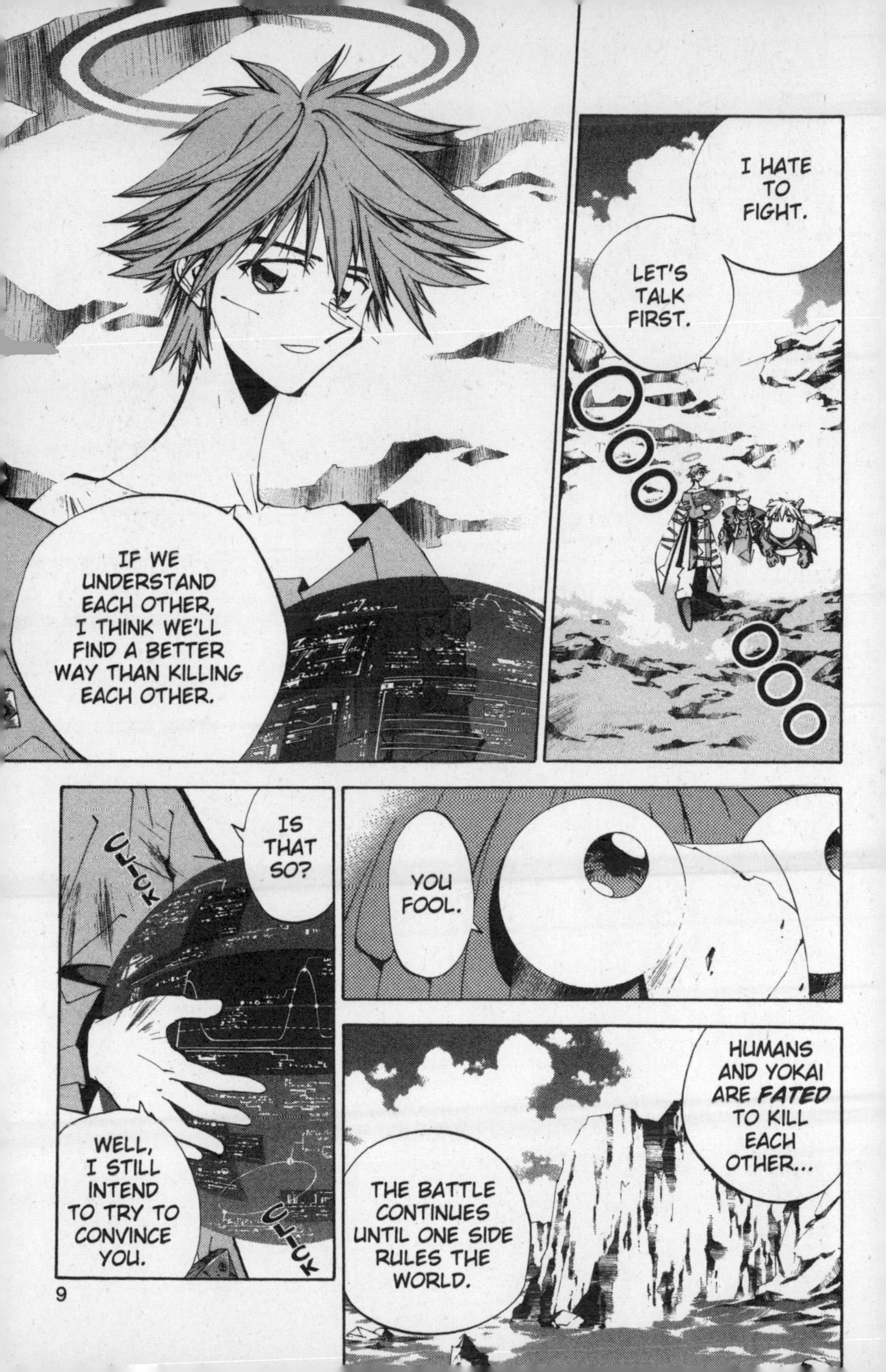
I HATE TO FIGHT.
LET'S TALK FIRST.
IF WE UNDERSTAND EACH OTHER, I THINK WE'LL FIND A BETTER WAY THAN KILLING EACH OTHER.
YOU FOOL.
HUMANS AND YOKAI ARE *FATED* TO KILL EACH OTHER...
THE BATTLE CONTINUES UNTIL ONE SIDE RULES THE WORLD.
IS THAT SO?
CLICK
WELL, I STILL INTEND TO TRY TO CONVINCE YOU.
CLICK

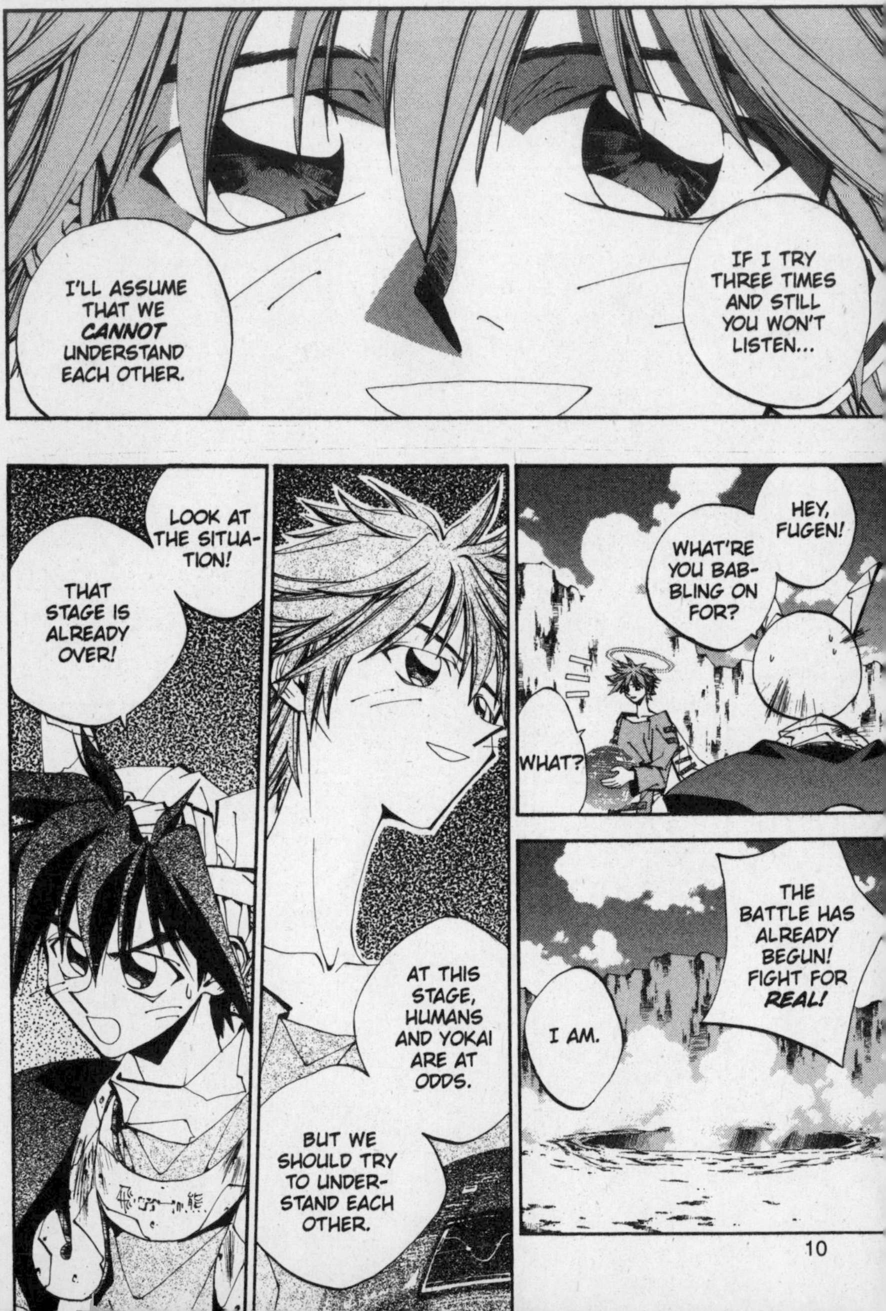
IF I TRY THREE TIMES AND STILL YOU WON'T LISTEN...
I'LL ASSUME THAT WE *CANNOT* UNDERSTAND EACH OTHER.
HEY, FUGEN!
WHAT'RE YOU BAB-BLING ON FOR?
WHAT?
THE BATTLE HAS ALREADY BEGUN! FIGHT FOR ***REAL!***
I AM.
AT THIS STAGE, HUMANS AND YOKAI ARE AT ODDS.
BUT WE SHOULD TRY TO UNDER-STAND EACH OTHER.
LOOK AT THE SITUA-TION!
THAT STAGE IS ALREADY OVER!

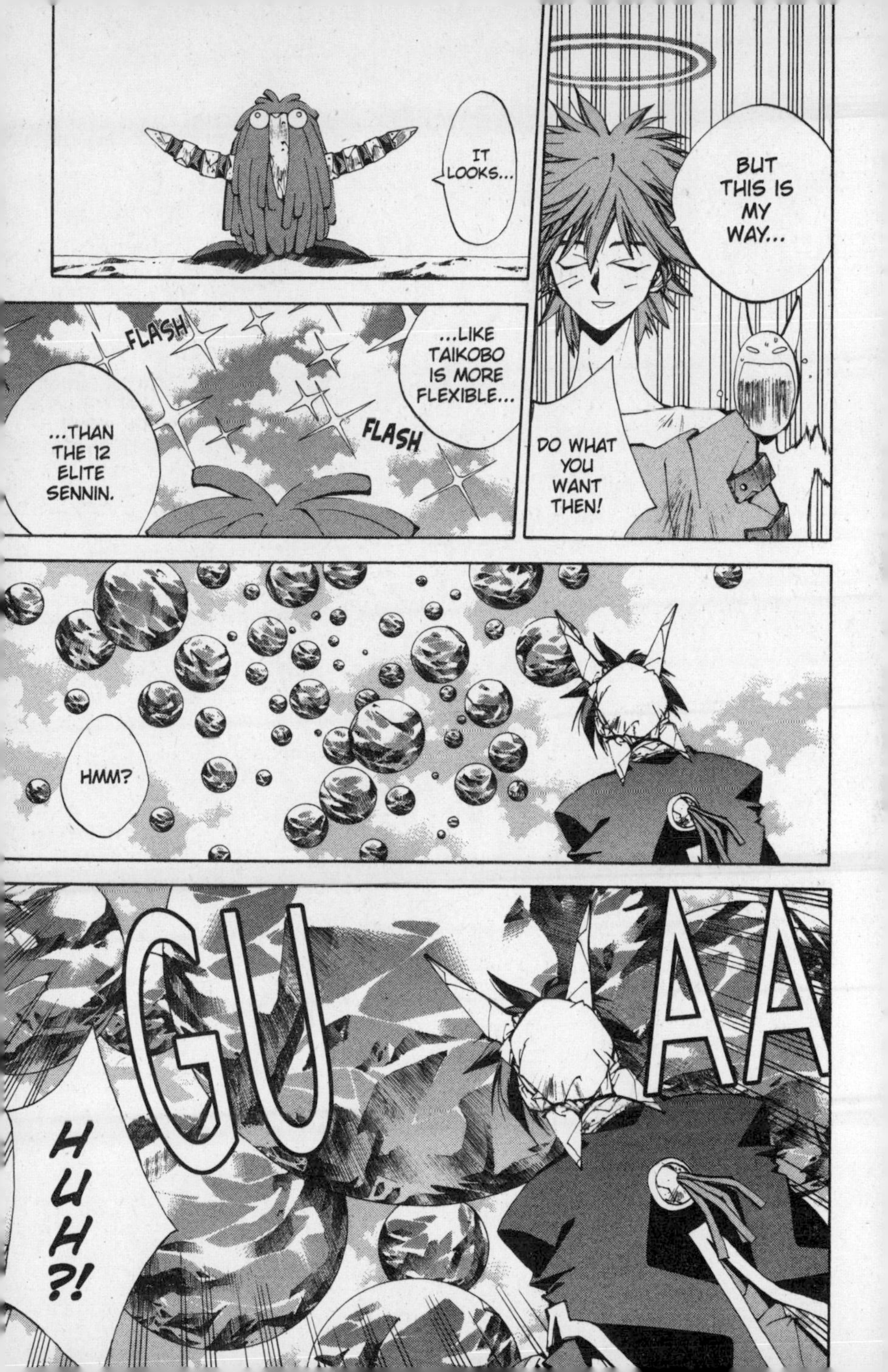
BUT THIS IS MY WAY...
DO WHAT YOU WANT THEN!
IT LOOKS...
...LIKE TAIKOBO IS MORE FLEXIBLE...
FLASH
FLASH
...THAN THE 12 ELITE SENNIN.
HMM?
GU
AA
HUH?!

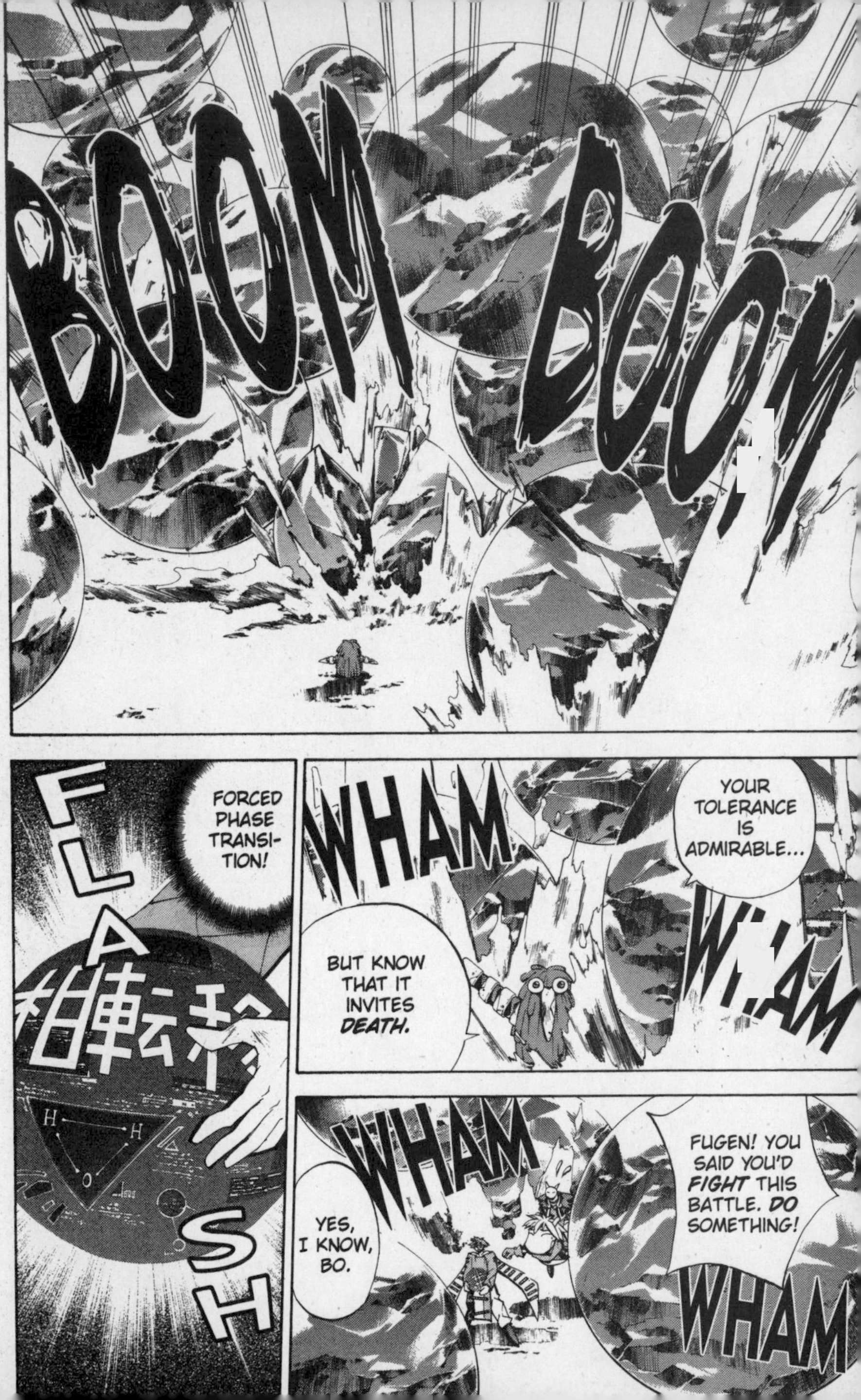

BOOM
BOOM
YOUR TOLERANCE IS ADMIRABLE...
WHAM
BUT KNOW THAT IT INVITES *DEATH.*
FUGEN! YOU SAID YOU'D *FIGHT* THIS BATTLE. *DO* SOMETHING!
WHAM
WHAM
YES, I KNOW, BO.
FORCED PHASE TRANSITION!
FLASH
相転移

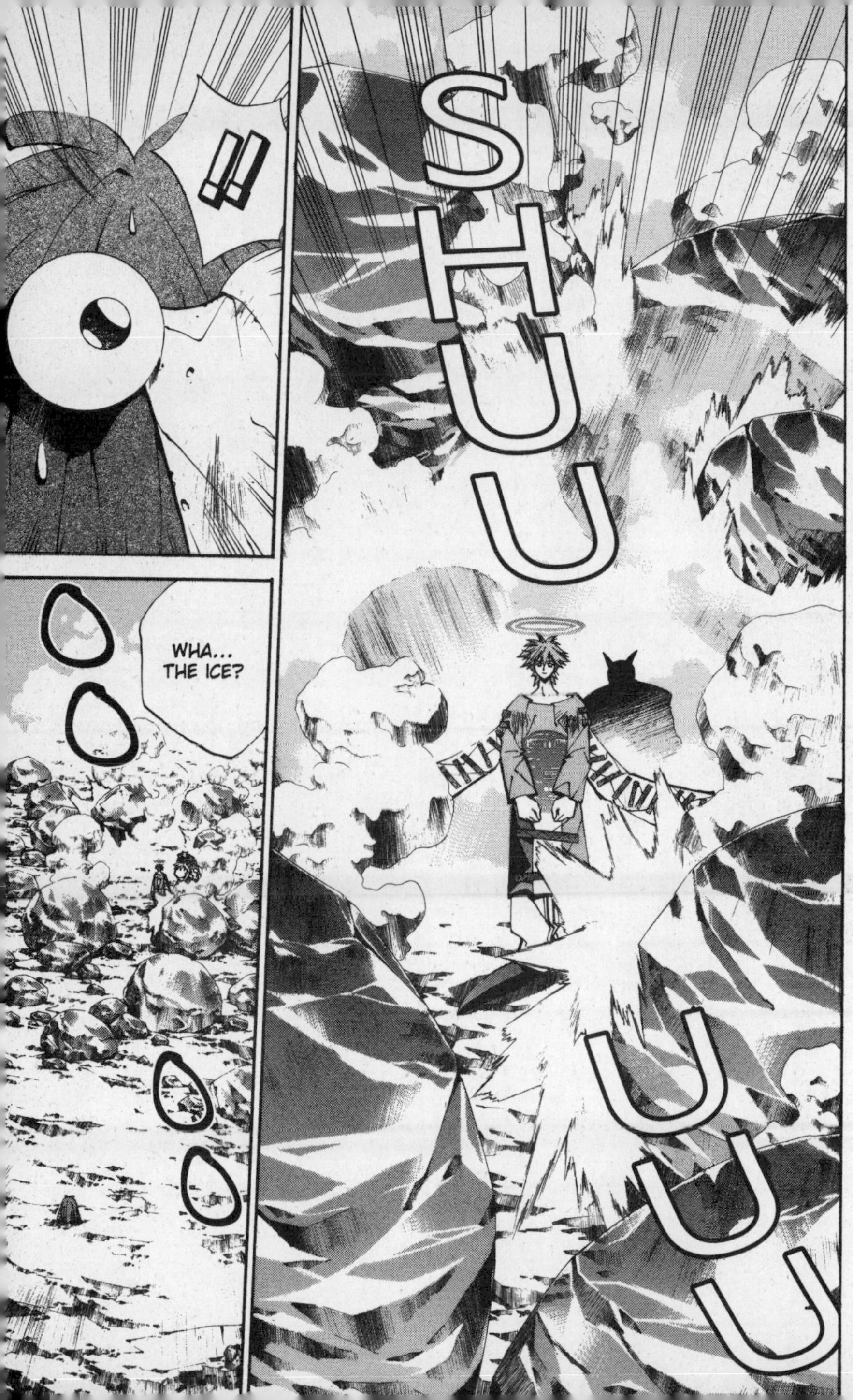
SHUU
UUU
!!
WHA... THE ICE?

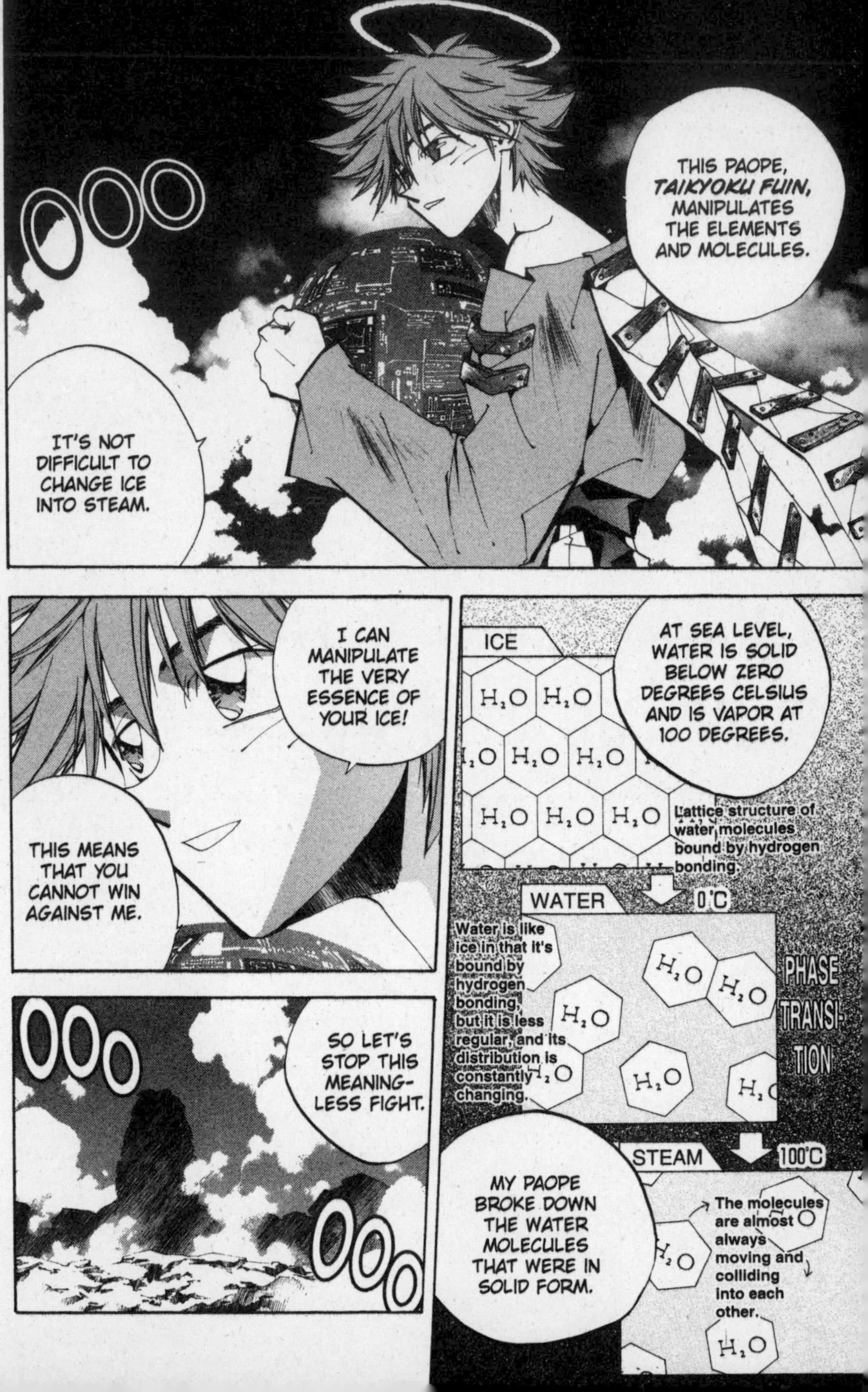
OOO
THIS PAOPE, *TAIKYOKU FUIN*, MANIPULATES THE ELEMENTS AND MOLECULES.
IT'S NOT DIFFICULT TO CHANGE ICE INTO STEAM.
AT SEA LEVEL, WATER IS SOLID BELOW ZERO DEGREES CELSIUS AND IS VAPOR AT 100 DEGREES.
ICE
Lattice structure of water molecules bound by hydrogen bonding.
WATER
0°C
Water is like ice in that it's bound by hydrogen bonding, but it is less regular, and its distribution is constantly changing.
PHASE TRANSITION
STEAM
100°C
MY PAOPE BROKE DOWN THE WATER MOLECULES THAT WERE IN SOLID FORM.
The molecules are almost always moving and colliding into each other.
I CAN MANIPULATE THE VERY ESSENCE OF YOUR ICE!
THIS MEANS THAT YOU CANNOT WIN AGAINST ME.
OOO
SO LET'S STOP THIS MEANINGLESS FIGHT.
OOO

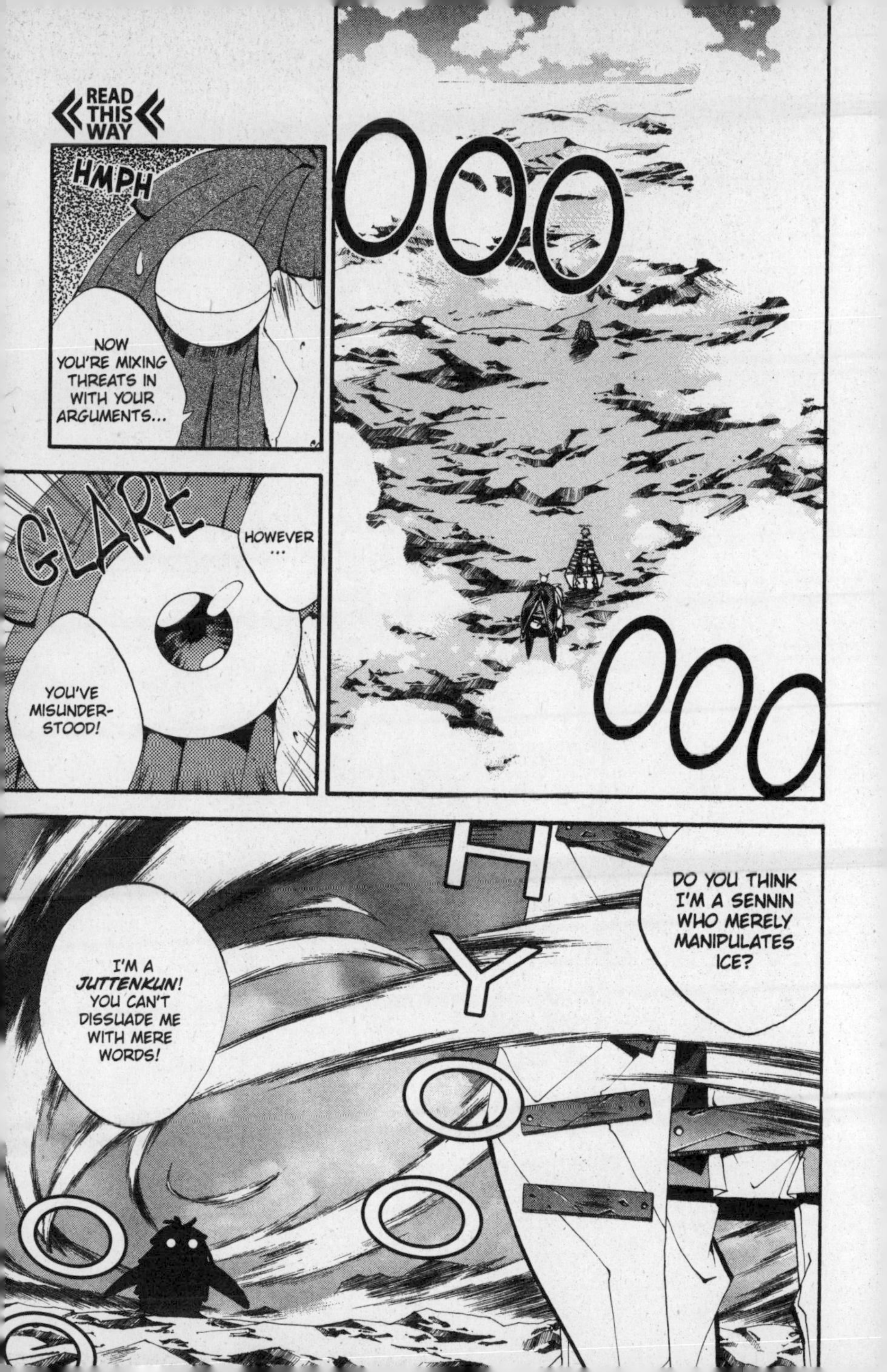
READ THIS WAY
OOO
OOO
HMPH
NOW YOU'RE MIXING THREATS IN WITH YOUR ARGUMENTS...
GLARE
HOWEVER...
YOU'VE MISUNDERSTOOD!
HY
DO YOU THINK I'M A SENNIN WHO MERELY MANIPULATES ICE?
I'M A *JUTTENKUN*! YOU CAN'T DISSUADE ME WITH MERE WORDS!

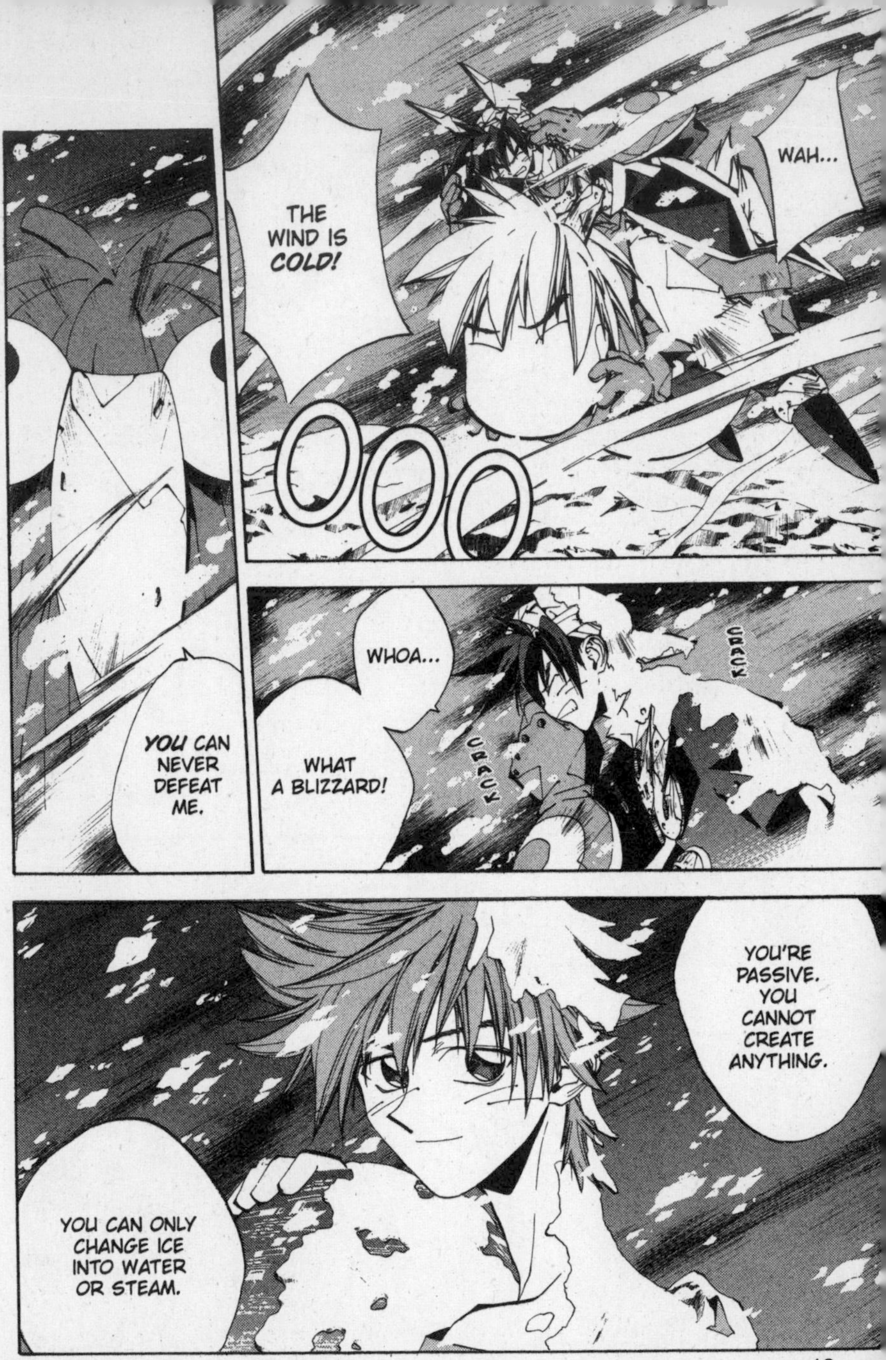
WAH...
THE WIND IS COLD!
WHOA...
WHAT A BLIZZARD!
CRACK
CRACK
YOU CAN NEVER DEFEAT ME.
YOU'RE PASSIVE. YOU CANNOT CREATE ANYTHING.
YOU CAN ONLY CHANGE ICE INTO WATER OR STEAM.

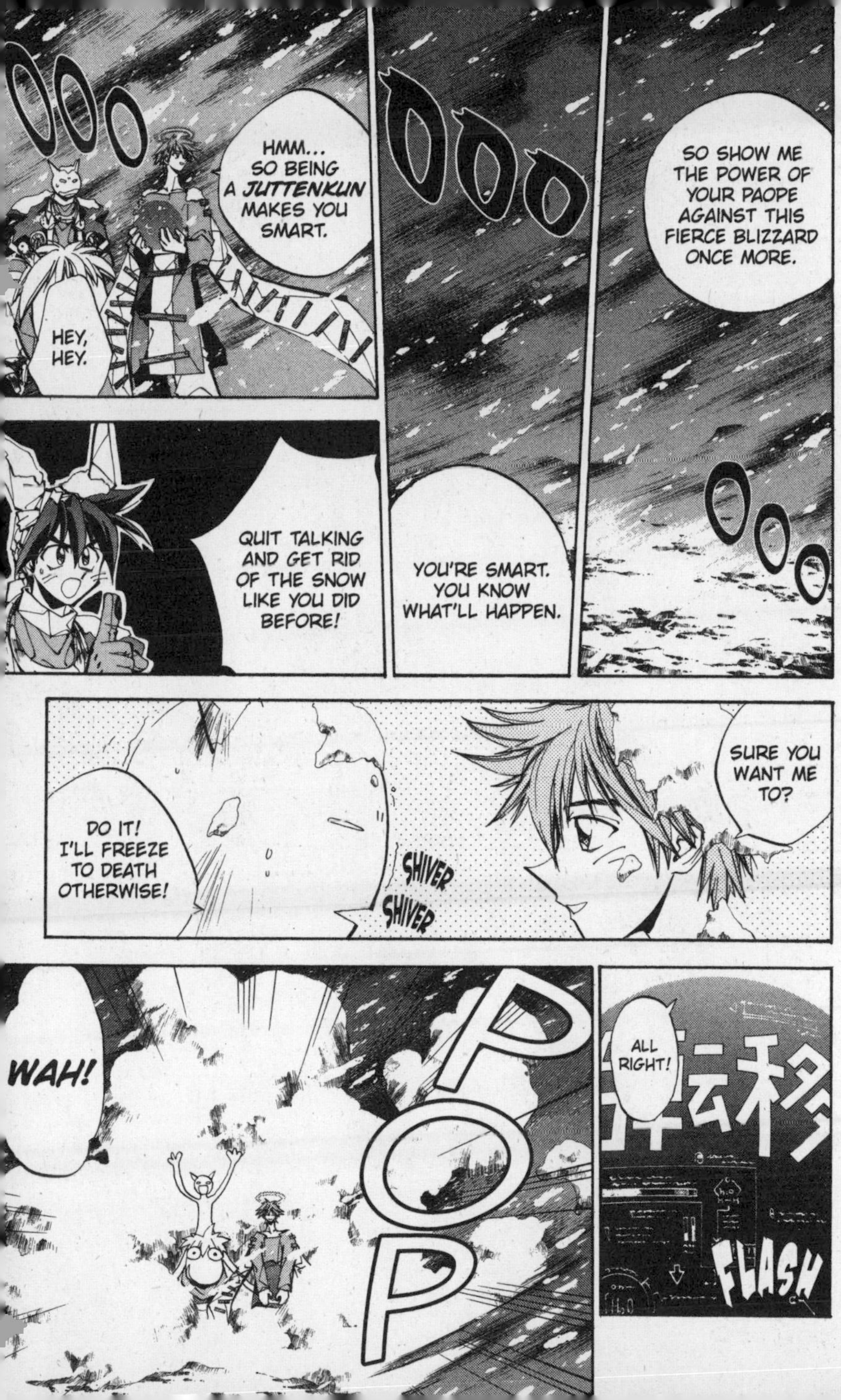

SO SHOW ME THE POWER OF YOUR PAOPE AGAINST THIS FIERCE BLIZZARD ONCE MORE.
YOU'RE SMART. YOU KNOW WHAT'LL HAPPEN.
HMM... SO BEING A *JUTTENKUN* MAKES YOU SMART.
HEY, HEY.
QUIT TALKING AND GET RID OF THE SNOW LIKE YOU DID BEFORE!
SURE YOU WANT ME TO?
SHIVER
SHIVER
DO IT! I'LL FREEZE TO DEATH OTHERWISE!
ALL RIGHT!
FLASH
POP
WAH!

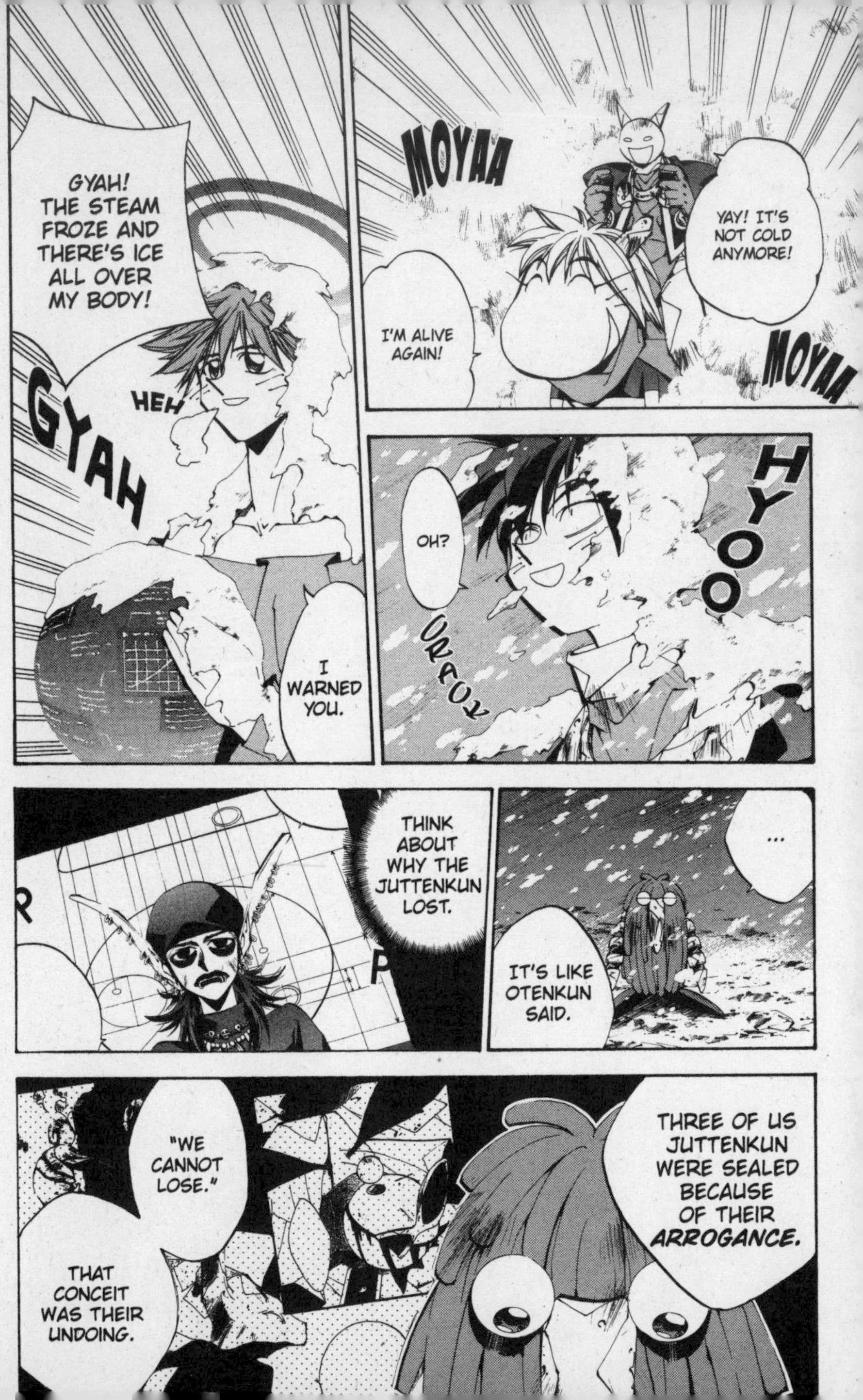
MOYAA
YAY! IT'S NOT COLD ANYMORE!
I'M ALIVE AGAIN!
MOYAA
HYOOO
OH?
GYAH! THE STEAM FROZE AND THERE'S ICE ALL OVER MY BODY!
HEH
GYAH
I WARNED YOU.
...
IT'S LIKE OTENKUN SAID.
THINK ABOUT WHY THE JUTTENKUN LOST.
THREE OF US JUTTENKUN WERE SEALED BECAUSE OF THEIR ARROGANCE.
"WE CANNOT LOSE."
THAT CONCEIT WAS THEIR UNDOING.

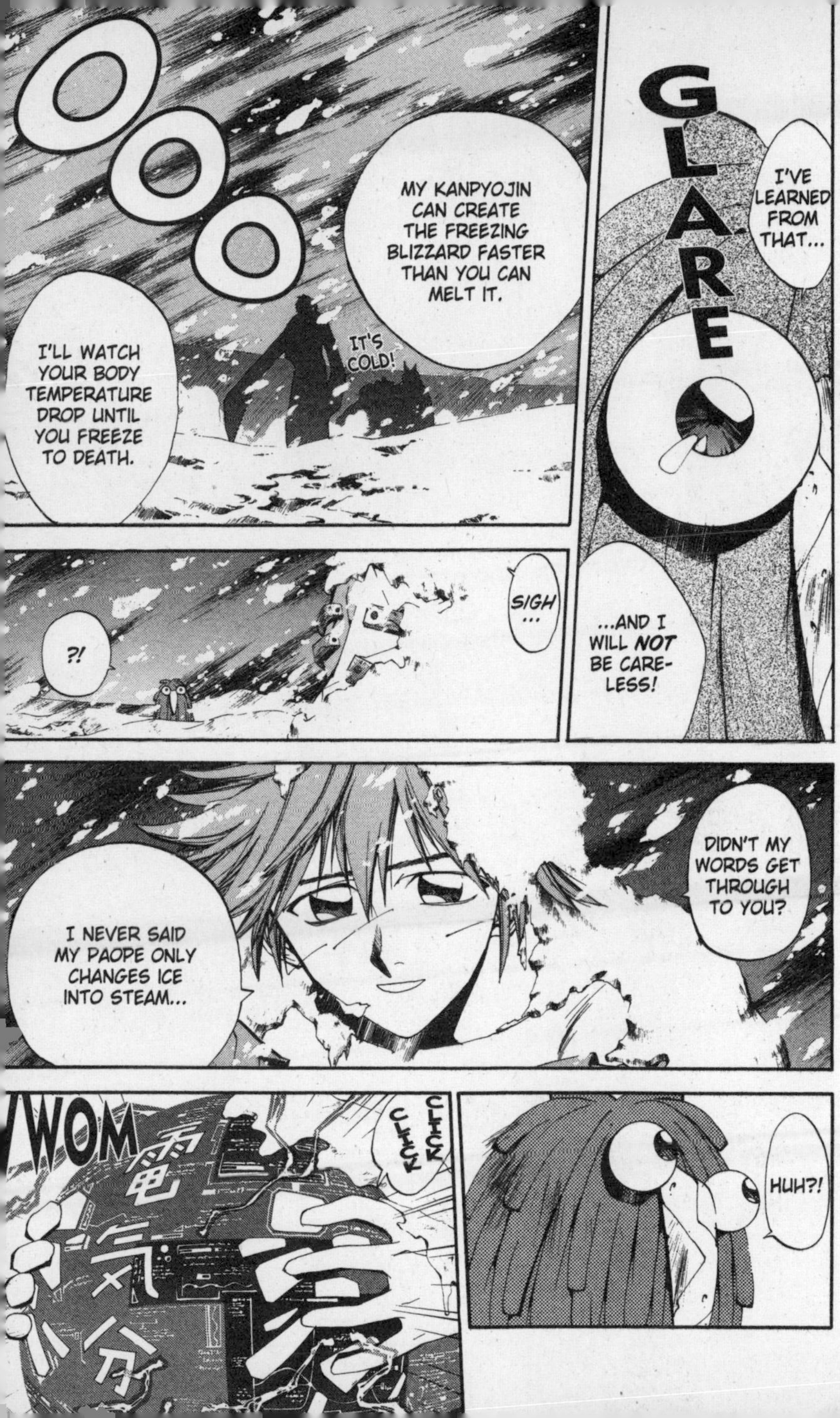
GLARE
I'VE LEARNED FROM THAT...
...AND I WILL *NOT* BE CARE-LESS!
OOOO
MY KANPYOJIN CAN CREATE THE FREEZING BLIZZARD FASTER THAN YOU CAN MELT IT.
IT'S COLD!
I'LL WATCH YOUR BODY TEMPERATURE DROP UNTIL YOU FREEZE TO DEATH.
SIGH...
?!
DIDN'T MY WORDS GET THROUGH TO YOU?
I NEVER SAID MY PAOPE ONLY CHANGES ICE INTO STEAM...
HUH?!
CLICK CLICK
WOM

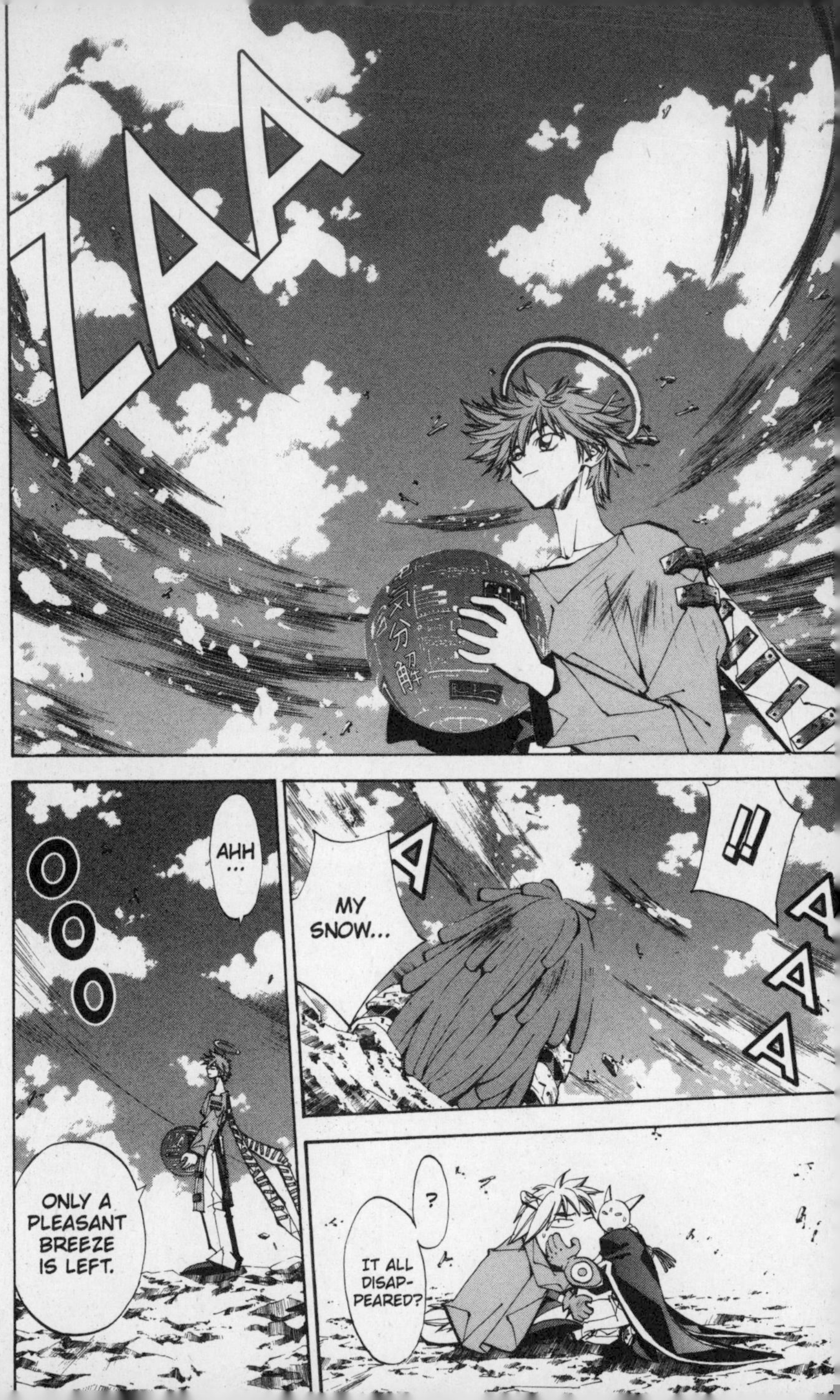
ZAA
!!
AAA
MY SNOW...
A
?
IT ALL DISAP-PEARED?
AHH ...
OOO
ONLY A PLEASANT BREEZE IS LEFT.

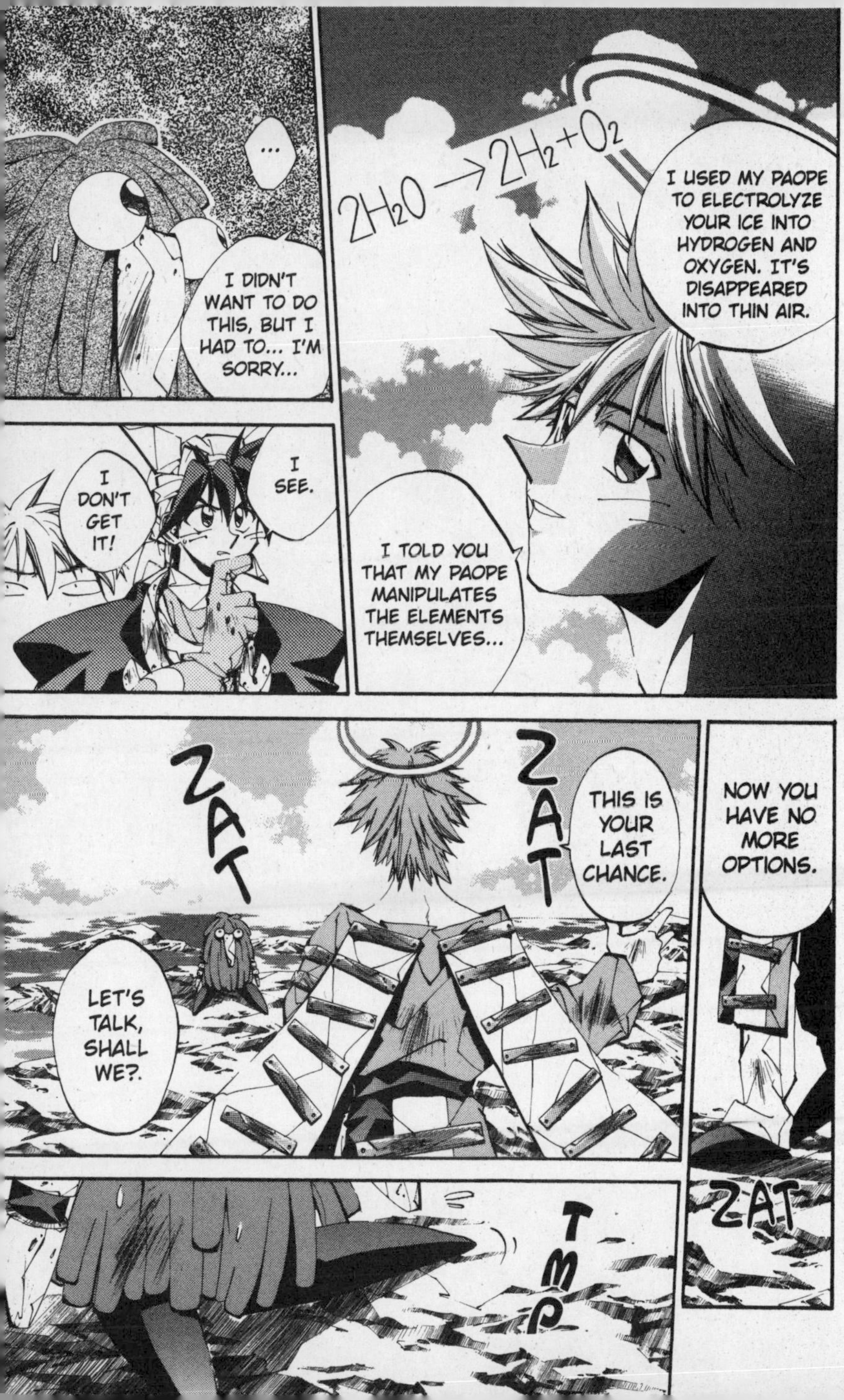
$2H_2O \rightarrow 2H_2 + O_2$
I USED MY PAOPE TO ELECTROLYZE YOUR ICE INTO HYDROGEN AND OXYGEN. IT'S DISAPPEARED INTO THIN AIR.
I TOLD YOU THAT MY PAOPE MANIPULATES THE ELEMENTS THEMSELVES...
...
I DIDN'T WANT TO DO THIS, BUT I HAD TO... I'M SORRY...
I SEE.
I DON'T GET IT!
NOW YOU HAVE NO MORE OPTIONS.
ZAT
THIS IS YOUR LAST CHANCE.
ZAT
LET'S TALK, SHALL WE?.
ZAT
TMP

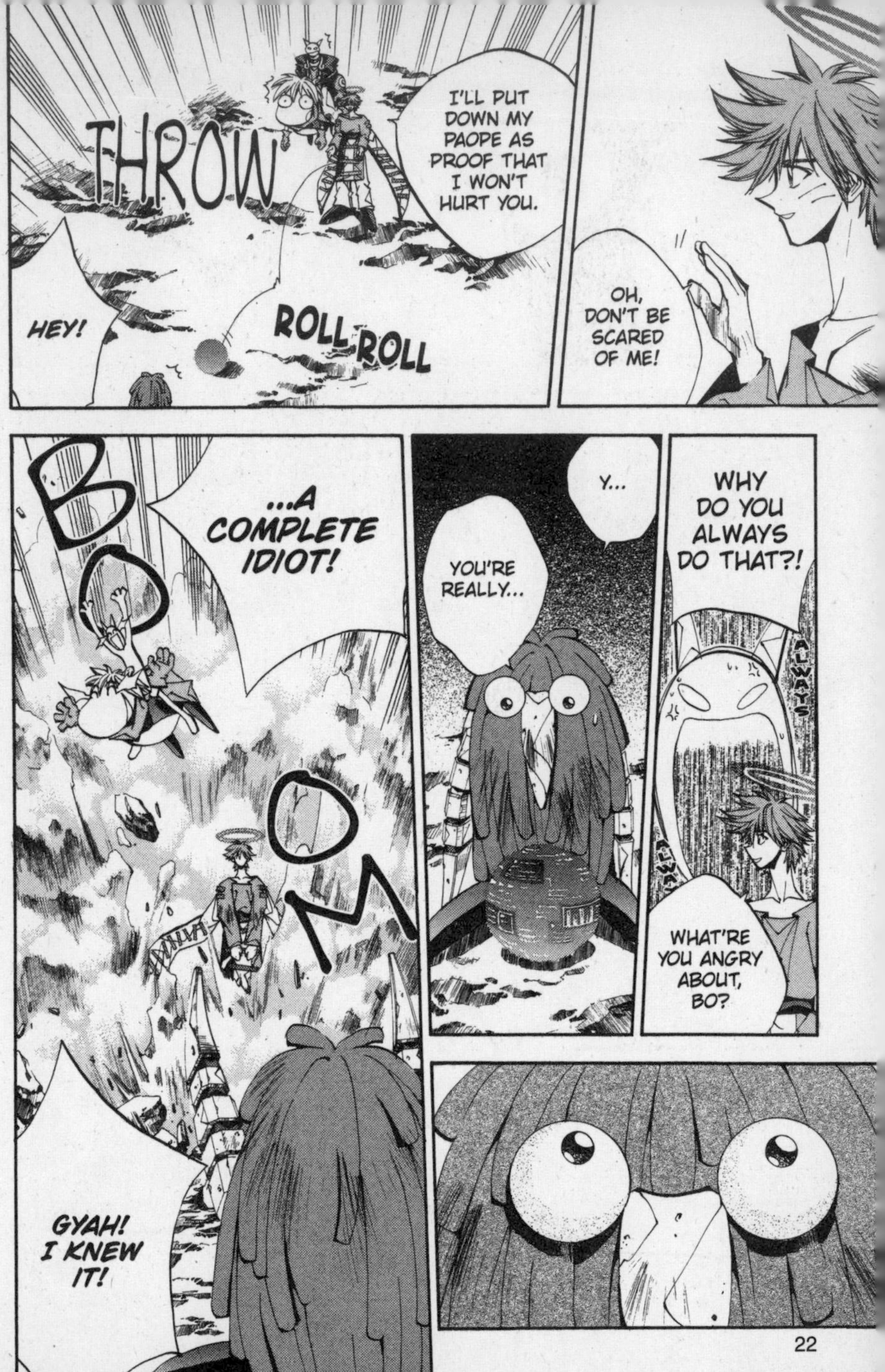
OH, DON'T BE SCARED OF ME!
I'LL PUT DOWN MY PAOPE AS PROOF THAT I WON'T HURT YOU.
THROW
ROLL ROLL
HEY!
WHY DO YOU ALWAYS DO THAT?!
ALWAYS
ALWAYS
WHAT'RE YOU ANGRY ABOUT, BO?
Y...
YOU'RE REALLY...
BOOM
...A COMPLETE IDIOT!
GYAH! I KNEW IT!

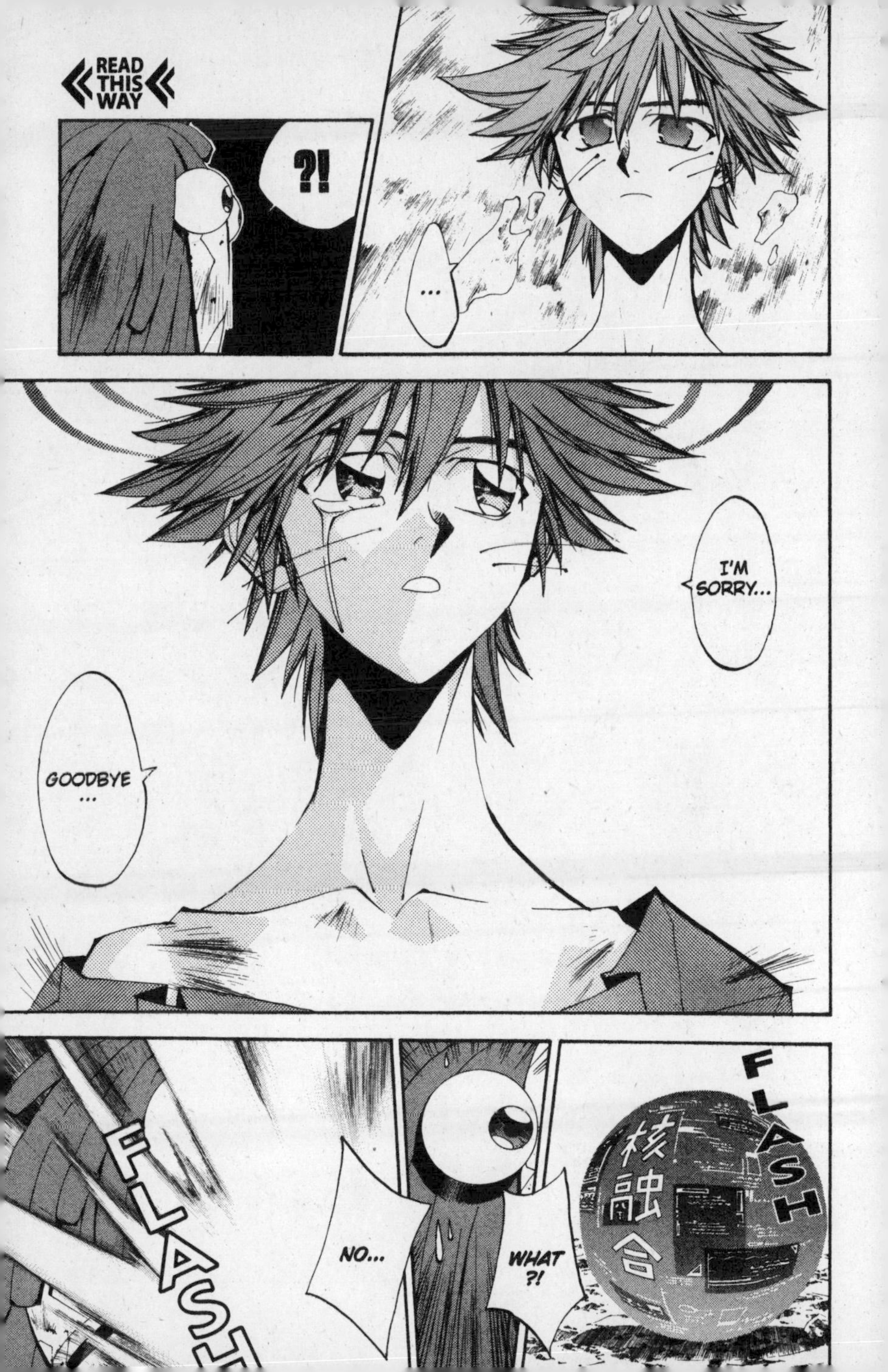
READ THIS WAY
…
?!
I'M SORRY…
GOODBYE …
FLASH
核融合
WHAT ?!
NO…
FLASH

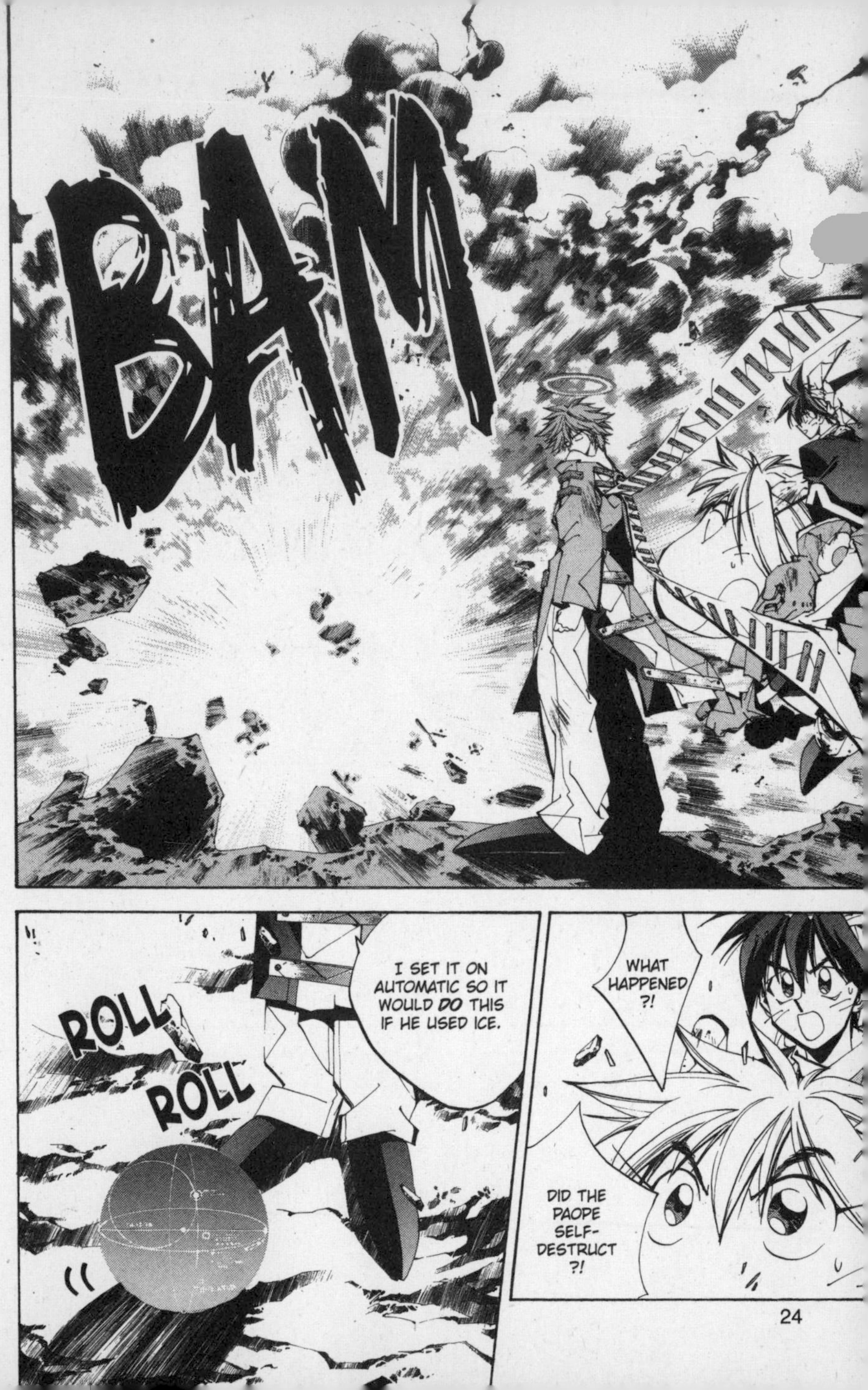
BAM
WHAT HAPPENED ?!
DID THE PAOPE SELF-DESTRUCT ?!
I SET IT ON AUTOMATIC SO IT WOULD *DO* THIS IF HE USED ICE.
ROLL
ROLL

READ THIS WAY

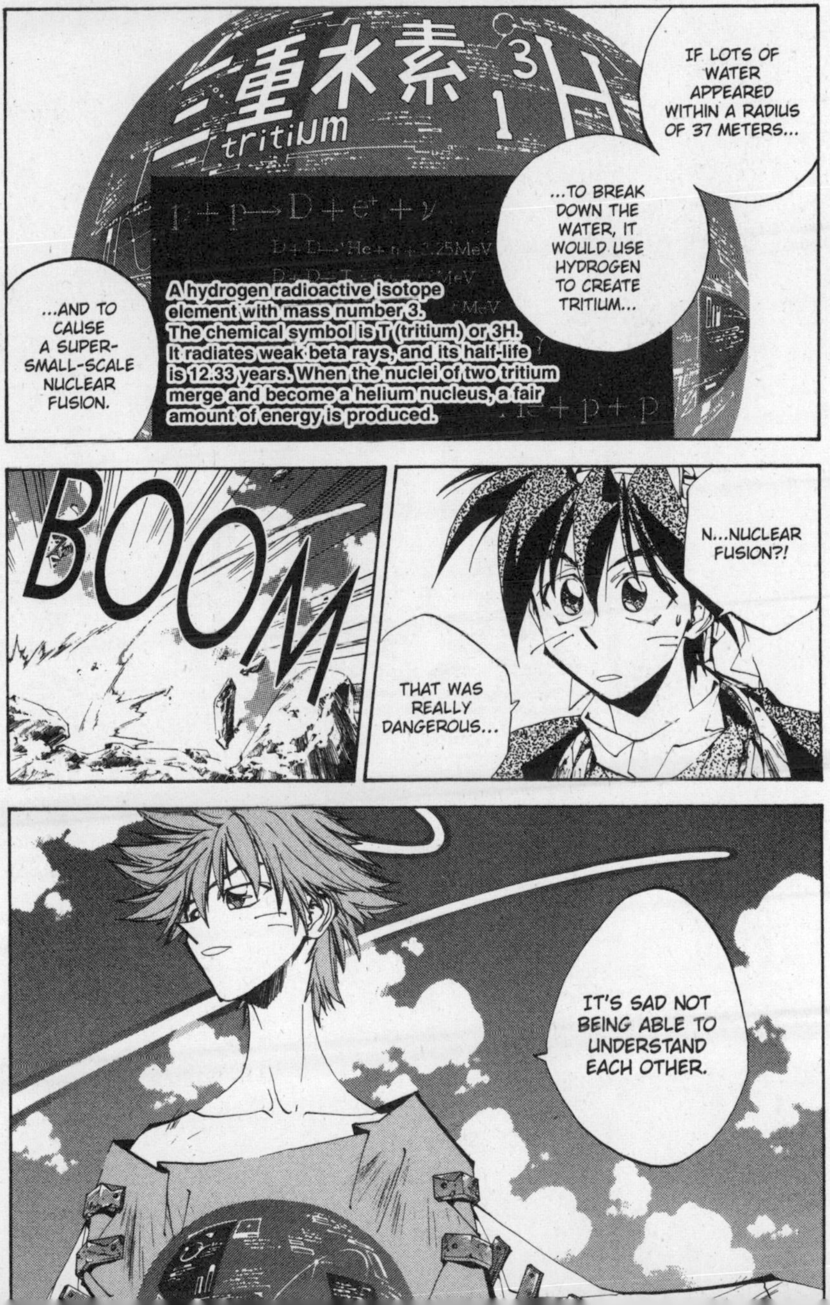
IF LOTS OF WATER APPEARED WITHIN A RADIUS OF 37 METERS...
...TO BREAK DOWN THE WATER, IT WOULD USE HYDROGEN TO CREATE TRITIUM...
...AND TO CAUSE A SUPER-SMALL-SCALE NUCLEAR FUSION.
三重水素 tritium
A hydrogen radioactive isotope element with mass number 3. The chemical symbol is T (tritium) or 3H. It radiates weak beta rays, and its half-life is 12.33 years. When the nuclei of two tritium merge and become a helium nucleus, a fair amount of energy is produced.
N...NUCLEAR FUSION?!
THAT WAS REALLY DANGEROUS...
BOOM
IT'S SAD NOT BEING ABLE TO UNDERSTAND EACH OTHER.

封神演義

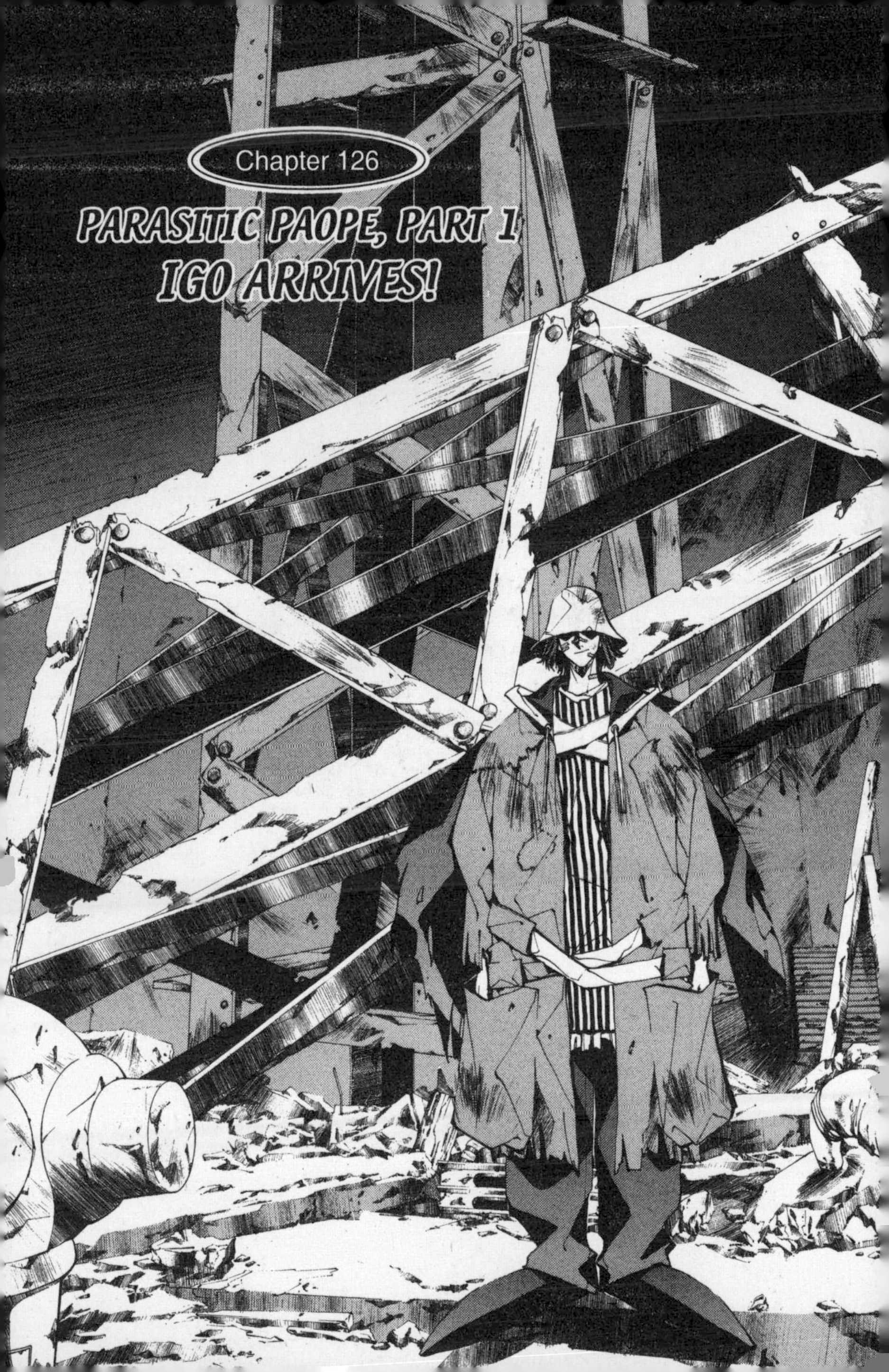
Chapter 126
PARASITIC PAOPE, PART 1
IGO ARRIVES!

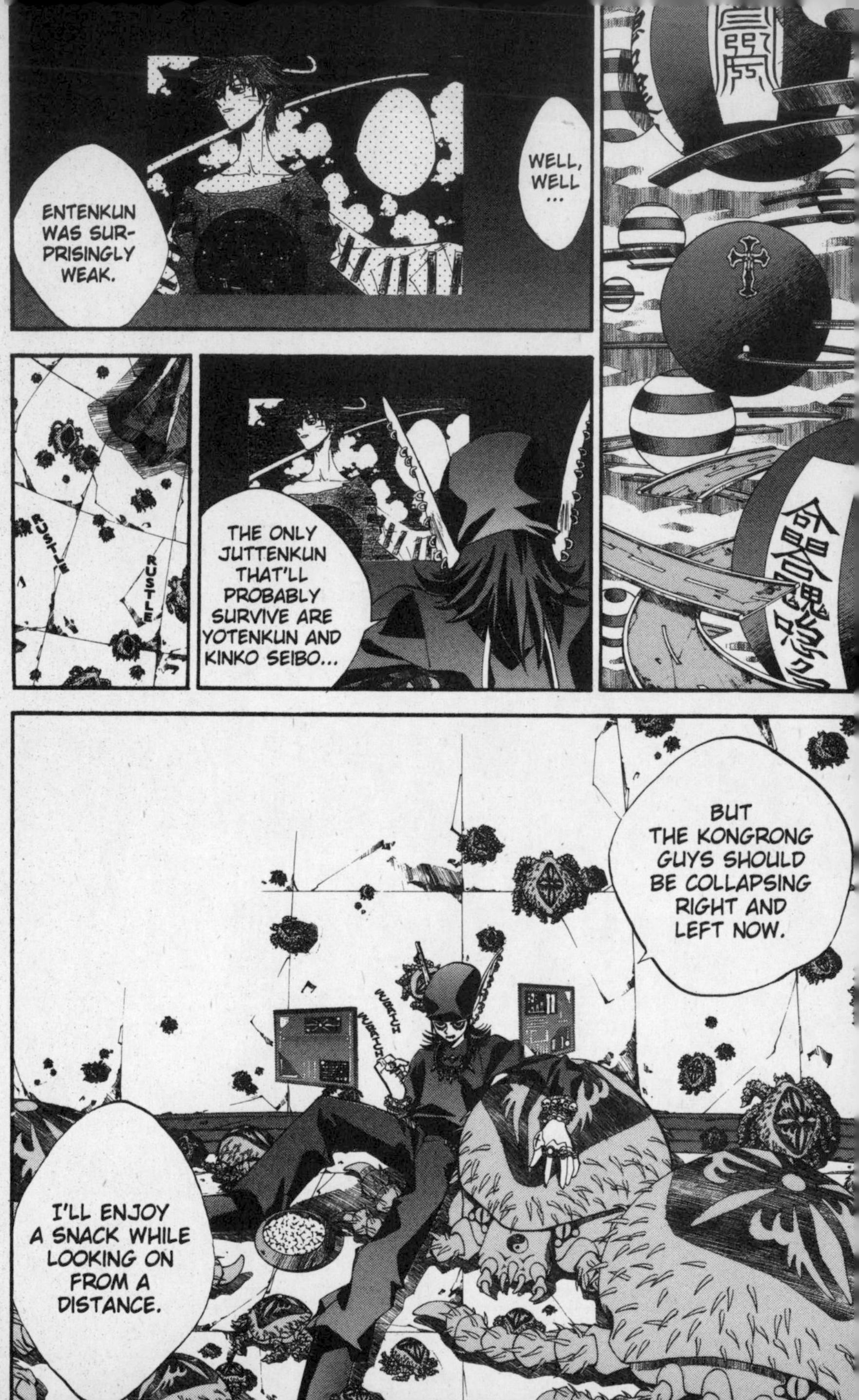
WELL, WELL...
ENTENKUN WAS SURPRISINGLY WEAK.
THE ONLY JUTTENKUN THAT'LL PROBABLY SURVIVE ARE YOTENKUN AND KINKO SEIBO...
RUSTLE
RUSTLE
BUT THE KONGRONG GUYS SHOULD BE COLLAPSING RIGHT AND LEFT NOW.
I'LL ENJOY A SNACK WHILE LOOKING ON FROM A DISTANCE.

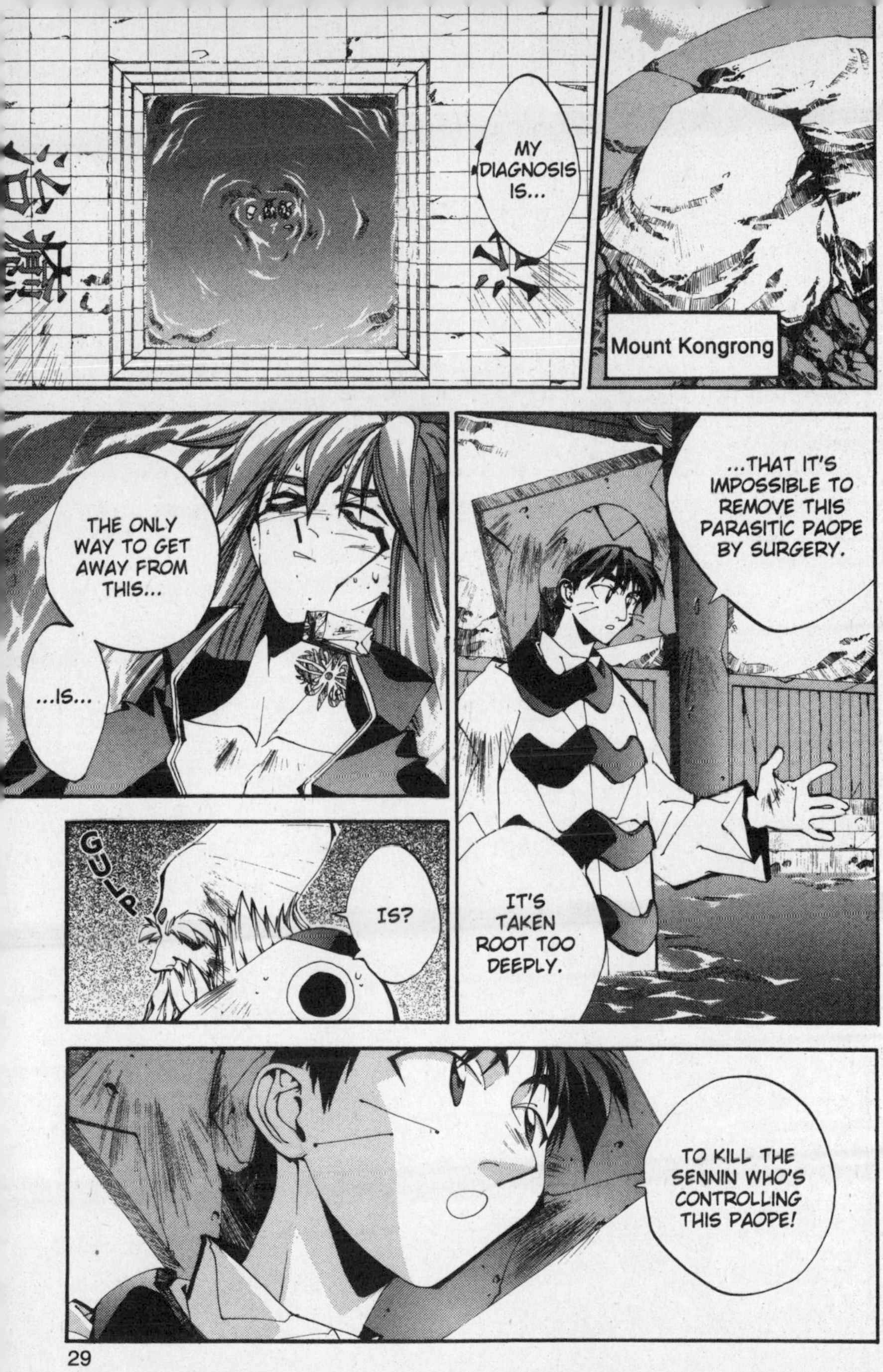
Mount Kongrong
MY DIAGNOSIS IS...
...THAT IT'S IMPOSSIBLE TO REMOVE THIS PARASITIC PAOPE BY SURGERY.
IT'S TAKEN ROOT TOO DEEPLY.
THE ONLY WAY TO GET AWAY FROM THIS...
...IS...
GULP
IS?
TO KILL THE SENNIN WHO'S CONTROLLING THIS PAOPE!

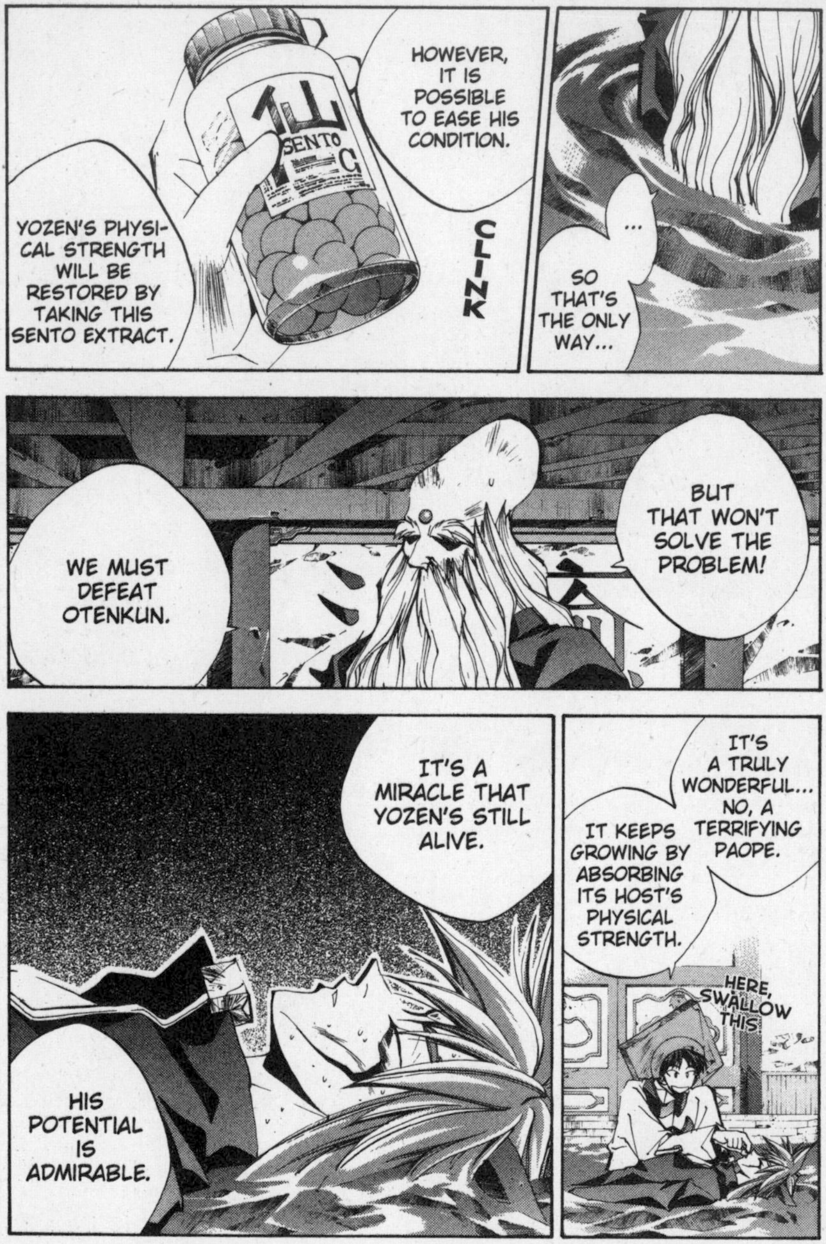
...
SO THAT'S THE ONLY WAY...
HOWEVER, IT IS POSSIBLE TO EASE HIS CONDITION.
SENTO
CLINK
YOZEN'S PHYSICAL STRENGTH WILL BE RESTORED BY TAKING THIS SENTO EXTRACT.
BUT THAT WON'T SOLVE THE PROBLEM!
WE MUST DEFEAT OTENKUN.
IT'S A TRULY WONDERFUL... NO, A TERRIFYING PAOPE.
IT KEEPS GROWING BY ABSORBING ITS HOST'S PHYSICAL STRENGTH.
HERE, SWALLOW THIS.
IT'S A MIRACLE THAT YOZEN'S STILL ALIVE.
HIS POTENTIAL IS ADMIRABLE.

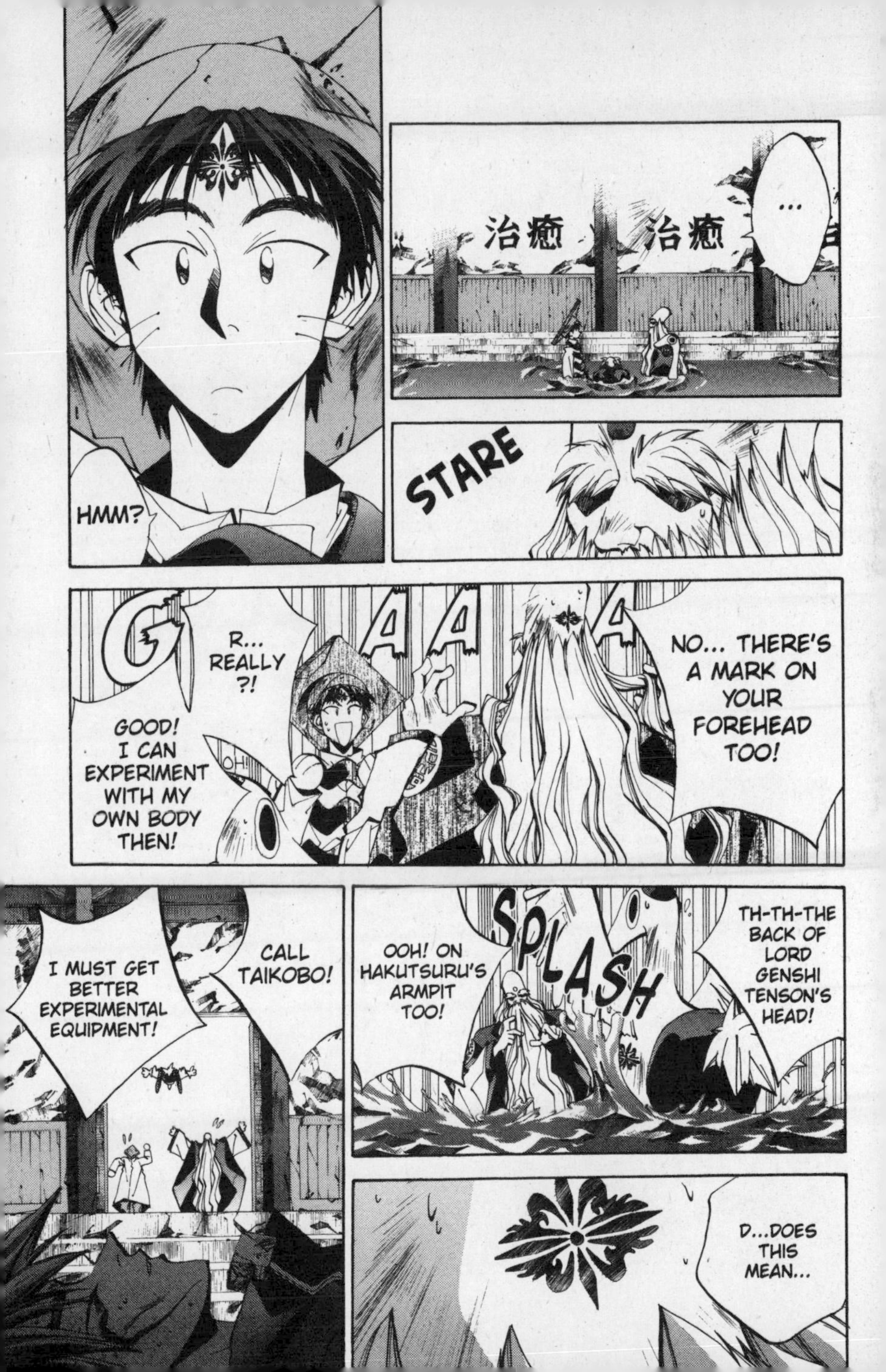
...
治癒 治癒
STARE
HMM?
NO... THERE'S A MARK ON YOUR FOREHEAD TOO!
GAAA
R... REALLY ?!
GOOD! I CAN EXPERIMENT WITH MY OWN BODY THEN!
OH!
TH-TH-THE BACK OF LORD GENSHI TENSON'S HEAD!
SPLASH
OOH! ON HAKUTSURU'S ARMPIT TOO!
D...DOES THIS MEAN...
CALL TAIKOBO!
I MUST GET BETTER EXPERIMENTAL EQUIPMENT!

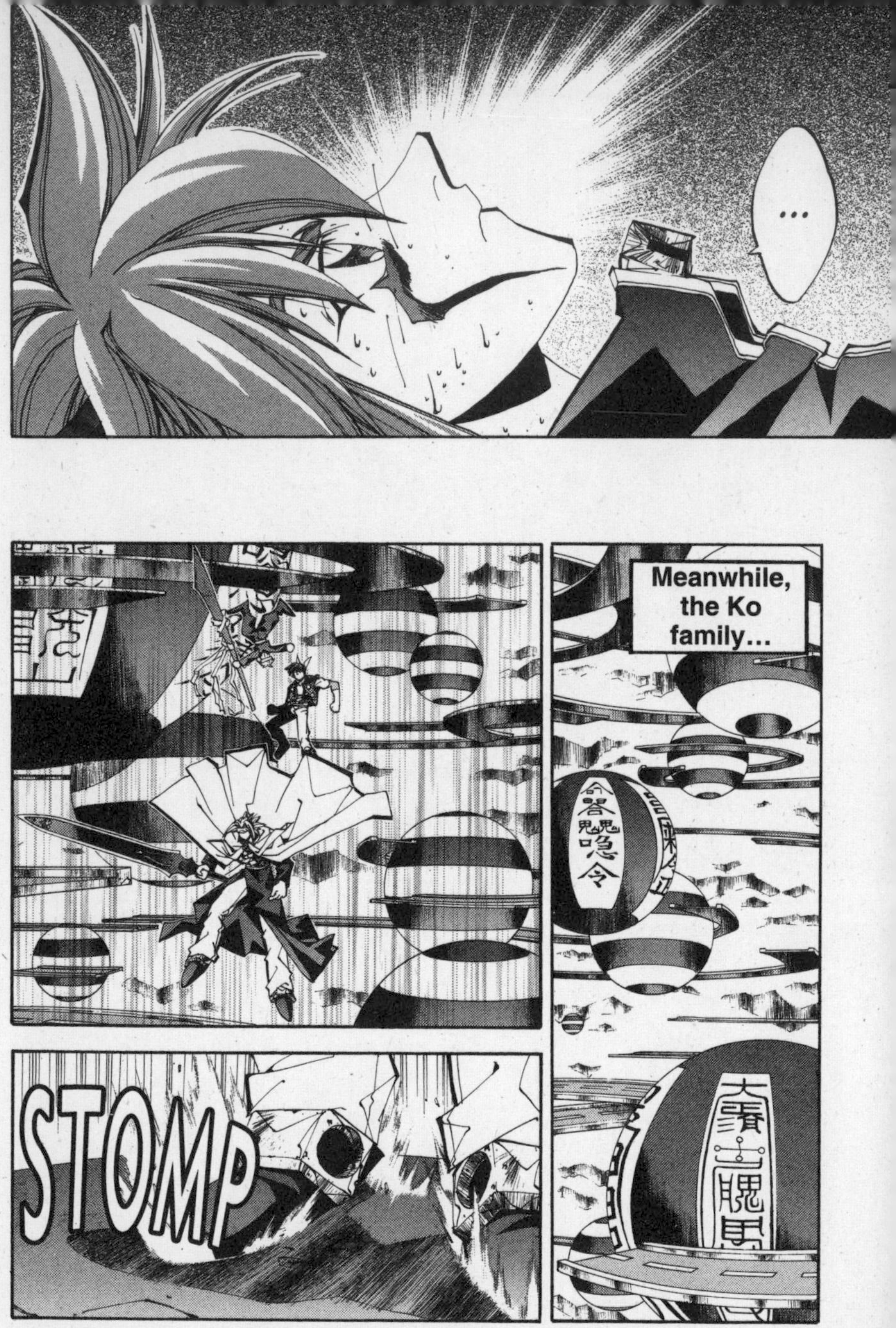
...
Meanwhile, the Ko family...
STOMP

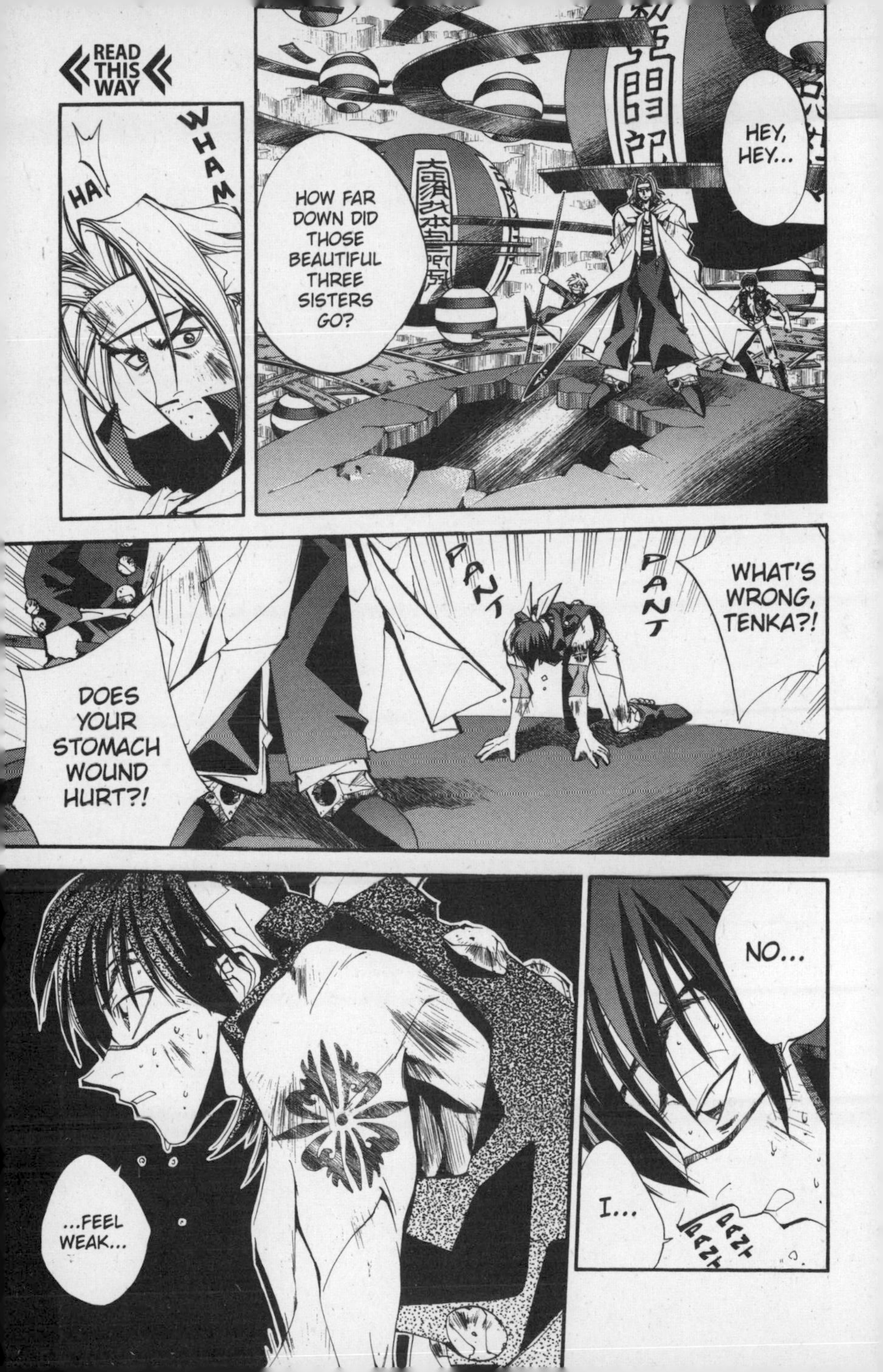
READ THIS WAY
HEY, HEY...
HOW FAR DOWN DID THOSE BEAUTIFUL THREE SISTERS GO?
WHAM
HA
WHAT'S WRONG, TENKA?!
PANT
PANT
DOES YOUR STOMACH WOUND HURT?!
NO...
I...
...FEEL WEAK...

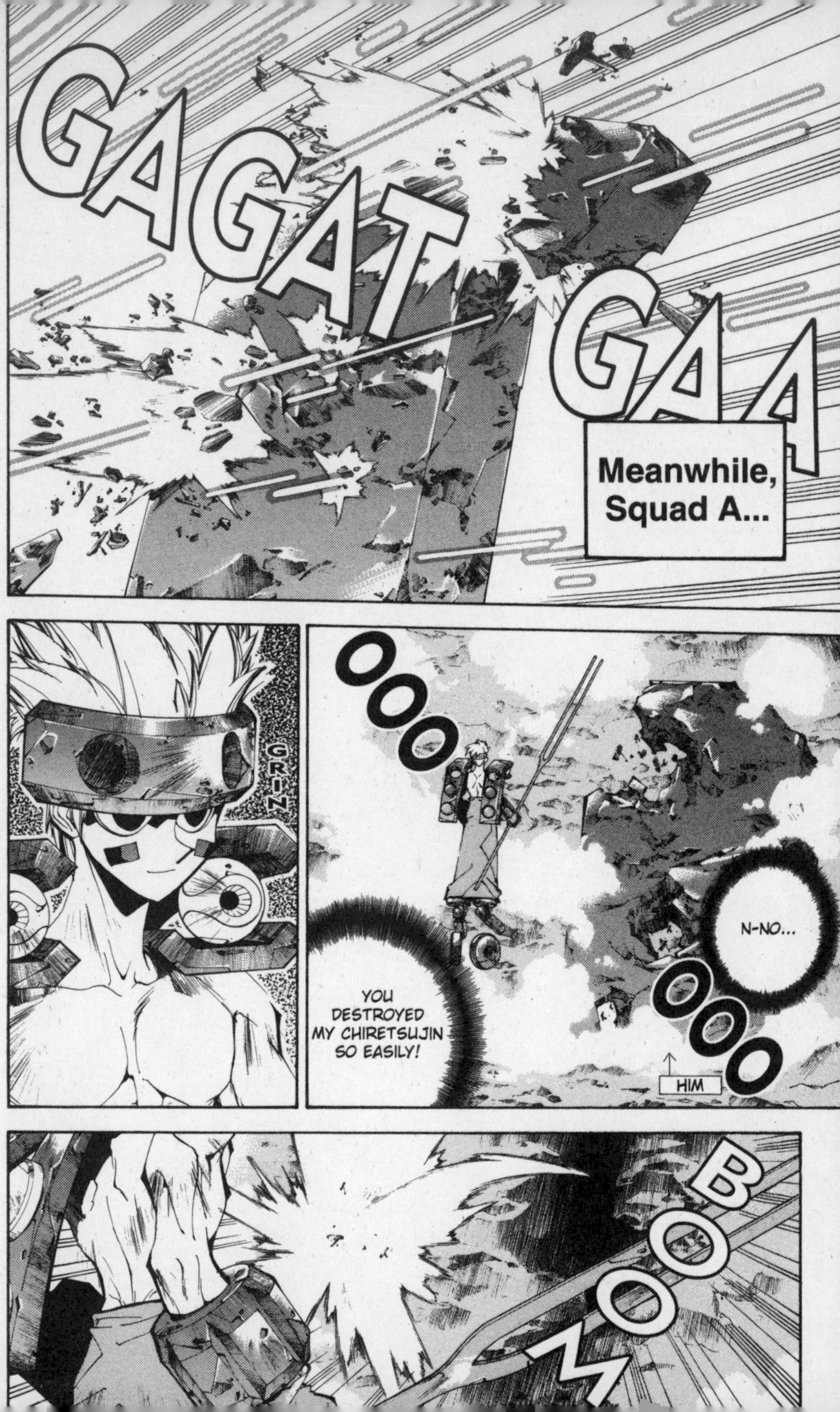
GAGAT
GAA
Meanwhile, Squad A...
OOO
N-NO...
OOOO
YOU DESTROYED MY CHIRETSUJIN SO EASILY!
HIM
GRIN
BOOOM

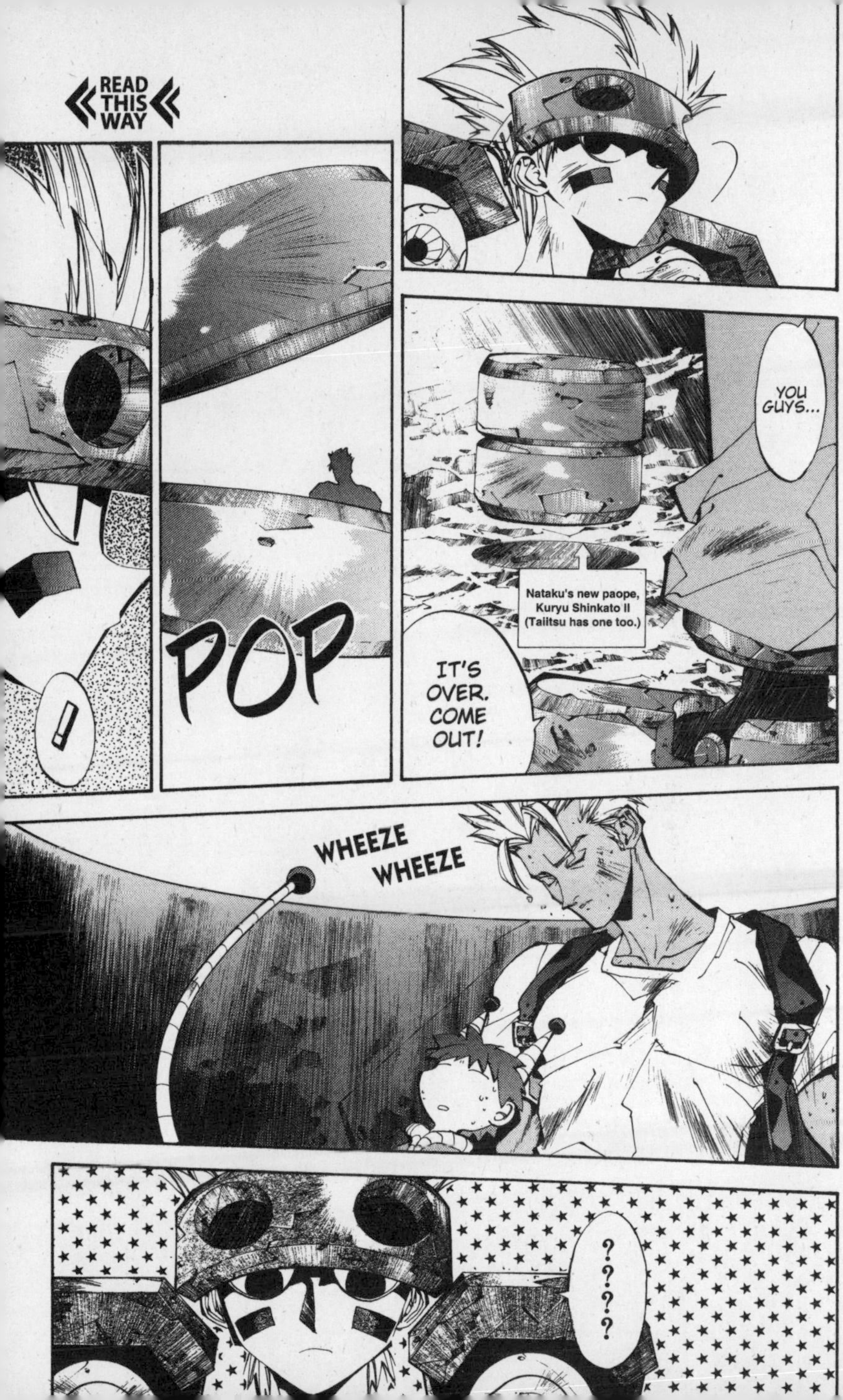
READ THIS WAY
YOU GUYS...
Nataku's new paope, Kuryu Shinkato II (Taiitsu has one too.)
IT'S OVER. COME OUT!
POP
!
WHEEZE WHEEZE
????

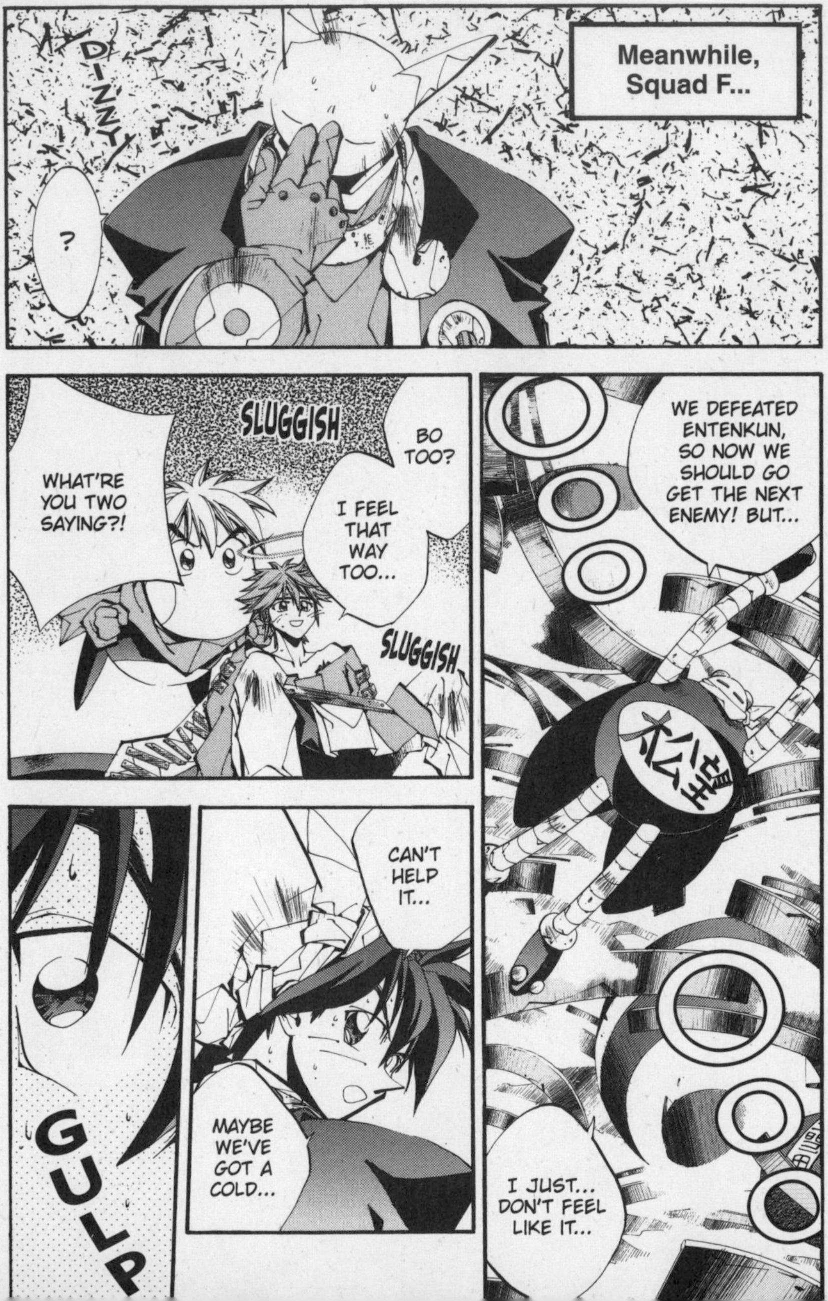
Meanwhile, Squad F...
DIZZY
?
WE DEFEATED ENTENKUN, SO NOW WE SHOULD GO GET THE NEXT ENEMY! BUT...
I JUST... DON'T FEEL LIKE IT...
BO TOO?
SLUGGISH
I FEEL THAT WAY TOO...
SLUGGISH
WHAT'RE YOU TWO SAYING?!
CAN'T HELP IT...
MAYBE WE'VE GOT A COLD...
GULP

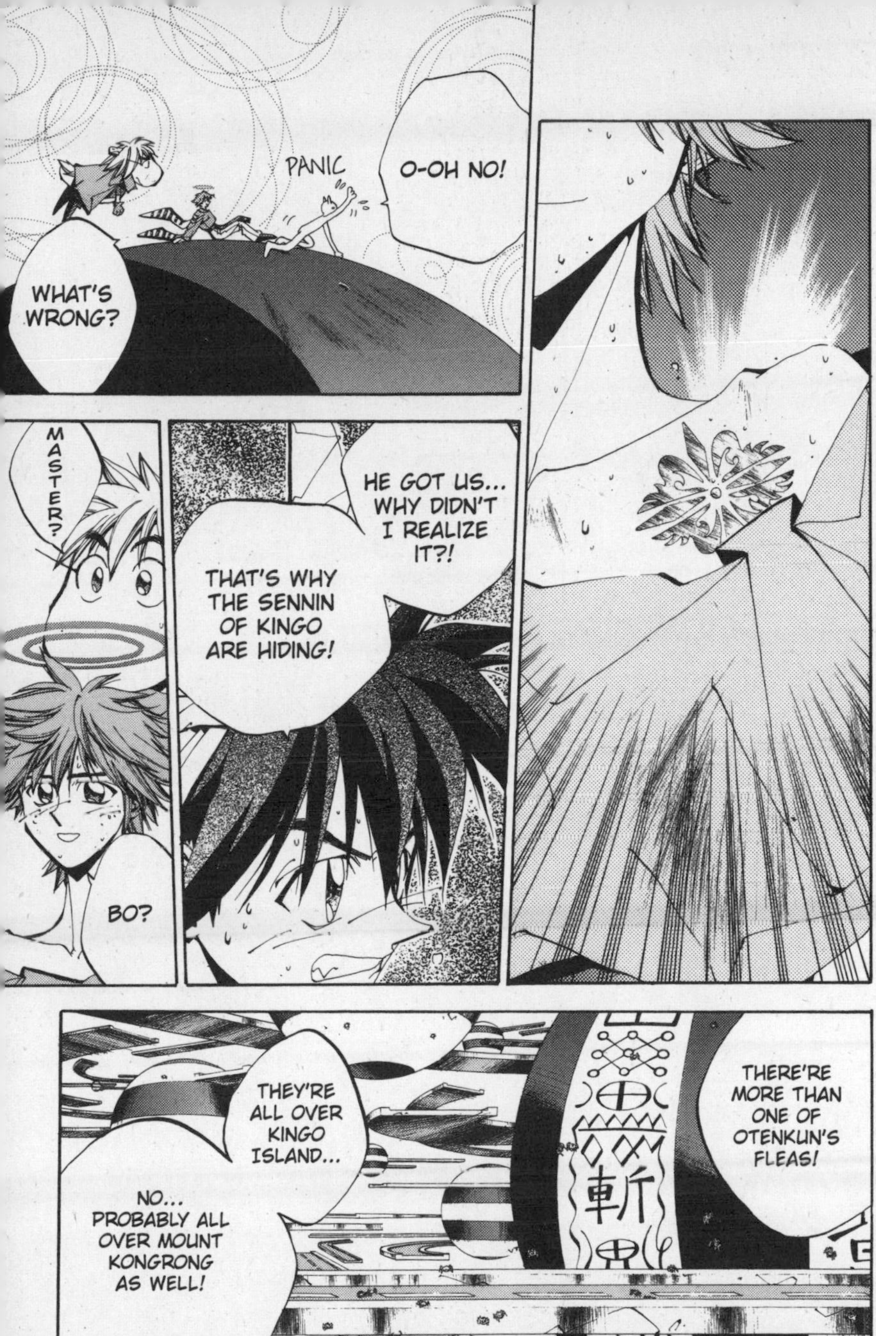
O-OH NO!
PANIC
WHAT'S WRONG?
HE GOT US... WHY DIDN'T I REALIZE IT?!
THAT'S WHY THE SENNIN OF KINGO ARE HIDING!
MASTER?
BO?
THERE'RE MORE THAN ONE OF OTENKUN'S FLEAS!
THEY'RE ALL OVER KINGO ISLAND...
NO... PROBABLY ALL OVER MOUNT KONGRONG AS WELL!

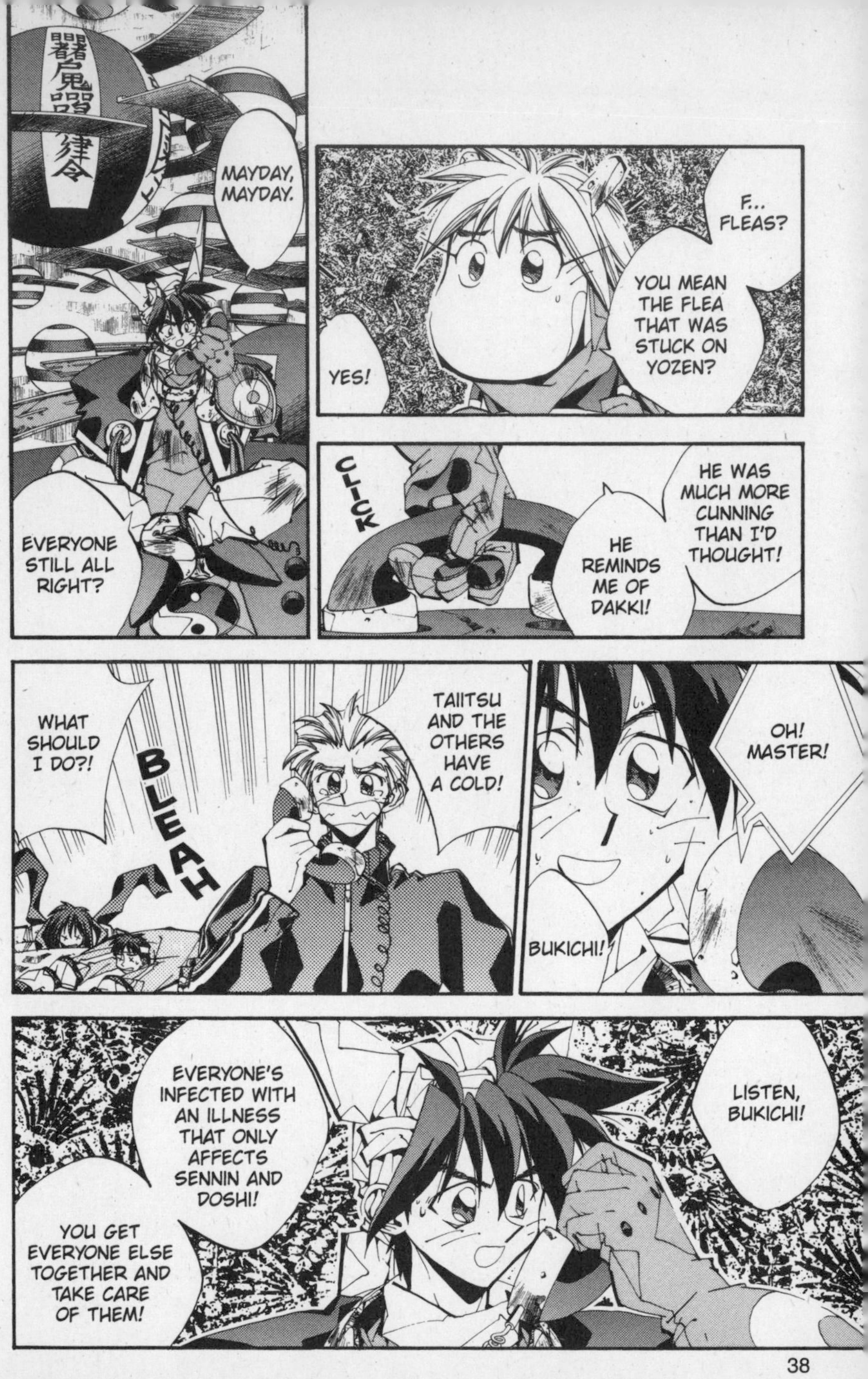
F... FLEAS?
YOU MEAN THE FLEA THAT WAS STUCK ON YOZEN?
YES!
HE WAS MUCH MORE CUNNING THAN I'D THOUGHT!
HE REMINDS ME OF DAKKI!
CLICK
MAYDAY, MAYDAY.
EVERYONE STILL ALL RIGHT?
OH! MASTER!
BUKICHI!
TAIITSU AND THE OTHERS HAVE A COLD!
BLEAH
WHAT SHOULD I DO?!
LISTEN, BUKICHI!
EVERYONE'S INFECTED WITH AN ILLNESS THAT ONLY AFFECTS SENNIN AND DOSHI!
YOU GET EVERYONE ELSE TOGETHER AND TAKE CARE OF THEM!

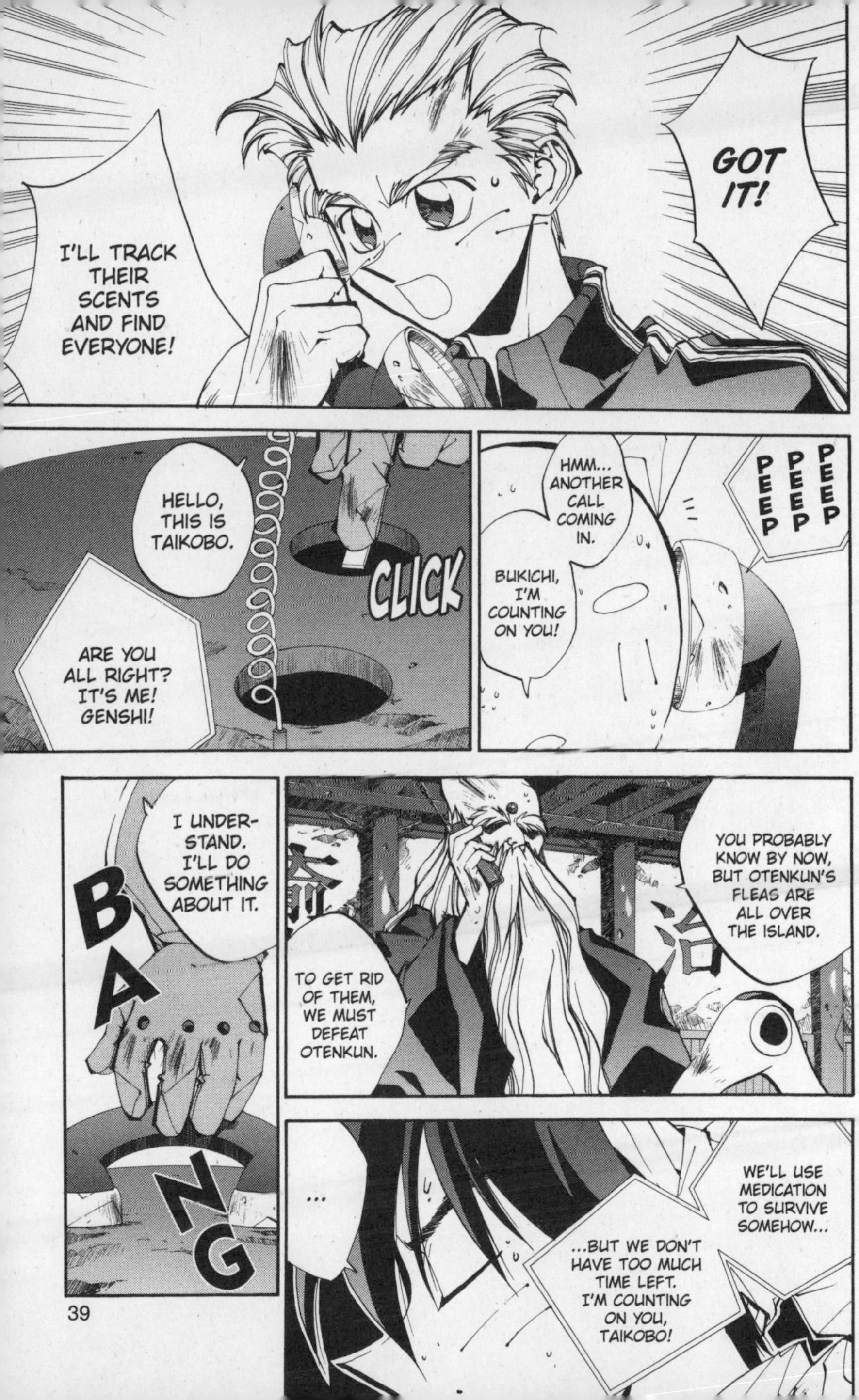
GOT IT!
I'LL TRACK THEIR SCENTS AND FIND EVERYONE!
PEEP PEEP PEEP
HMM... ANOTHER CALL COMING IN.
BUKICHI, I'M COUNTING ON YOU!
HELLO, THIS IS TAIKOBO.
CLICK
ARE YOU ALL RIGHT? IT'S ME! GENSHI!
YOU PROBABLY KNOW BY NOW, BUT OTENKUN'S FLEAS ARE ALL OVER THE ISLAND.
TO GET RID OF THEM, WE MUST DEFEAT OTENKUN.
WE'LL USE MEDICATION TO SURVIVE SOMEHOW...
...BUT WE DON'T HAVE TOO MUCH TIME LEFT. I'M COUNTING ON YOU, TAIKOBO!
...
I UNDER-STAND. I'LL DO SOMETHING ABOUT IT.
BANG

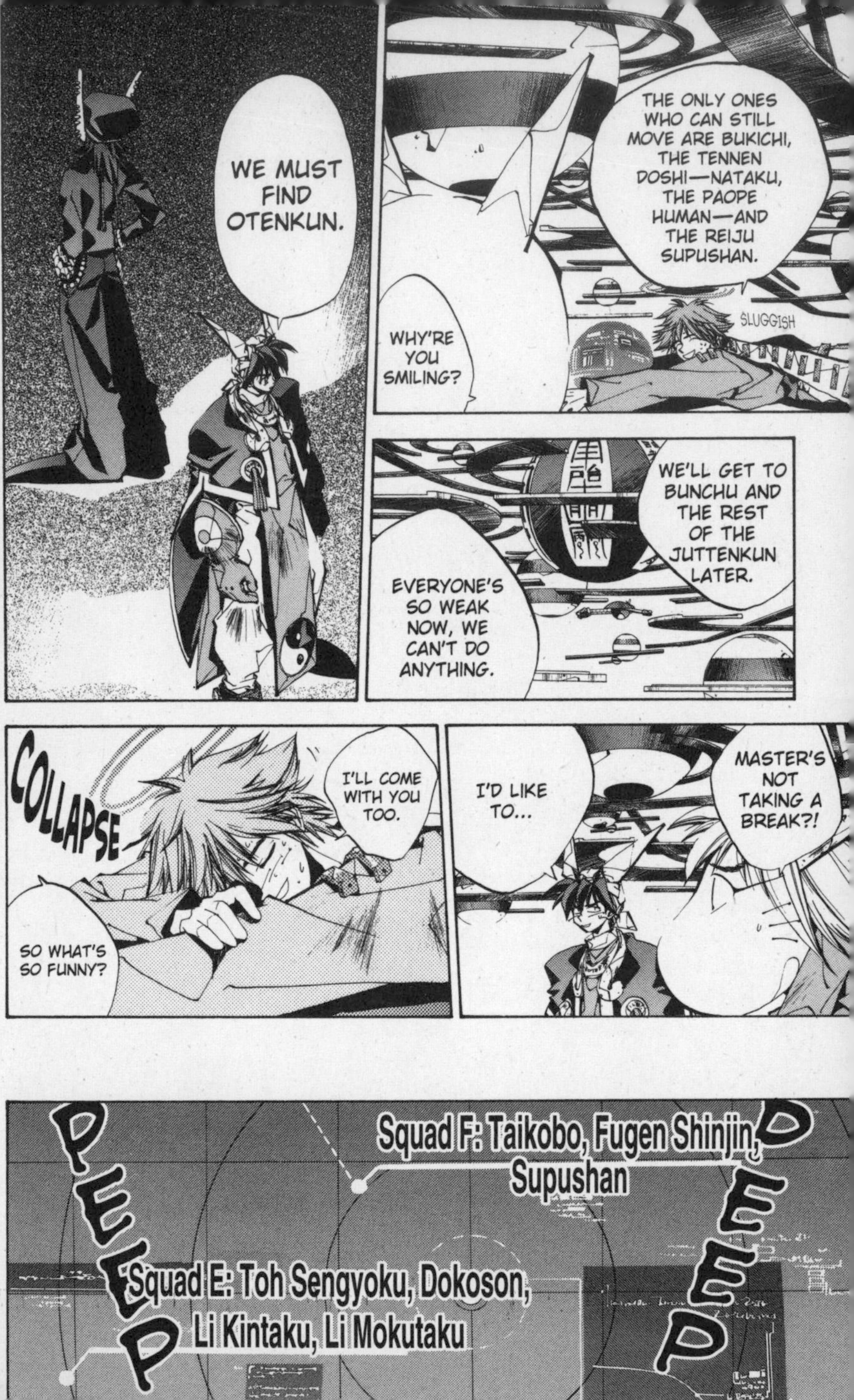
THE ONLY ONES WHO CAN STILL MOVE ARE BUKICHI, THE TENNEN DOSHI—NATAKU, THE PAOPE HUMAN—AND THE REIJU SUPUSHAN.
SLUGGISH
WHY'RE YOU SMILING?
WE'LL GET TO BUNCHU AND THE REST OF THE JUTTENKUN LATER.
EVERYONE'S SO WEAK NOW, WE CAN'T DO ANYTHING.
WE MUST FIND OTENKUN.
MASTER'S NOT TAKING A BREAK?!
I'D LIKE TO...
I'LL COME WITH YOU TOO.
COLLAPSE
SO WHAT'S SO FUNNY?
PEEP
Squad F: Taikobo, Fugen Shinjin, Supushan
Squad E: Toh Sengyoku, Dokoson, Li Kintaku, Li Mokutaku
PEEP

READ THIS WAY

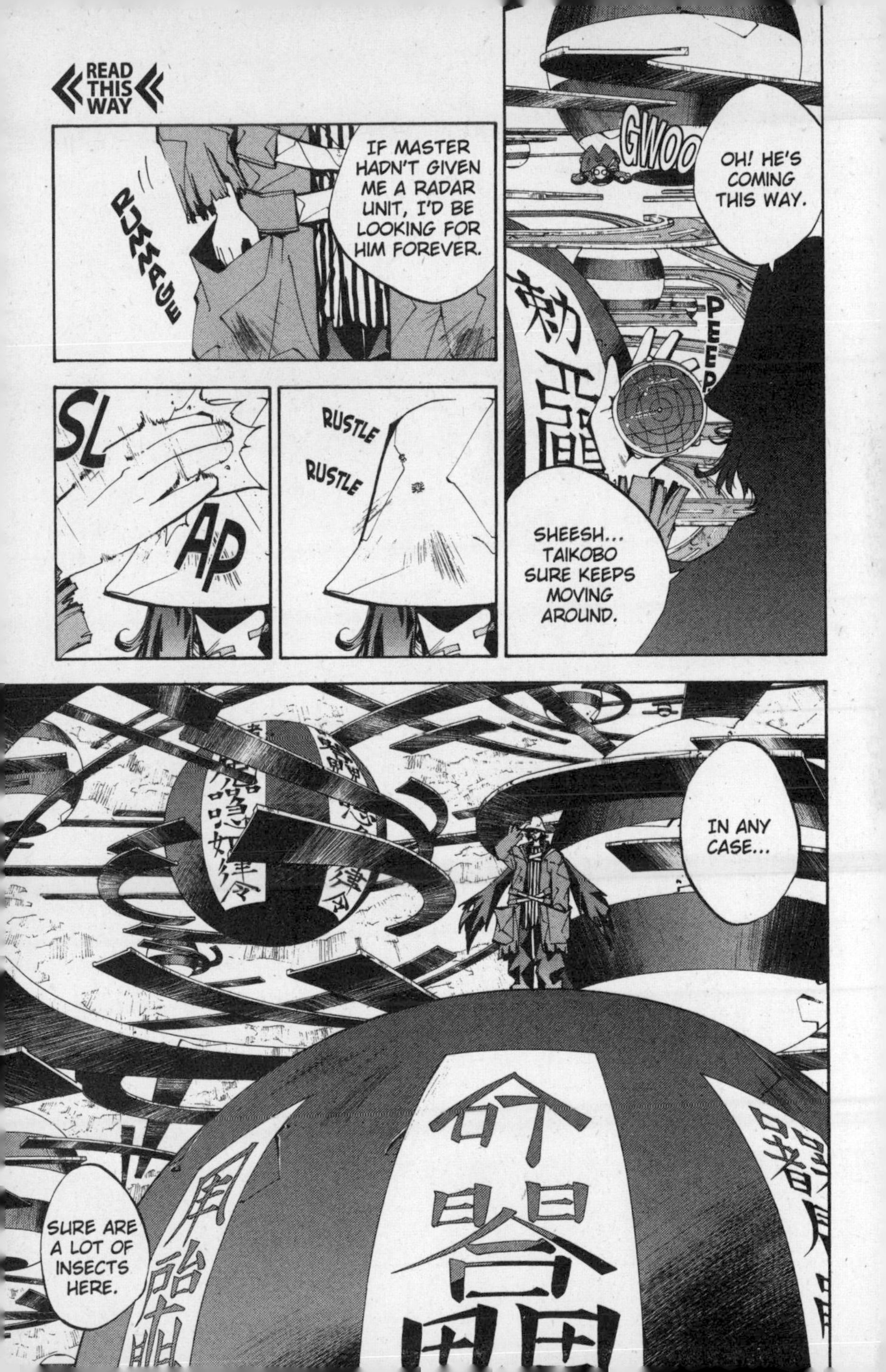
GWOO
OH! HE'S COMING THIS WAY.
PEEP
SHEESH... TAIKOBO SURE KEEPS MOVING AROUND.
IF MASTER HADN'T GIVEN ME A RADAR UNIT, I'D BE LOOKING FOR HIM FOREVER.
RUMMAGE
RUSTLE
RUSTLE
SLAP
IN ANY CASE...
SURE ARE A LOT OF INSECTS HERE.

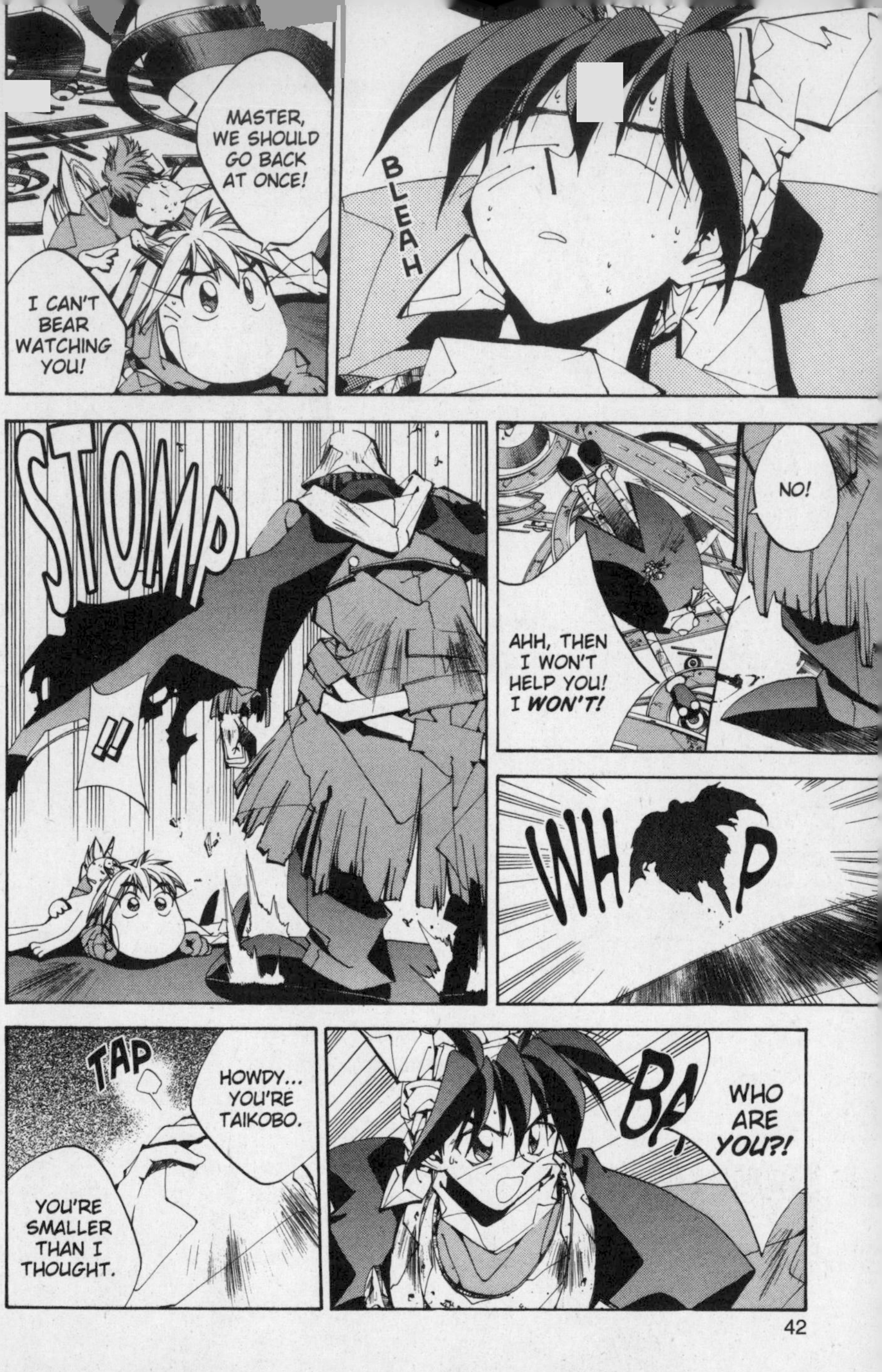
BLEAH
MASTER, WE SHOULD GO BACK AT ONCE!
I CAN'T BEAR WATCHING YOU!
NO!
AHH, THEN I WON'T HELP YOU! I *WON'T!*
WH P
STOMP
!!
BA
WHO ARE *YOU?!*
TAP
HOWDY... YOU'RE TAIKOBO.
YOU'RE SMALLER THAN I THOUGHT.

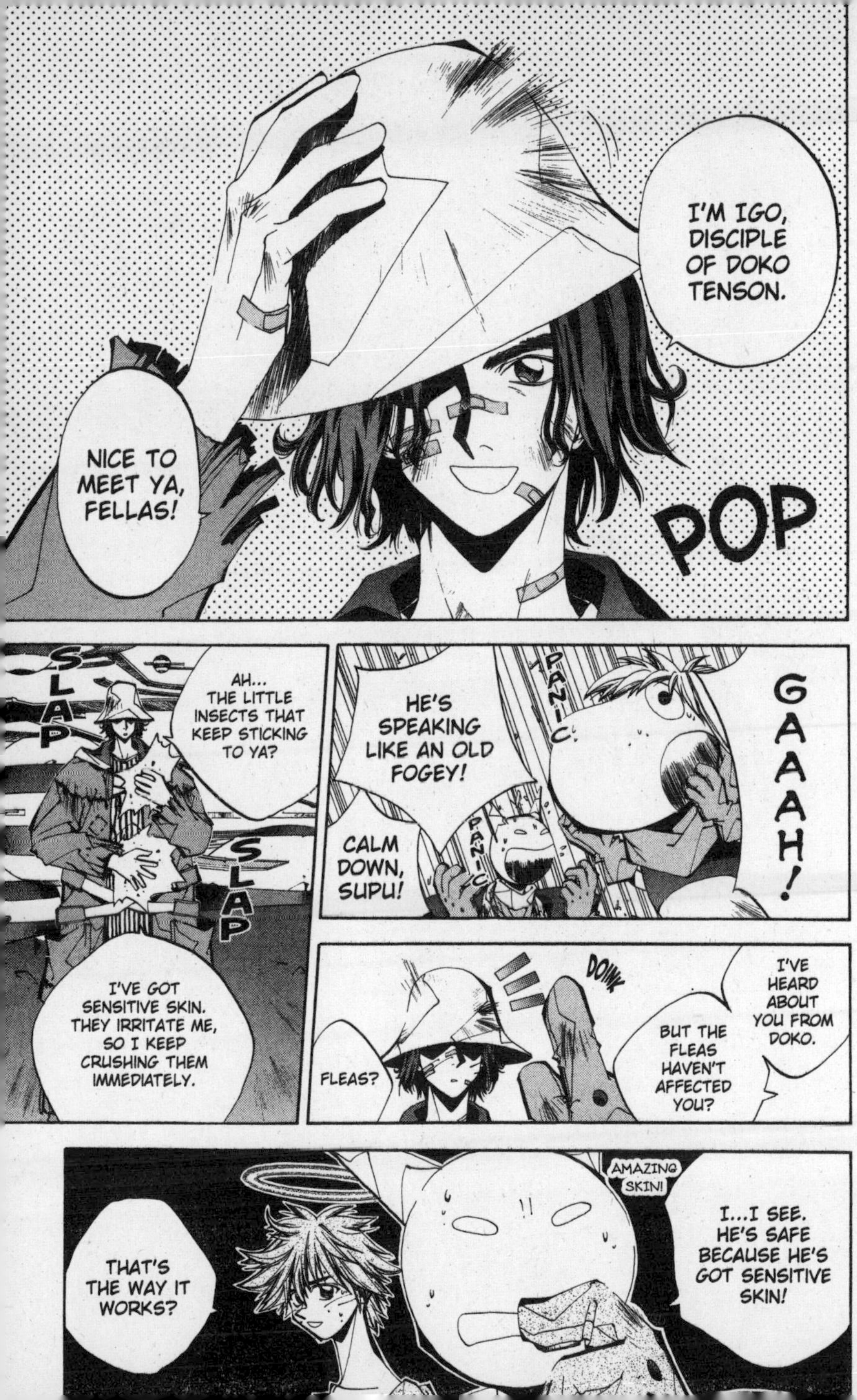
I'M IGO, DISCIPLE OF DOKO TENSON.
POP
NICE TO MEET YA, FELLAS!
GAAAH!
PANIC
HE'S SPEAKING LIKE AN OLD FOGEY!
PANIC
CALM DOWN, SUPU!
I'VE HEARD ABOUT YOU FROM DOKO.
BUT THE FLEAS HAVEN'T AFFECTED YOU?
DOINK
FLEAS?
SLAP
AH... THE LITTLE INSECTS THAT KEEP STICKING TO YA?
SLAP
I'VE GOT SENSITIVE SKIN. THEY IRRITATE ME, SO I KEEP CRUSHING THEM IMMEDIATELY.
AMAZING SKIN!
I...I SEE. HE'S SAFE BECAUSE HE'S GOT SENSITIVE SKIN!
THAT'S THE WAY IT WORKS?

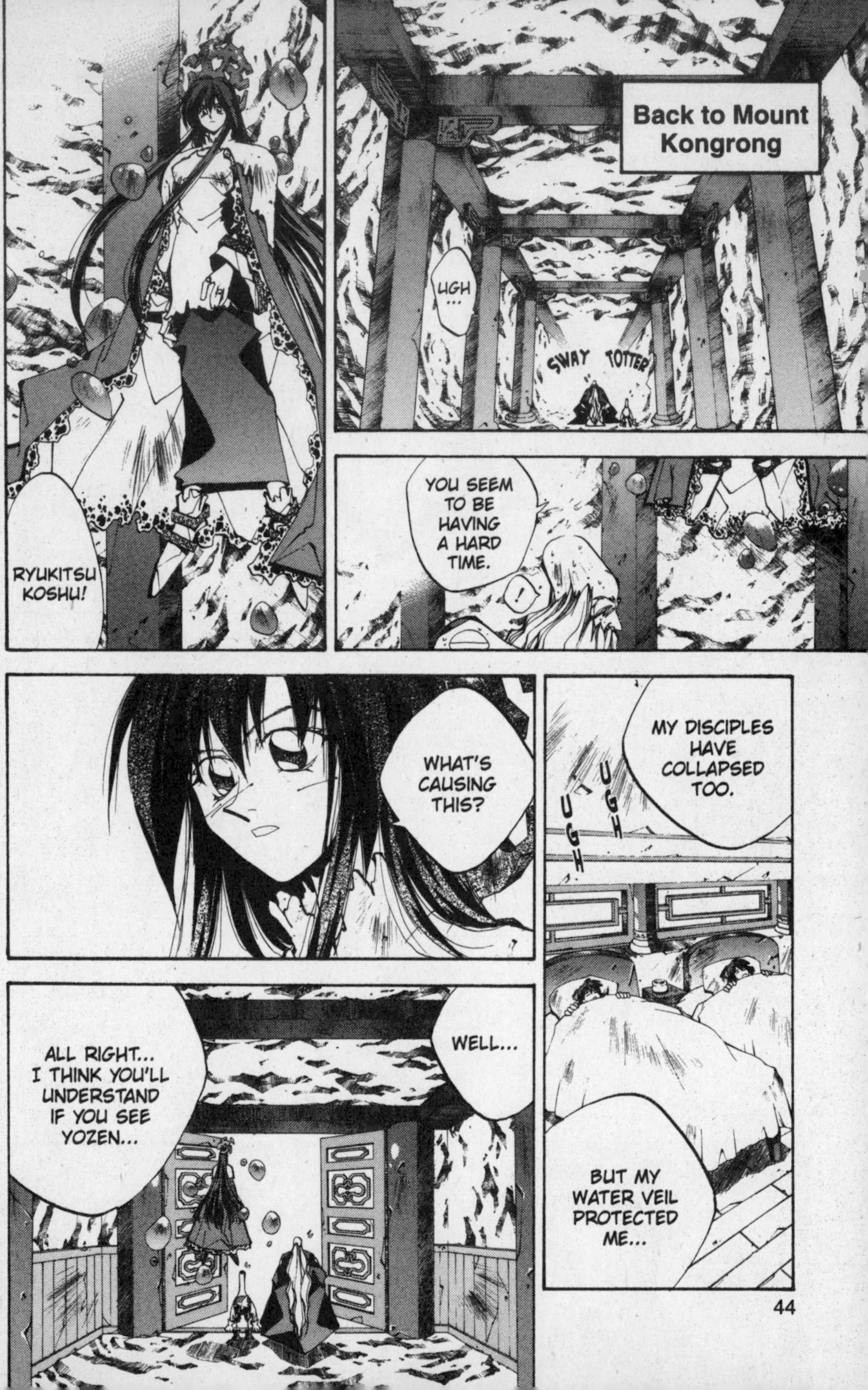
Back to Mount Kongrong
UGH...
SWAY
TOTTER
YOU SEEM TO BE HAVING A HARD TIME.
!
RYUKITSU KOSHU!
MY DISCIPLES HAVE COLLAPSED TOO.
UGH
UGH
BUT MY WATER VEIL PROTECTED ME...
WHAT'S CAUSING THIS?
WELL...
ALL RIGHT... I THINK YOU'LL UNDERSTAND IF YOU SEE YOZEN...

READ THIS WAY

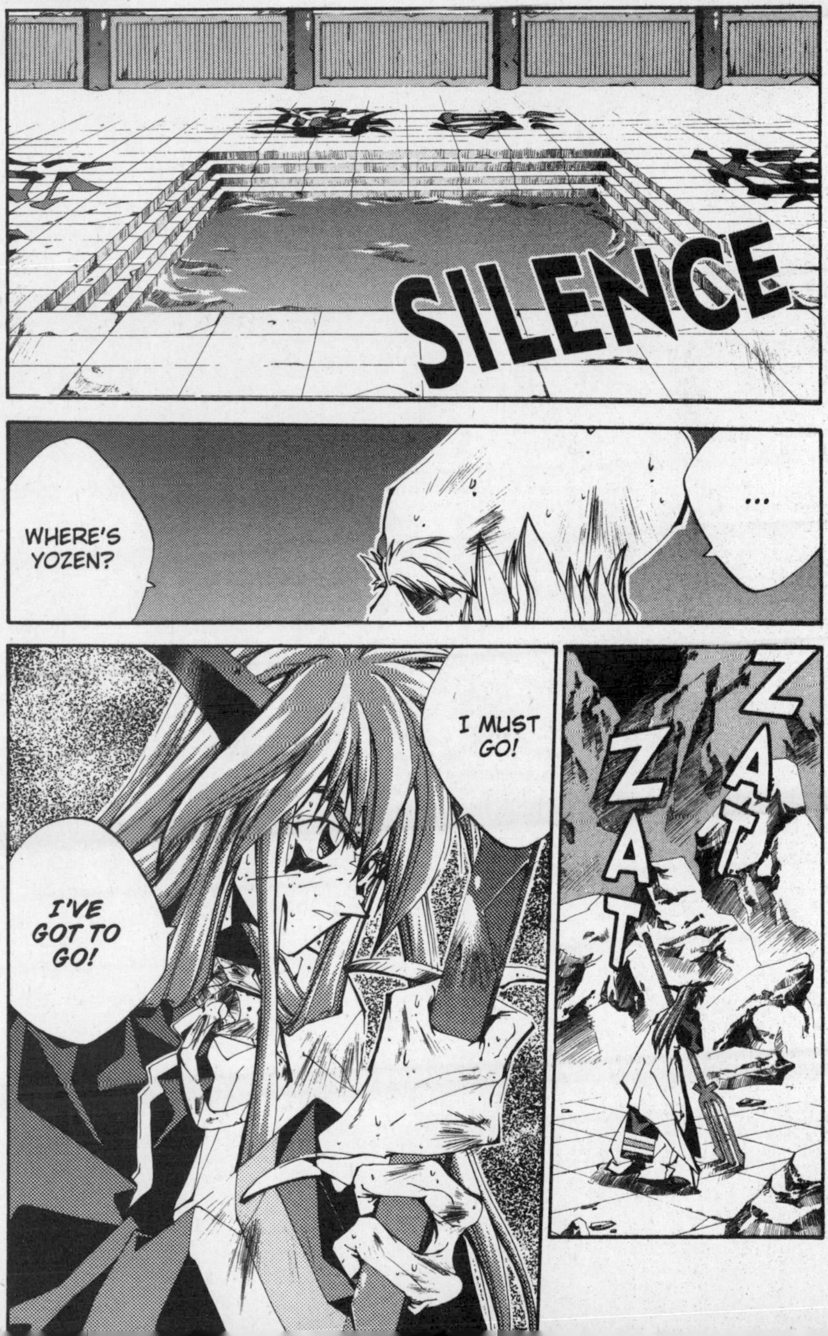
SILENCE
...
WHERE'S YOZEN?
ZAT
ZAT
I MUST GO!
I'VE GOT TO GO!

封神演義

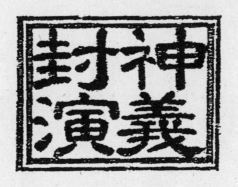

THE BATTLE OF THE JUZETSUJIN "KINKOJIN" & "RAKKONJIN" NATAKU, YOZEN AND IGO JOIN FORCES!

Mount Kongrong

Yozen

Squad A

Squad F

Otenkun

The core

Bunchu

The Ko Family

Where They Are Now

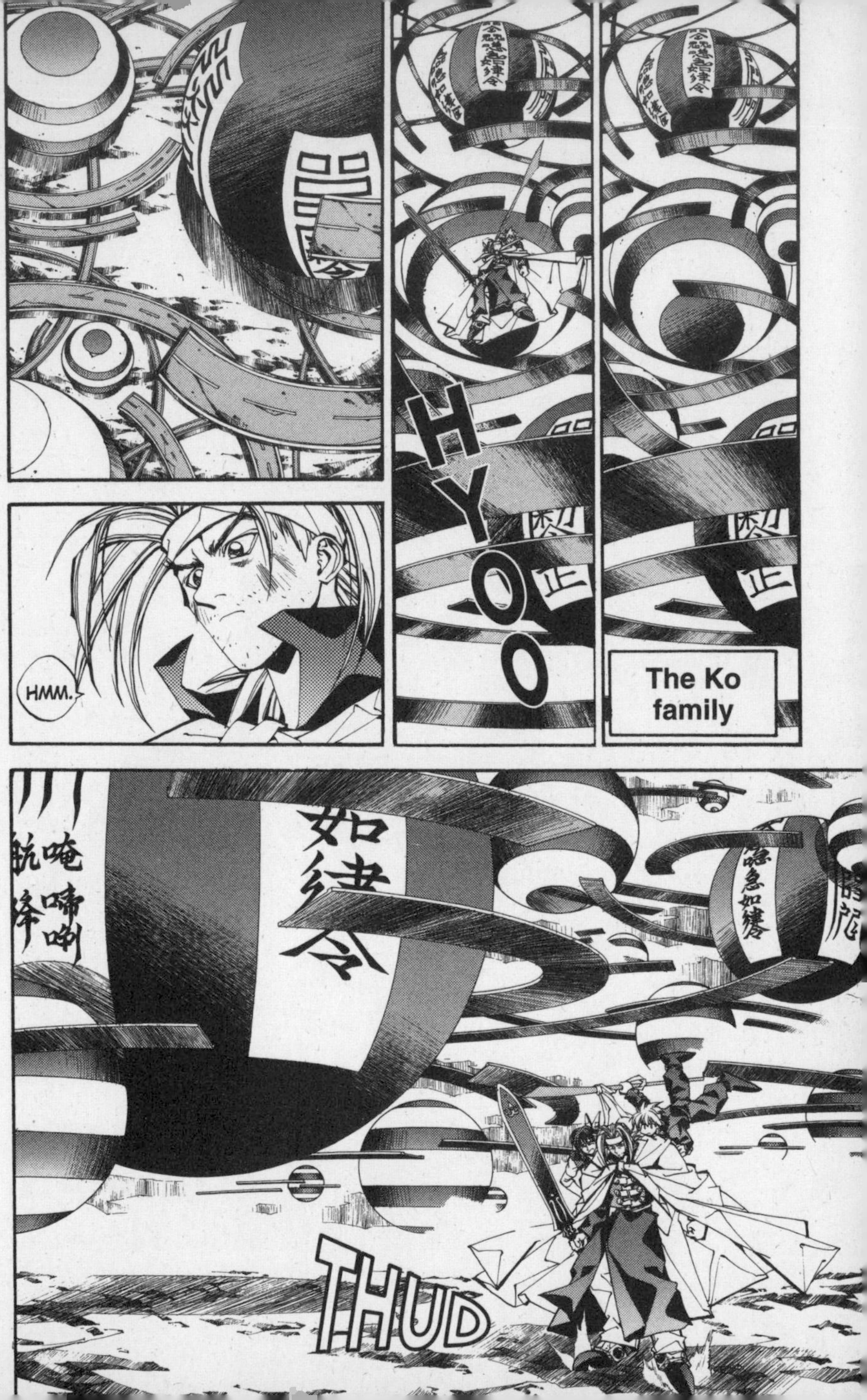
The Ko family
HYOOO
HMM.
THUD

READ THIS WAY

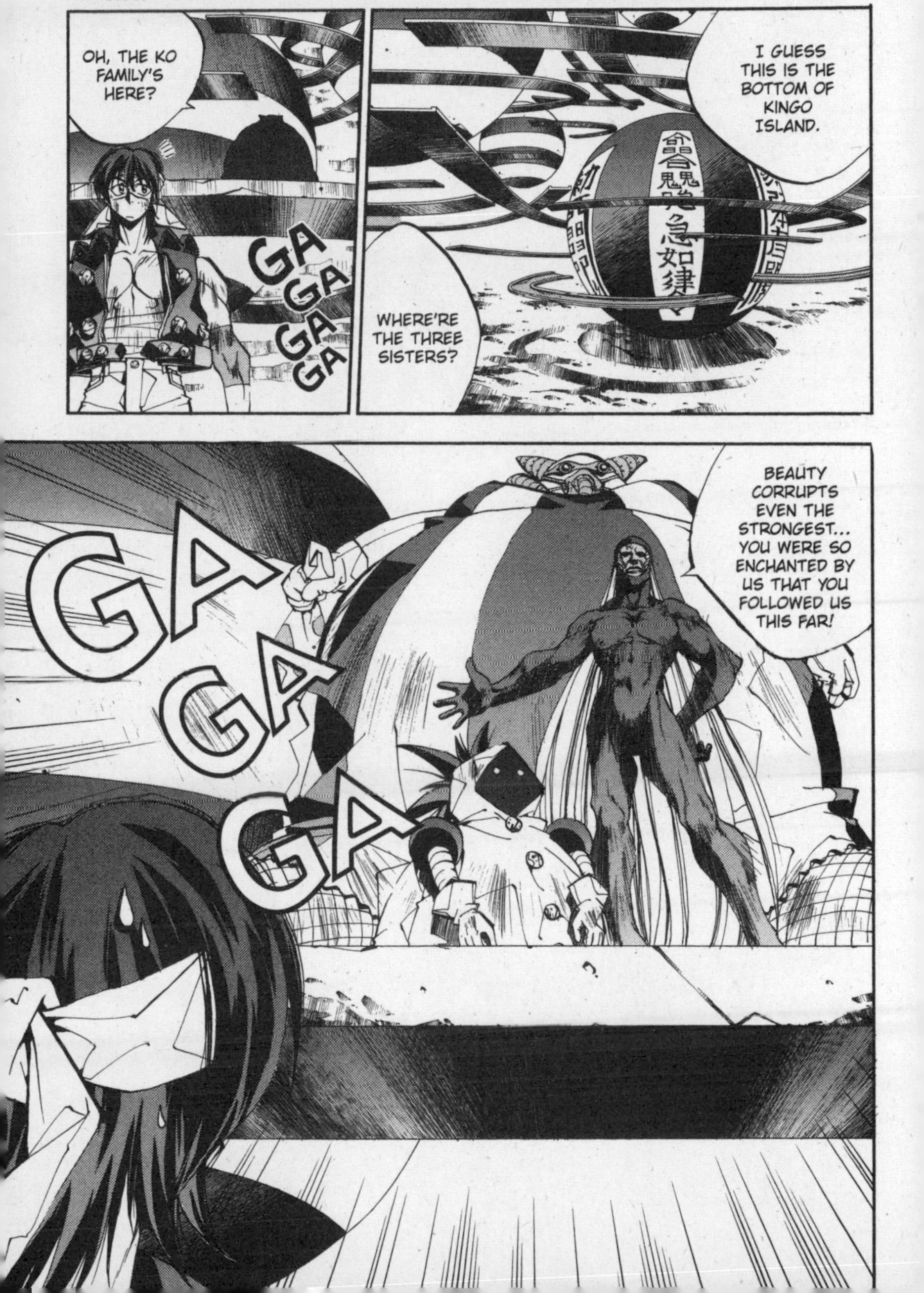
I GUESS THIS IS THE BOTTOM OF KINGO ISLAND.
WHERE'RE THE THREE SISTERS?
OH, THE KO FAMILY'S HERE?
GA GA GA GA
BEAUTY CORRUPTS EVEN THE STRONGEST... YOU WERE SO ENCHANTED BY US THAT YOU FOLLOWED US THIS FAR!
GA GA GA

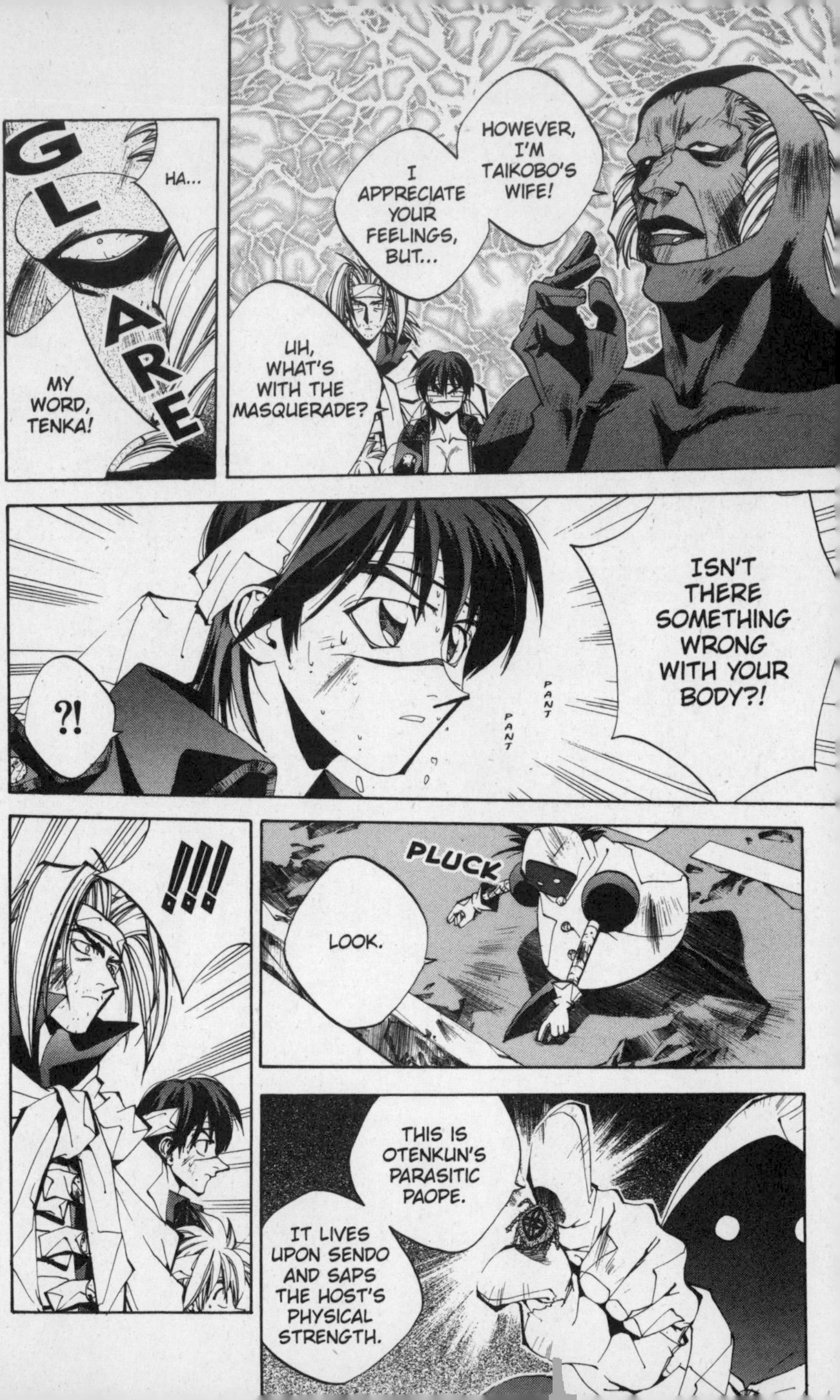
HOWEVER, I'M TAIKOBO'S WIFE!
I APPRECIATE YOUR FEELINGS, BUT...
UH, WHAT'S WITH THE MASQUERADE?
HA...
GLARE
MY WORD, TENKA!
ISN'T THERE SOMETHING WRONG WITH YOUR BODY?!
PANT PANT
?!
PLUCK
LOOK.
THIS IS OTENKUN'S PARASITIC PAOPE.
IT LIVES UPON SENDO AND SAPS THE HOST'S PHYSICAL STRENGTH.
!!!

READ THIS WAY

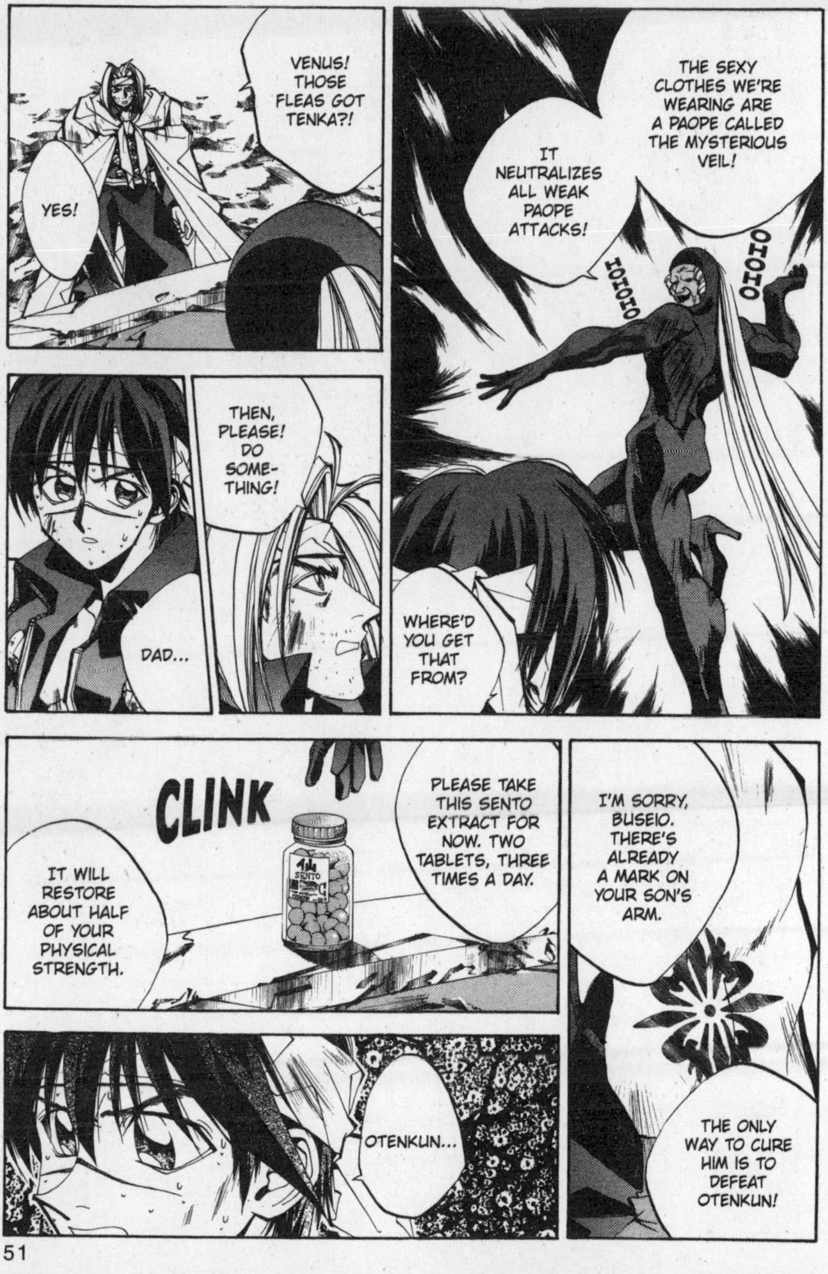
THE SEXY CLOTHES WE'RE WEARING ARE A PAOPE CALLED THE MYSTERIOUS VEIL!
IT NEUTRALIZES ALL WEAK PAOPE ATTACKS!
OHOHO
HOHOHO
WHERE'D YOU GET THAT FROM?
VENUS! THOSE FLEAS GOT TENKA?!
YES!
THEN, PLEASE! DO SOME-THING!
DAD...
I'M SORRY, BUSEIO. THERE'S ALREADY A MARK ON YOUR SON'S ARM.
THE ONLY WAY TO CURE HIM IS TO DEFEAT OTENKUN!
PLEASE TAKE THIS SENTO EXTRACT FOR NOW. TWO TABLETS, THREE TIMES A DAY.
CLINK
SENTO
IT WILL RESTORE ABOUT HALF OF YOUR PHYSICAL STRENGTH.
OTENKUN...

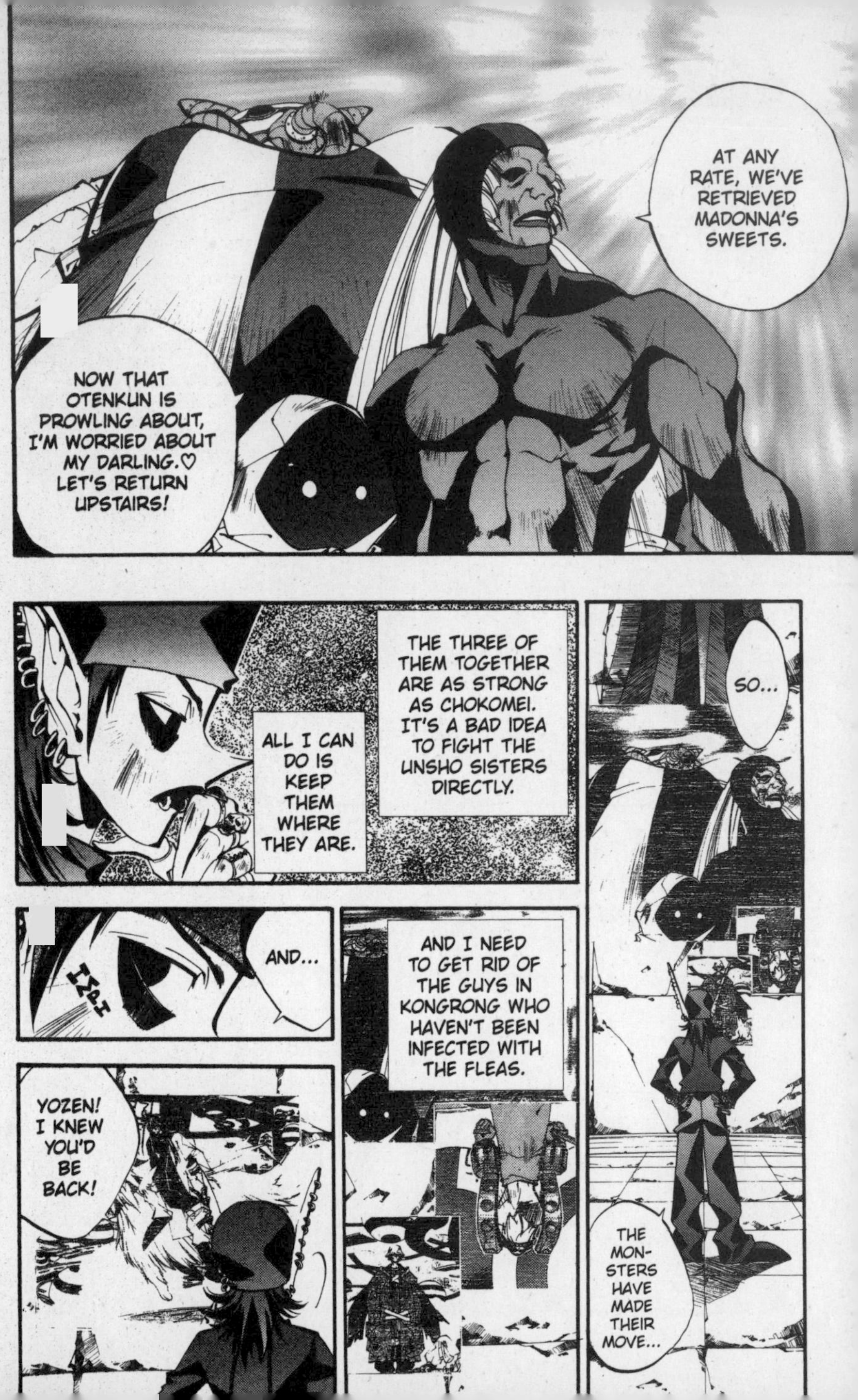
AT ANY RATE, WE'VE RETRIEVED MADONNA'S SWEETS.
NOW THAT OTENKUN IS PROWLING ABOUT, I'M WORRIED ABOUT MY DARLING.♡ LET'S RETURN UPSTAIRS!
SO...
THE MONSTERS HAVE MADE THEIR MOVE...
THE THREE OF THEM TOGETHER ARE AS STRONG AS CHOKOMEI. IT'S A BAD IDEA TO FIGHT THE UNSHO SISTERS DIRECTLY.
ALL I CAN DO IS KEEP THEM WHERE THEY ARE.
AND I NEED TO GET RID OF THE GUYS IN KONGRONG WHO HAVEN'T BEEN INFECTED WITH THE FLEAS.
AND...
YOZEN! I KNEW YOU'D BE BACK!

READ THIS WAY

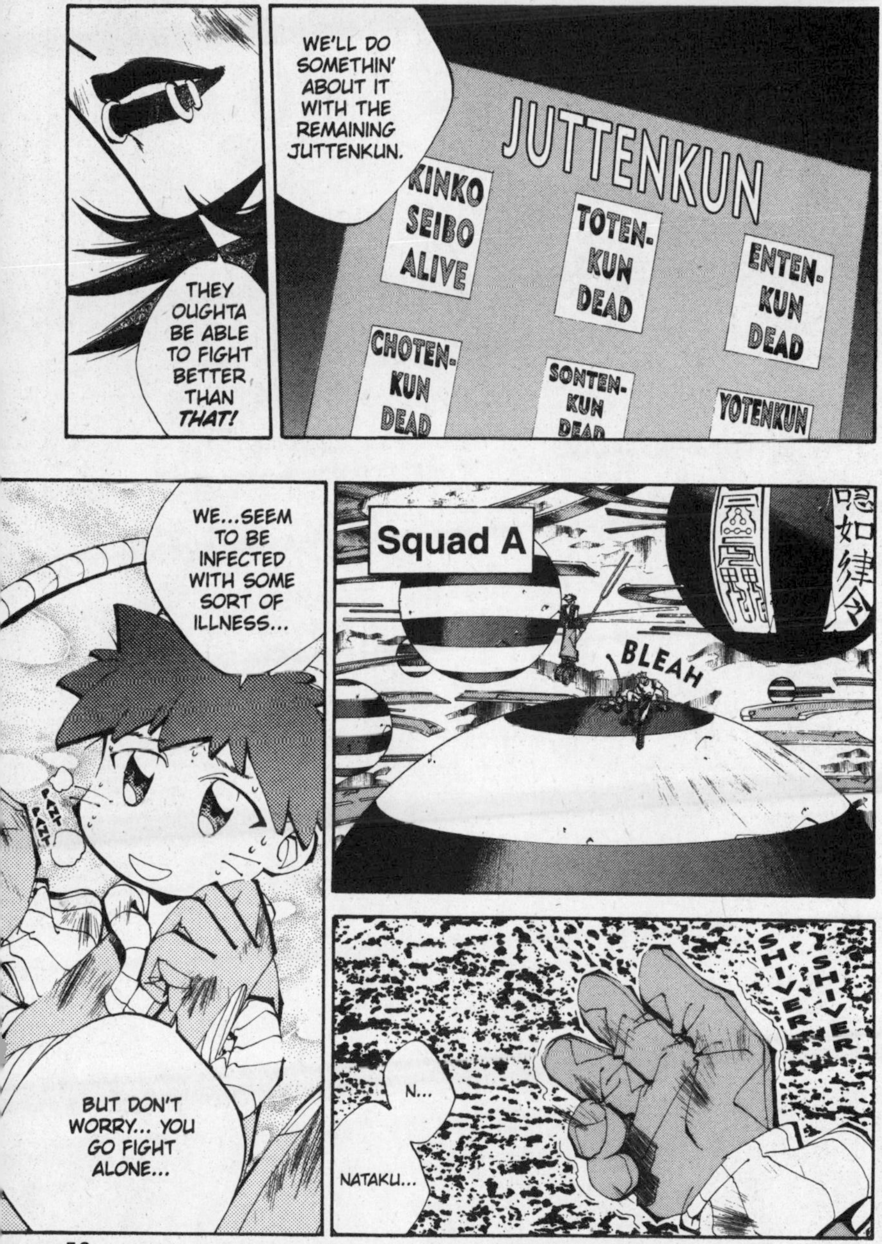
WE'LL DO SOMETHIN' ABOUT IT WITH THE REMAINING JUTTENKUN.
JUTTENKUN
KINKO SEIBO ALIVE
TOTEN-KUN DEAD
ENTEN-KUN DEAD
CHOTEN-KUN DEAD
SONTEN-KUN DEAD
YOTENKUN
THEY OUGHTA BE ABLE TO FIGHT BETTER THAN *THAT!*
Squad A
BLEAH
SHIVER SHIVER
N...
NATAKU...
WE...SEEM TO BE INFECTED WITH SOME SORT OF ILLNESS...
PANT PANT
BUT DON'T WORRY... YOU GO FIGHT ALONE...

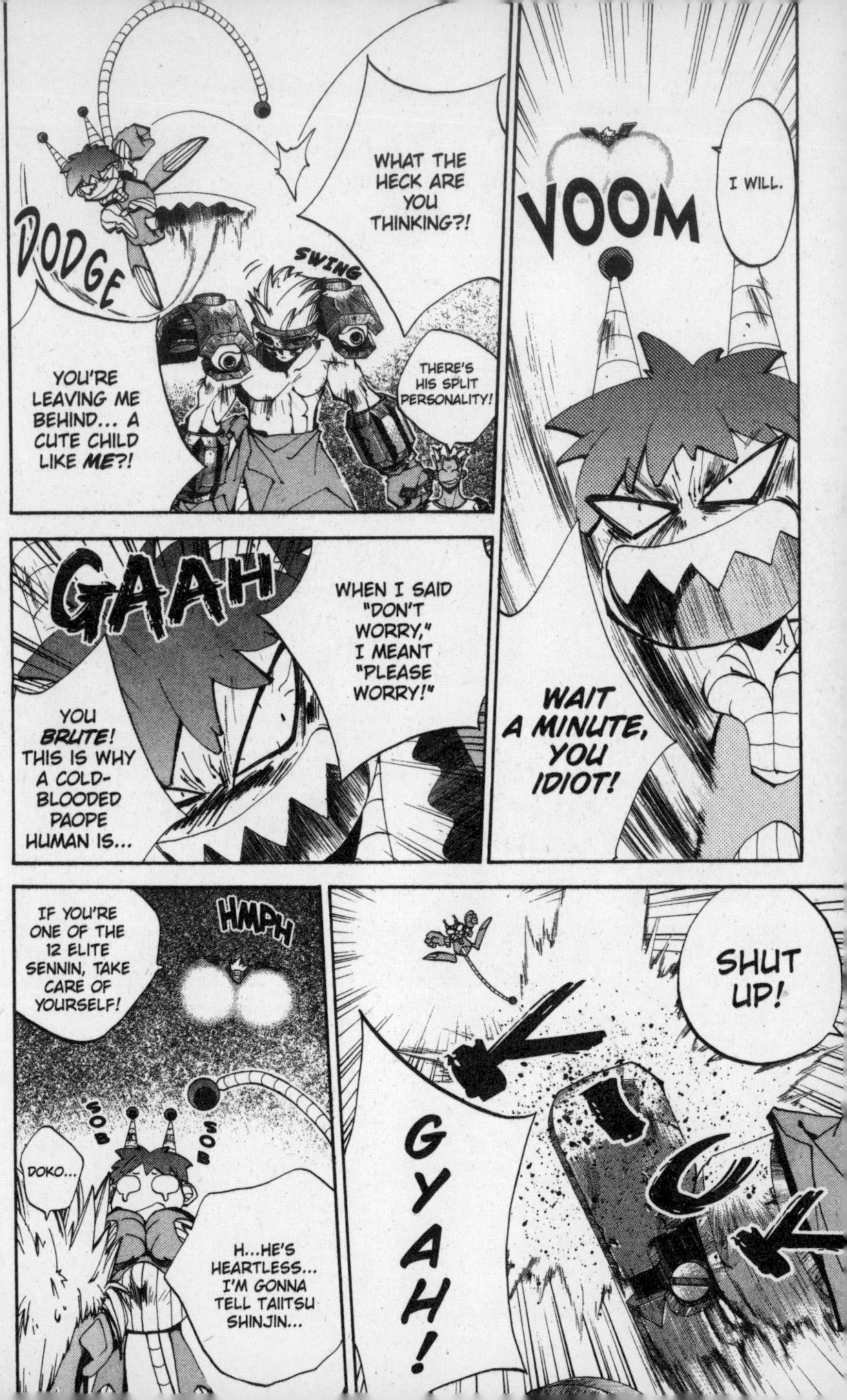
I WILL.
VOOM
WAIT A MINUTE, YOU IDIOT!
WHAT THE HECK ARE YOU THINKING?!
DODGE
SWING
THERE'S HIS SPLIT PERSONALITY!
YOU'RE LEAVING ME BEHIND... A CUTE CHILD LIKE *ME*?!
WHEN I SAID "DON'T WORRY," I MEANT "PLEASE WORRY!"
GAAH
YOU *BRUTE*! THIS IS WHY A COLD-BLOODED PAOPE HUMAN IS...
SHUT UP!
CK
GYAH!
HMPH
IF YOU'RE ONE OF THE 12 ELITE SENNIN, TAKE CARE OF YOURSELF!
SOB
SOB
DOKO...
H...HE'S HEARTLESS... I'M GONNA TELL TAIITSU SHINJIN...

READ THIS WAY

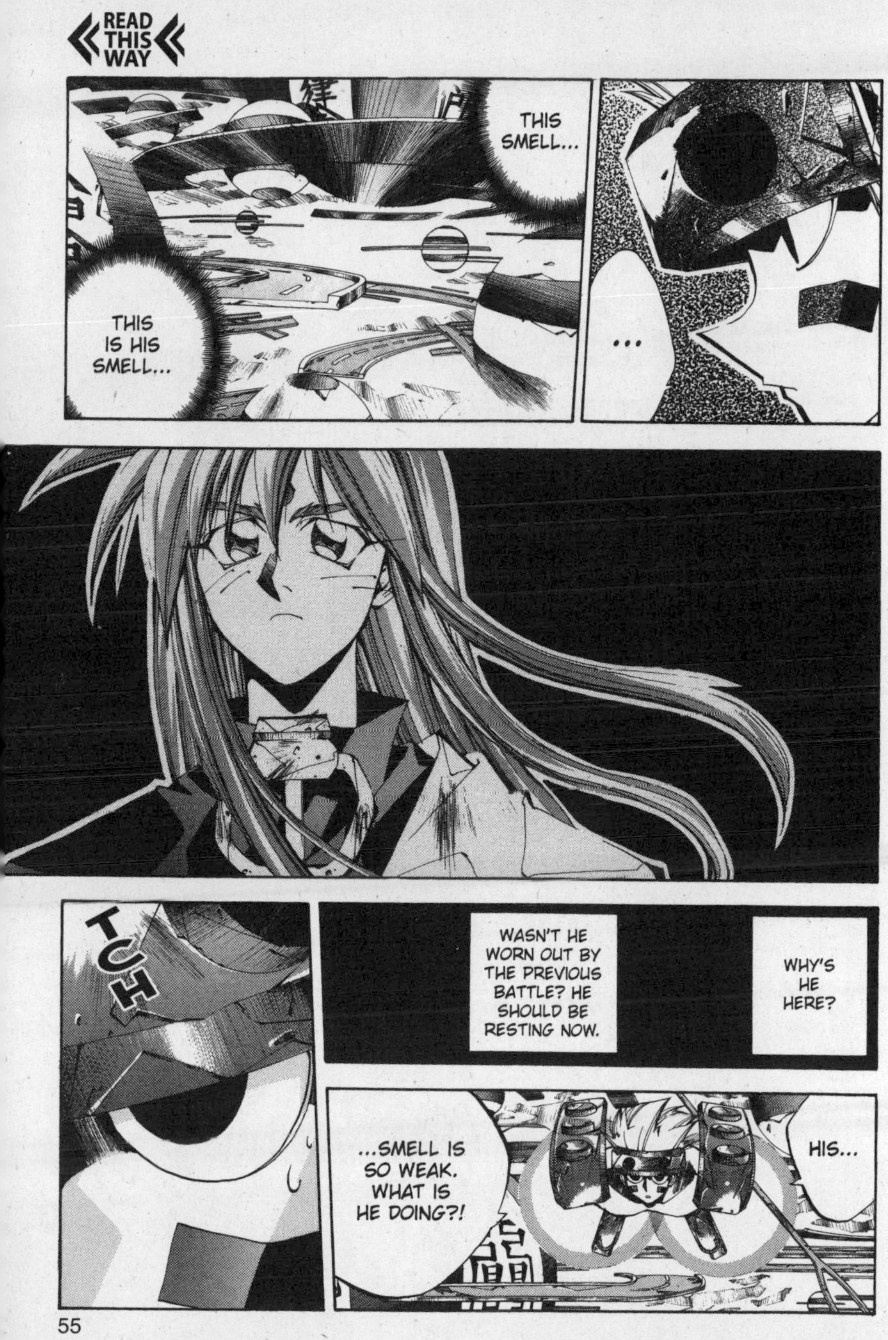
...
THIS SMELL...
THIS IS HIS SMELL...
WHY'S HE HERE?
WASN'T HE WORN OUT BY THE PREVIOUS BATTLE? HE SHOULD BE RESTING NOW.
HIS...
...SMELL IS SO WEAK. WHAT IS HE DOING?!
TCH

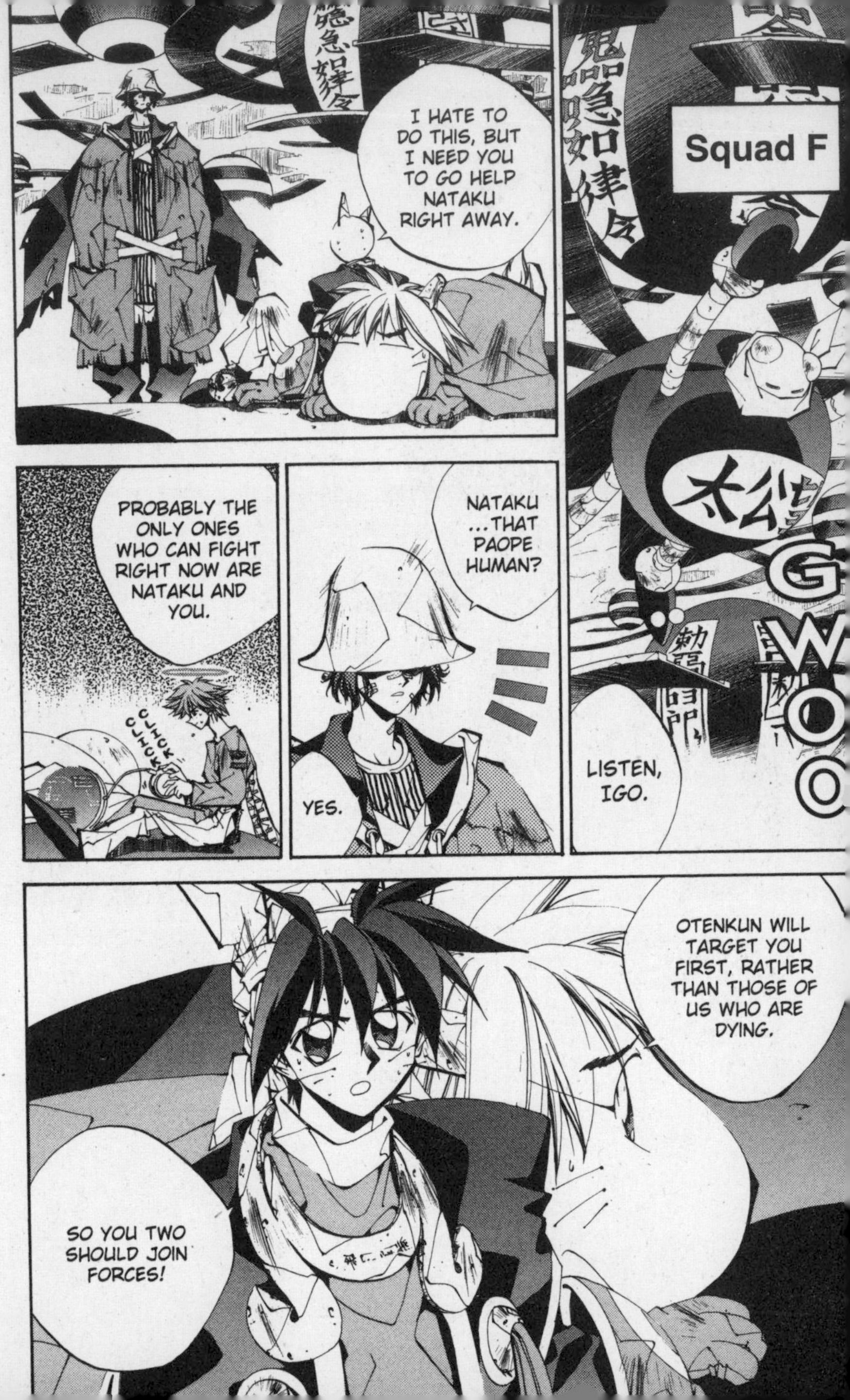
Squad F
GWOO
LISTEN, IGO.
I HATE TO DO THIS, BUT I NEED YOU TO GO HELP NATAKU RIGHT AWAY.
NATAKU ...THAT PAOPE HUMAN?
YES.
PROBABLY THE ONLY ONES WHO CAN FIGHT RIGHT NOW ARE NATAKU AND YOU.
CLICK CLICK
OTENKUN WILL TARGET YOU FIRST, RATHER THAN THOSE OF US WHO ARE DYING.
SO YOU TWO SHOULD JOIN FORCES!

READ THIS WAY

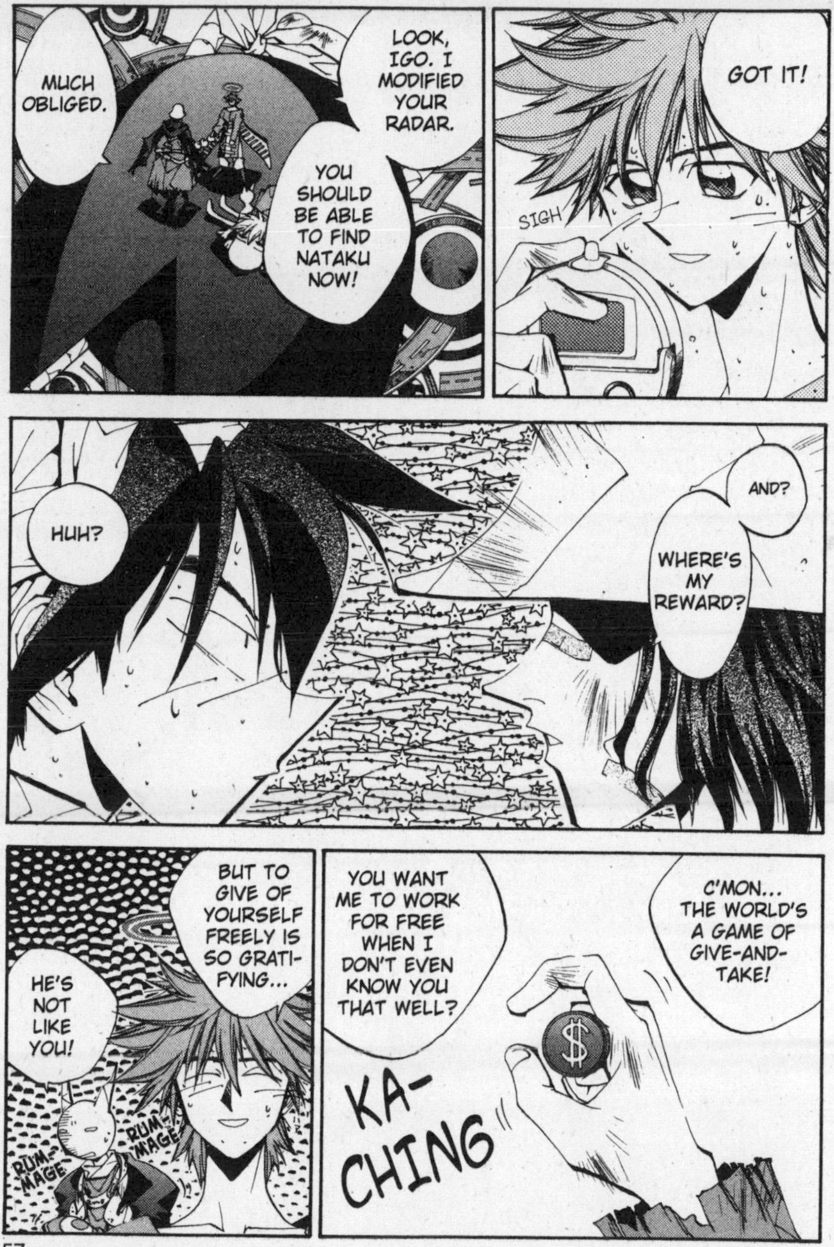
GOT IT!
SIGH
LOOK, IGO. I MODIFIED YOUR RADAR.
YOU SHOULD BE ABLE TO FIND NATAKU NOW!
MUCH OBLIGED.
AND?
WHERE'S MY REWARD?
HUH?
C'MON... THE WORLD'S A GAME OF GIVE-AND-TAKE!
KA-CHING
YOU WANT ME TO WORK FOR FREE WHEN I DON'T EVEN KNOW YOU THAT WELL?
BUT TO GIVE OF YOURSELF FREELY IS SO GRATI-FYING...
HE'S NOT LIKE YOU!
RUM-MAGE
RUM-MAGE

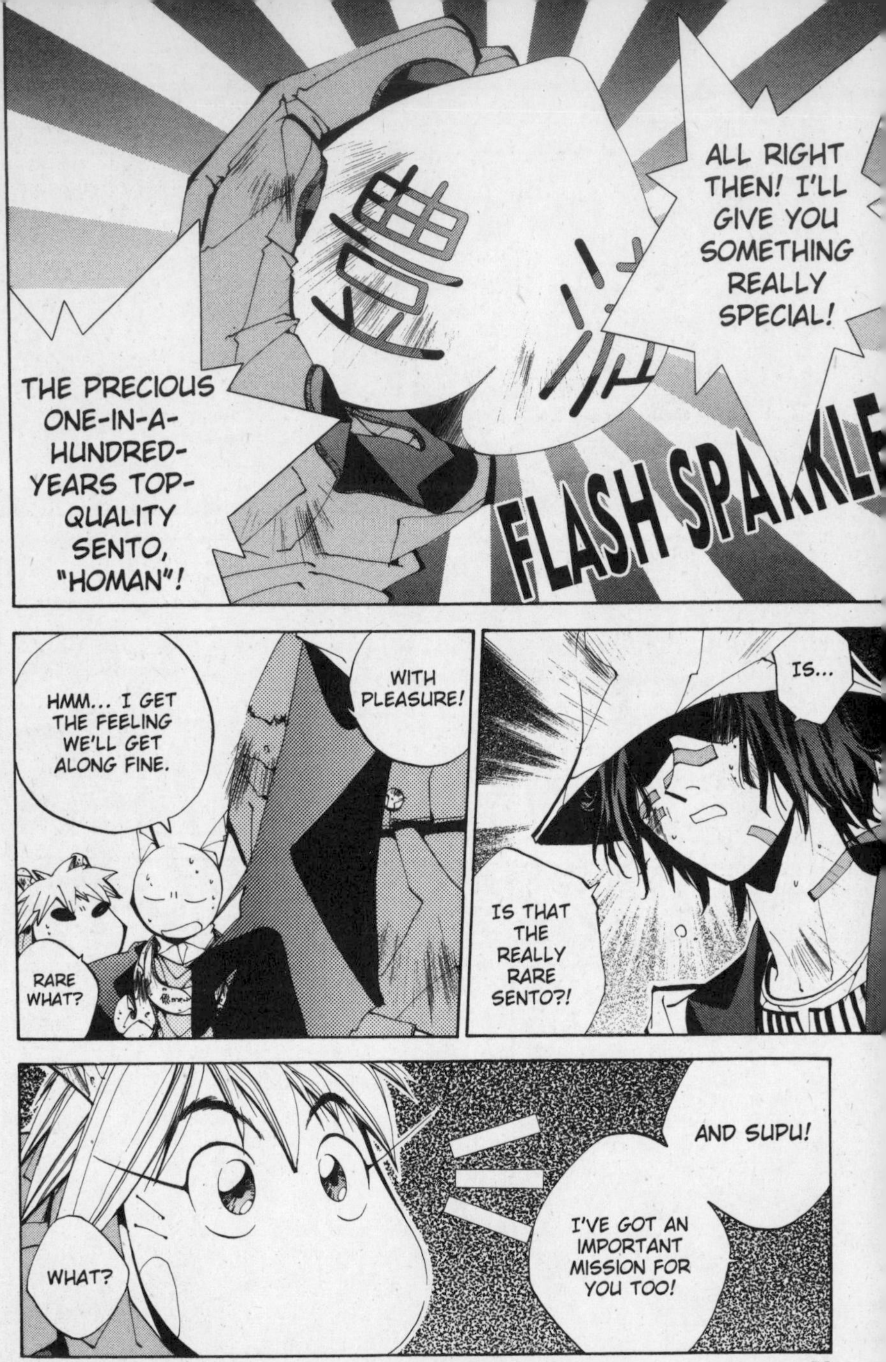
ALL RIGHT THEN! I'LL GIVE YOU SOMETHING REALLY SPECIAL!
FLASH SPARKLE
THE PRECIOUS ONE-IN-A-HUNDRED-YEARS TOP-QUALITY SENTO, "HOMAN"!
IS...
IS THAT THE REALLY RARE SENTO?!
WITH PLEASURE!
HMM... I GET THE FEELING WE'LL GET ALONG FINE.
RARE WHAT?
AND SUPU!
I'VE GOT AN IMPORTANT MISSION FOR YOU TOO!
WHAT?

READ THIS WAY

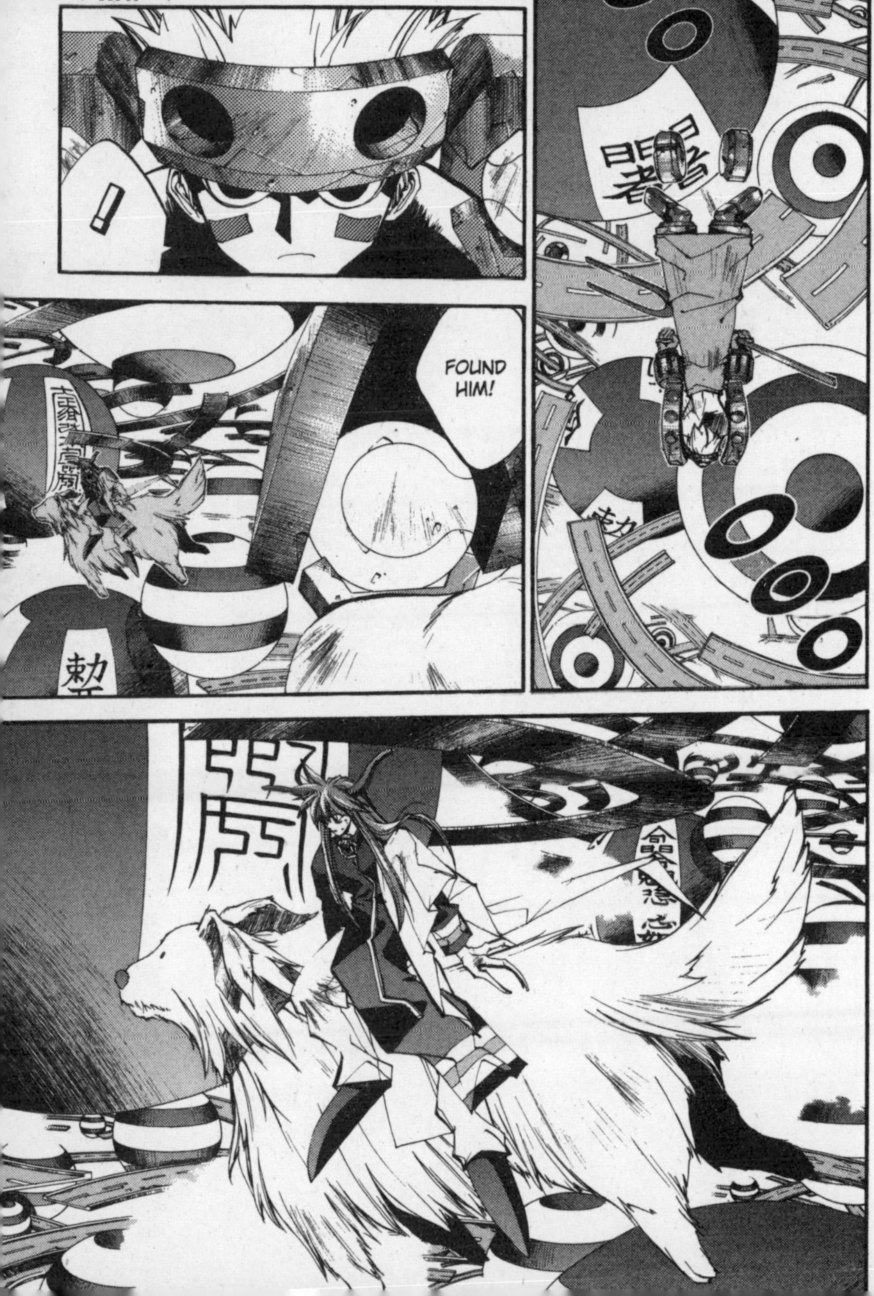
!
FOUND HIM!

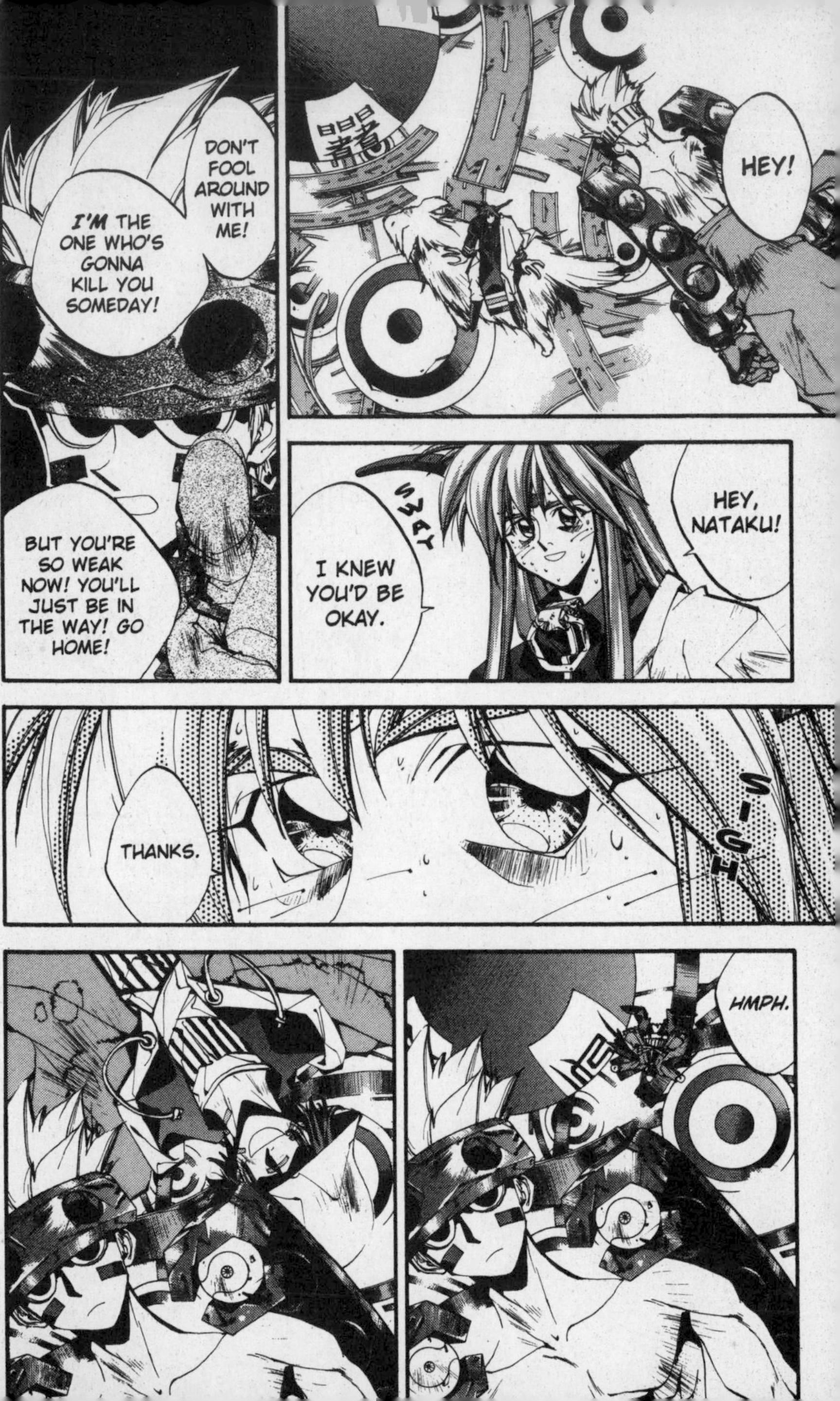
HEY!
HEY, NATAKU!
SWAY
I KNEW YOU'D BE OKAY.
DON'T FOOL AROUND WITH ME!
I'M THE ONE WHO'S GONNA KILL YOU SOMEDAY!
BUT YOU'RE SO WEAK NOW! YOU'LL JUST BE IN THE WAY! GO HOME!
SIGH
THANKS.
HMPH.

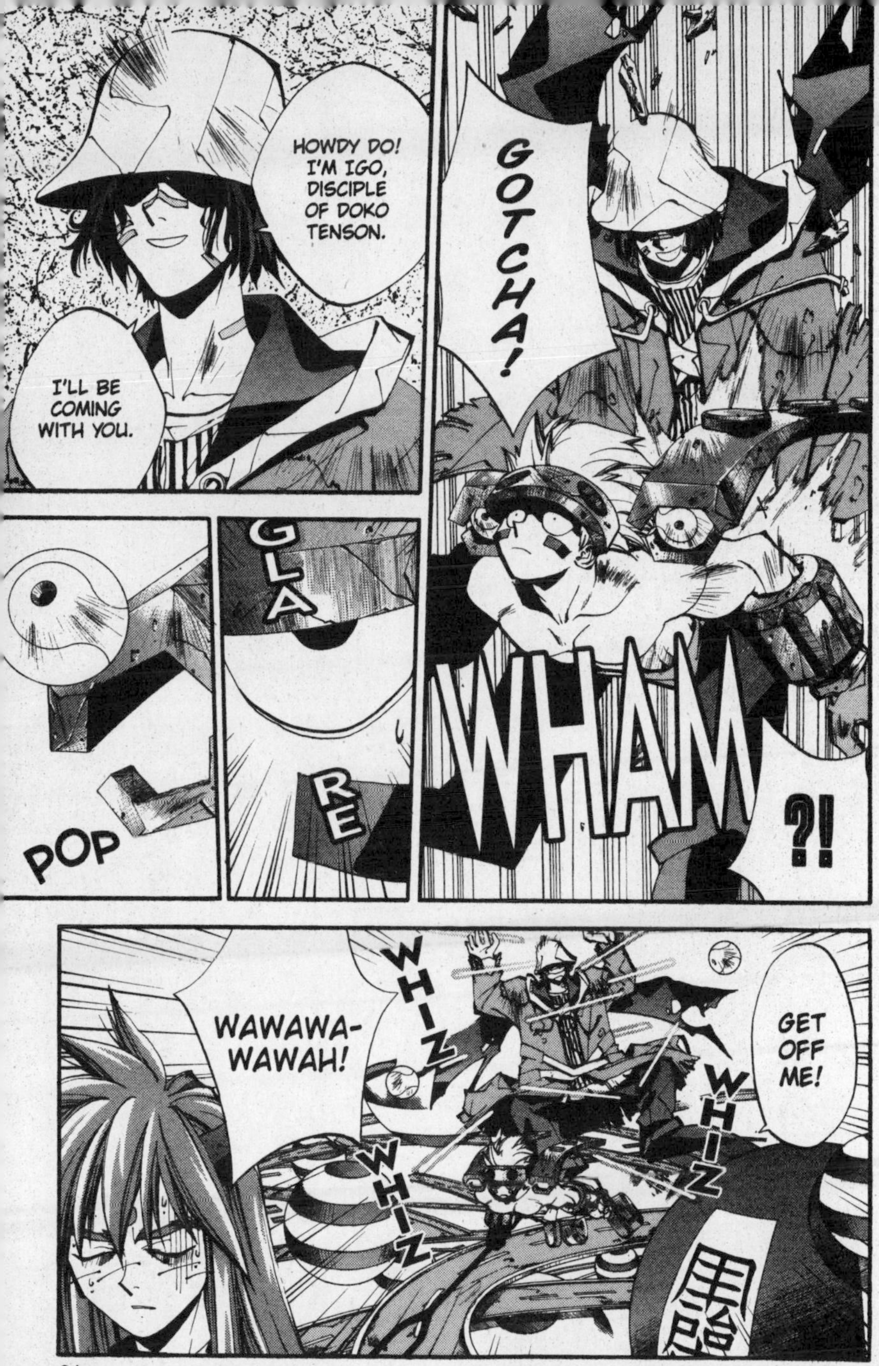
GOTCHA!
WHAM
?!
HOWDY DO! I'M IGO, DISCIPLE OF DOKO TENSON.
I'LL BE COMING WITH YOU.
GLARE
POP
GET OFF ME!
WHIZ
WHIZ
WAWAWA-WAWAH!
WHIZ

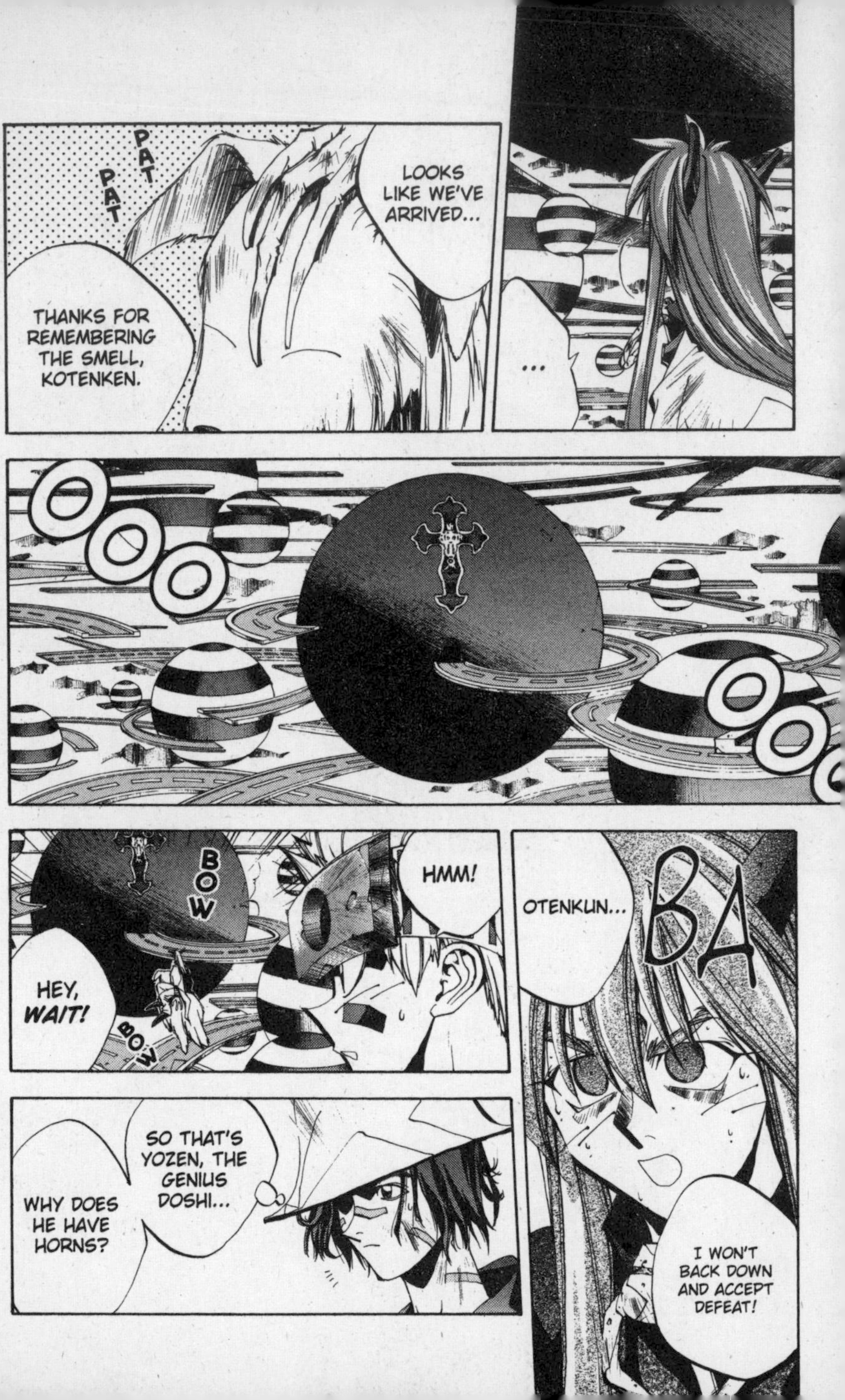
...
LOOKS LIKE WE'VE ARRIVED...
PAT
PAT
THANKS FOR REMEMBERING THE SMELL, KOTENKEN.
OOOO
OOOO
OTENKUN...
BA
I WON'T BACK DOWN AND ACCEPT DEFEAT!
HMM!
BOW
HEY, WAIT!
BOW
SO THAT'S YOZEN, THE GENIUS DOSHI...
WHY DOES HE HAVE HORNS?

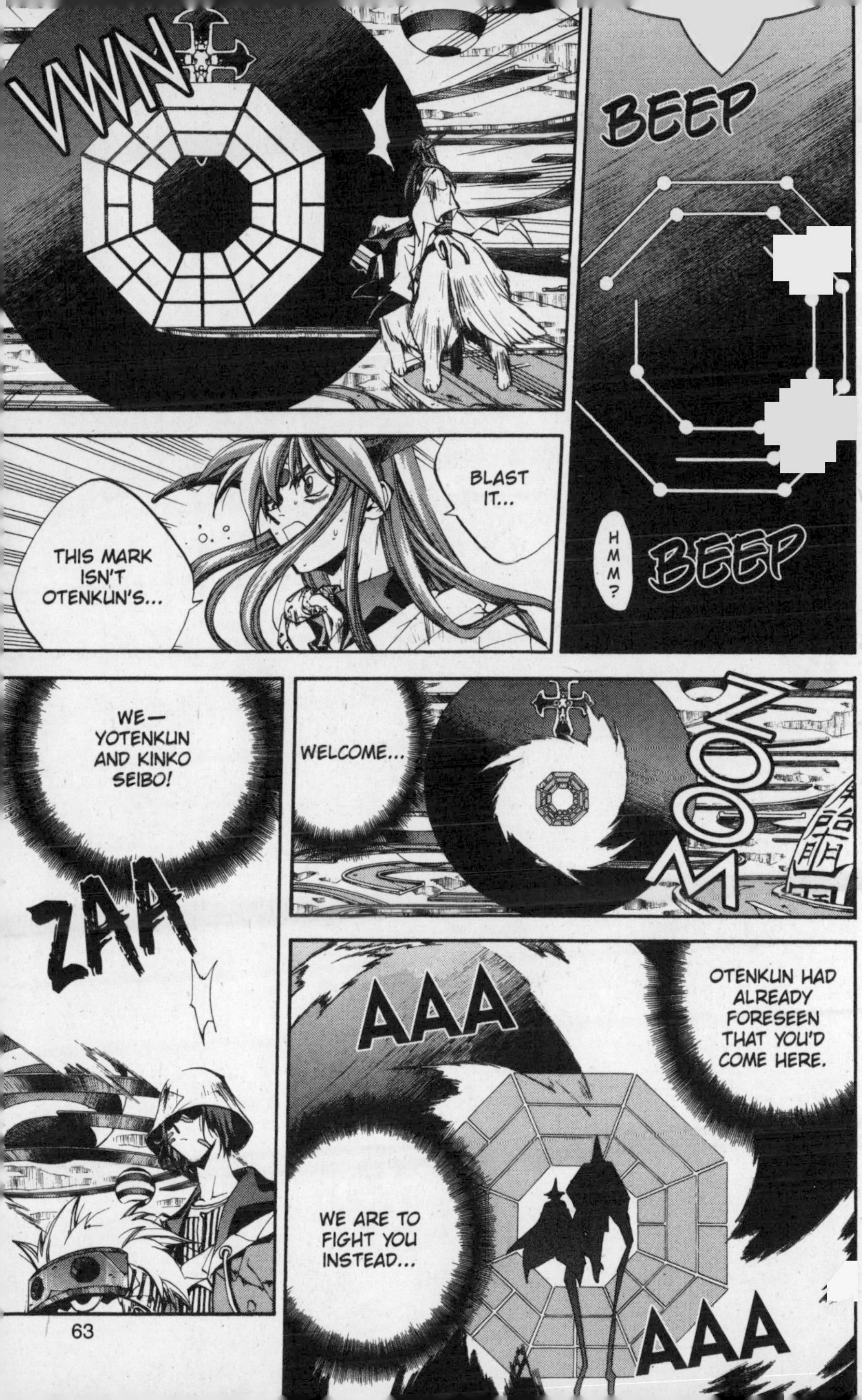
BEEP
HMM?
BEEP
VWN
BLAST IT...
THIS MARK ISN'T OTENKUN'S...
WELCOME...
ZOOM
AAA
OTENKUN HAD ALREADY FORESEEN THAT YOU'D COME HERE.
WE ARE TO FIGHT YOU INSTEAD...
AAA
WE— YOTENKUN AND KINKO SEIBO!
ZAA

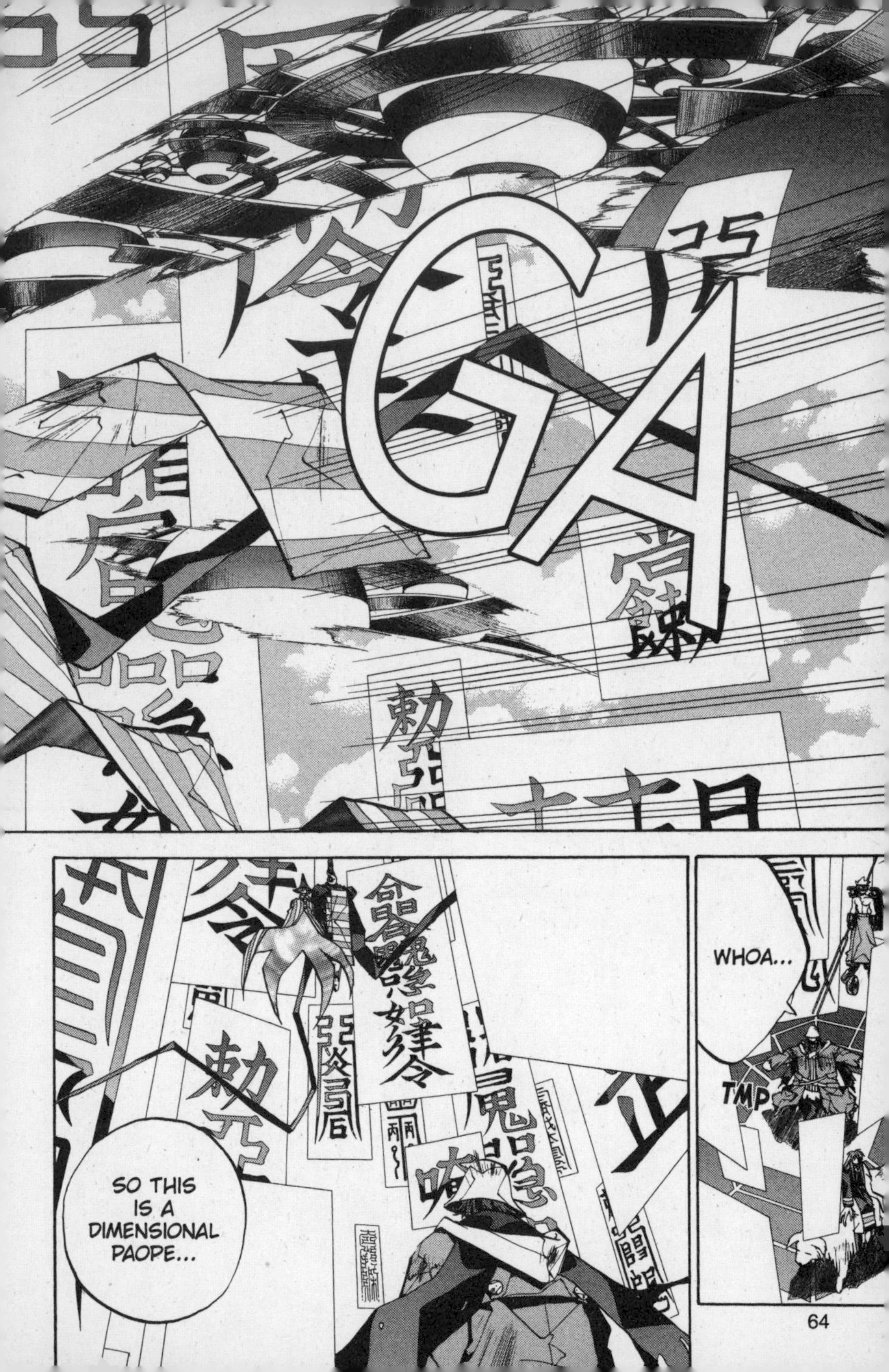
GA
WHOA...
TMP
SO THIS IS A DIMENSIONAL PAOPE...

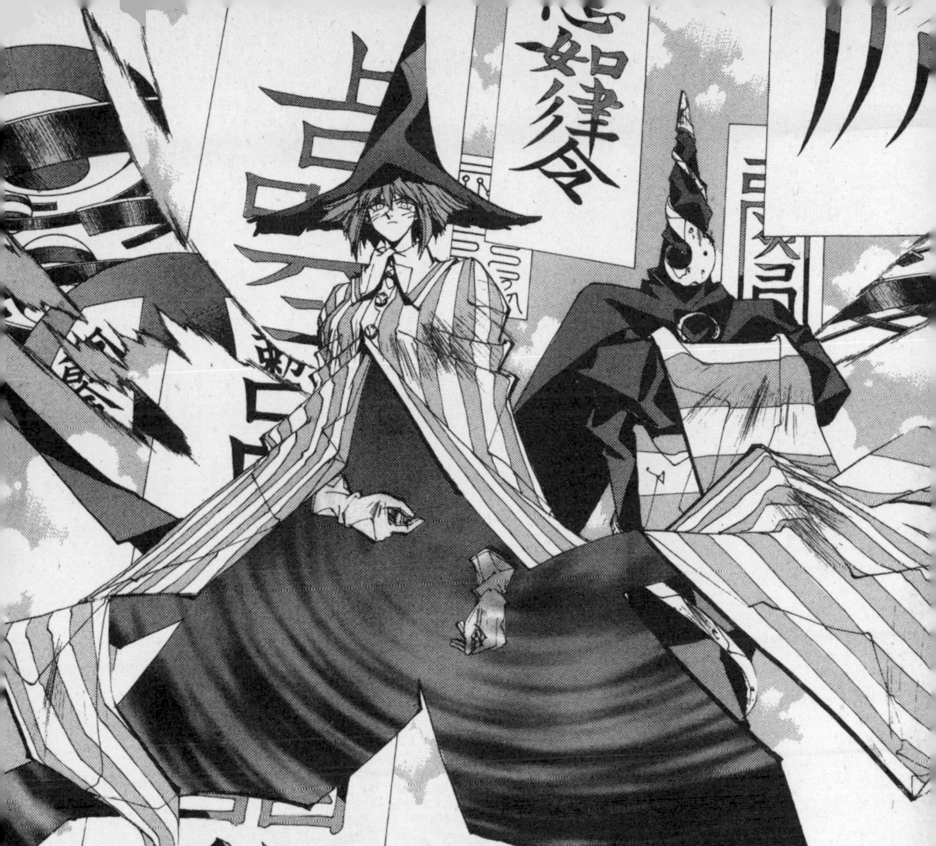

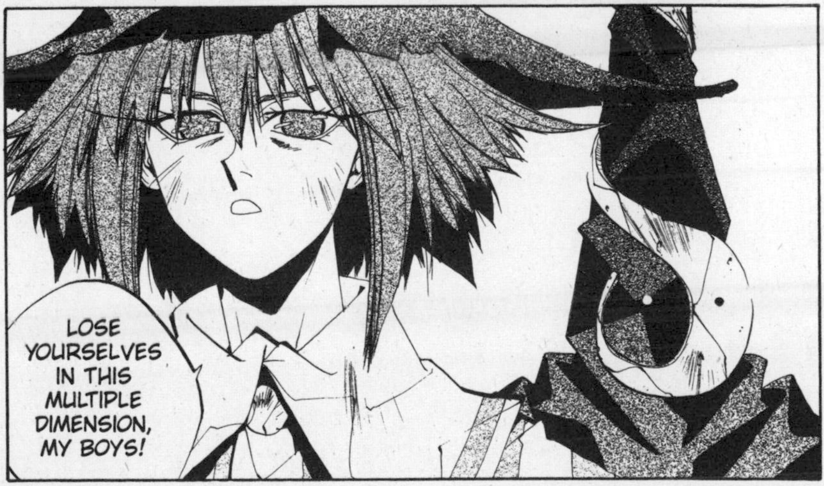
LOSE YOURSELVES IN THIS MULTIPLE DIMENSION, MY BOYS!

封神演義

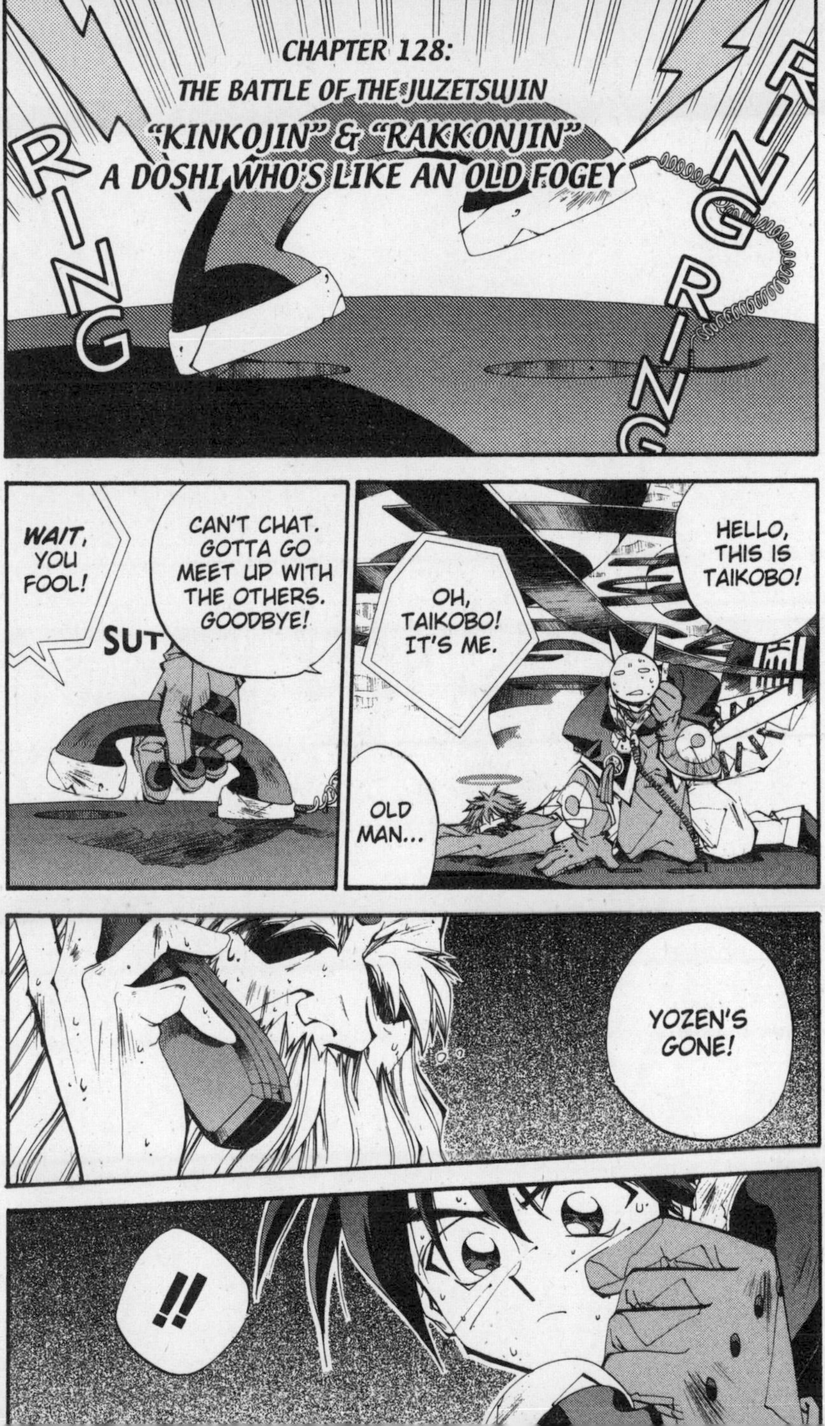
CHAPTER 128:
THE BATTLE OF THE JUZETSUJIN
"KINKOJIN" & "RAKKONJIN"
A DOSHI WHO'S LIKE AN OLD FOGEY
RING RING
RING
RING
HELLO, THIS IS TAIKOBO!
OH, TAIKOBO! IT'S ME.
OLD MAN...
CAN'T CHAT. GOTTA GO MEET UP WITH THE OTHERS. GOODBYE!
WAIT, YOU FOOL!
SUT
YOZEN'S GONE!
!!

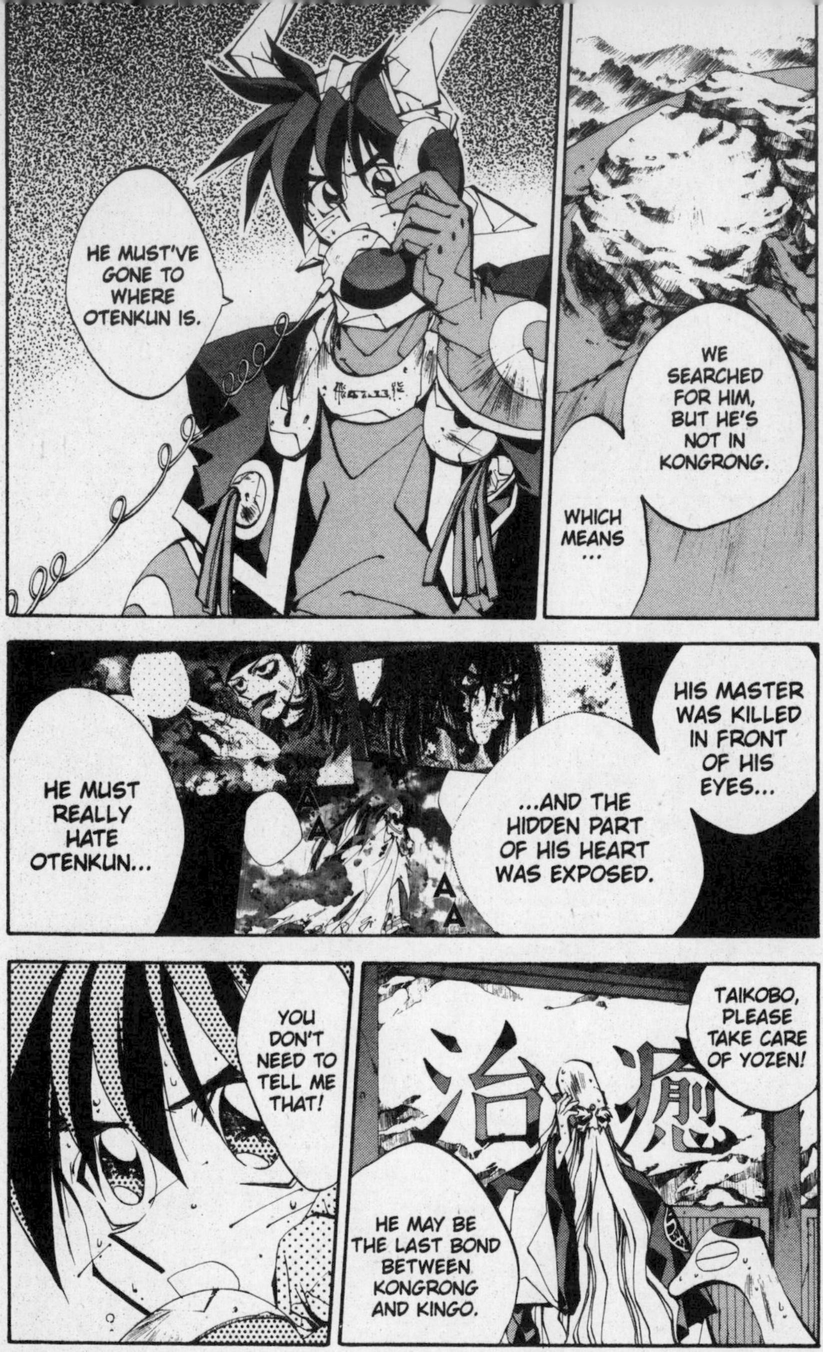
WE SEARCHED FOR HIM, BUT HE'S NOT IN KONGRONG.
WHICH MEANS ...
HE MUST'VE GONE TO WHERE OTENKUN IS.
HIS MASTER WAS KILLED IN FRONT OF HIS EYES...
...AND THE HIDDEN PART OF HIS HEART WAS EXPOSED.
HE MUST REALLY HATE OTENKUN...
TAIKOBO, PLEASE TAKE CARE OF YOZEN!
治癒
HE MAY BE THE LAST BOND BETWEEN KONGRONG AND KINGO.
YOU DON'T NEED TO TELL ME THAT!

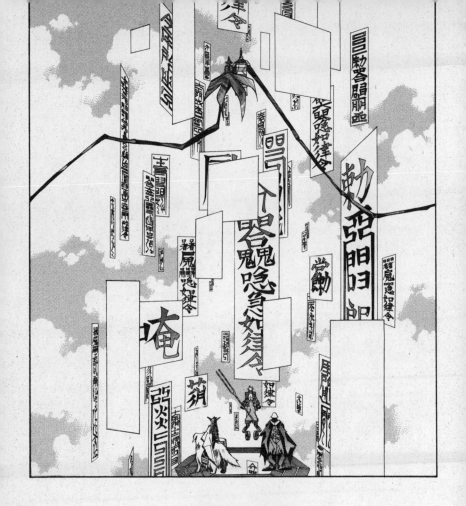

Chapter 128

THE BATTLE OF THE JUZETSUJIN
"KINKOJIN" & "RAKKONJIN"
A DOSHI WHO'S LIKE AN OLD FOGEY

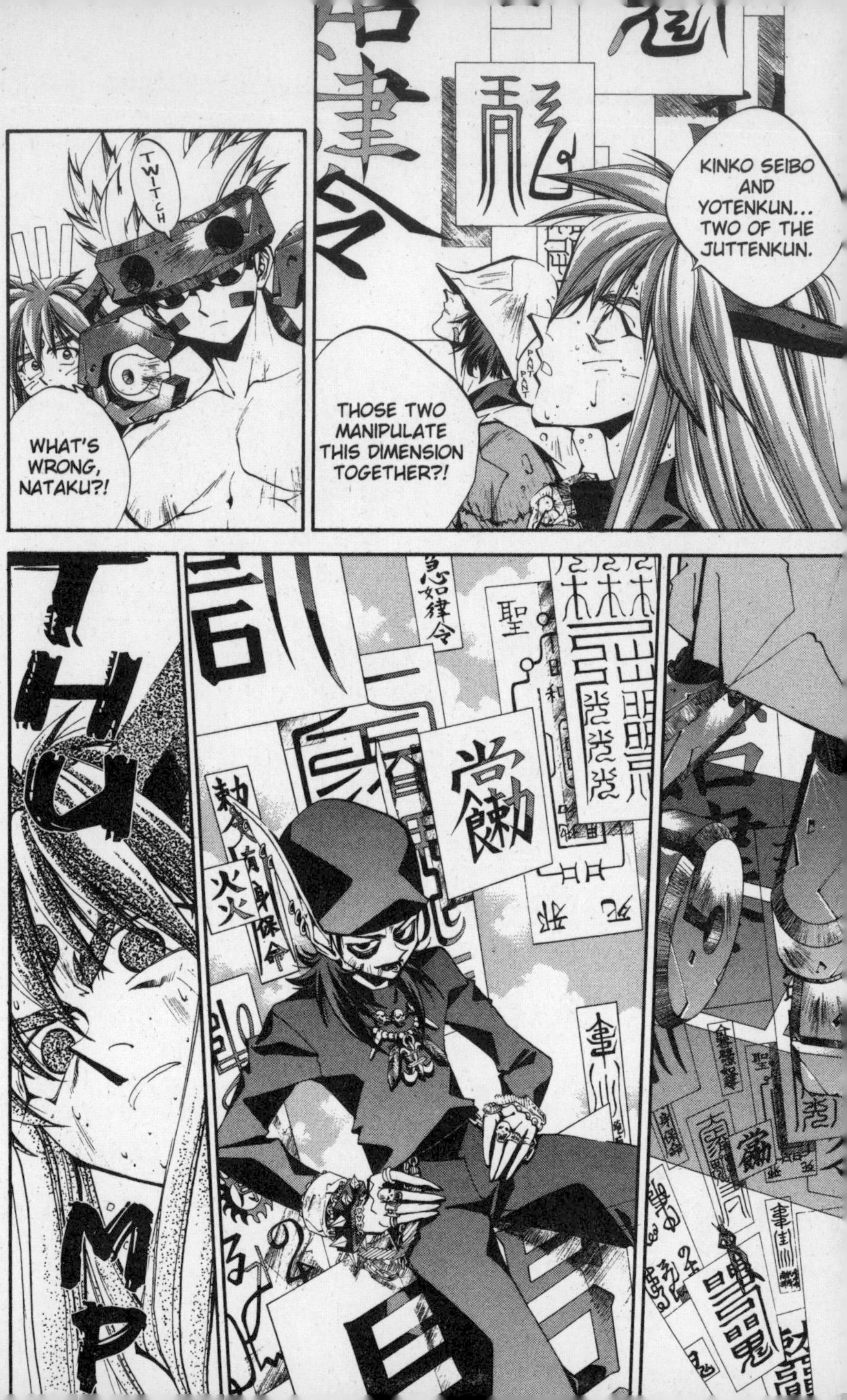

KINKO SEIBO AND YOTENKUN... TWO OF THE JUTTENKUN.
PANT PANT
THOSE TWO MANIPULATE THIS DIMENSION TOGETHER?!
TWITCH
WHAT'S WRONG, NATAKU?!
THUMP

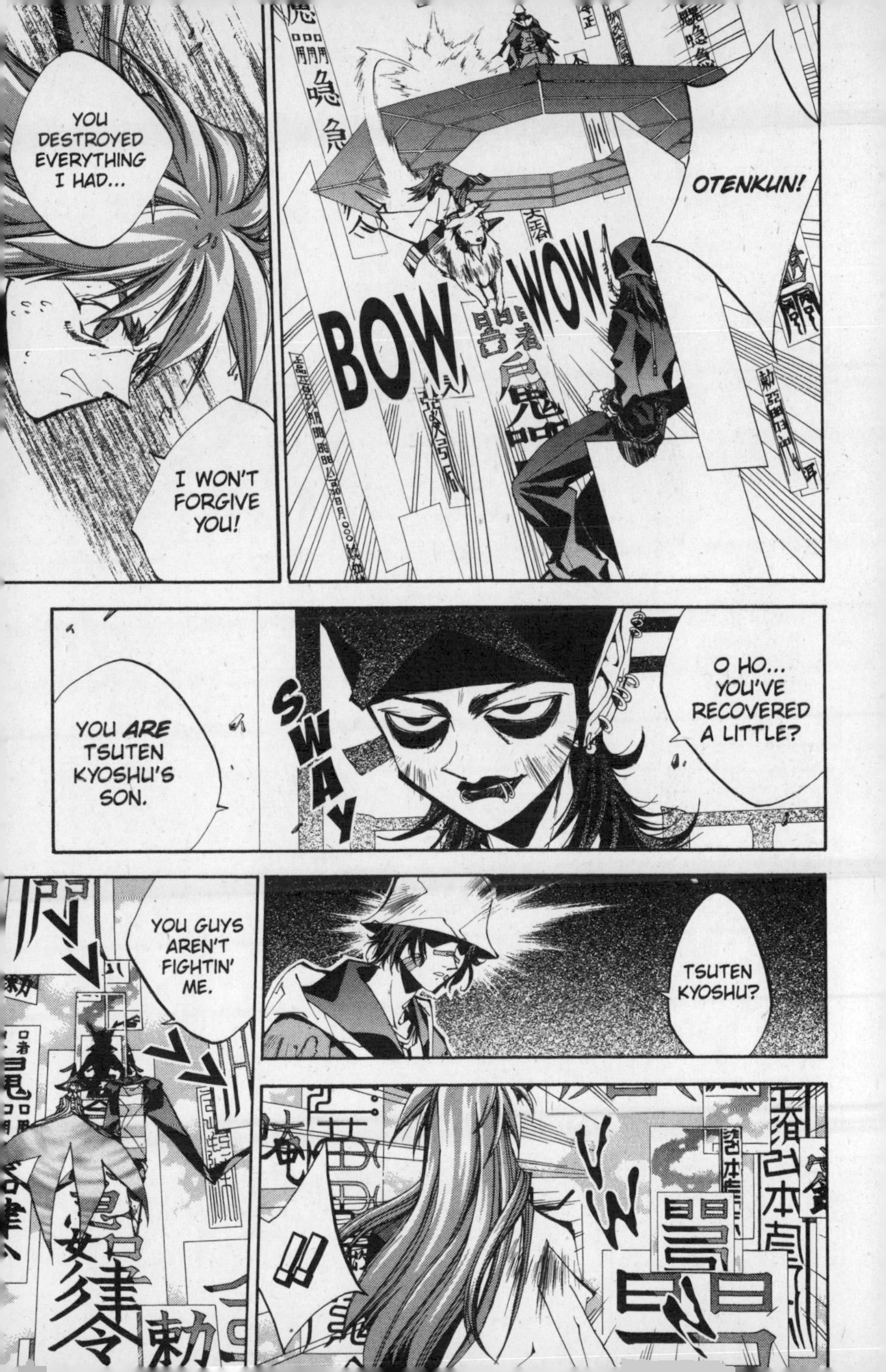
OTENKUN!
BOW WOW
YOU DESTROYED EVERYTHING I HAD...
I WON'T FORGIVE YOU!
O HO... YOU'VE RECOVERED A LITTLE?
SWAY
YOU *ARE* TSUTEN KYOSHU'S SON.
TSUTEN KYOSHU?
!!
YOU GUYS AREN'T FIGHTIN' ME.

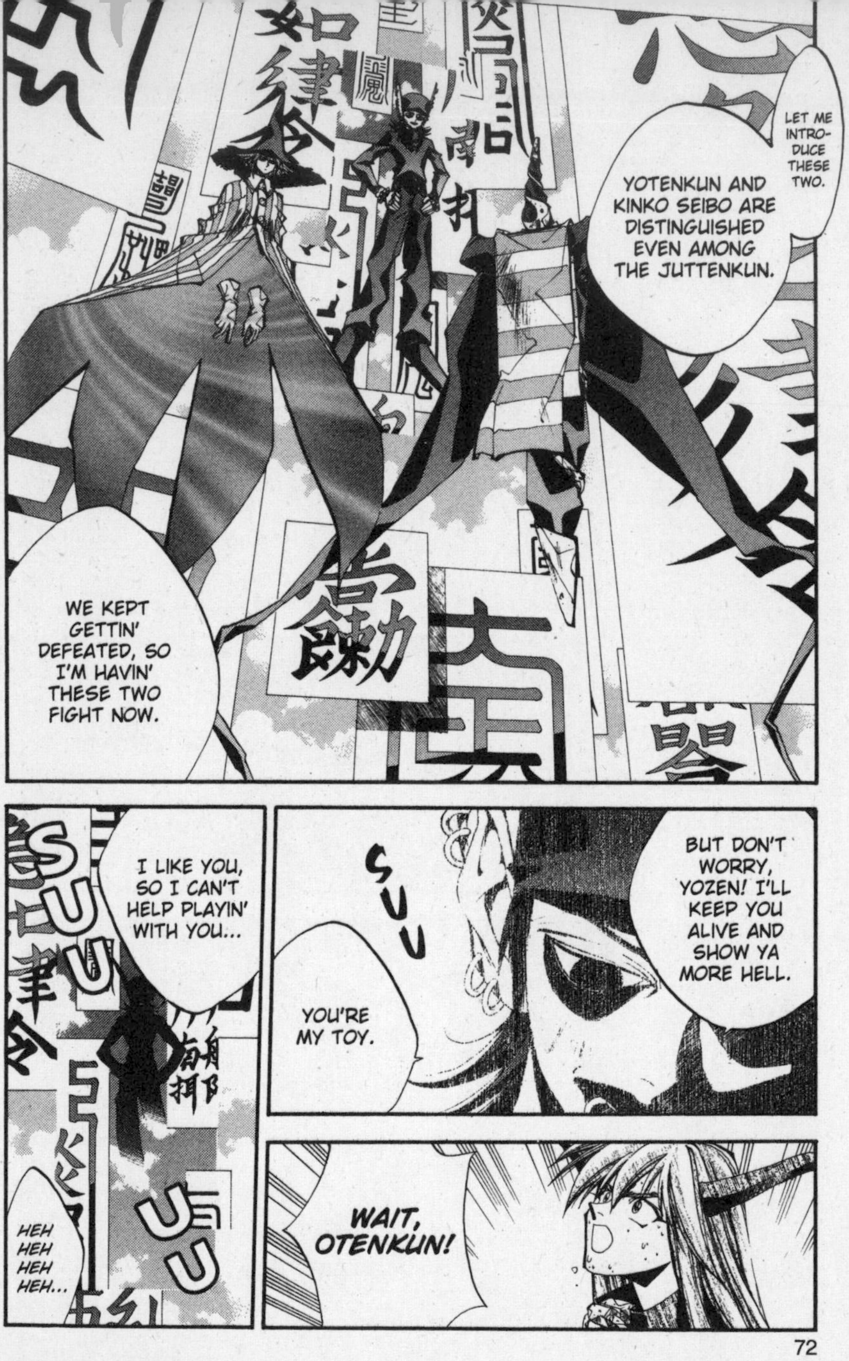

LET ME INTRODUCE THESE TWO.
YOTENKUN AND KINKO SEIBO ARE DISTINGUISHED EVEN AMONG THE JUTTENKUN.
WE KEPT GETTIN' DEFEATED, SO I'M HAVIN' THESE TWO FIGHT NOW.
BUT DON'T WORRY, YOZEN! I'LL KEEP YOU ALIVE AND SHOW YA MORE HELL.
SUU
YOU'RE MY TOY.
WAIT, OTENKUN!
SUU
I LIKE YOU, SO I CAN'T HELP PLAYIN' WITH YOU...
UU
HEH HEH HEH HEH...

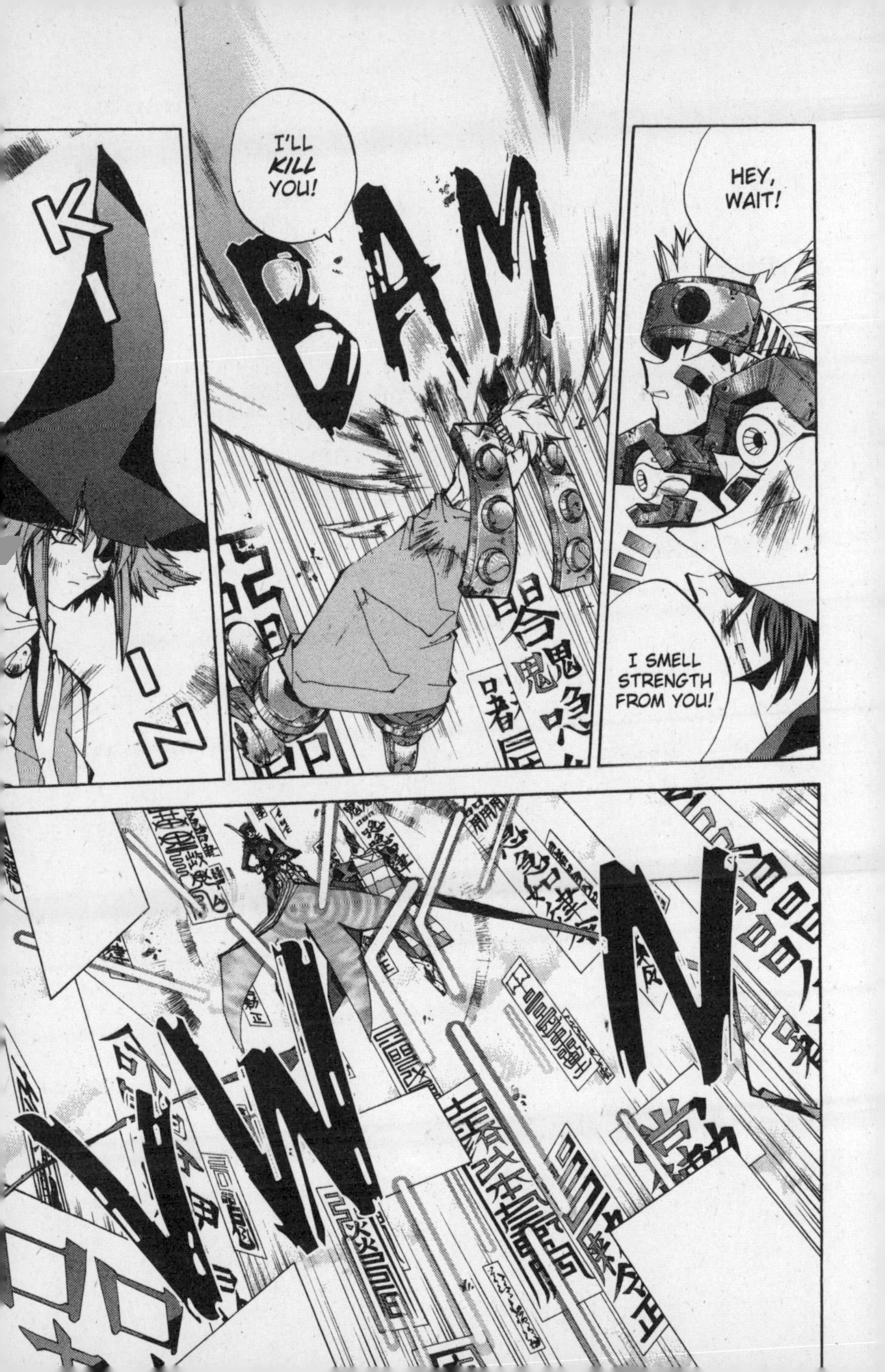
HEY, WAIT!
I SMELL STRENGTH FROM YOU!
I'LL *KILL* YOU!
BAM

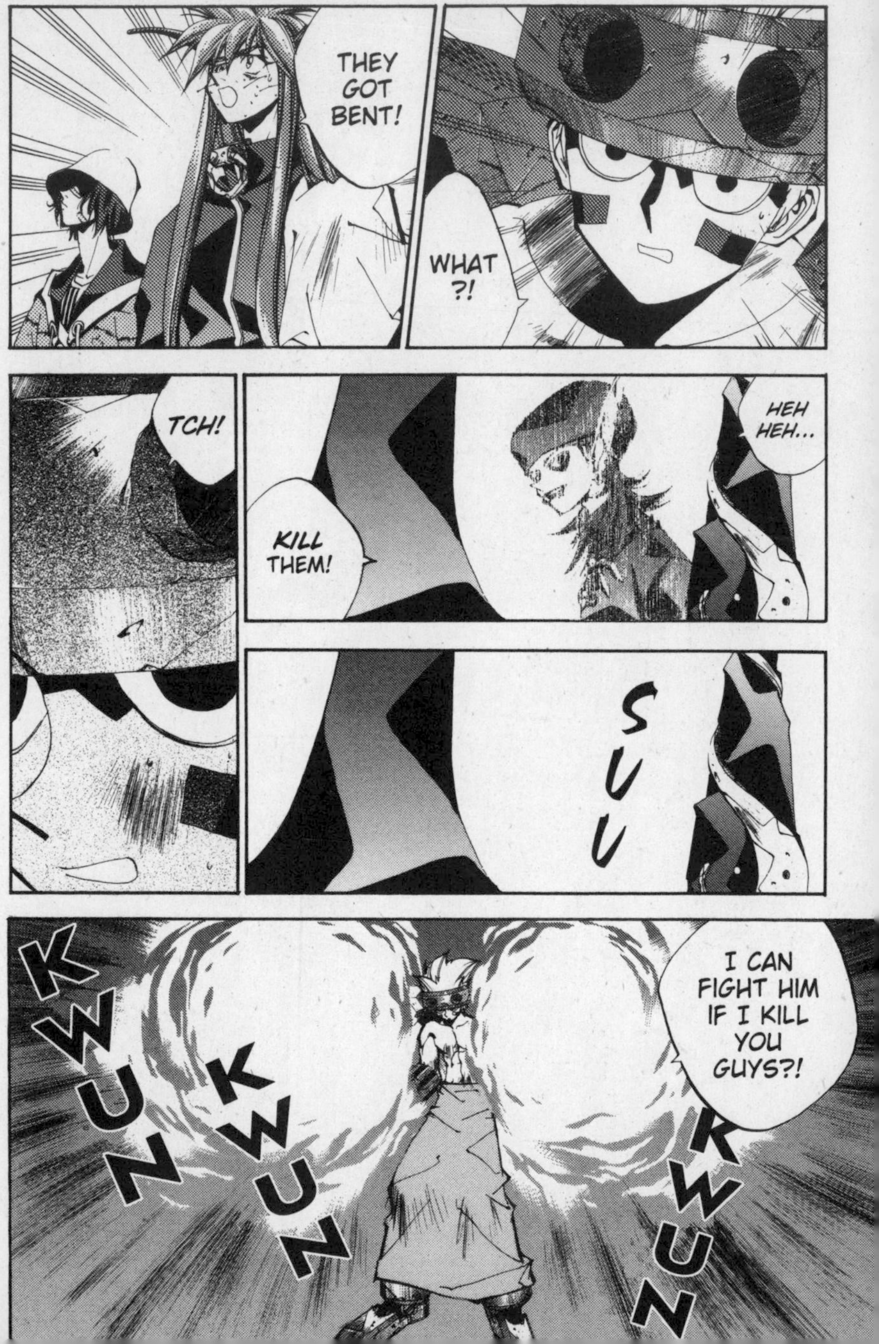
WHAT ?!
THEY GOT BENT!
HEH HEH...
KILL THEM!
SUU
TCH!
I CAN FIGHT HIM IF I KILL YOU GUYS?!
KWUN
KWUN
KWUN

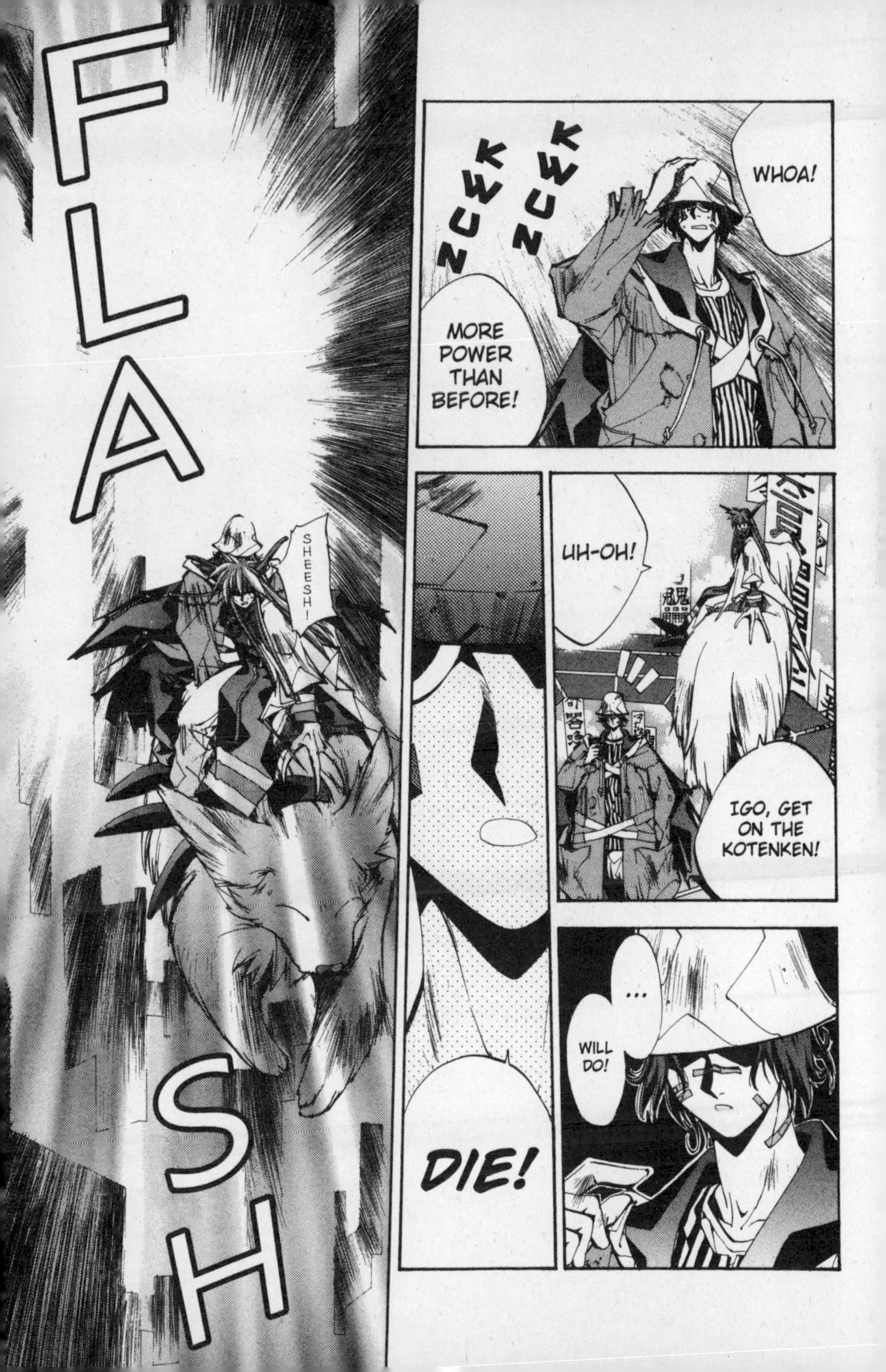
KWUNK
KWUNK
WHOA!
MORE POWER THAN BEFORE!
UH-OH!
IGO, GET ON THE KOTENKEN!
...
WILL DO!
DIE!
FLASH
SHEESH!

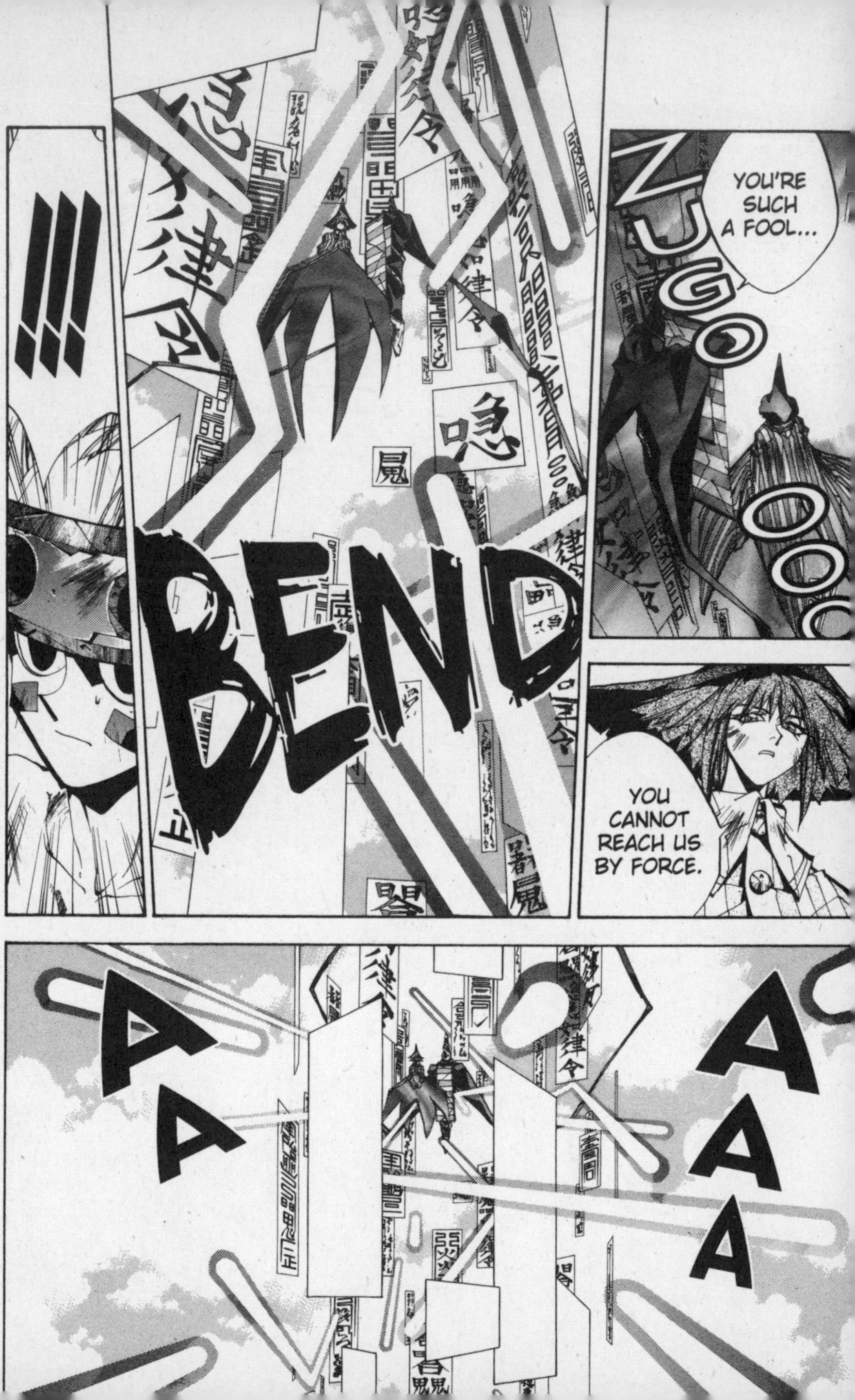
YOU'RE SUCH A FOOL...
ZUGOOOO
YOU CANNOT REACH US BY FORCE.
BEND
!!!
AAAA
AA

THEY'RE NOT HURT...

THEY'RE NOT HURT AT ALL!

EVEN THE TALISMANS AROUND THEM WEREN'T DESTROYED!

...

VWOOM

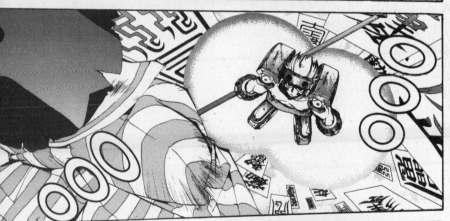

AH...

NO, NATAKU!

YOU THINK YOU'LL HIT ME AT CLOSE RANGE?

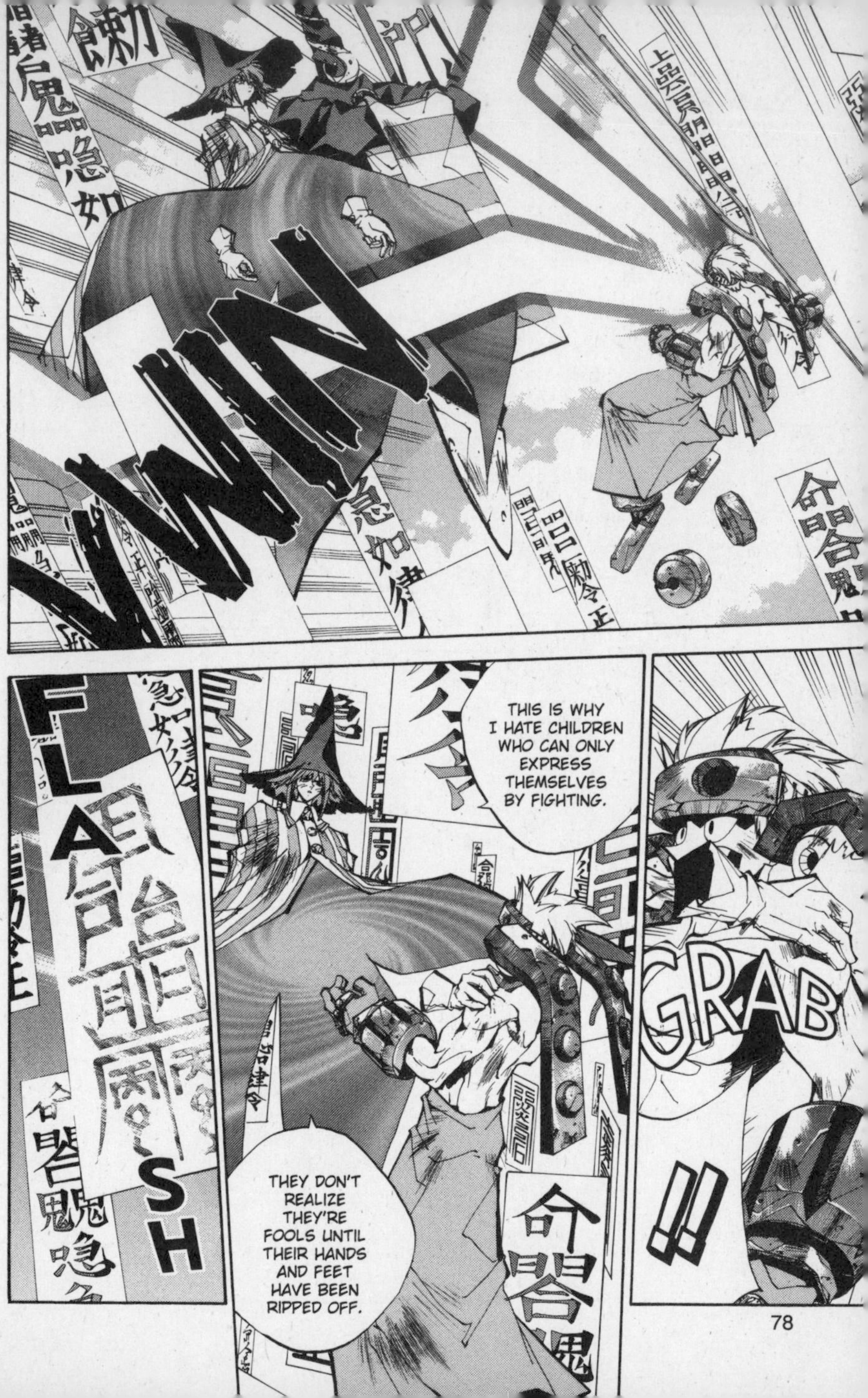
GRAB
!!
THIS IS WHY I HATE CHILDREN WHO CAN ONLY EXPRESS THEMSELVES BY FIGHTING.
THEY DON'T REALIZE THEY'RE FOOLS UNTIL THEIR HANDS AND FEET HAVE BEEN RIPPED OFF.
FLASH

READ THIS WAY

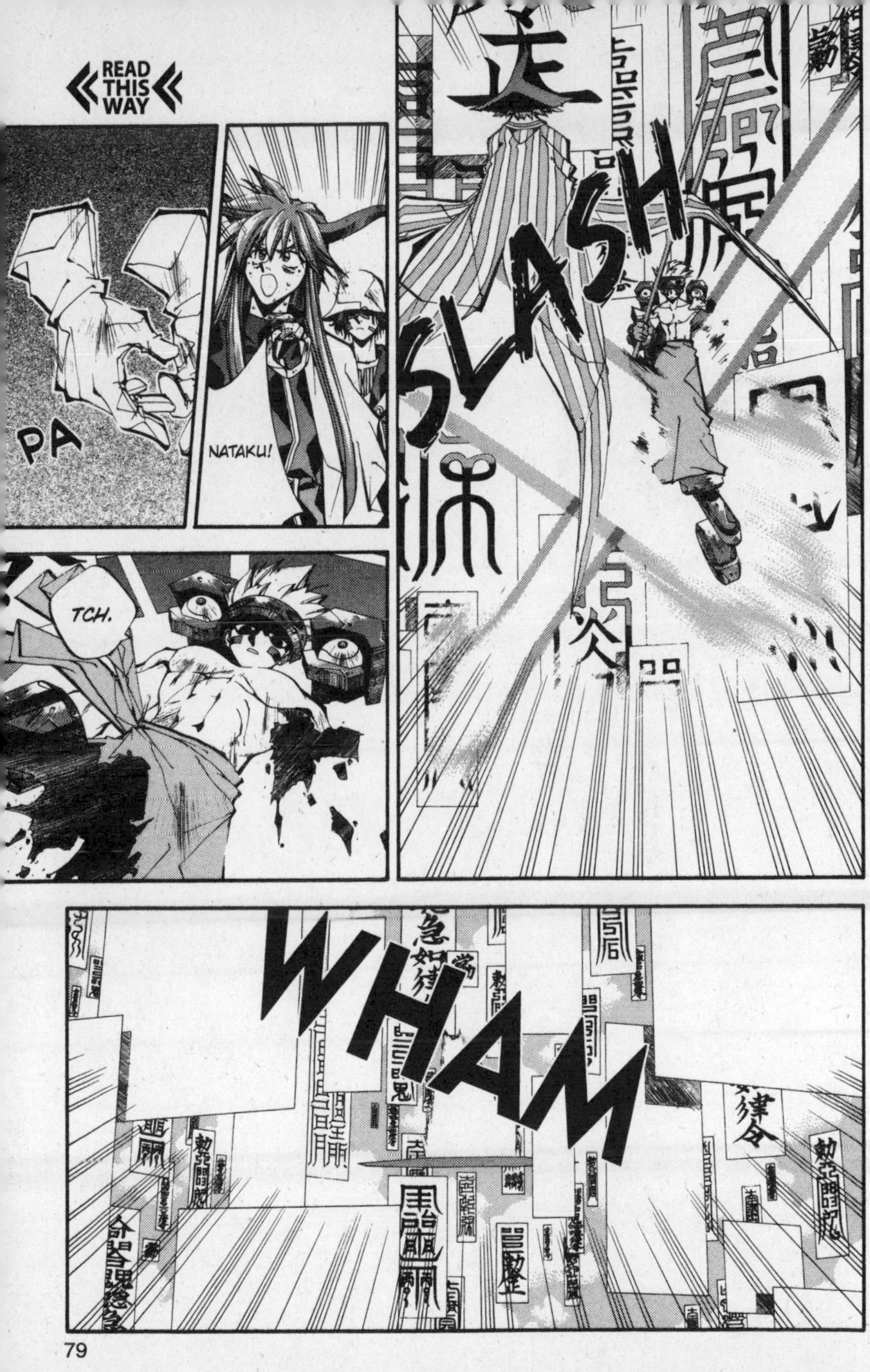

SLASH
NATAKU!
PA
TCH.
WHAM

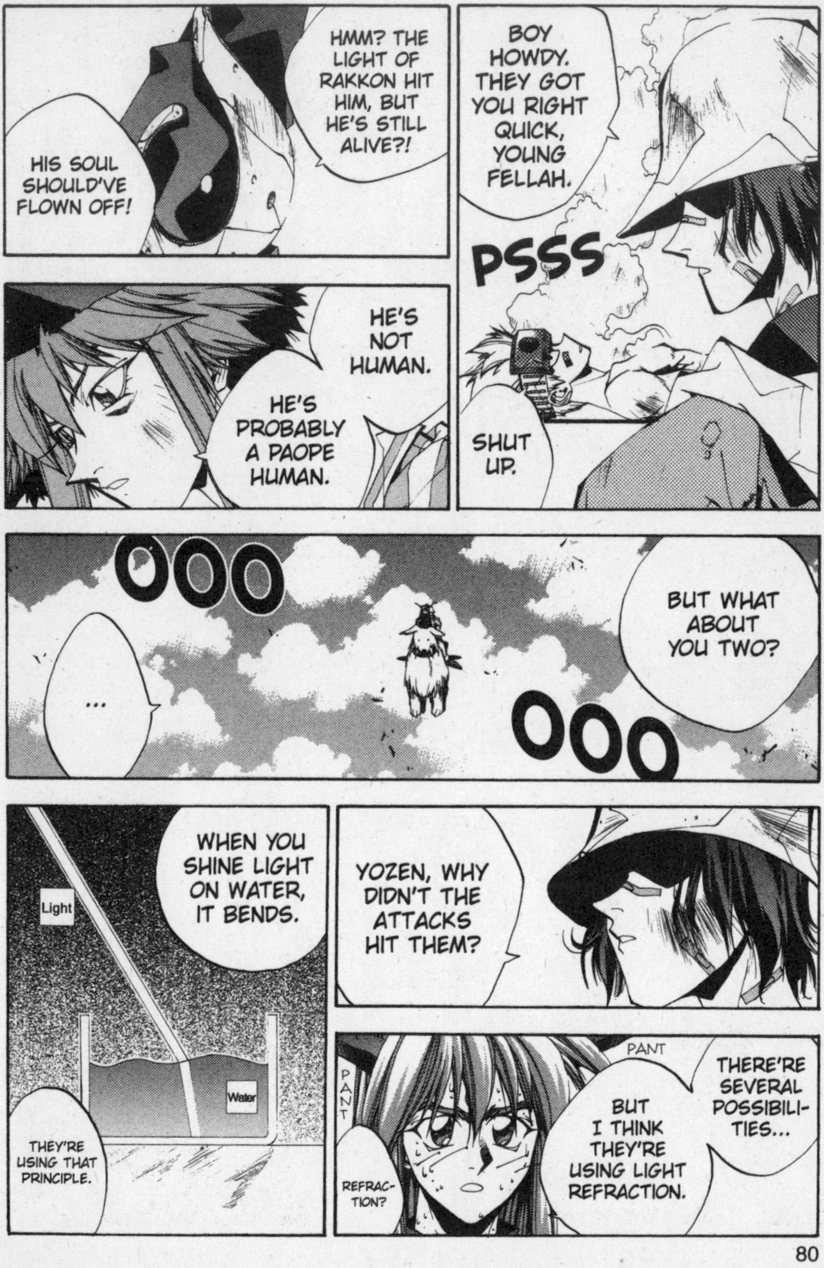
BOY HOWDY. THEY GOT YOU RIGHT QUICK, YOUNG FELLAH.
PSSS
SHUT UP.
HMM? THE LIGHT OF RAKKON HIT HIM, BUT HE'S STILL ALIVE?!
HIS SOUL SHOULD'VE FLOWN OFF!
HE'S NOT HUMAN.
HE'S PROBABLY A PAOPE HUMAN.
BUT WHAT ABOUT YOU TWO?
OOO
OOO
...
YOZEN, WHY DIDN'T THE ATTACKS HIT THEM?
PANT
PANT
THERE'RE SEVERAL POSSIBILI-TIES...
BUT I THINK THEY'RE USING LIGHT REFRACTION.
REFRAC-TION?
WHEN YOU SHINE LIGHT ON WATER, IT BENDS.
Light
Water
THEY'RE USING THAT PRINCIPLE.

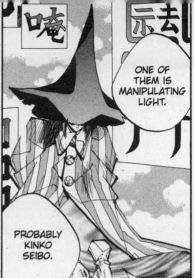

ONE OF THEM IS MANIPULATING LIGHT.
PROBABLY KINKO SEIBO.
THIS IS GOING TO BE DIFFICULT.
IT MAY MEAN THAT THIS DIMENSION ITSELF IS AN ILLUSION.
WHAT DO YOU MEAN?
WELL...
HE STINKS...
OUR EYES SEE THINGS BY SENSING LIGHT.
Ciliary zonule
Conjunctiva
Iris
Ora serrata
Pupil
Crystalline lens
Anterior eye chamber
Cornea
Central fovea
Optic nerves
Retina
Choroid coat
Sclera
COLOR, SHAPE AND EVERYTHING IS INFORMATION THAT LIGHT GIVES TO THE OPTIC NERVES. THE BRAIN THEN RECOGNIZES THEM.
IF THE LIGHT THAT OUR EYES RECEIVE IS ALSO BENT...
BEND
BEND
BEND
...THIS HAND YOU SEE HERE MAY NOT EVEN EXIST.
SO IF WE ATTACK THEM...
PERCEPTION
YAH
SWING
WE MAY BE SWINGING AT NOTHING...
REALITY
YAH
SWING
STUPID

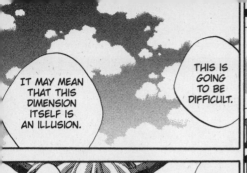

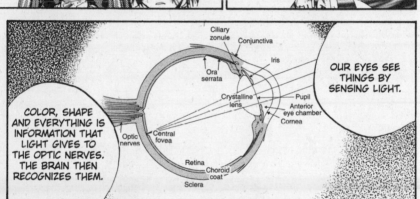

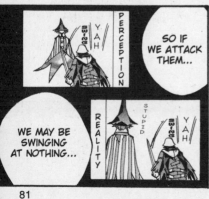

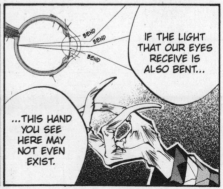

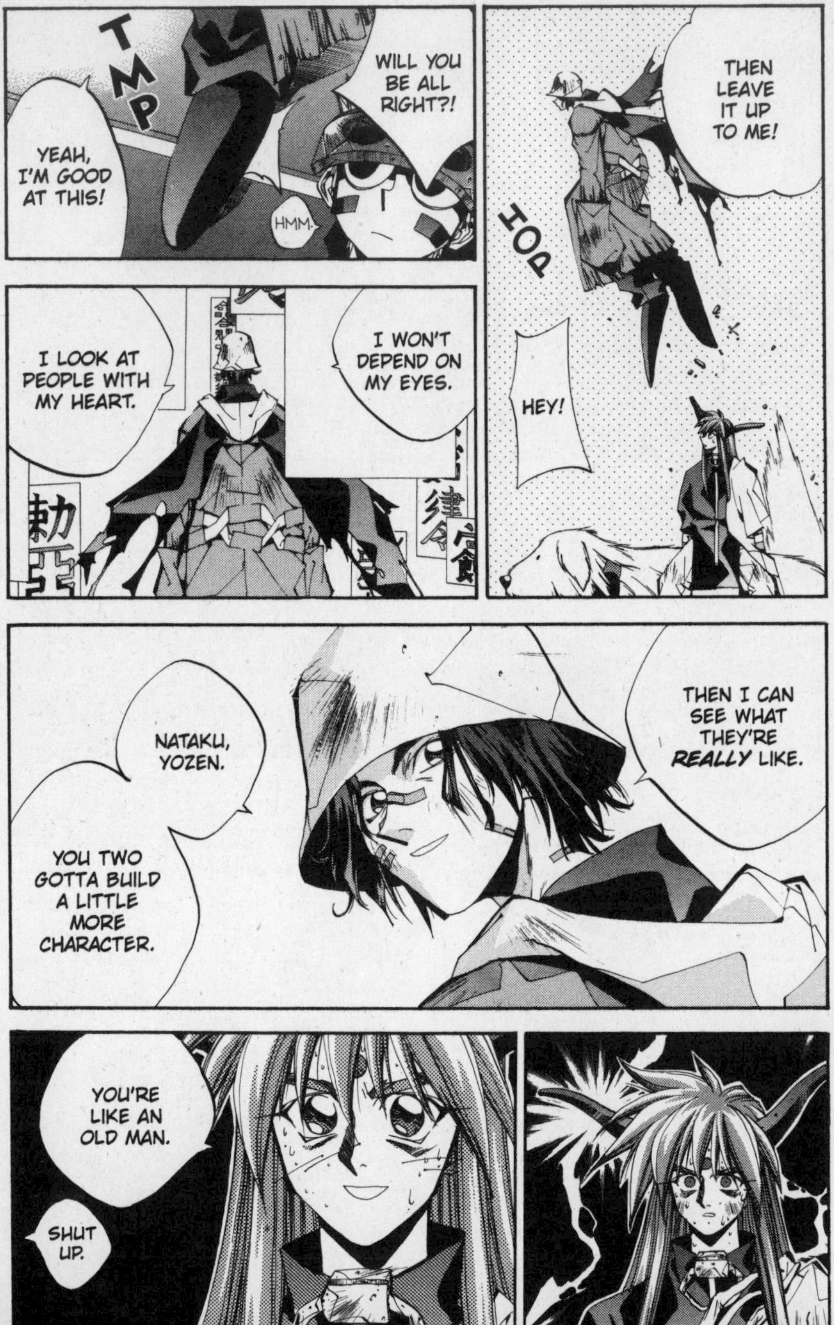

THEN LEAVE IT UP TO ME!
HOP
HEY!
WILL YOU BE ALL RIGHT?!
TMP
YEAH, I'M GOOD AT THIS!
HMM.
I WON'T DEPEND ON MY EYES.
I LOOK AT PEOPLE WITH MY HEART.
THEN I CAN SEE WHAT THEY'RE *REALLY* LIKE.
NATAKU, YOZEN.
YOU TWO GOTTA BUILD A LITTLE MORE CHARACTER.
YOU'RE LIKE AN OLD MAN.
SHUT UP.

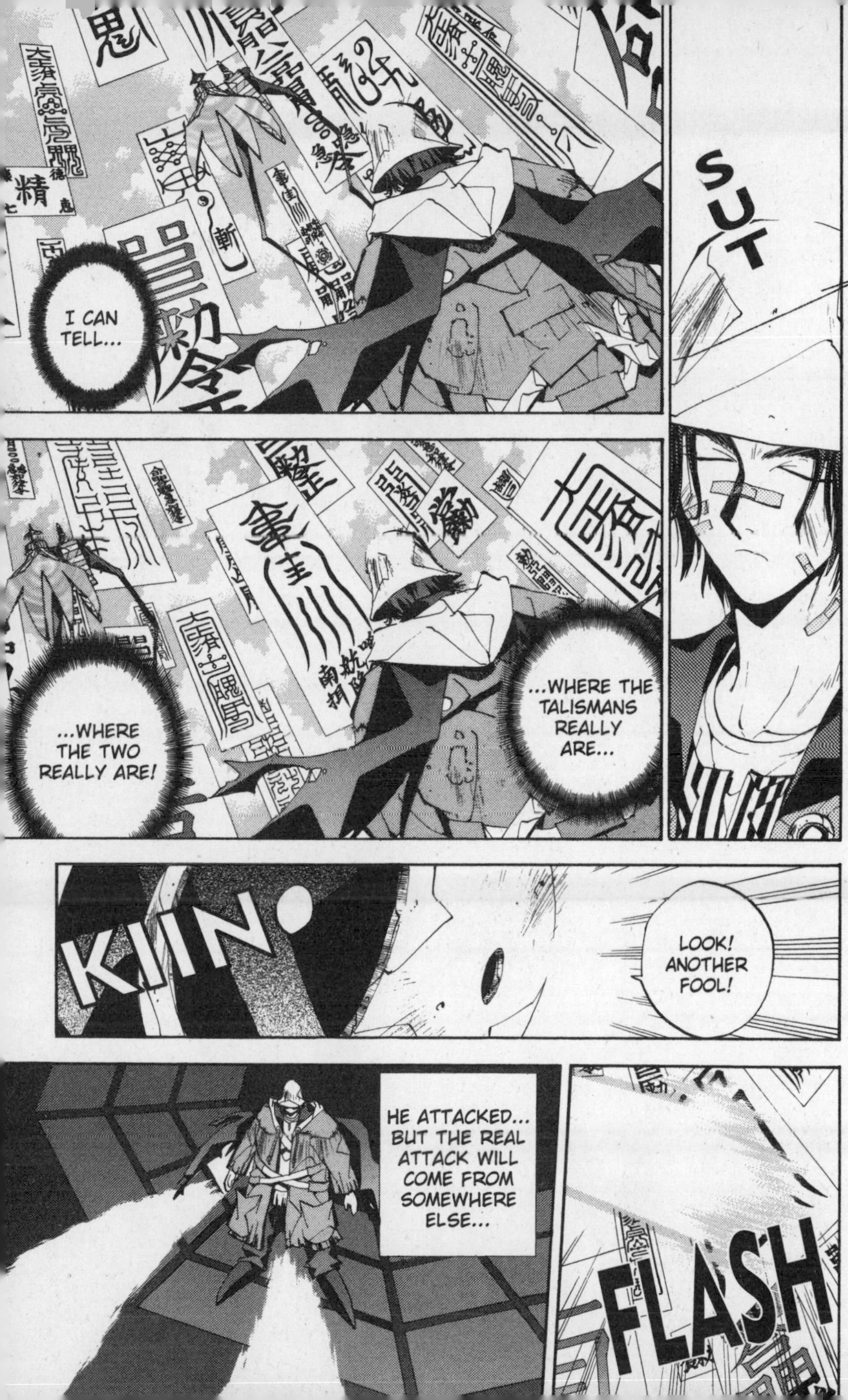
SUT
I CAN TELL...
...WHERE THE TALISMANS REALLY ARE...
...WHERE THE TWO REALLY ARE!
LOOK! ANOTHER FOOL!
KIIN
FLASH
HE ATTACKED... BUT THE REAL ATTACK WILL COME FROM SOMEWHERE ELSE...

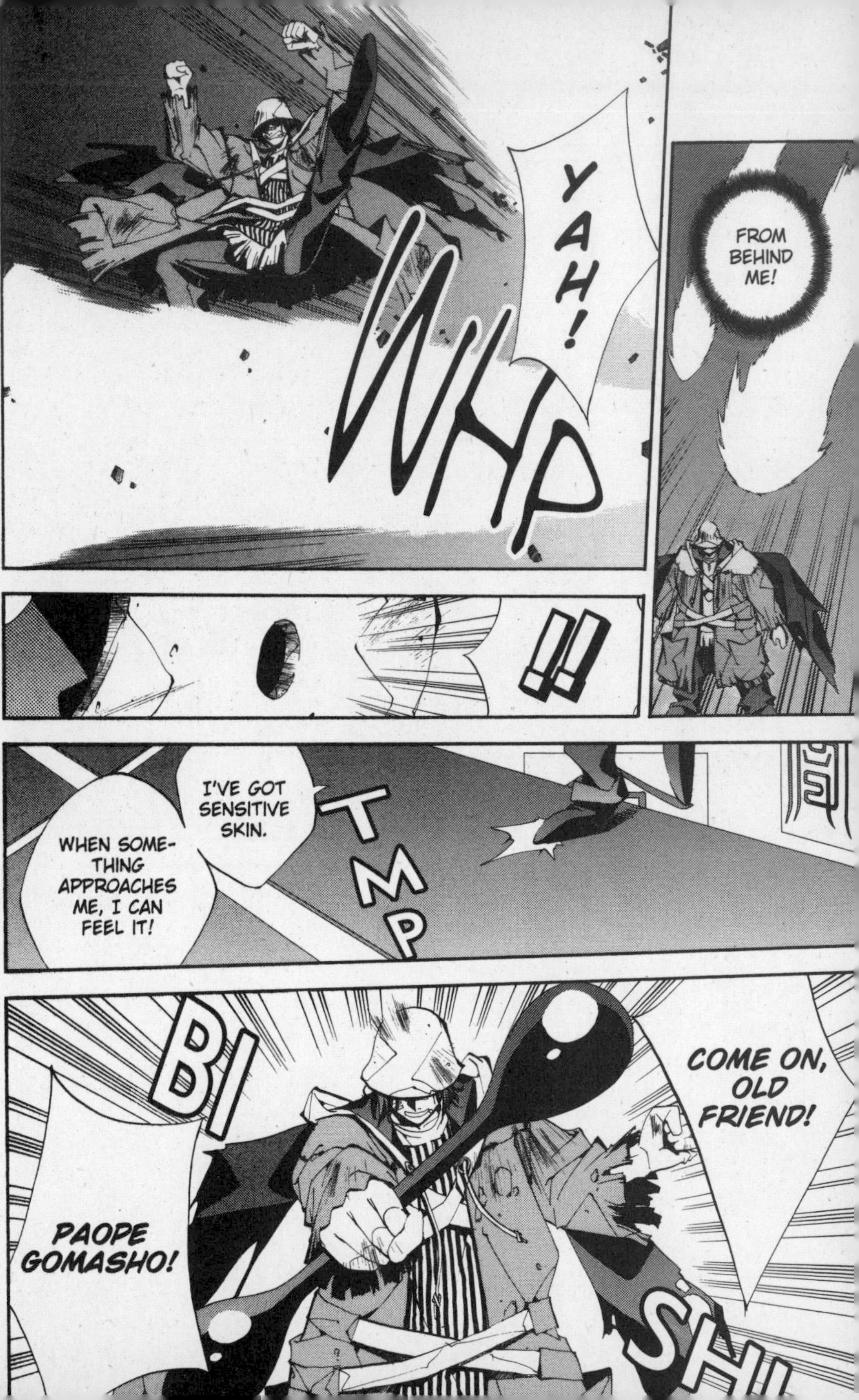
FROM BEHIND ME!
YAH!
WHP
!!
I'VE GOT SENSITIVE SKIN.
WHEN SOME-THING APPROACHES ME, I CAN FEEL IT!
TMP
COME ON, OLD FRIEND!
BI
PAOPE GOMASHO!
SHI

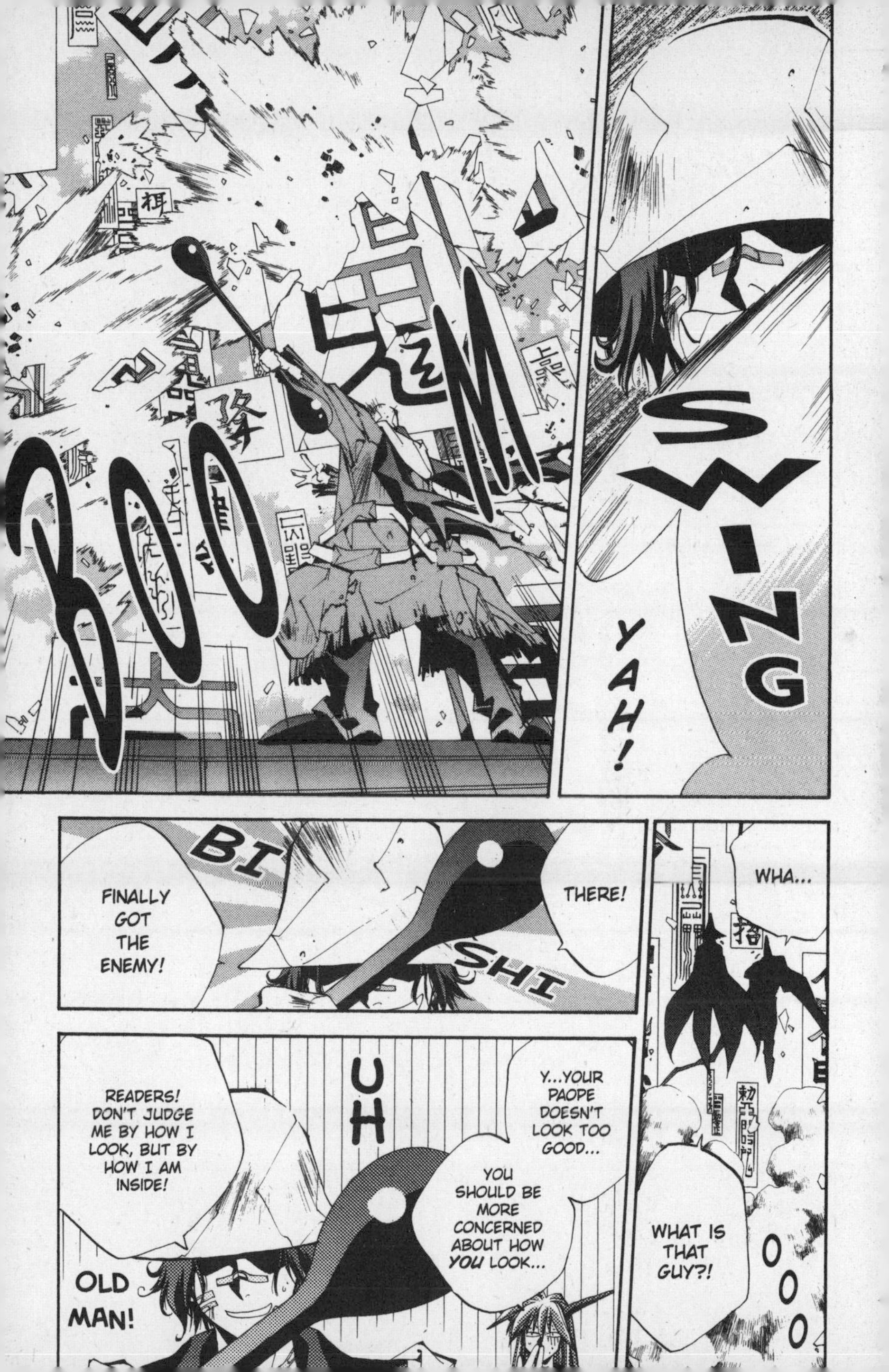
SWING
YAH!
BOOM
WHA...
WHAT IS THAT GUY?!
OOO
THERE!
BI SHI
FINALLY GOT THE ENEMY!
Y...YOUR PAOPE DOESN'T LOOK TOO GOOD...
UH
READERS! DON'T JUDGE ME BY HOW I LOOK, BUT BY HOW I AM INSIDE!
YOU SHOULD BE MORE CONCERNED ABOUT HOW *YOU* LOOK...
OLD MAN!

封神演義

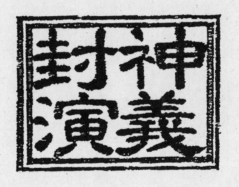

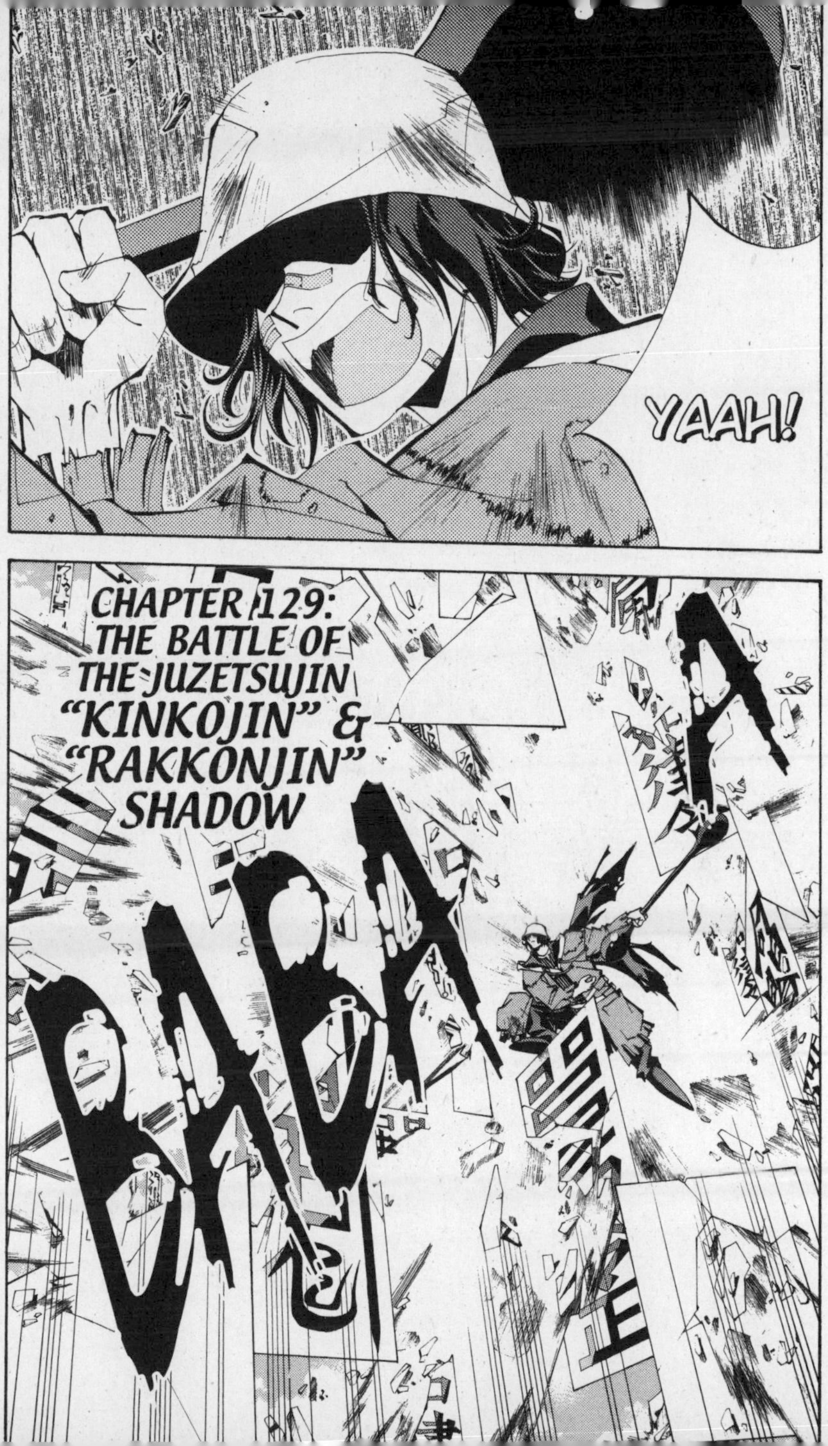
YAAH!
CHAPTER 129: THE BATTLE OF THE JUZETSUJIN "KINKOJIN" & "RAKKONJIN" SHADOW

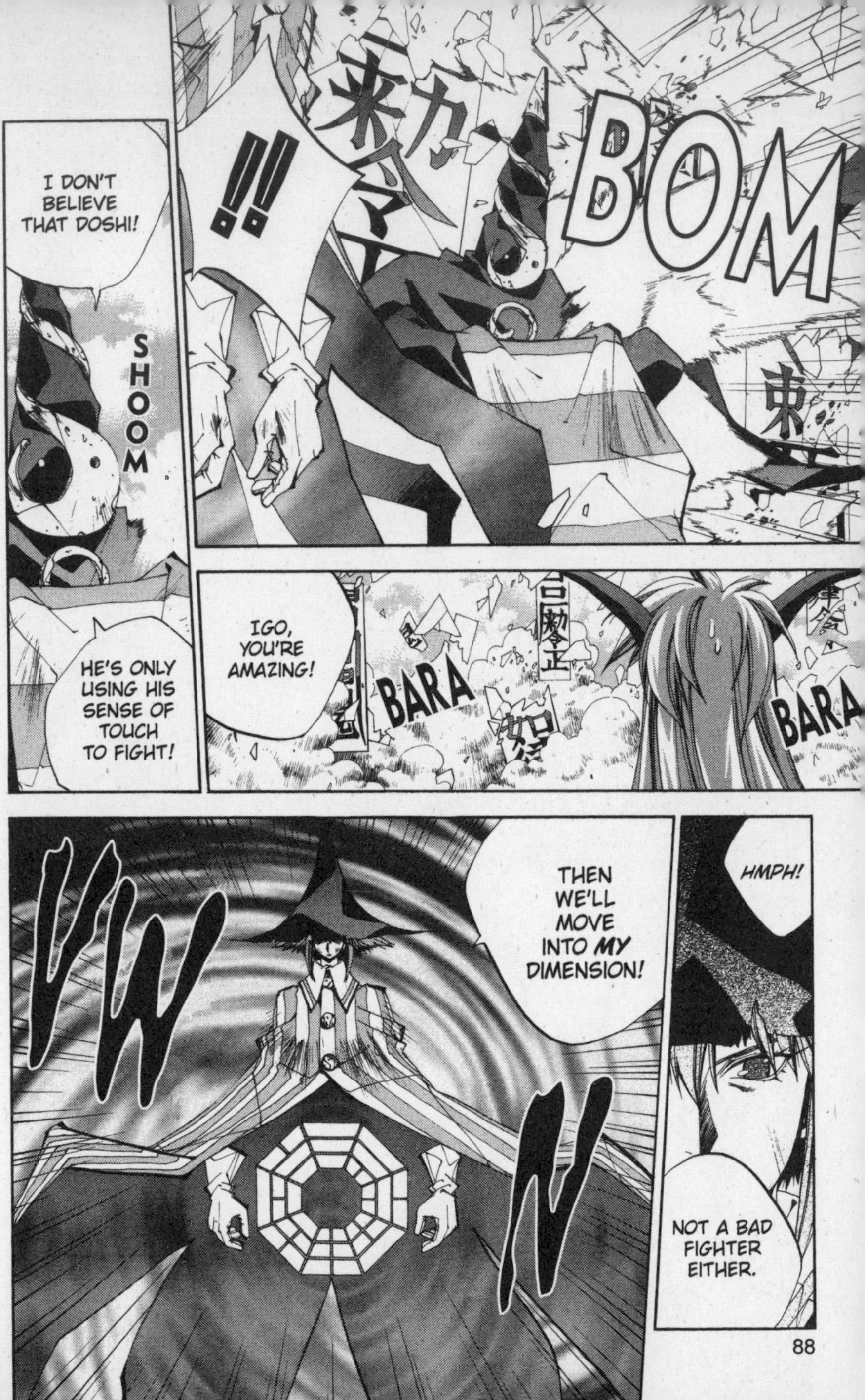
!!
BOM
BARA
IGO, YOU'RE AMAZING!
BARA
I DON'T BELIEVE THAT DOSHI!
SHOOM
HE'S ONLY USING HIS SENSE OF TOUCH TO FIGHT!
HMPH!
NOT A BAD FIGHTER EITHER.
THEN WE'LL MOVE INTO *MY* DIMENSION!
VWN

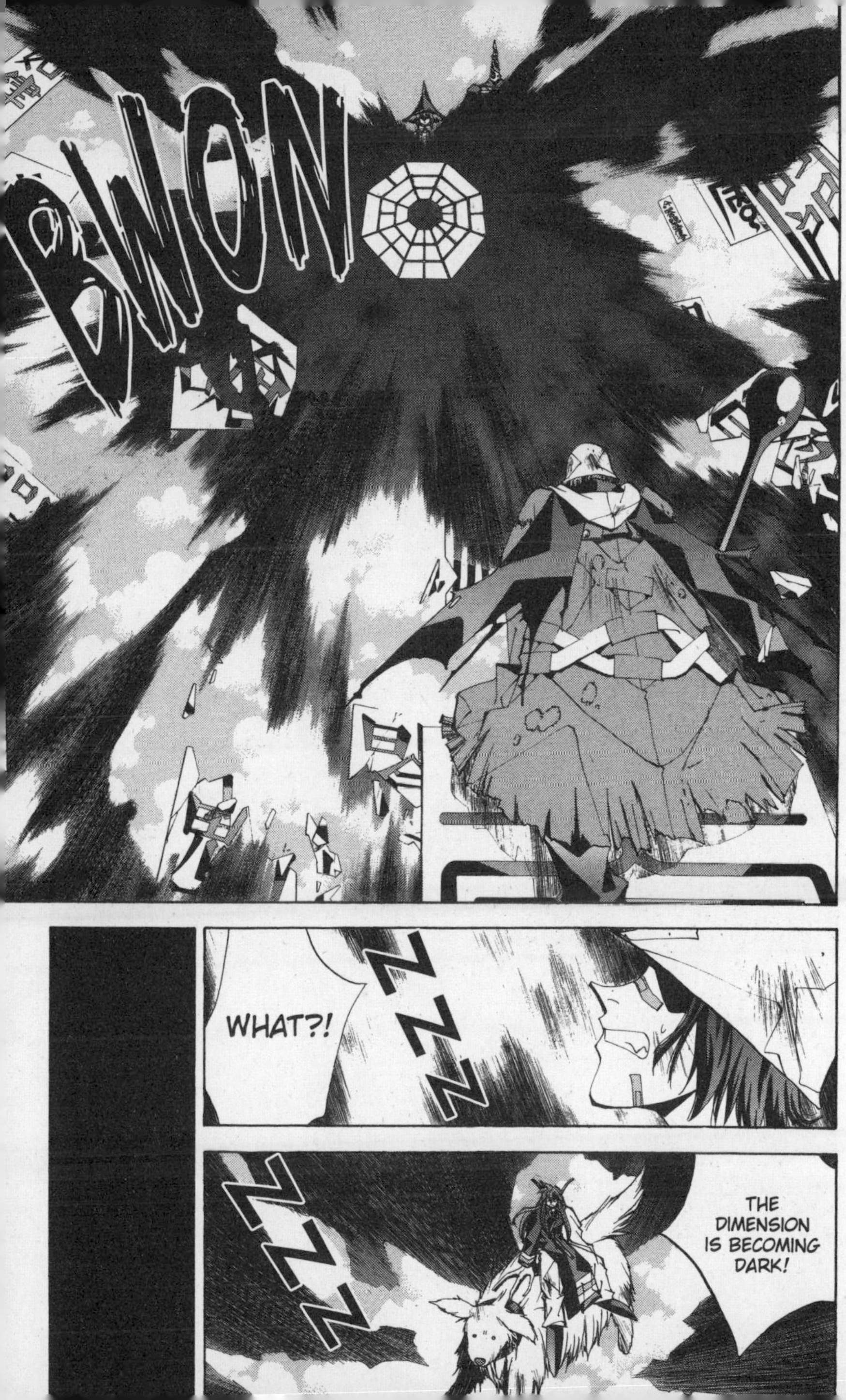
BWON
WHAT?!
ZZZ
THE DIMENSION IS BECOMING DARK!
ZZZ

Chapter 129

THE BATTLE OF THE JUZETSUJIN "KINKOJIN" & "RAKKONJIN" SHADOW

Recent Characters
Igo
A disciple of Doko Tenson, one of Kongrong's 12 Elite Sennin.

Wields the paope "Gomasho."
He's got sensitive skin, so he's good at sensing the enemy's presence.
It seems that he's joined the Sennin World only recently.

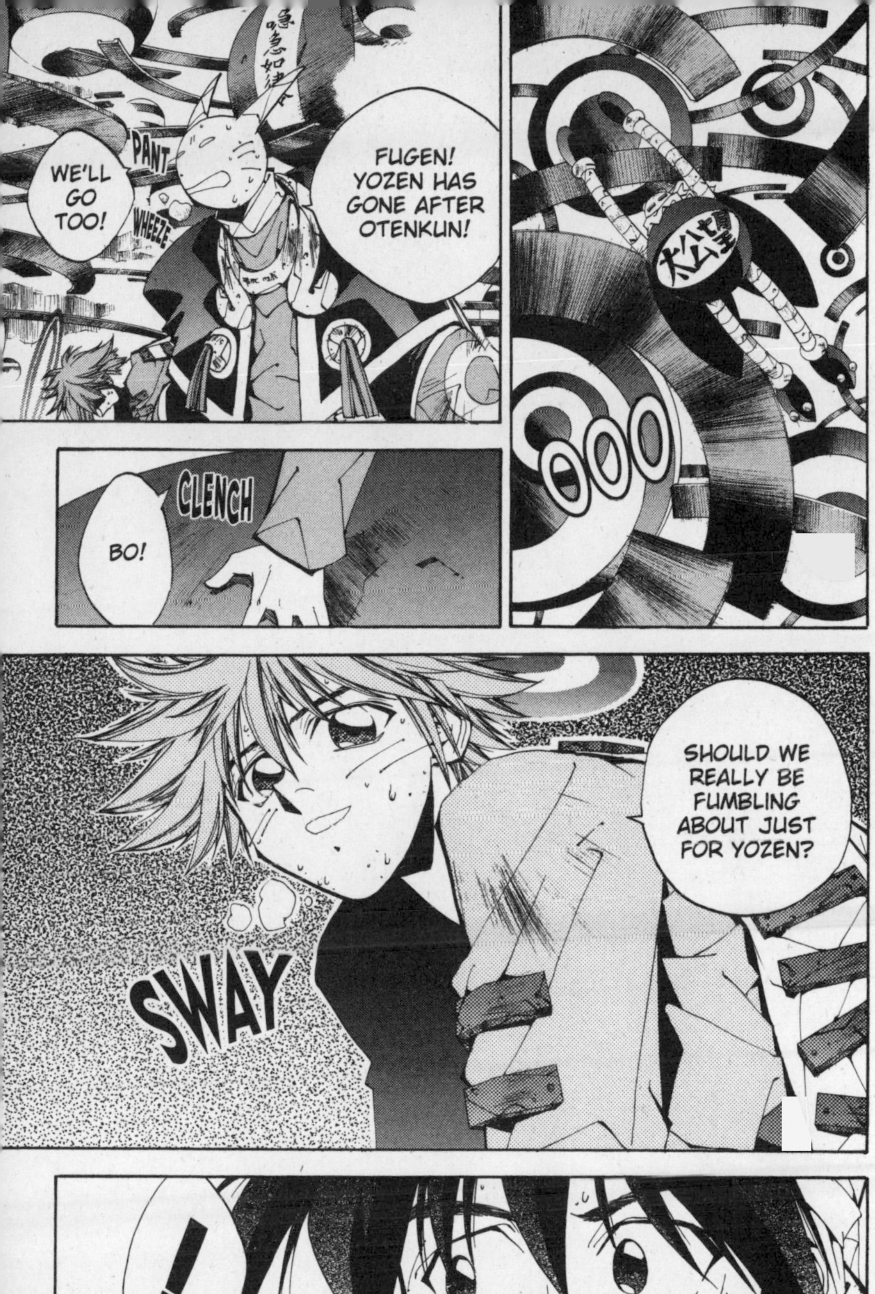
FUGEN! YOZEN HAS GONE AFTER OTENKUN!
PANT
WHEEZE
WE'LL GO TOO!
CLENCH
BO!
SHOULD WE REALLY BE FUMBLING ABOUT JUST FOR YOZEN?
SWAY
!

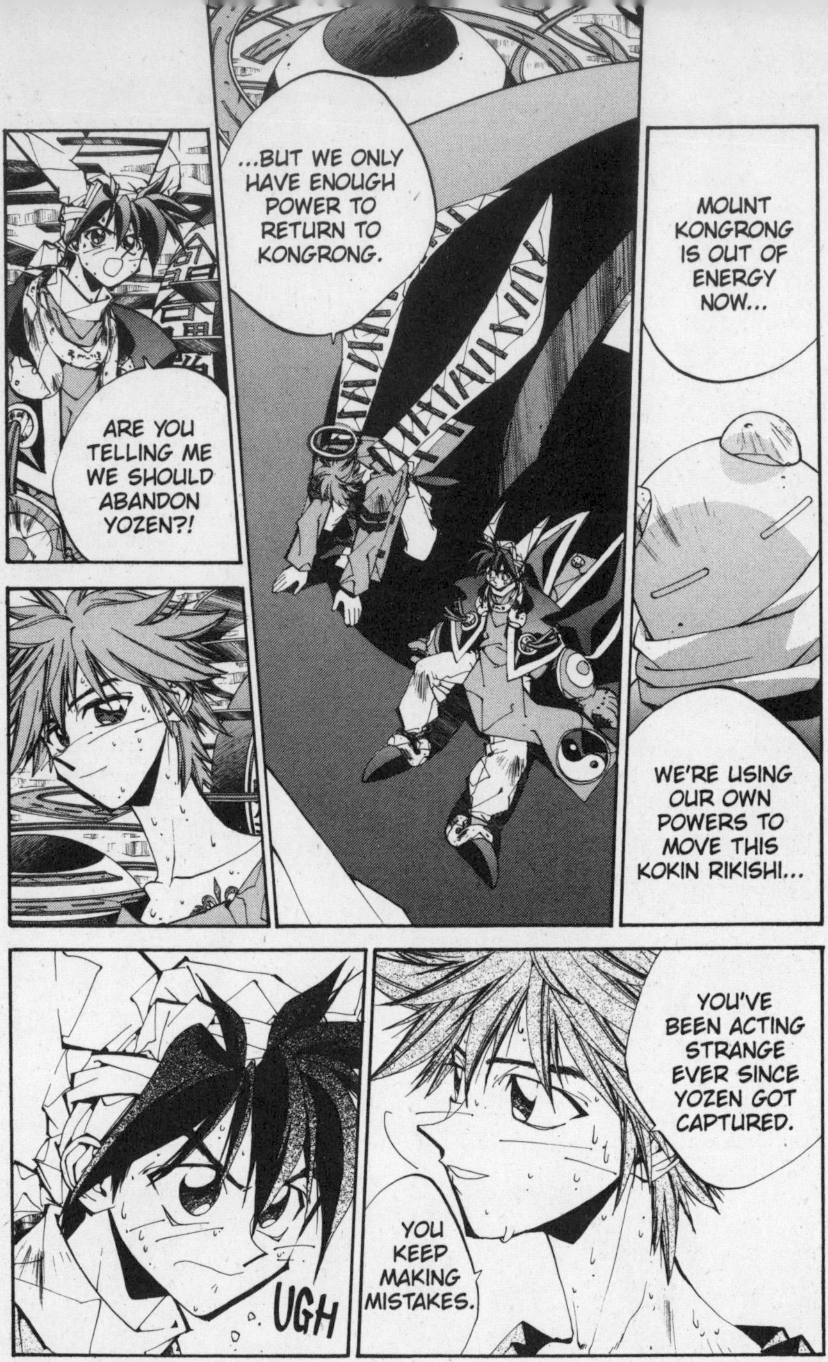
MOUNT KONGRONG IS OUT OF ENERGY NOW...
WE'RE USING OUR OWN POWERS TO MOVE THIS KOKIN RIKISHI...
...BUT WE ONLY HAVE ENOUGH POWER TO RETURN TO KONGRONG.
ARE YOU TELLING ME WE SHOULD ABANDON YOZEN?!
YOU'VE BEEN ACTING STRANGE EVER SINCE YOZEN GOT CAPTURED.
YOU KEEP MAKING MISTAKES.
UGH

READ THIS WAY

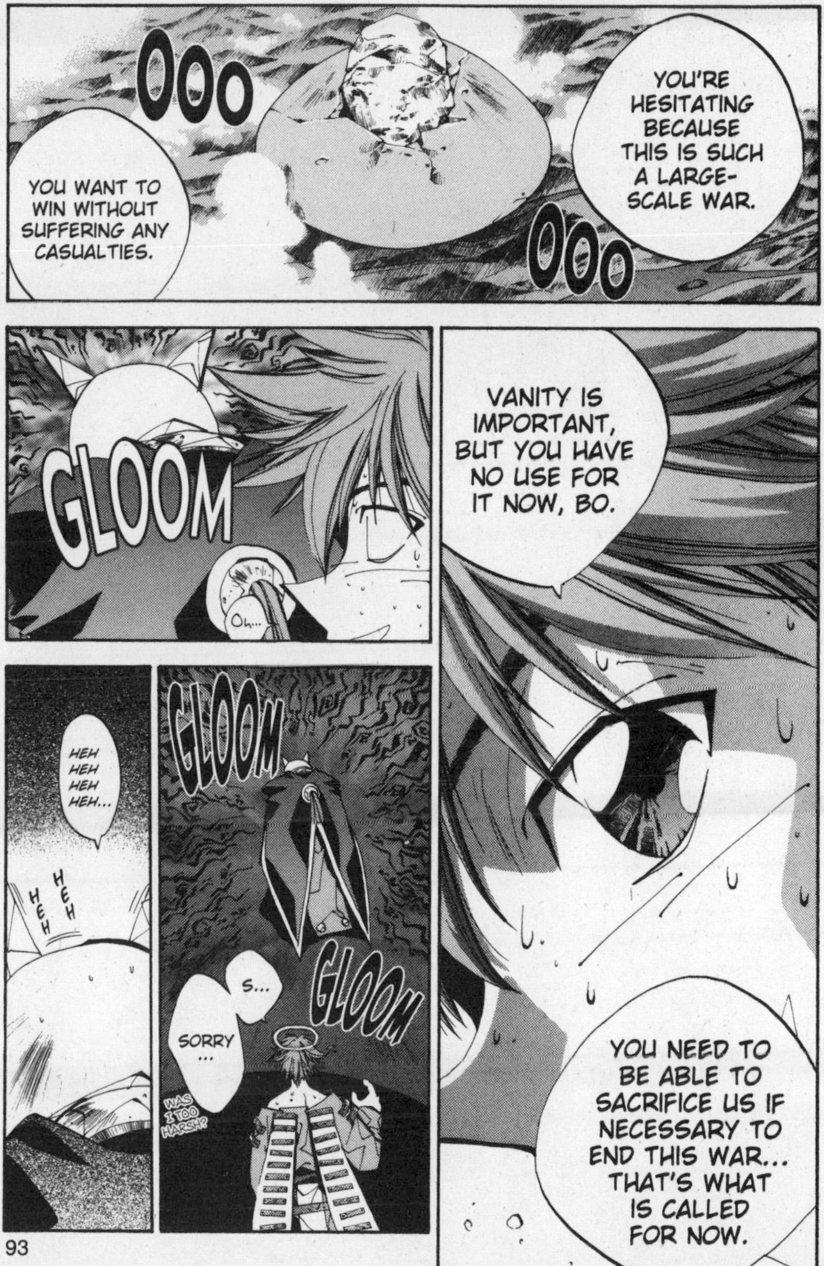

YOU'RE HESITATING BECAUSE THIS IS SUCH A LARGE-SCALE WAR.
OOO
OOO
YOU WANT TO WIN WITHOUT SUFFERING ANY CASUALTIES.
VANITY IS IMPORTANT, BUT YOU HAVE NO USE FOR IT NOW, BO.
YOU NEED TO BE ABLE TO SACRIFICE US IF NECESSARY TO END THIS WAR... THAT'S WHAT IS CALLED FOR NOW.
GLOOM
Oh...
GLOOM
S...
GLOOM
SORRY...
WAS I TOO HARSH?
HEH HEH HEH HEH...
HEH HEH HEH

HEHEH...

HEE
HEH
HEH
HEH
HEH...

GAAAA

BWA
HAHAHA
HAHAHA...

TWITCH

HAA
HAHA-
HAHA!

GAA

W-WHAT
SHOULD
I DO?

HA
HA
HA
HA
HA
HA
HA
HA

BO'S GONE
BONKERS...

HEH!

BWA
HAHAHA-
HAHA!

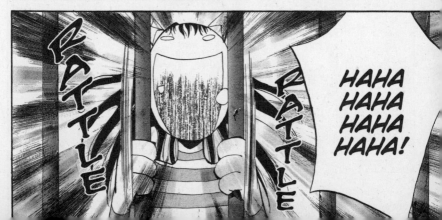

RATTLE

RATTLE

HAHA
HAHA
HAHA
HAHA!

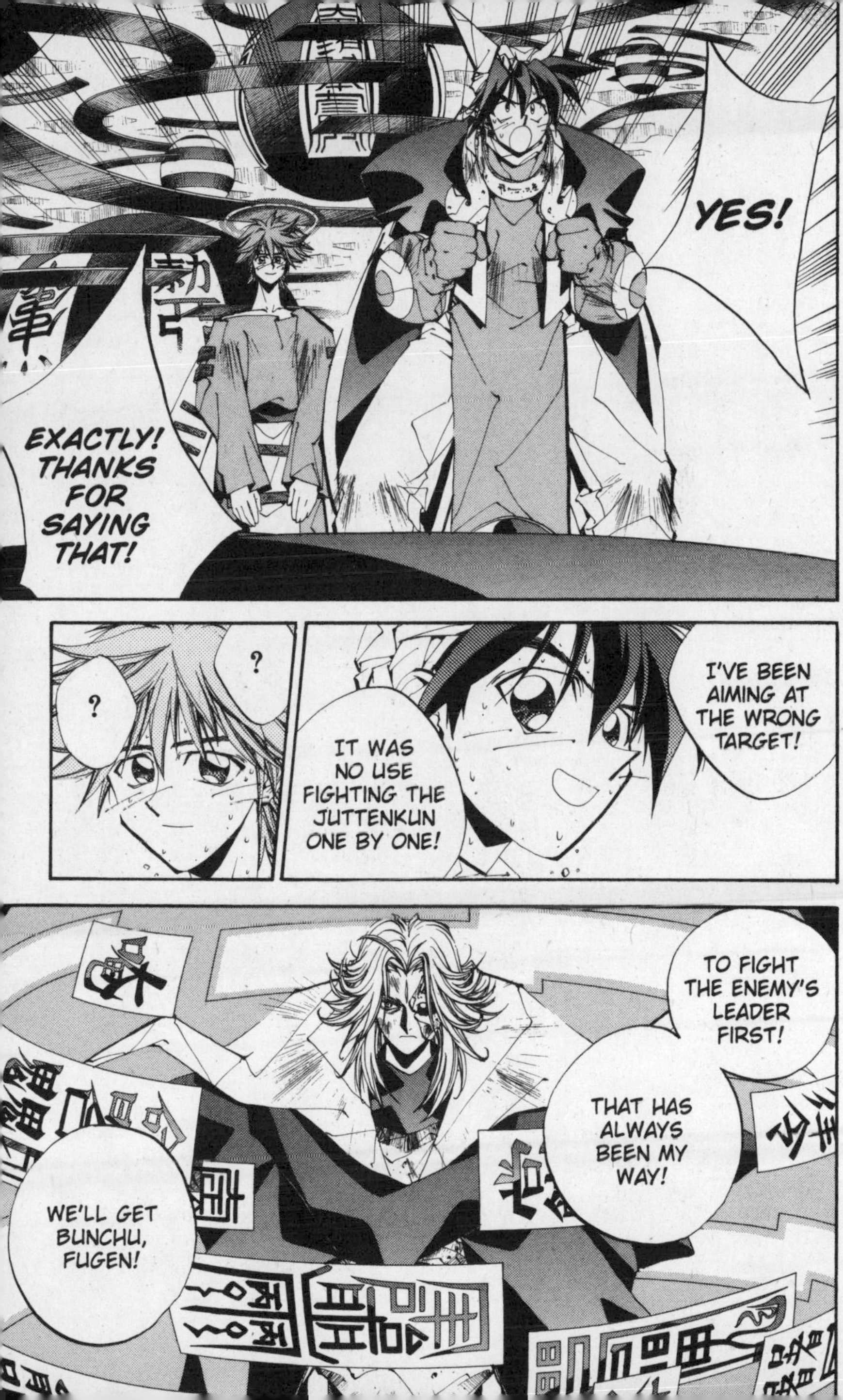
YES!
EXACTLY! THANKS FOR SAYING THAT!
I'VE BEEN AIMING AT THE WRONG TARGET!
IT WAS NO USE FIGHTING THE JUTTENKUN ONE BY ONE!
?
?
TO FIGHT THE ENEMY'S LEADER FIRST!
THAT HAS ALWAYS BEEN MY WAY!
WE'LL GET BUNCHU, FUGEN!

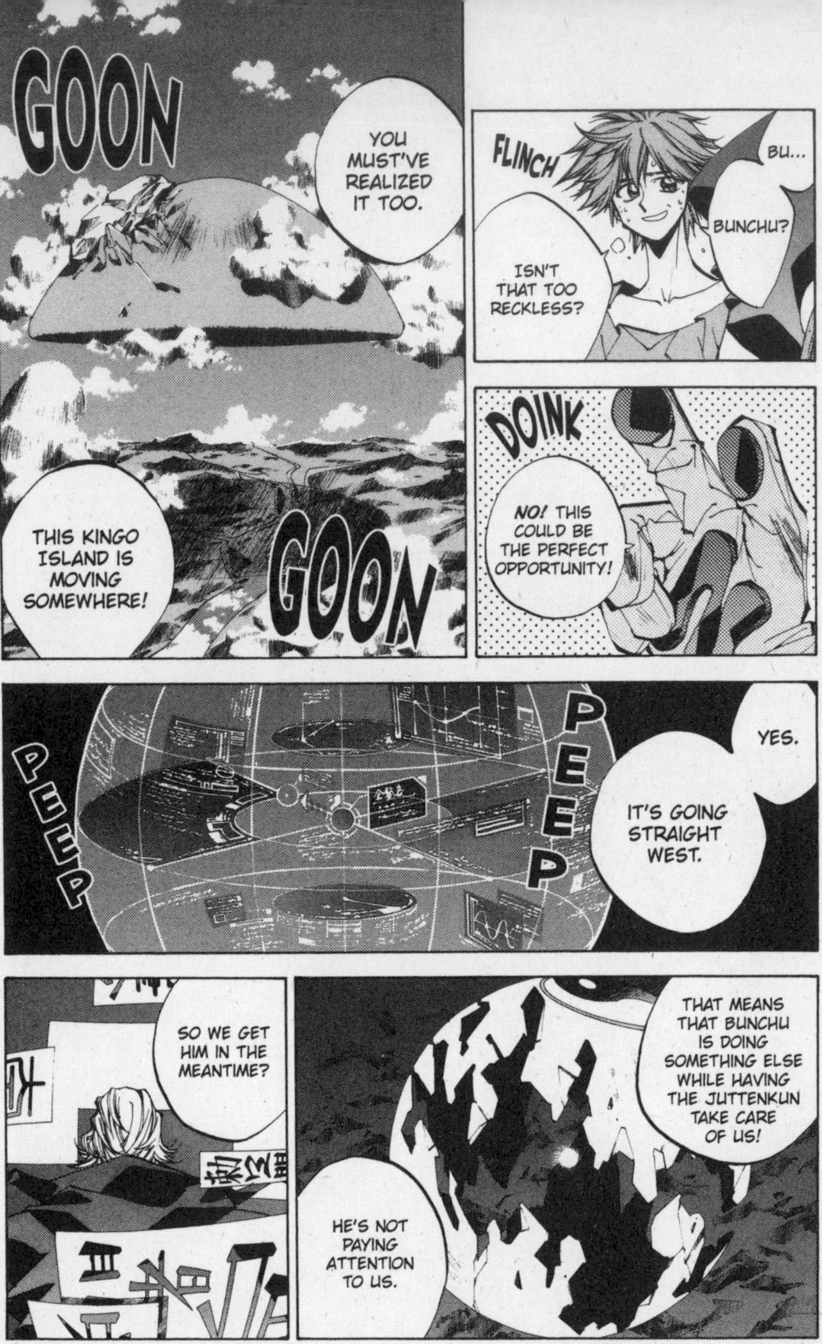
BU...
BUNCHU?
FLINCH
ISN'T THAT TOO RECKLESS?
DOINK
NO! THIS COULD BE THE PERFECT OPPORTUNITY!
GOON
YOU MUST'VE REALIZED IT TOO.
THIS KINGO ISLAND IS MOVING SOMEWHERE!
GOON
YES.
IT'S GOING STRAIGHT WEST.
PEEP
PEEP
THAT MEANS THAT BUNCHU IS DOING SOMETHING ELSE WHILE HAVING THE JUTTENKUN TAKE CARE OF US!
HE'S NOT PAYING ATTENTION TO US.
SO WE GET HIM IN THE MEANTIME?

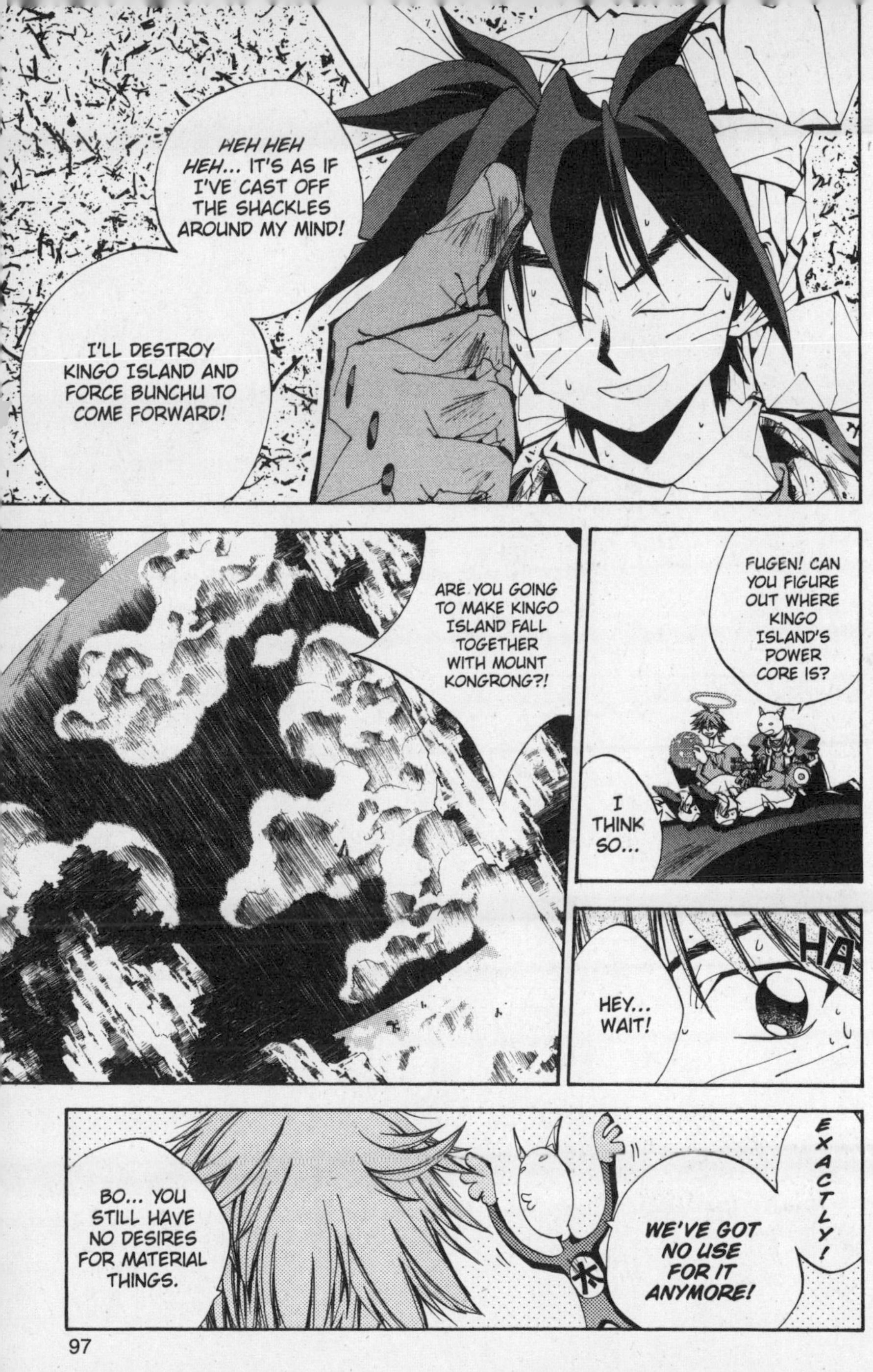
HEH HEH HEH... IT'S AS IF I'VE CAST OFF THE SHACKLES AROUND MY MIND!
I'LL DESTROY KINGO ISLAND AND FORCE BUNCHU TO COME FORWARD!
FUGEN! CAN YOU FIGURE OUT WHERE KINGO ISLAND'S POWER CORE IS?
I THINK SO...
HA
HEY... WAIT!
ARE YOU GOING TO MAKE KINGO ISLAND FALL TOGETHER WITH MOUNT KONGRONG?!
EXACTLY!
WE'VE GOT NO USE FOR IT ANYMORE!
BO... YOU STILL HAVE NO DESIRES FOR MATERIAL THINGS.

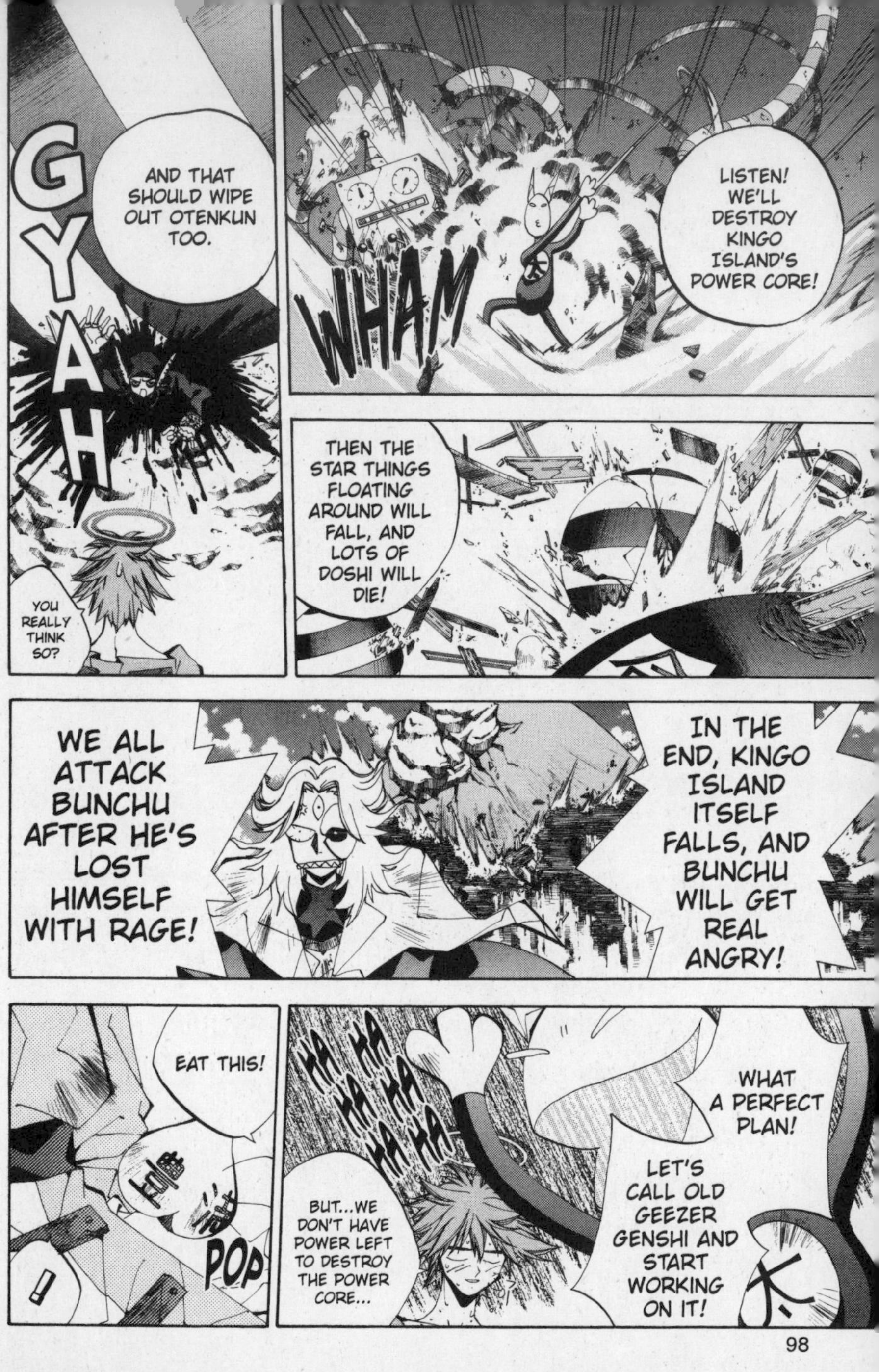
LISTEN! WE'LL DESTROY KINGO ISLAND'S POWER CORE!
WHAM
THEN THE STAR THINGS FLOATING AROUND WILL FALL, AND LOTS OF DOSHI WILL DIE!
AND THAT SHOULD WIPE OUT OTENKUN TOO.
GYAAH
YOU REALLY THINK SO?
IN THE END, KINGO ISLAND ITSELF FALLS, AND BUNCHU WILL GET REAL ANGRY!
WE ALL ATTACK BUNCHU AFTER HE'S LOST HIMSELF WITH RAGE!
WHAT A PERFECT PLAN!
LET'S CALL OLD GEEZER GENSHI AND START WORKING ON IT!
KA KA KA KA KA KA
BUT...WE DON'T HAVE POWER LEFT TO DESTROY THE POWER CORE...
EAT THIS!
POP
!

READ THIS WAY

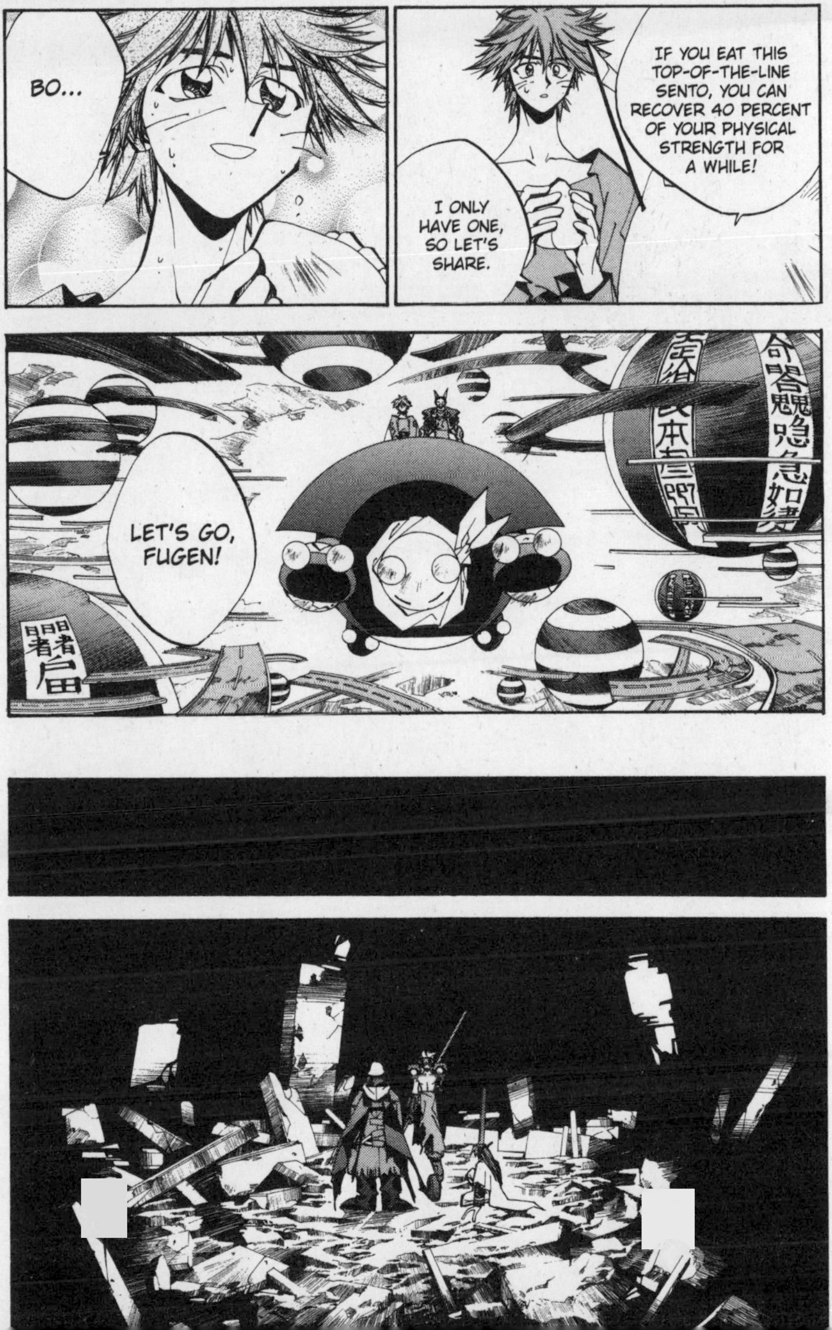
IF YOU EAT THIS TOP-OF-THE-LINE SENTO, YOU CAN RECOVER 40 PERCENT OF YOUR PHYSICAL STRENGTH FOR A WHILE!
I ONLY HAVE ONE, SO LET'S SHARE.
BO...
LET'S GO, FUGEN!

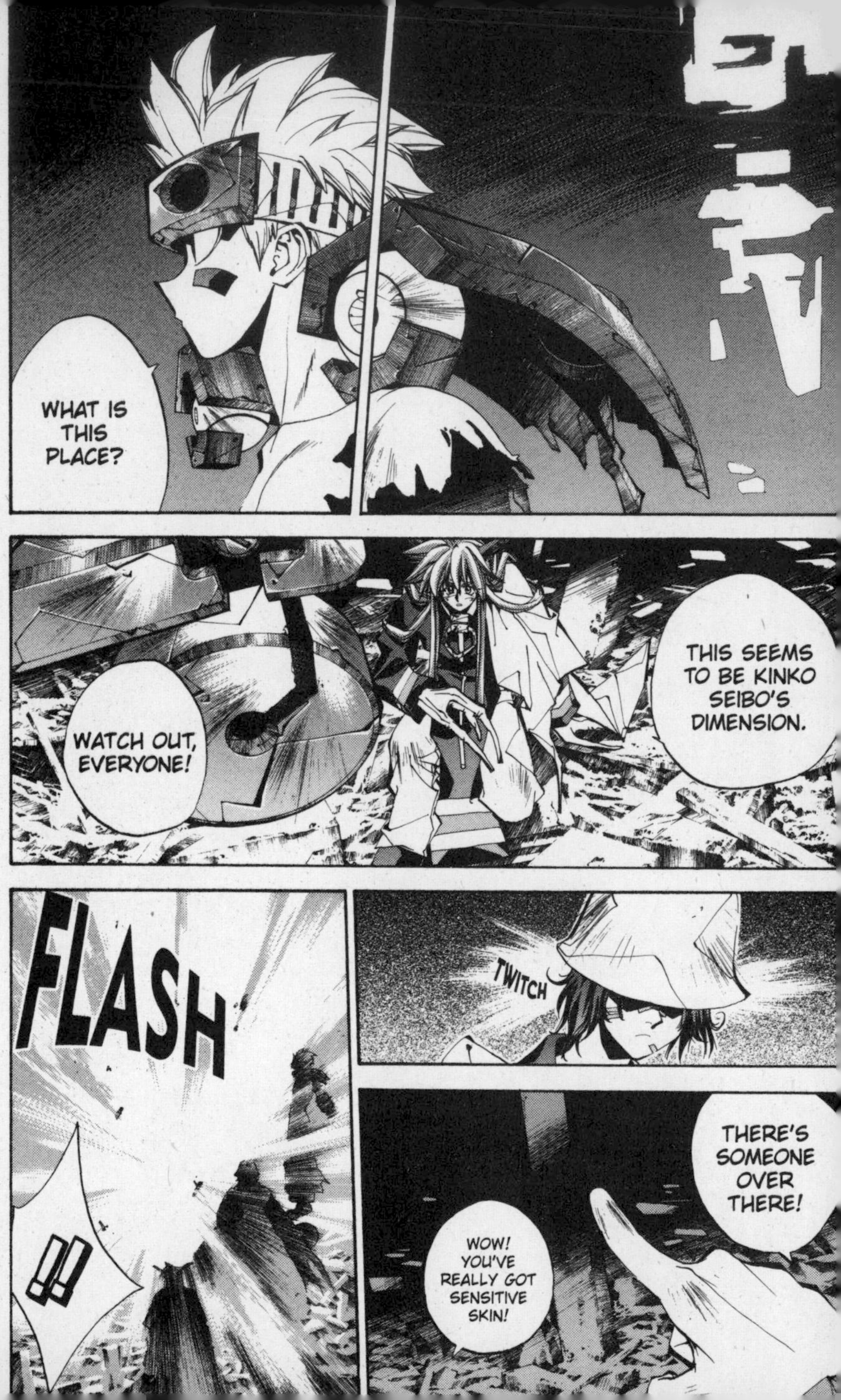

WHAT IS THIS PLACE?
THIS SEEMS TO BE KINKO SEIBO'S DIMENSION.
WATCH OUT, EVERYONE!
TWITCH
THERE'S SOMEONE OVER THERE!
WOW! YOU'VE REALLY GOT SENSITIVE SKIN!
FLASH
!!

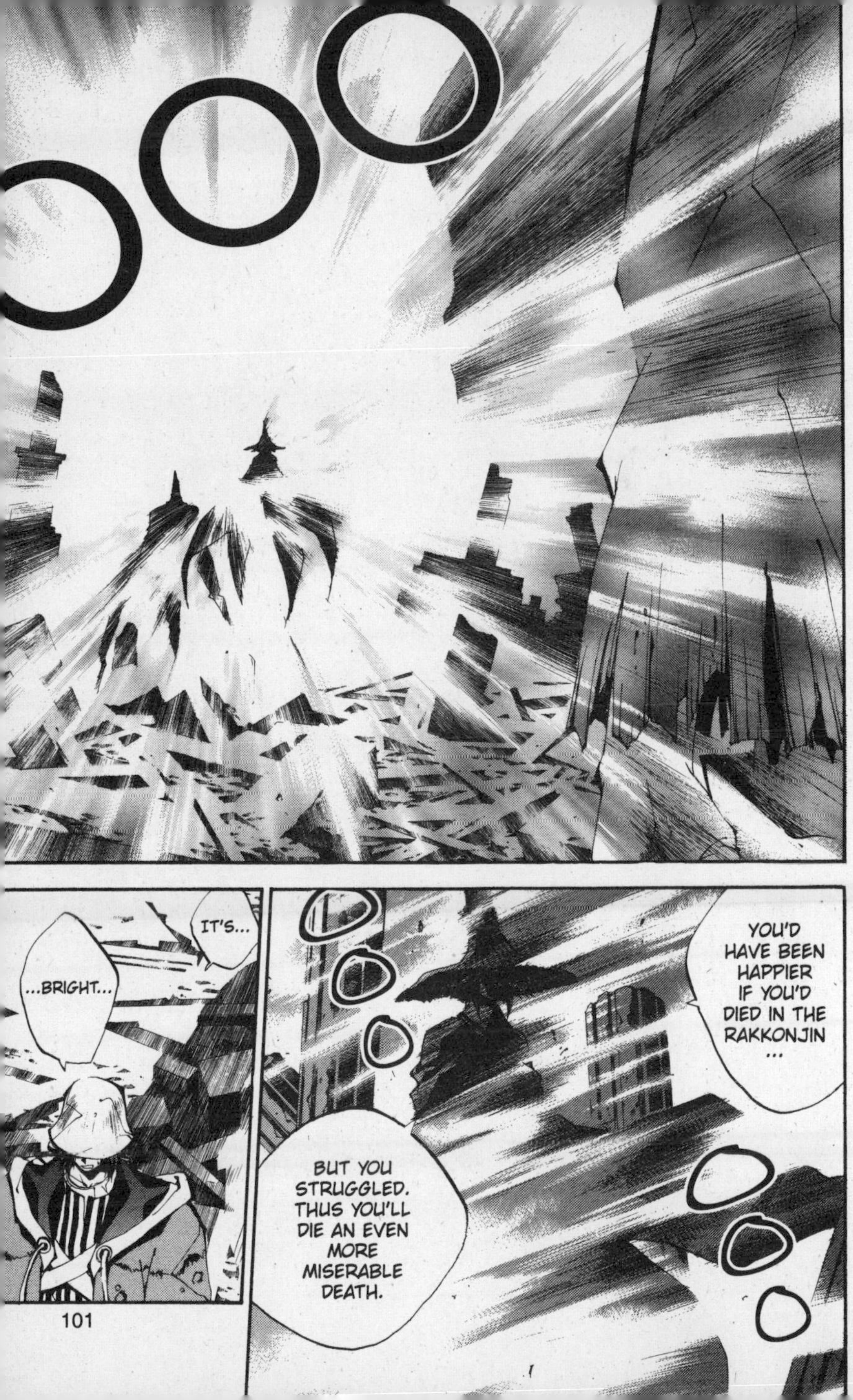
YOU'D HAVE BEEN HAPPIER IF YOU'D DIED IN THE RAKKONJIN ...
BUT YOU STRUGGLED. THUS YOU'LL DIE AN EVEN MORE MISERABLE DEATH.
IT'S...
...BRIGHT...

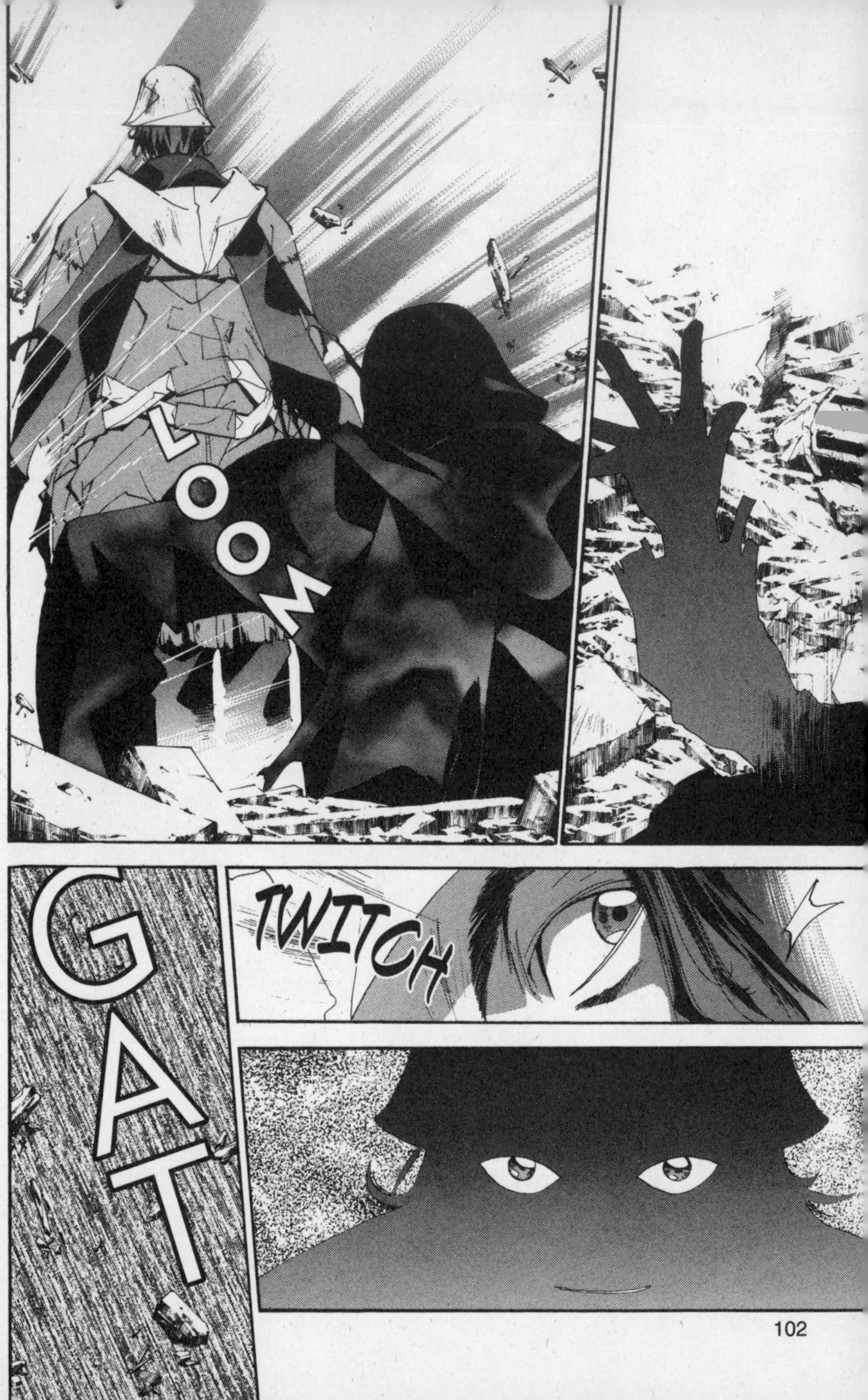
LOOM
TWITCH
GAT

READ THIS WAY

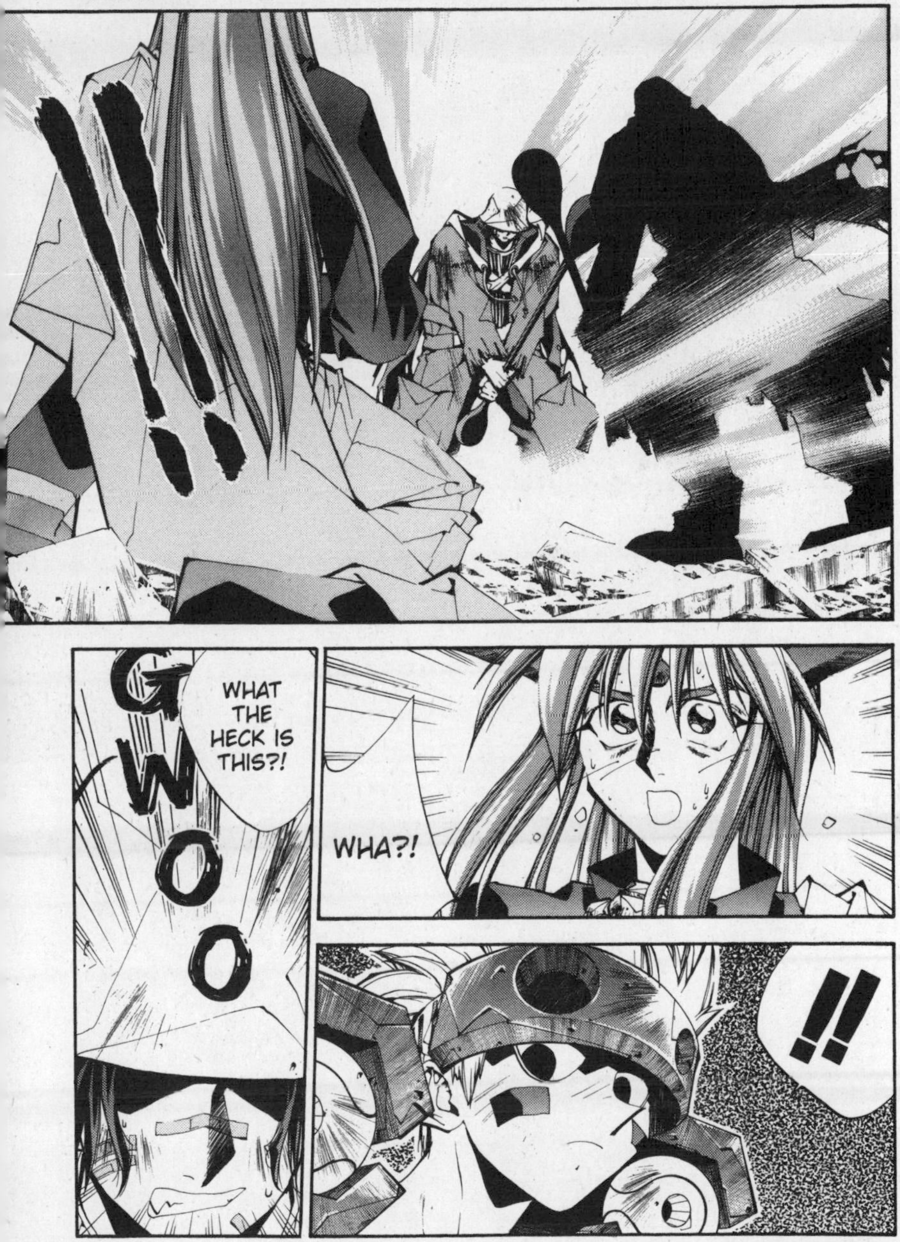

!!
WHA?!
!!
GWOO
WHAT THE HECK IS THIS?!

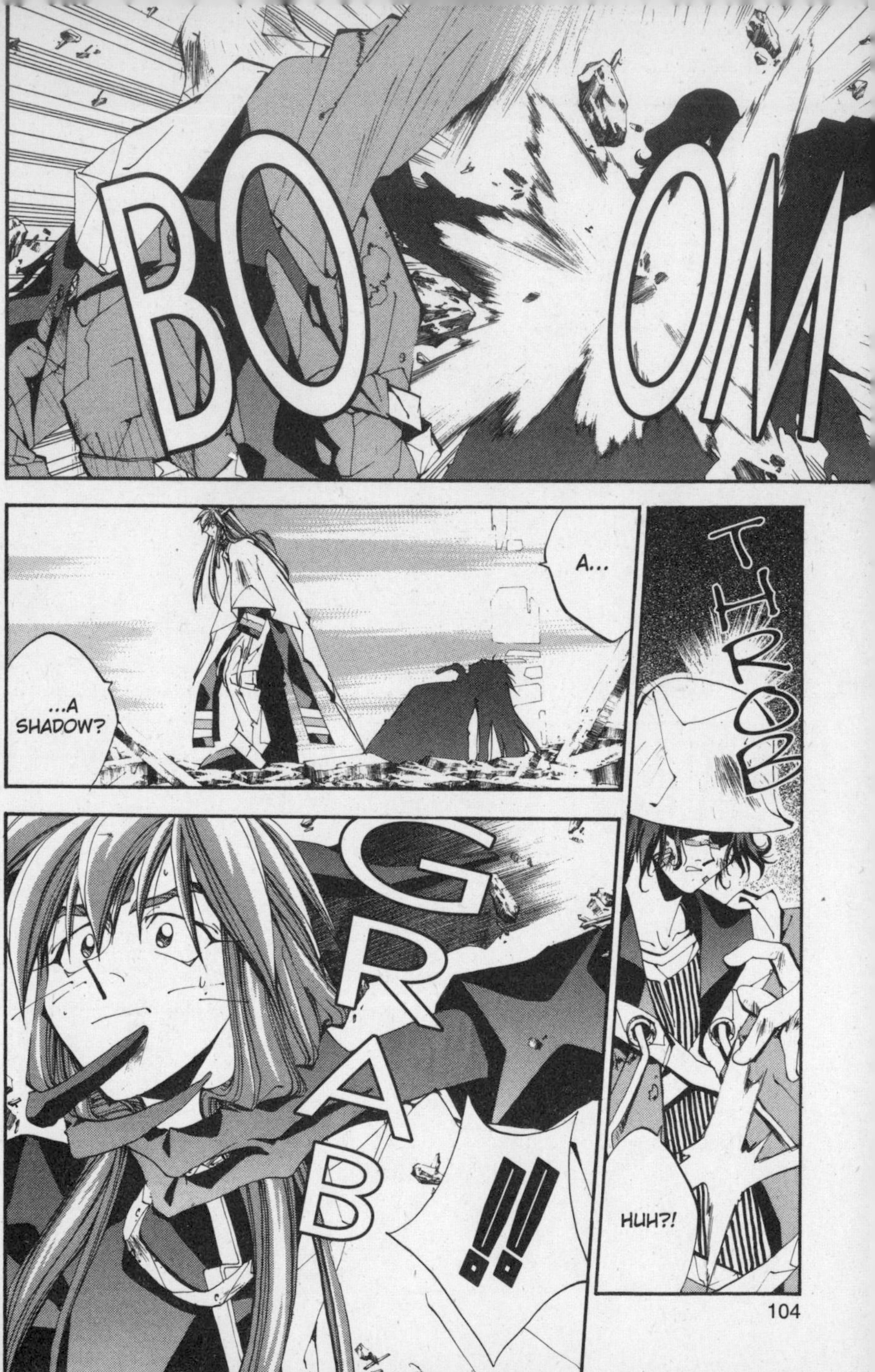
BOOM
THROB
HUH?!
A...
...A SHADOW?
GRAB!!

READ THIS WAY

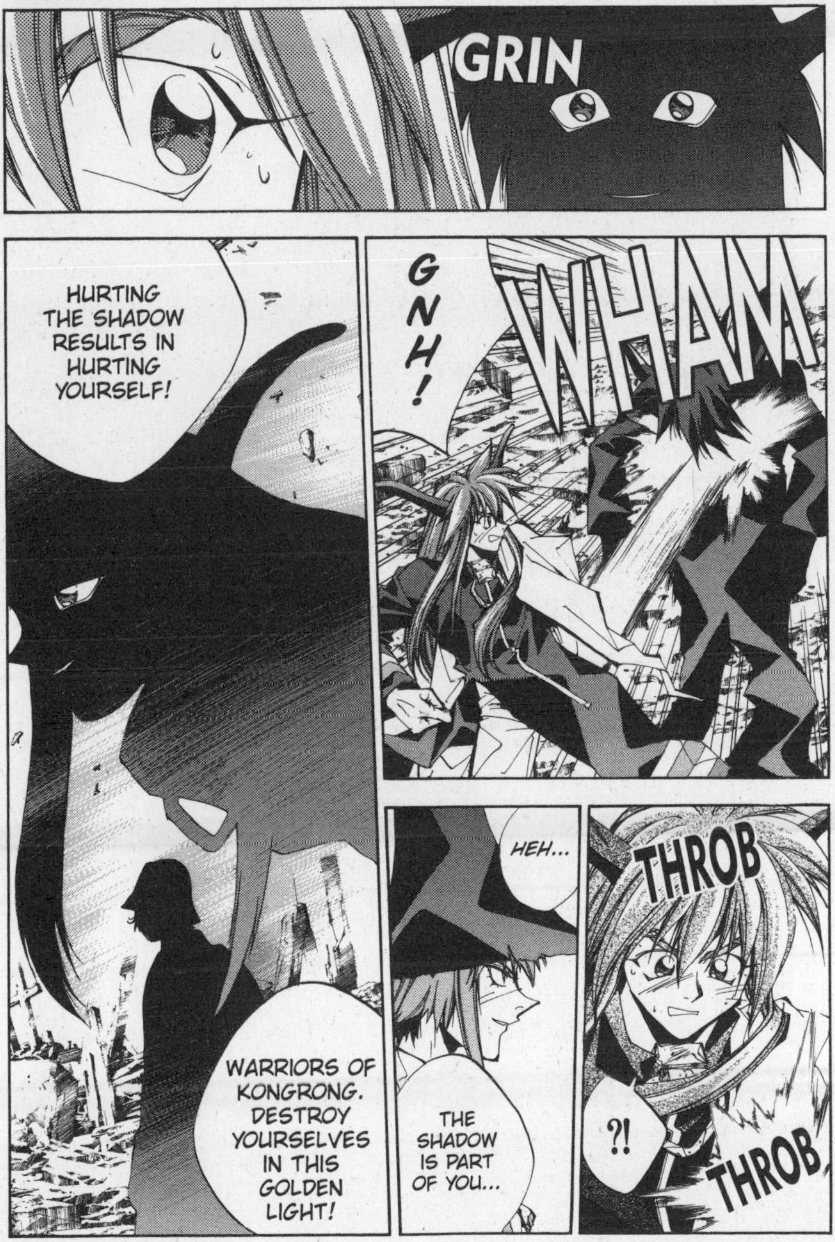
GRIN
GNH!
WHAM
THROB
?!
THROB
HEH...
THE SHADOW IS PART OF YOU...
HURTING THE SHADOW RESULTS IN HURTING YOURSELF!
WARRIORS OF KONGRONG. DESTROY YOURSELVES IN THIS GOLDEN LIGHT!

封神演義

Chapter 130

THE BATTLE OF THE JUZETSUJIN "KINKOJIN" & "RAKKONJIN" LIGHT

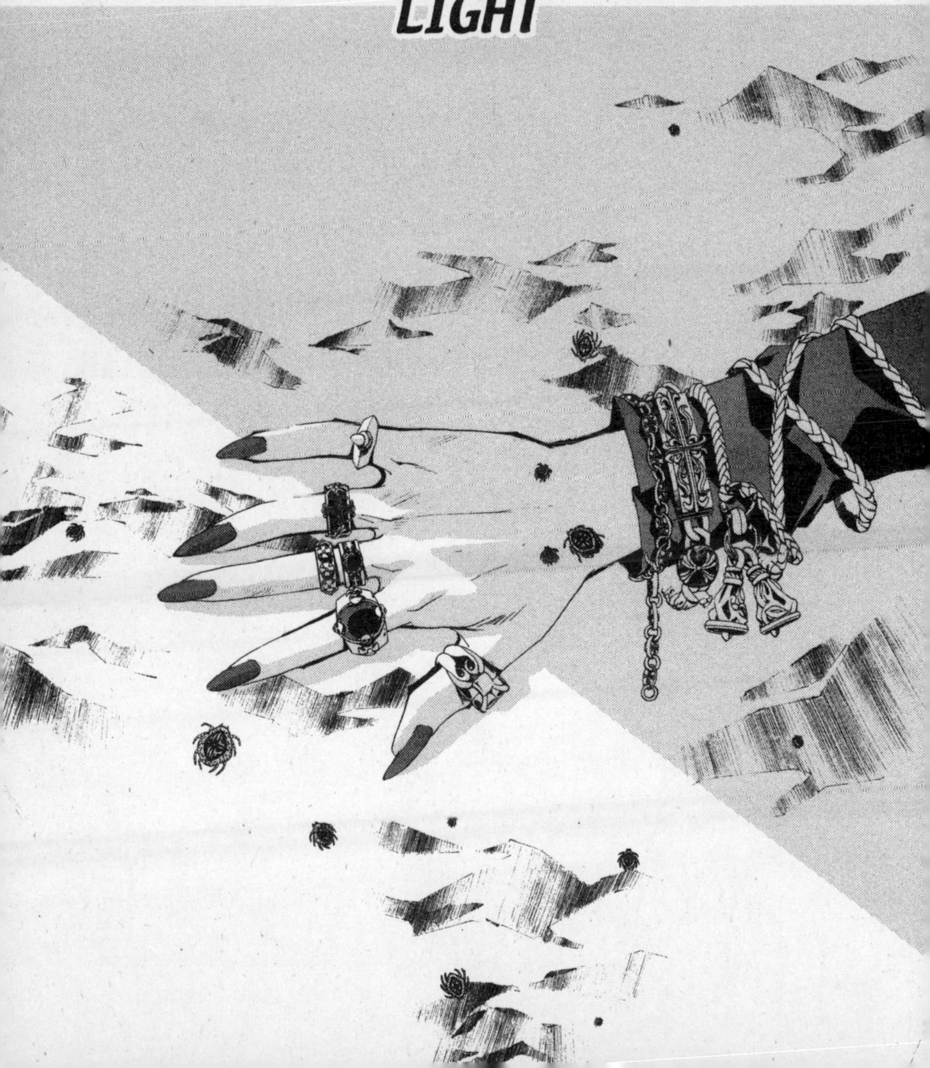

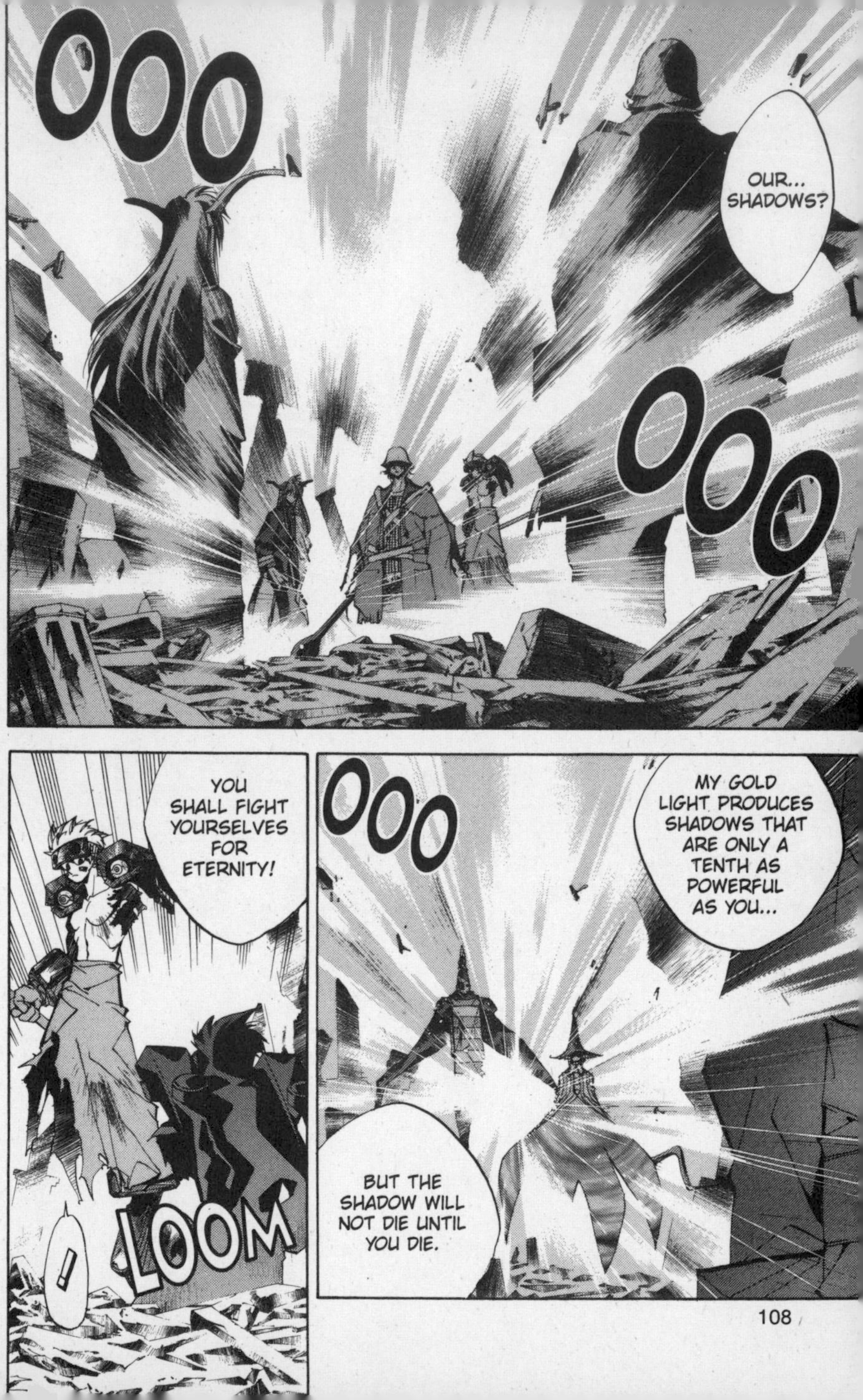
OUR... SHADOWS?
OOO
OOO
MY GOLD LIGHT PRODUCES SHADOWS THAT ARE ONLY A TENTH AS POWERFUL AS YOU...
OOO
BUT THE SHADOW WILL NOT DIE UNTIL YOU DIE.
YOU SHALL FIGHT YOURSELVES FOR ETERNITY!
!
LOOM

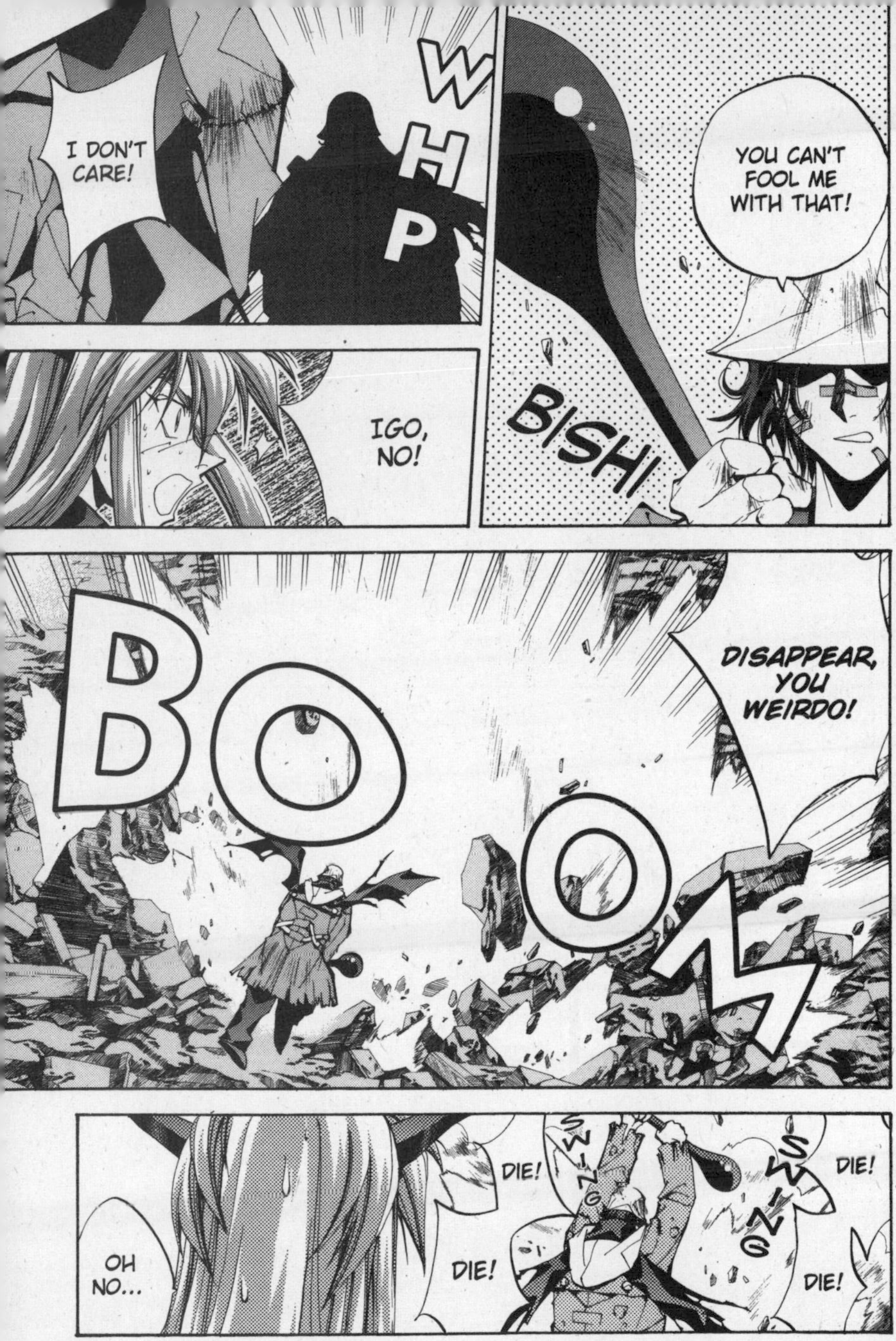
YOU CAN'T FOOL ME WITH THAT!
BISHI
WHP
I DON'T CARE!
IGO, NO!
BOOM
DISAPPEAR, YOU WEIRDO!
SWING
DIE!
DIE!
SWING
DIE!
DIE!
OH NO...

KOFF
...

SPURT

WAA HA-HAHAHA!

STOMP

GOTCHA!

SO IF THE SHADOW'S HURT, YOU GET HURT TOO.

WHAM

Igo's Hit Points
32,700/80,000

KWON

WHP

HEY, YOZEN, THAT'S UNFAIR!

IF YOU HIDE BEHIND SOMETHING, THE SHADOW WILL DISAPPEAR.

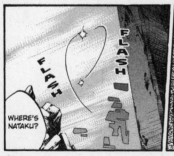

FLASH

FLASH

FLASH

WHERE'S NATAKU?

SIGH...

Yozen's Hit Points
28,630/150,320

↑ HE'S RECOVERED SLIGHTLY THANKS TO THE SENTO EXTRACT.

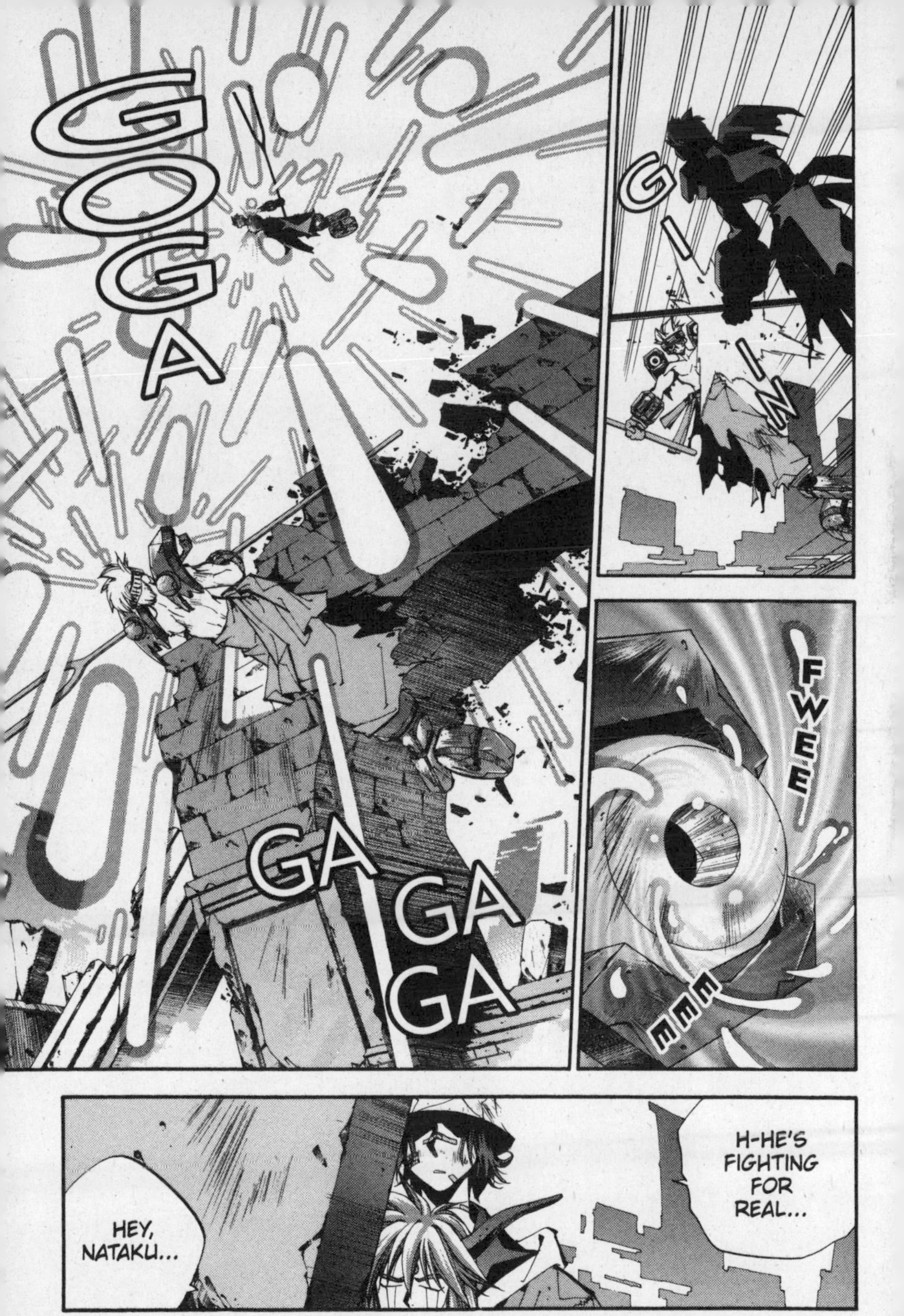
GIIN
FWEEEEEE
GOGA
GA GA GA
H-HE'S FIGHTING FOR REAL...
HEY, NATAKU...

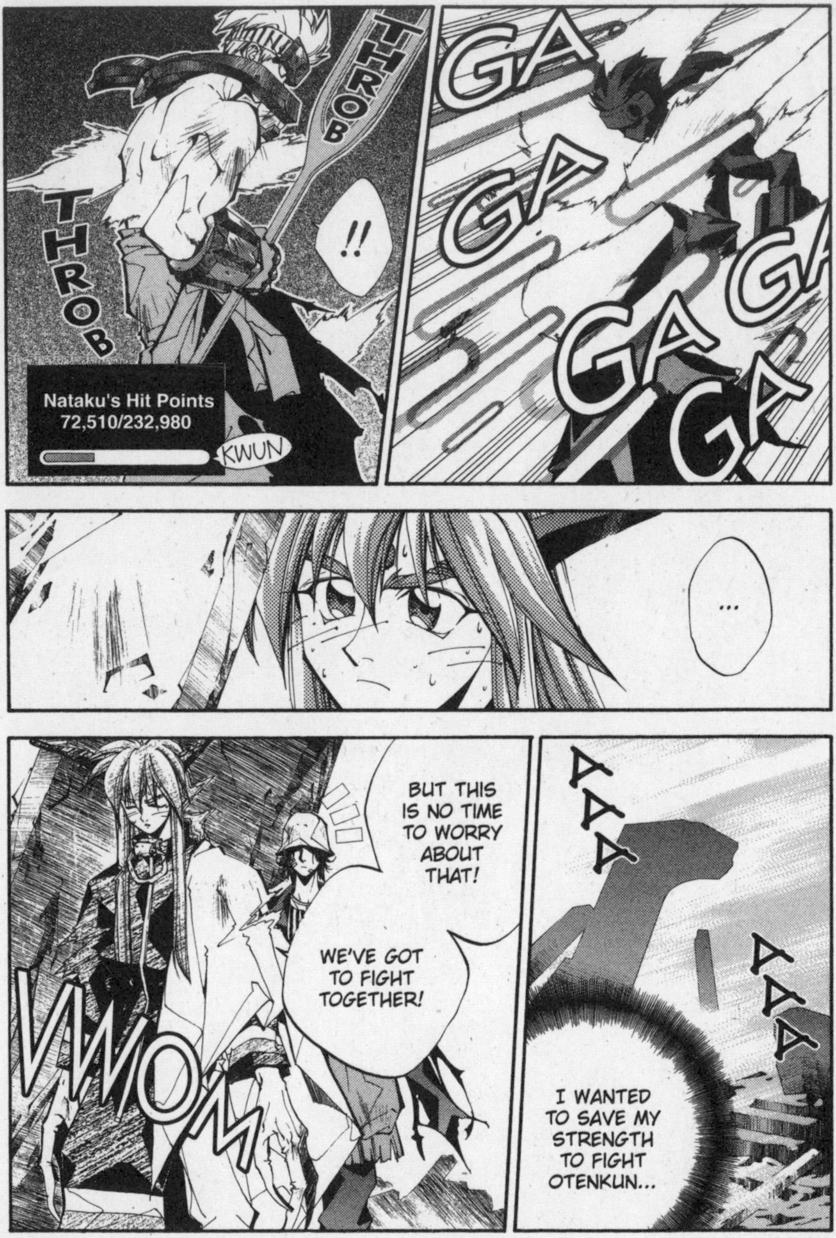
GA
GA
GA
GA
GA
GA
THROB
THROB
!!
Nataku's Hit Points
72,510/232,980
KWUN
...
I WANTED TO SAVE MY STRENGTH TO FIGHT OTENKUN...
BUT THIS IS NO TIME TO WORRY ABOUT THAT!
WE'VE GOT TO FIGHT TOGETHER!
VWOM

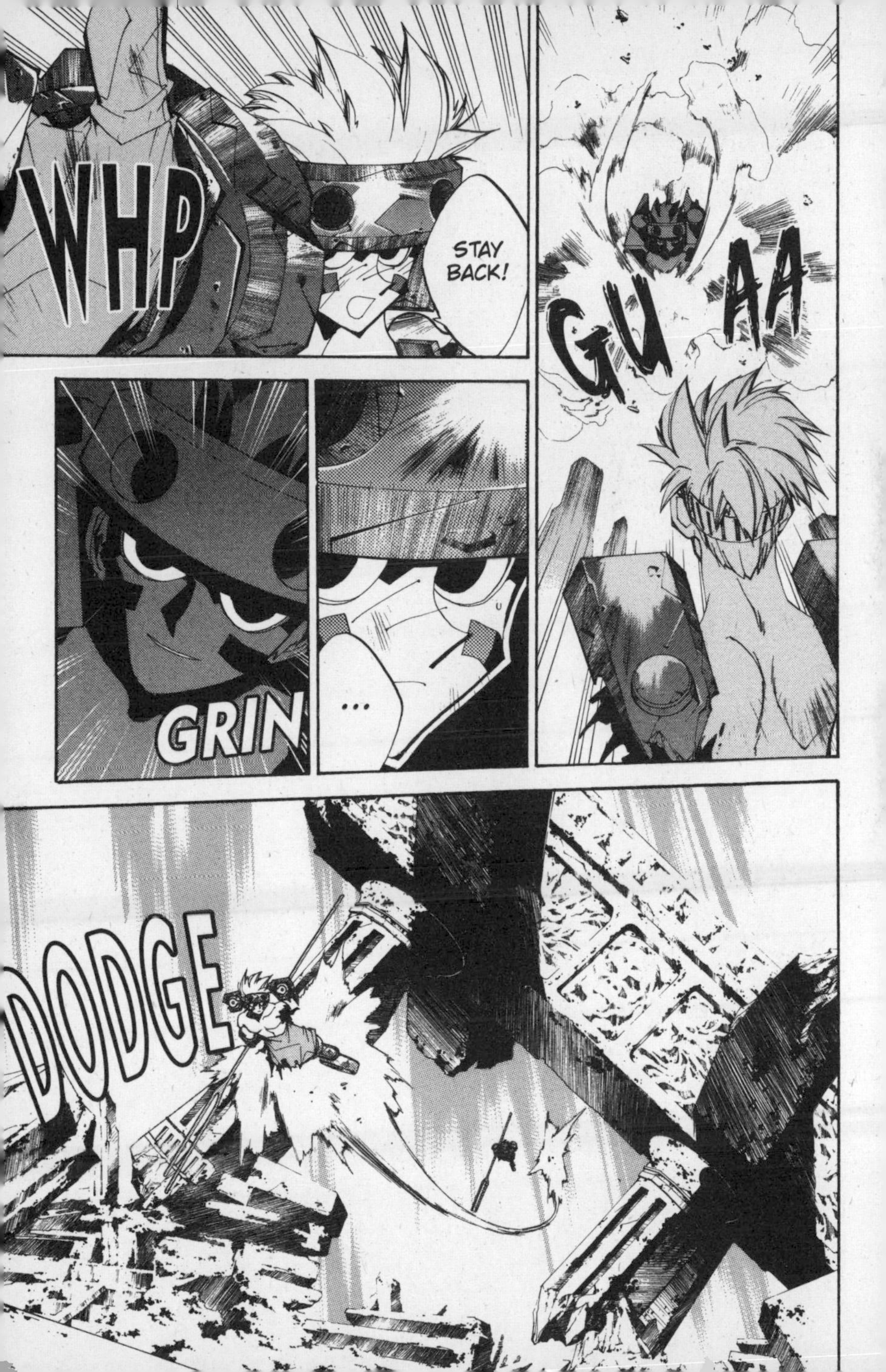
GU AA
WHP
STAY BACK!
...
GRIN
DODGE

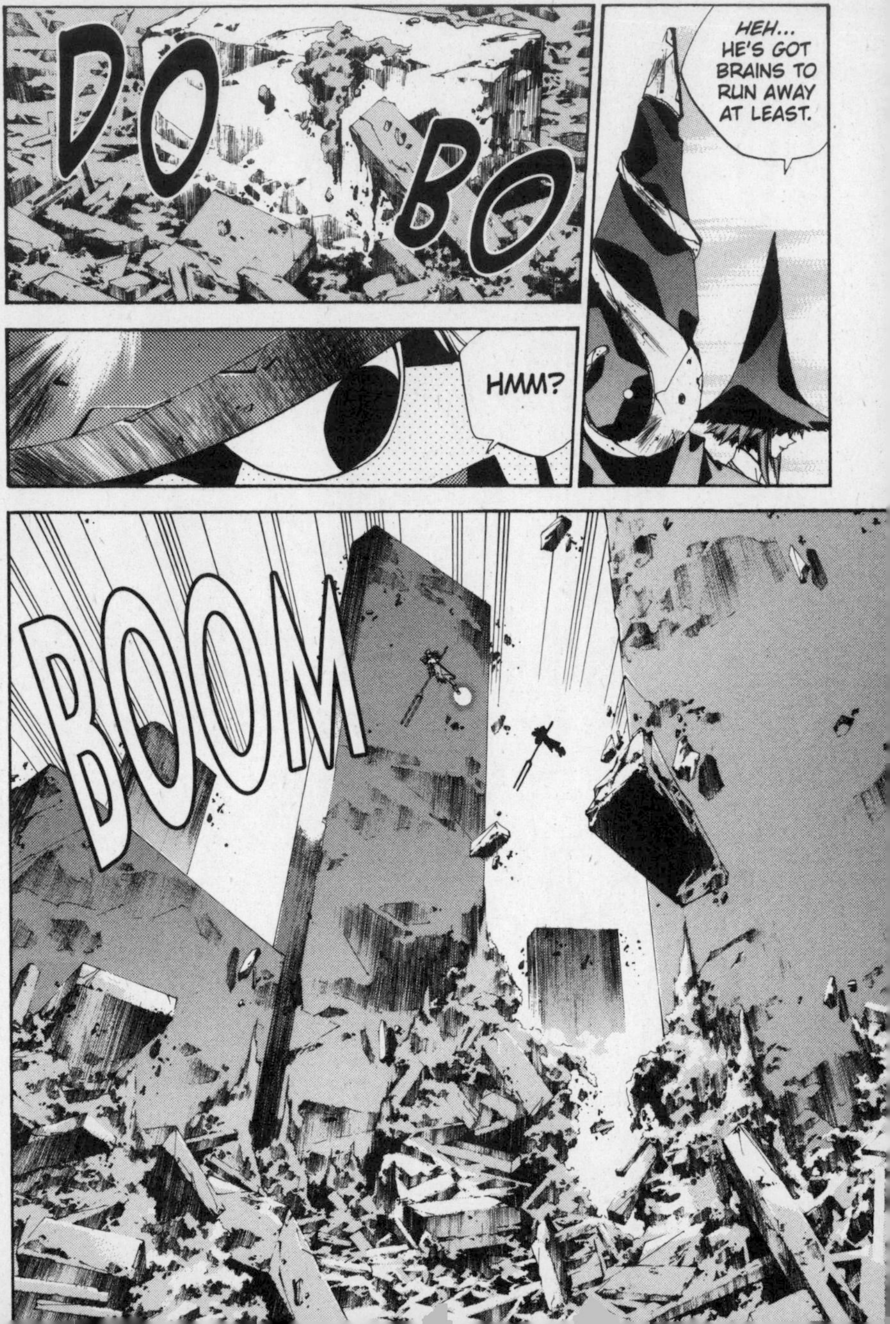
HEH... HE'S GOT BRAINS TO RUN AWAY AT LEAST.
DO BO
HMM?
BOOM

READ THIS WAY

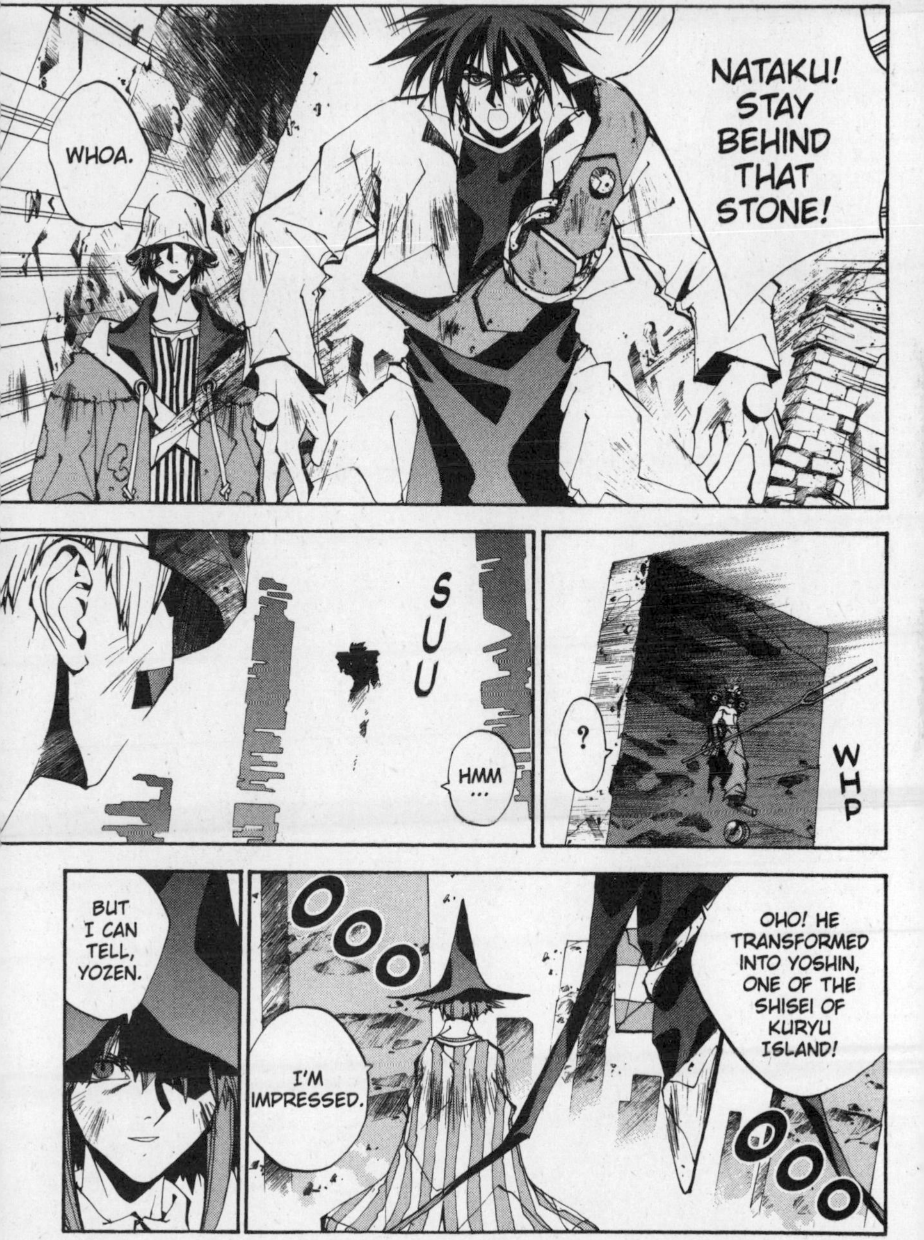
NATAKU! STAY BEHIND THAT STONE!
WHOA.
?
WHP
SUU
HMM...
OHO! HE TRANSFORMED INTO YOSHIN, ONE OF THE SHISEI OF KURYU ISLAND!
OOOO
I'M IMPRESSED.
OOOO
BUT I CAN TELL, YOZEN.

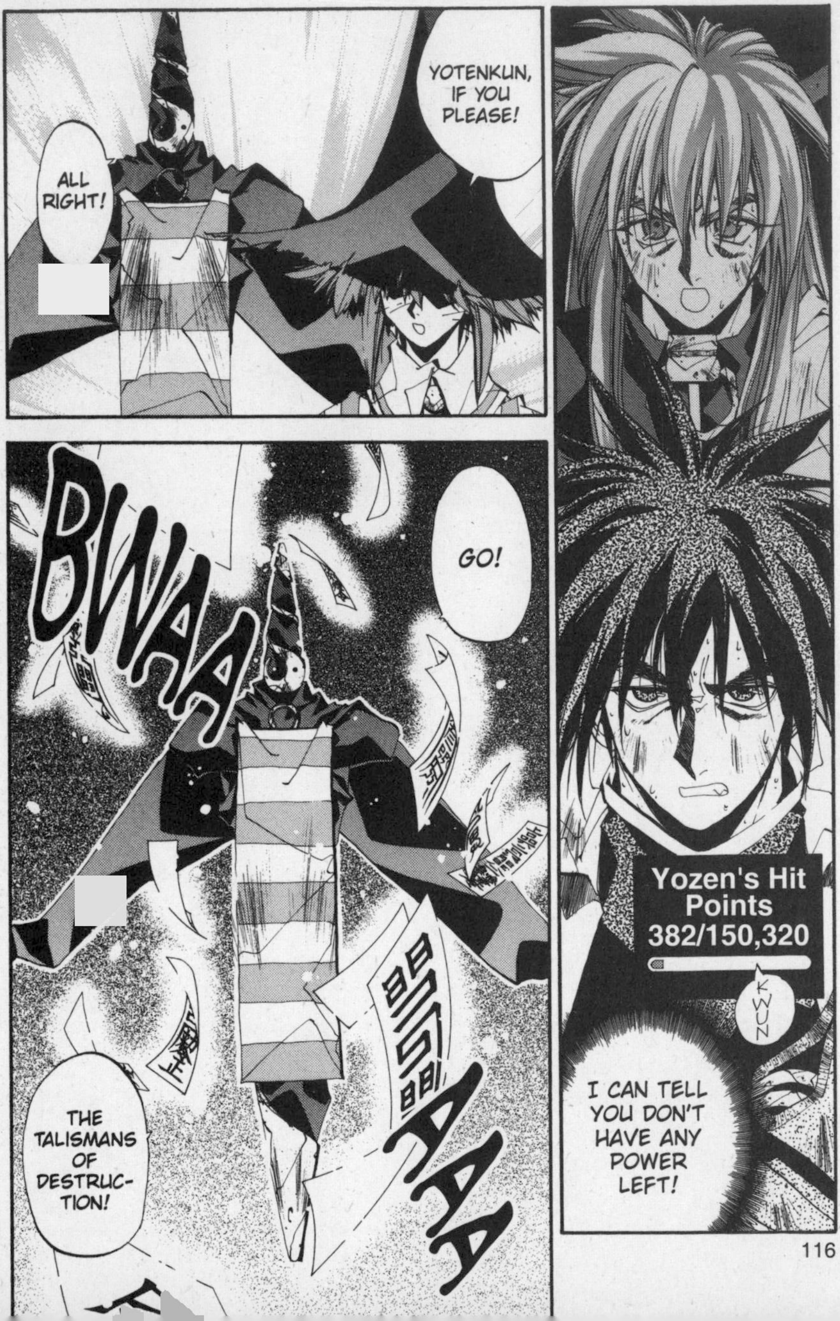
Yozen's Hit Points
382/150,320
KWUN
I CAN TELL YOU DON'T HAVE ANY POWER LEFT!
YOTENKUN, IF YOU PLEASE!
ALL RIGHT!
GO!
BWAAAAAA
THE TALISMANS OF DESTRUCTION!

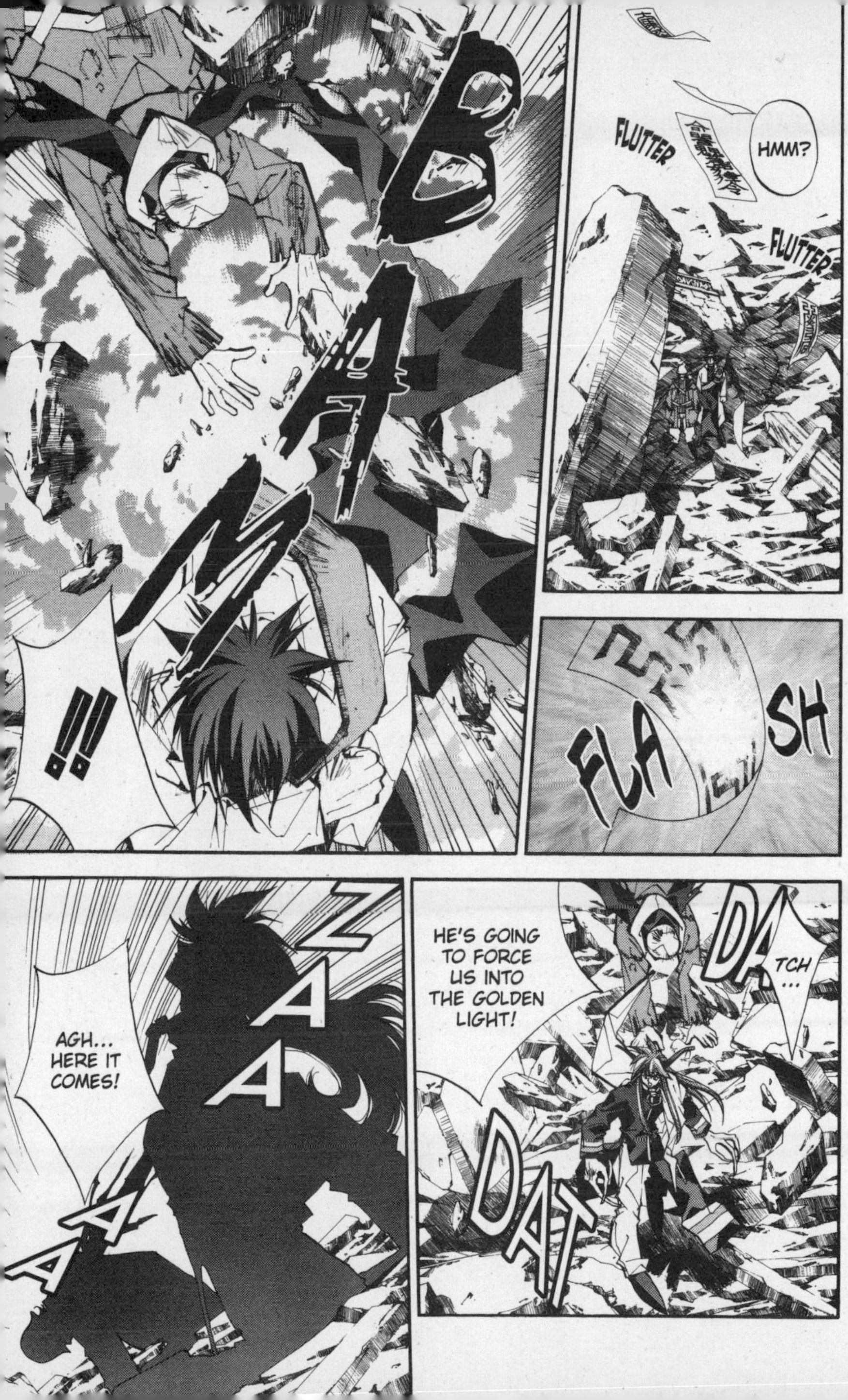
FLUTTER
HMM?
FLUTTER
FLASH
BAM
!!
DA
TCH...
HE'S GOING TO FORCE US INTO THE GOLDEN LIGHT!
DAT
ZAAA
AGH... HERE IT COMES!
AAA

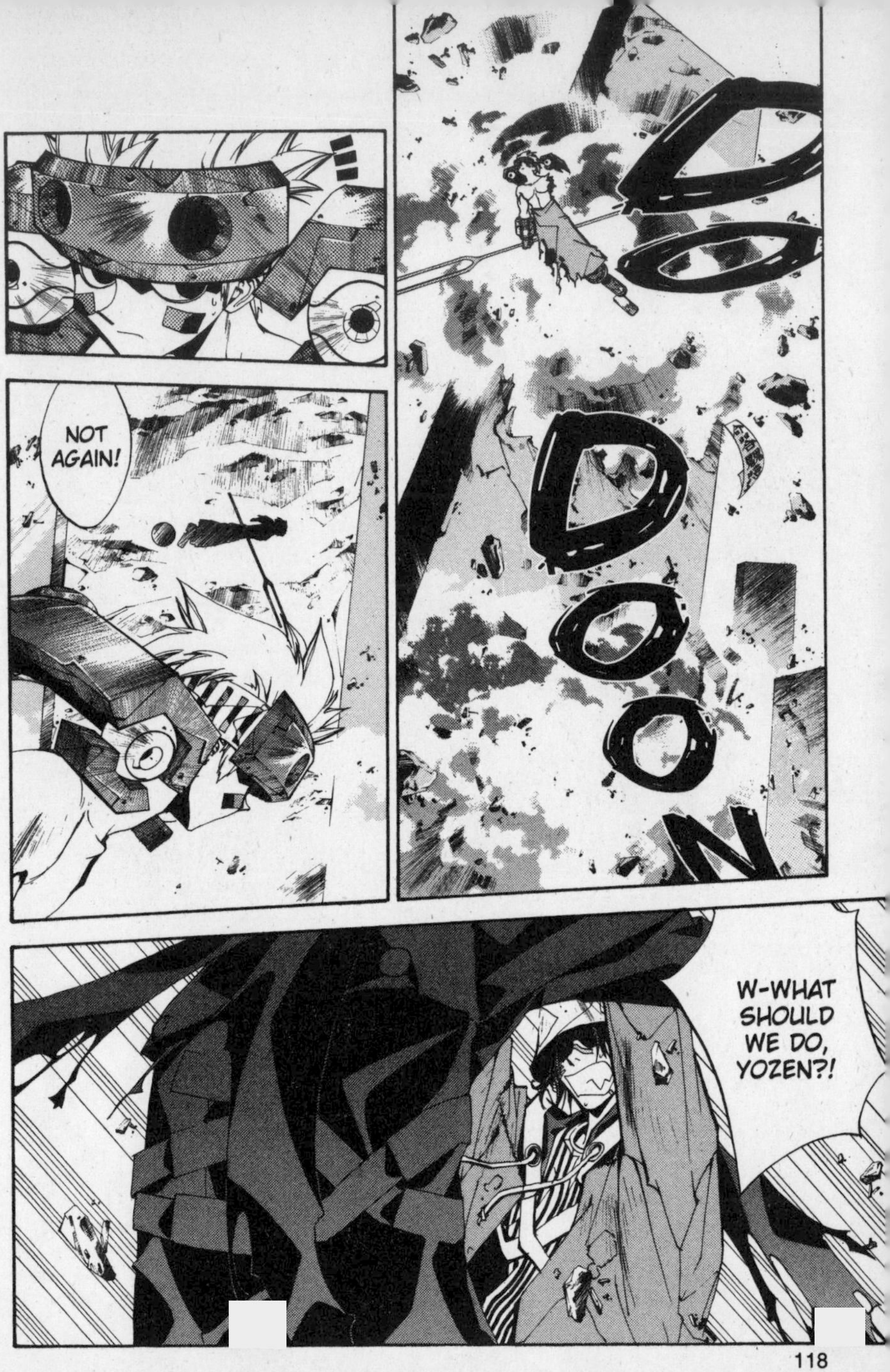
DOOON
NOT AGAIN!
W-WHAT SHOULD WE DO, YOZEN?!

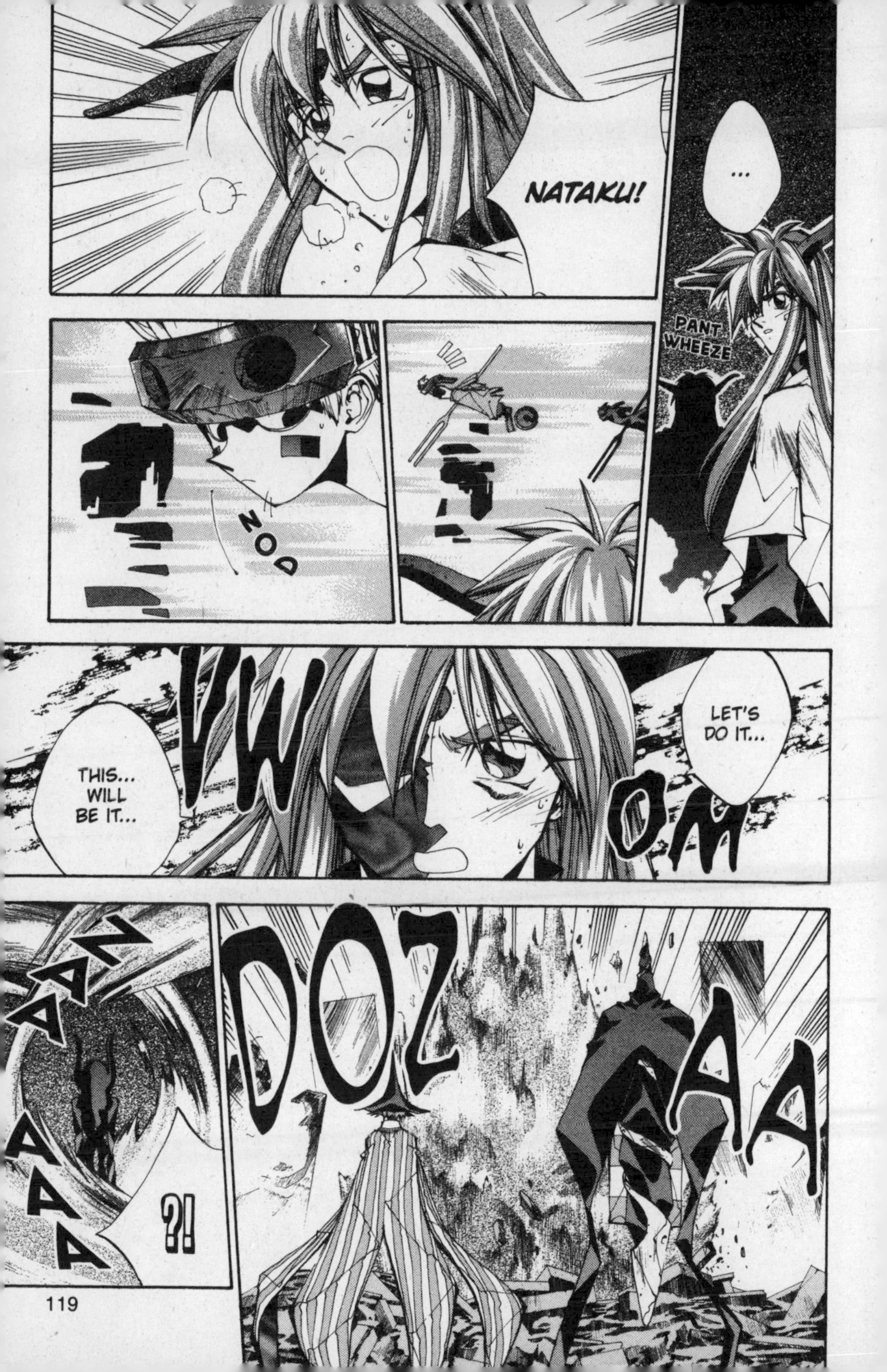
...
PANT WHEEZE
NATAKU!
ZOD
LET'S DO IT...
OM
VW
THIS... WILL BE IT...
DOZ
AA
ZAAAAAA
?!

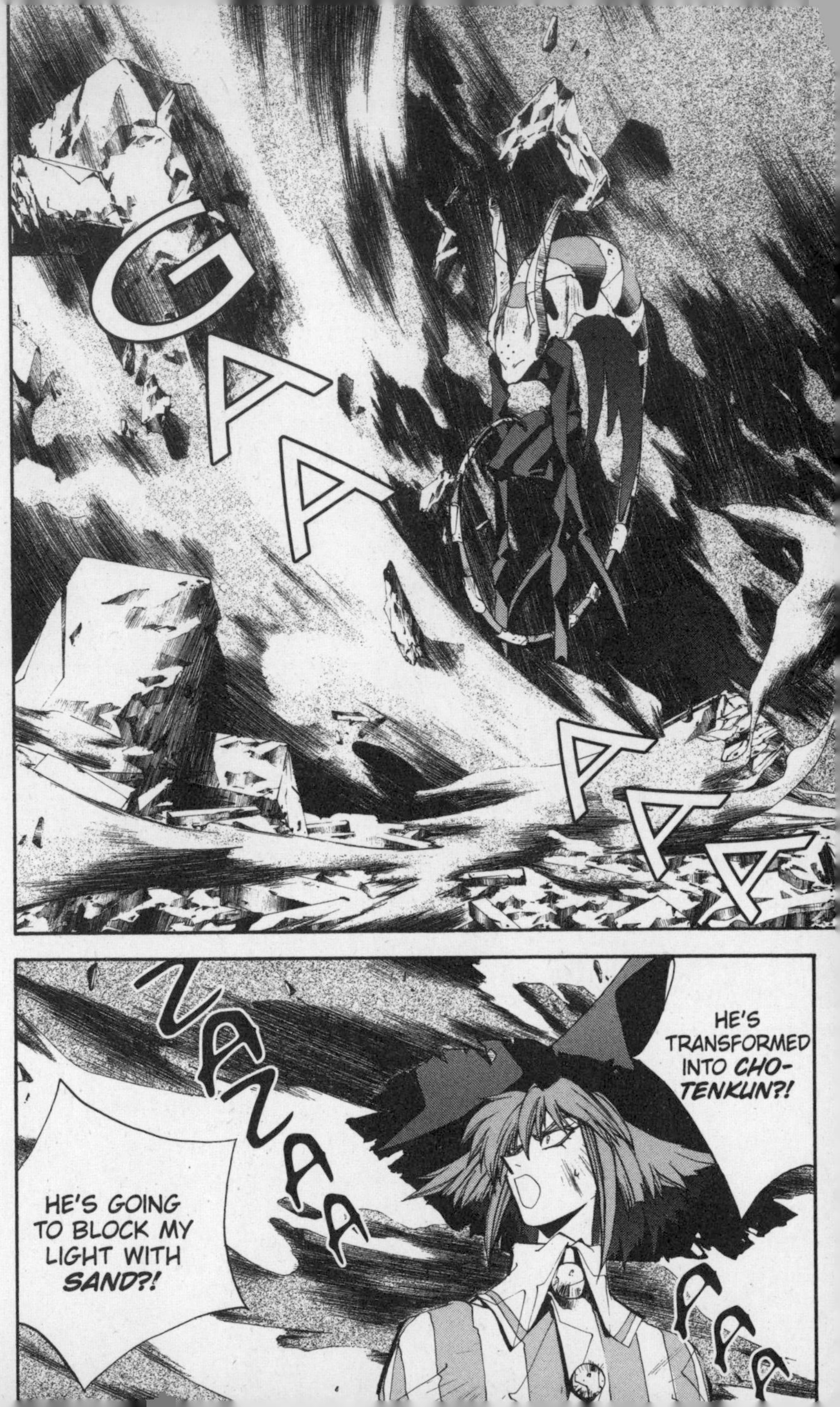
HE'S TRANSFORMED INTO *CHO-TENKUN*?!
HE'S GOING TO BLOCK MY LIGHT WITH *SAND*?!

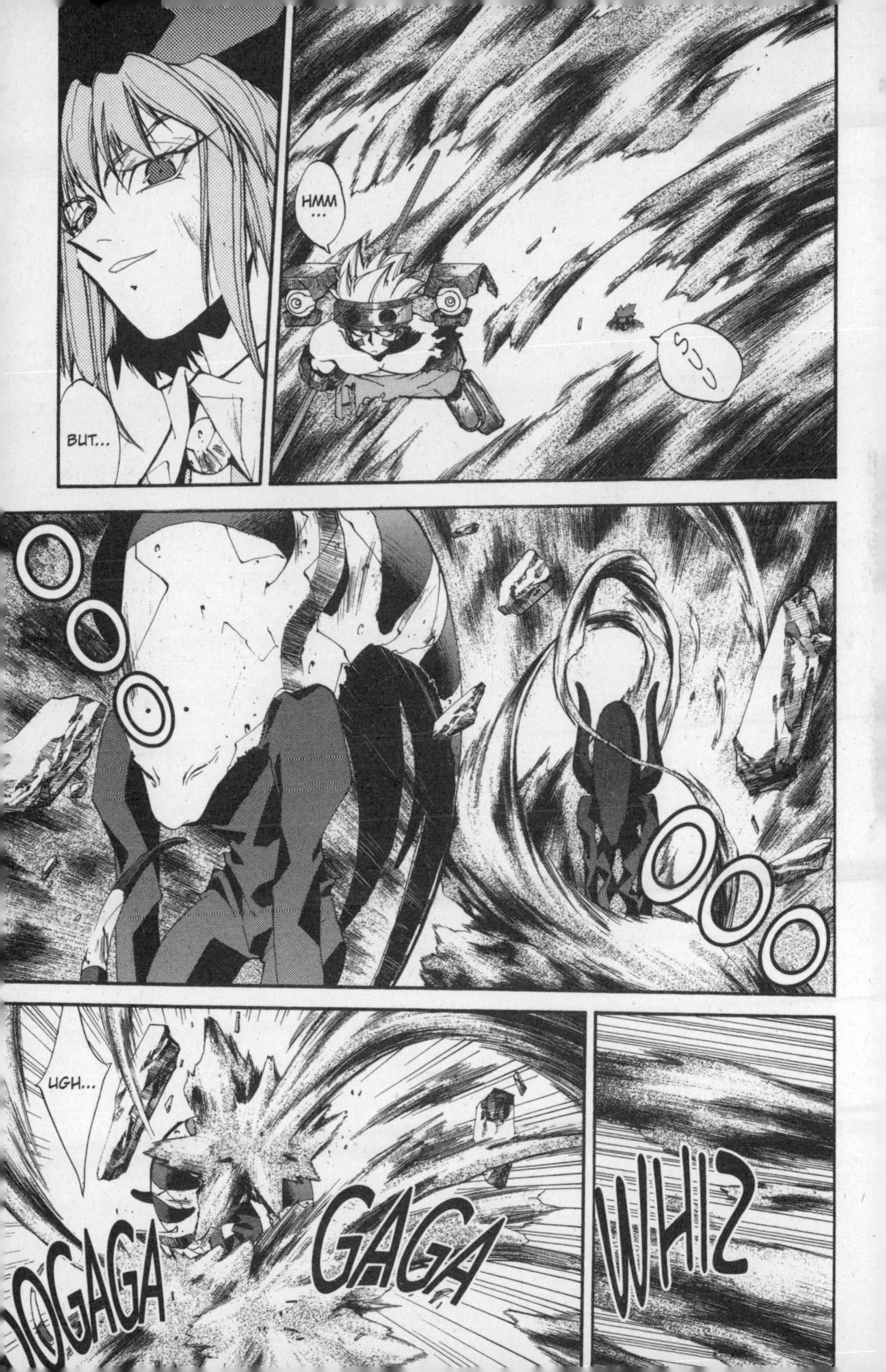
HMM...
BUT...
OOO
OOOO
WHIZ
UGH...
DOGAGA
GAGA

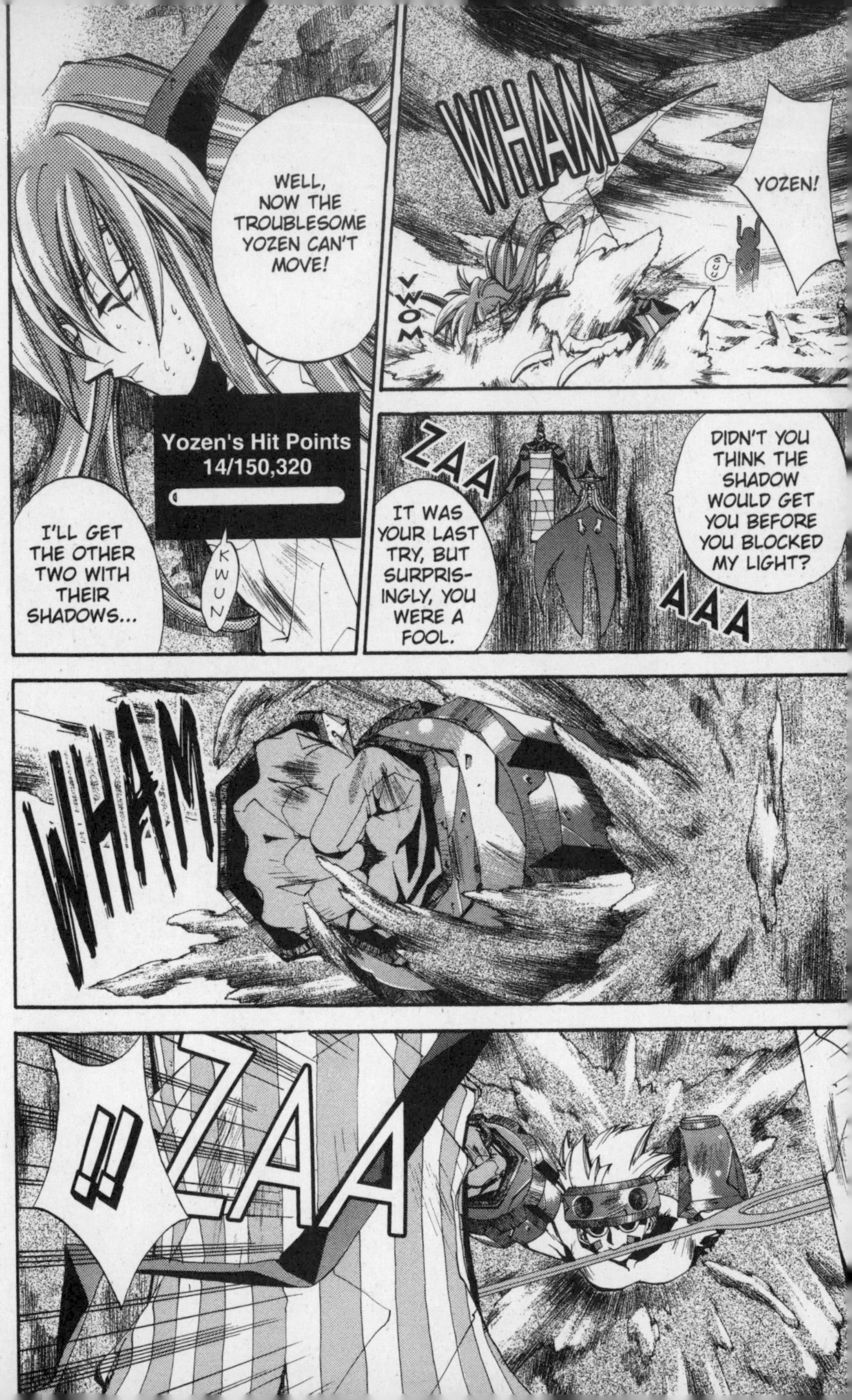
WHAM
YOZEN!
SUU
VWOM
ZAA
DIDN'T YOU THINK THE SHADOW WOULD GET YOU BEFORE YOU BLOCKED MY LIGHT?
IT WAS YOUR LAST TRY, BUT SURPRIS-INGLY, YOU WERE A FOOL.
AAA
WELL, NOW THE TROUBLESOME YOZEN CAN'T MOVE!
Yozen's Hit Points
14/150,320
I'LL GET THE OTHER TWO WITH THEIR SHADOWS...
KWUN
WHAM
ZAA
!!

READ THIS WAY

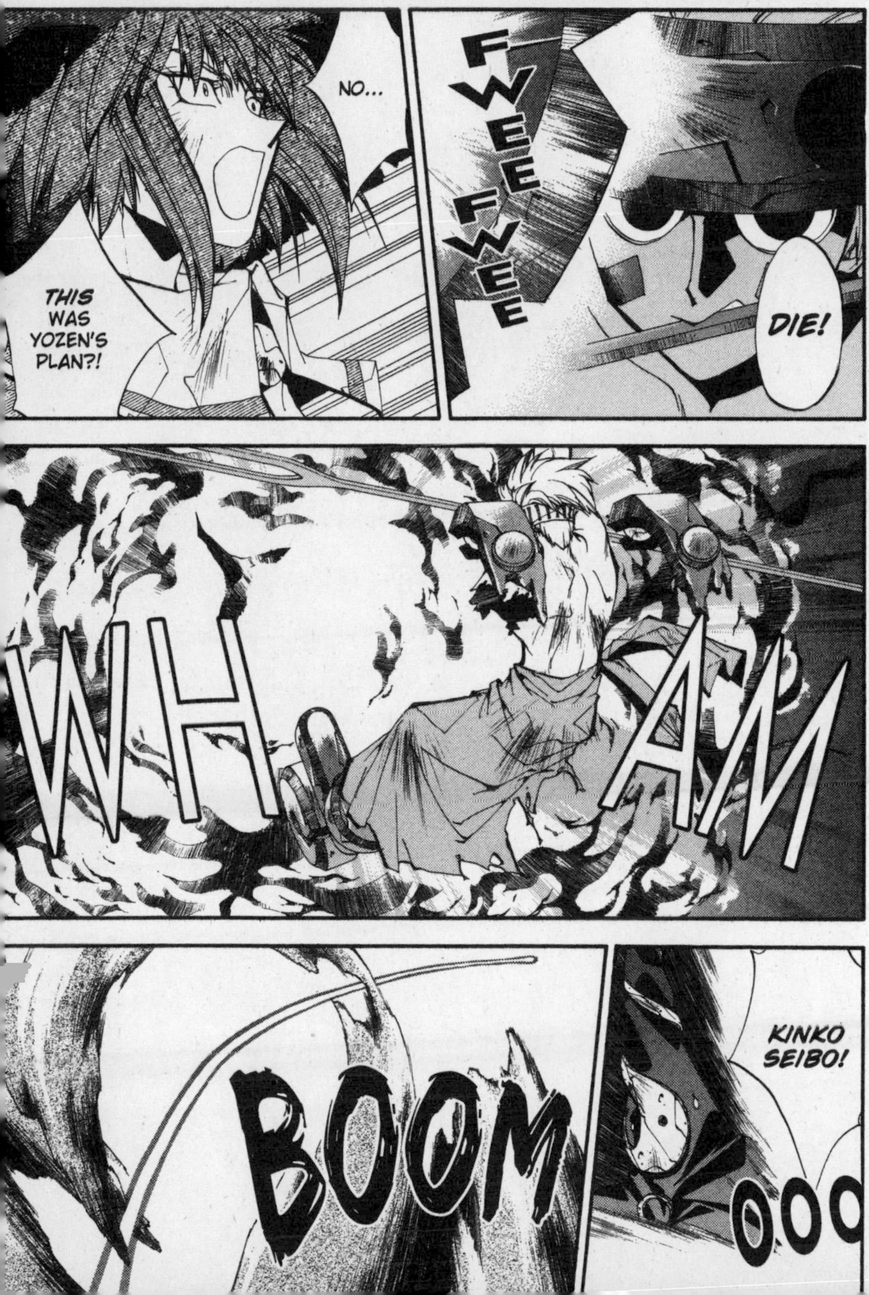
FWEE FWEE
DIE!
NO...
THIS WAS YOZEN'S PLAN?!
WHAM
KINKO SEIBO!
OOO
BOOM

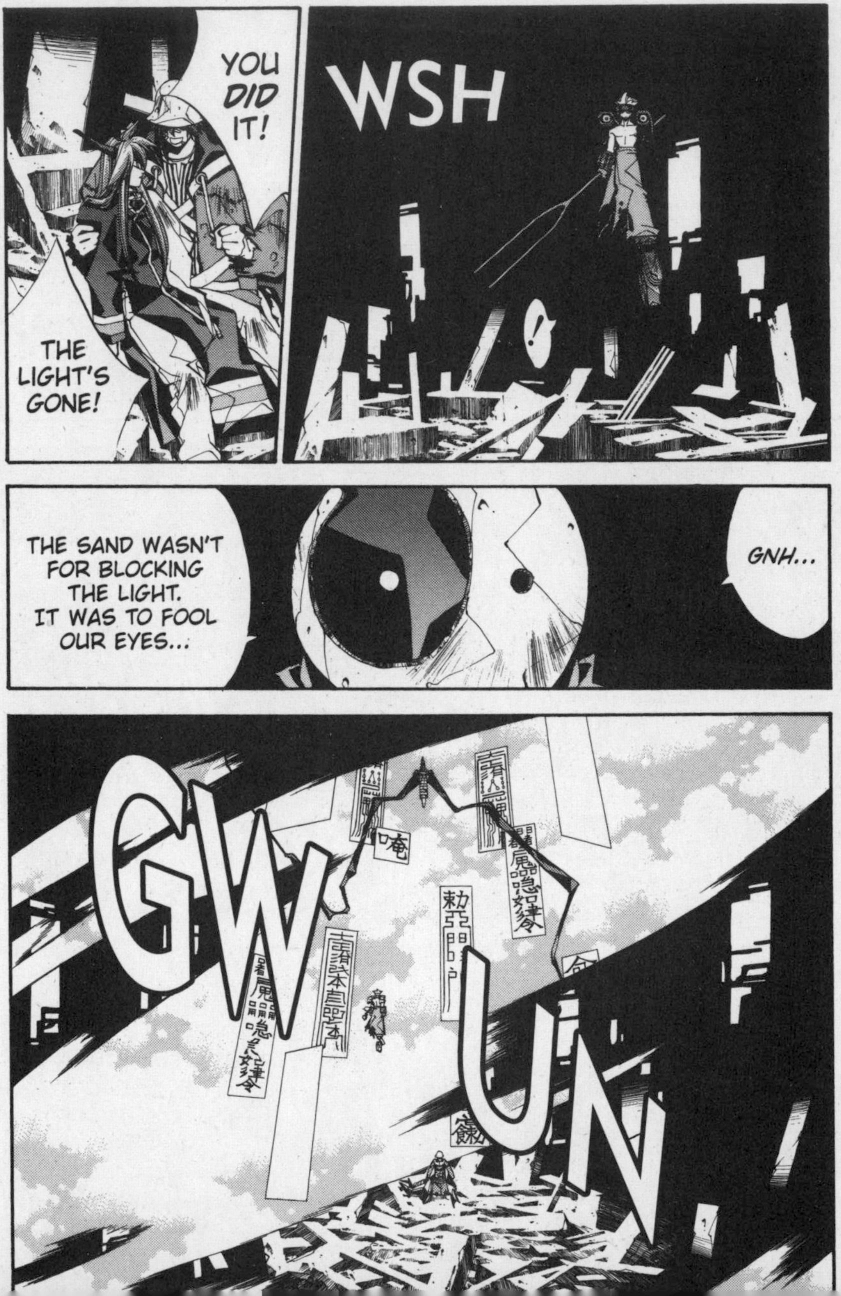
WSH
!
YOU DID IT!
THE LIGHT'S GONE!
GNH...
THE SAND WASN'T FOR BLOCKING THE LIGHT. IT WAS TO FOOL OUR EYES...
GWUN

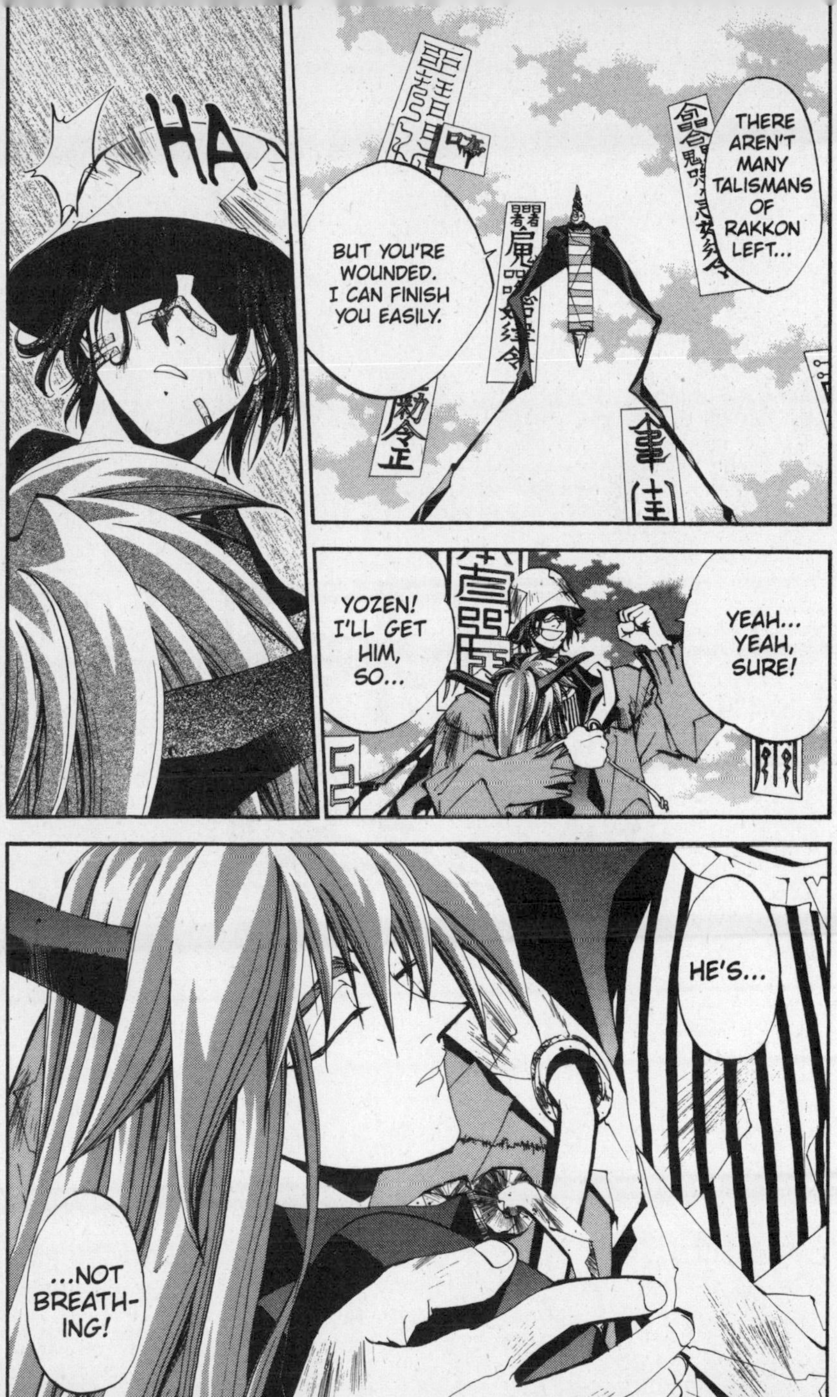
THERE AREN'T MANY TALISMANS OF RAKKON LEFT...
BUT YOU'RE WOUNDED. I CAN FINISH YOU EASILY.
YEAH... YEAH, SURE!
YOZEN! I'LL GET HIM, SO...
HA
HE'S...
...NOT BREATHING!

封神演義

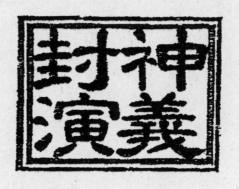

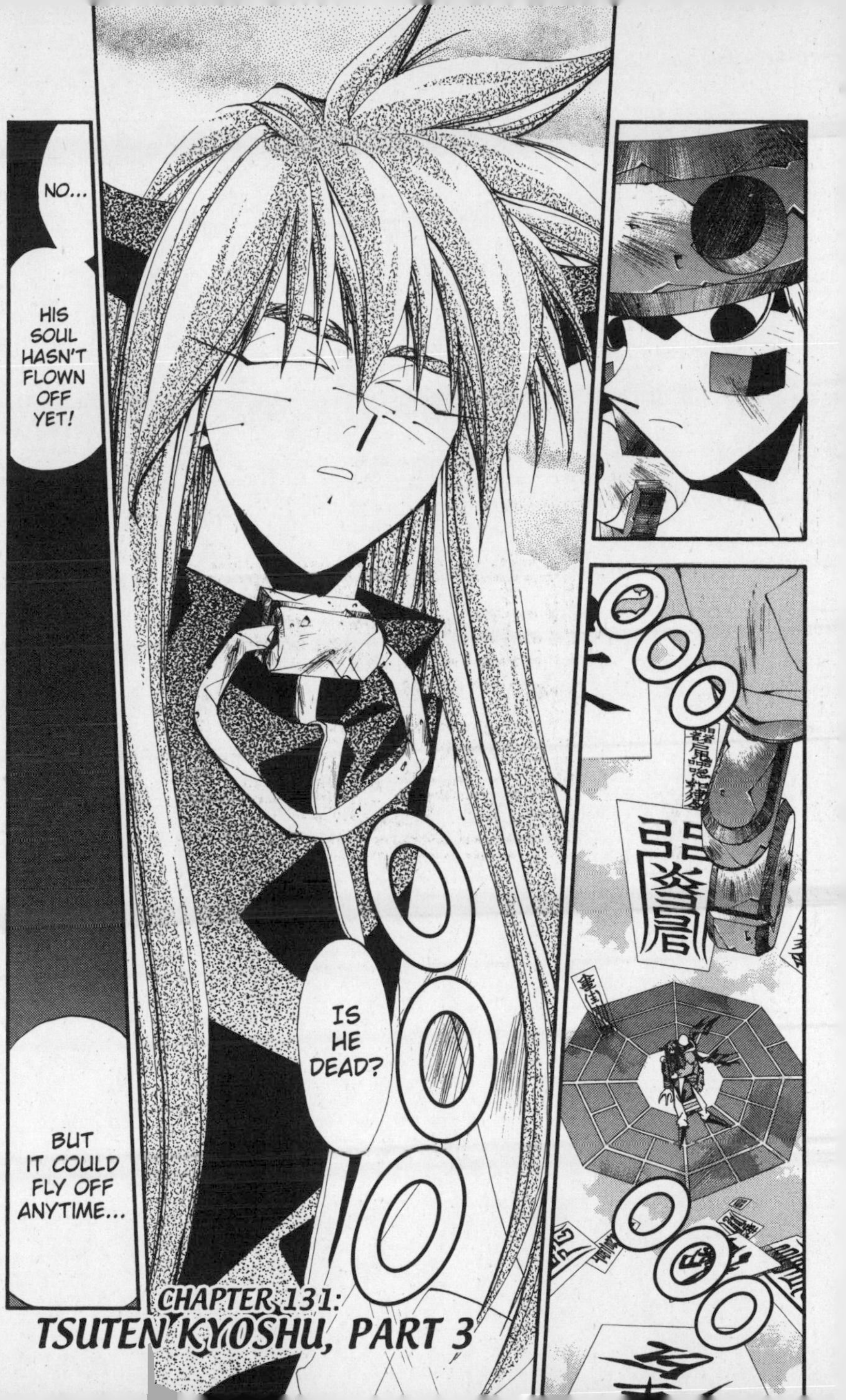
IS HE DEAD?
NO...
HIS SOUL HASN'T FLOWN OFF YET!
BUT IT COULD FLY OFF ANYTIME...
CHAPTER 131:
TSUTEN KYOSHU, PART 3

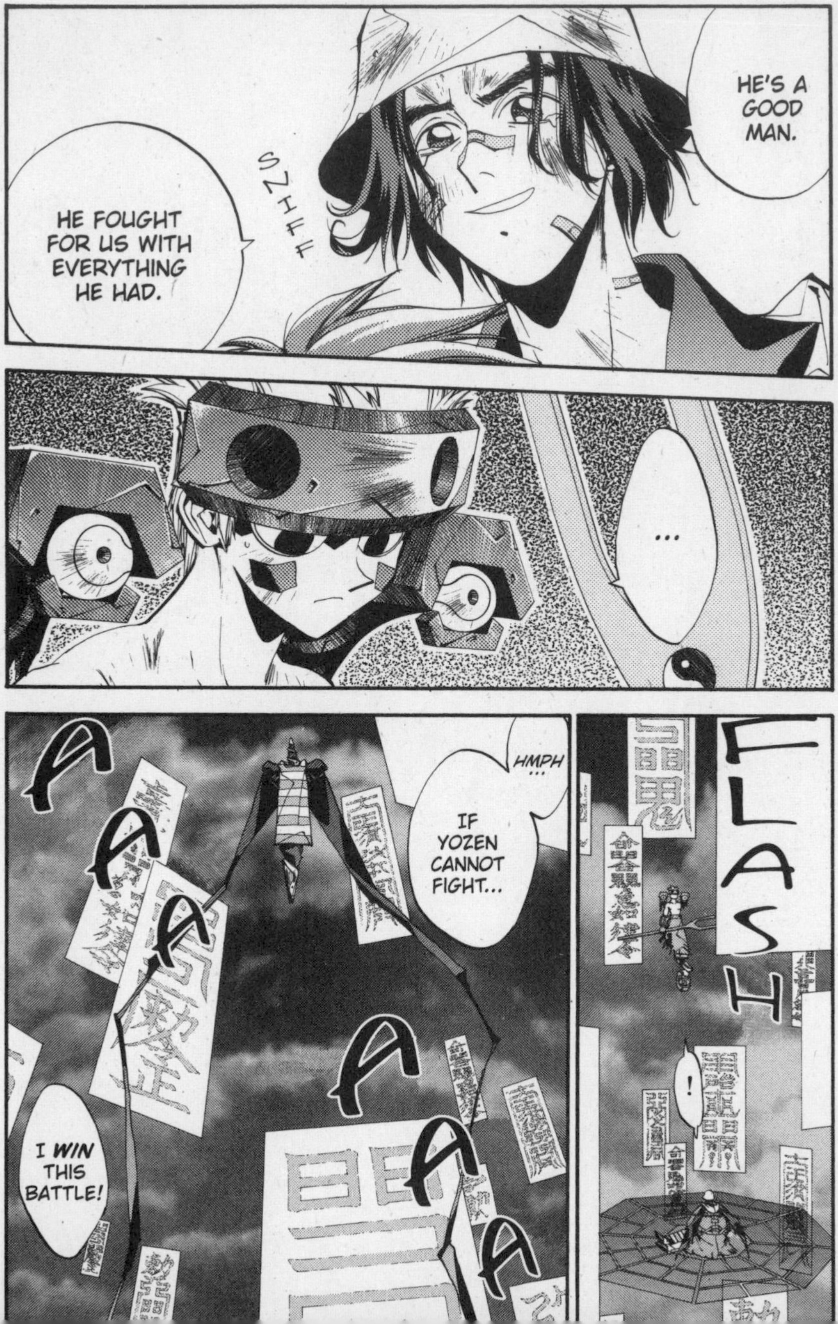
HE'S A GOOD MAN.
SNIFF
HE FOUGHT FOR US WITH EVERYTHING HE HAD.
...
FLASH
!
HMPH...
IF YOZEN CANNOT FIGHT...
AAAAAA
I *WIN* THIS BATTLE!

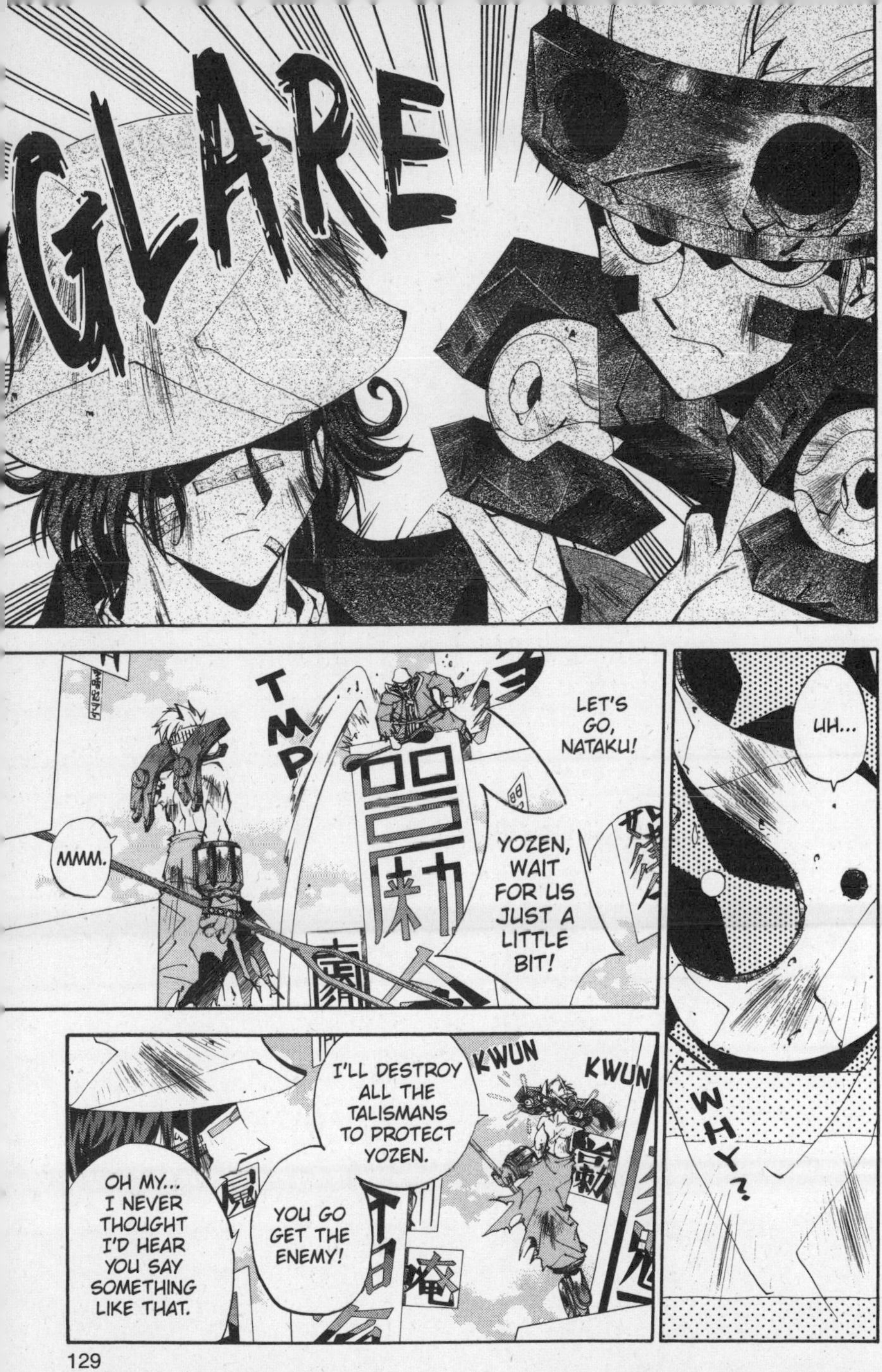
GLARE
UH...
WHY?
LET'S GO, NATAKU!
TMP
YOZEN, WAIT FOR US JUST A LITTLE BIT!
MMM.
KWUN
KWUN
I'LL DESTROY ALL THE TALISMANS TO PROTECT YOZEN.
YOU GO GET THE ENEMY!
OH MY... I NEVER THOUGHT I'D HEAR YOU SAY SOMETHING LIKE THAT.

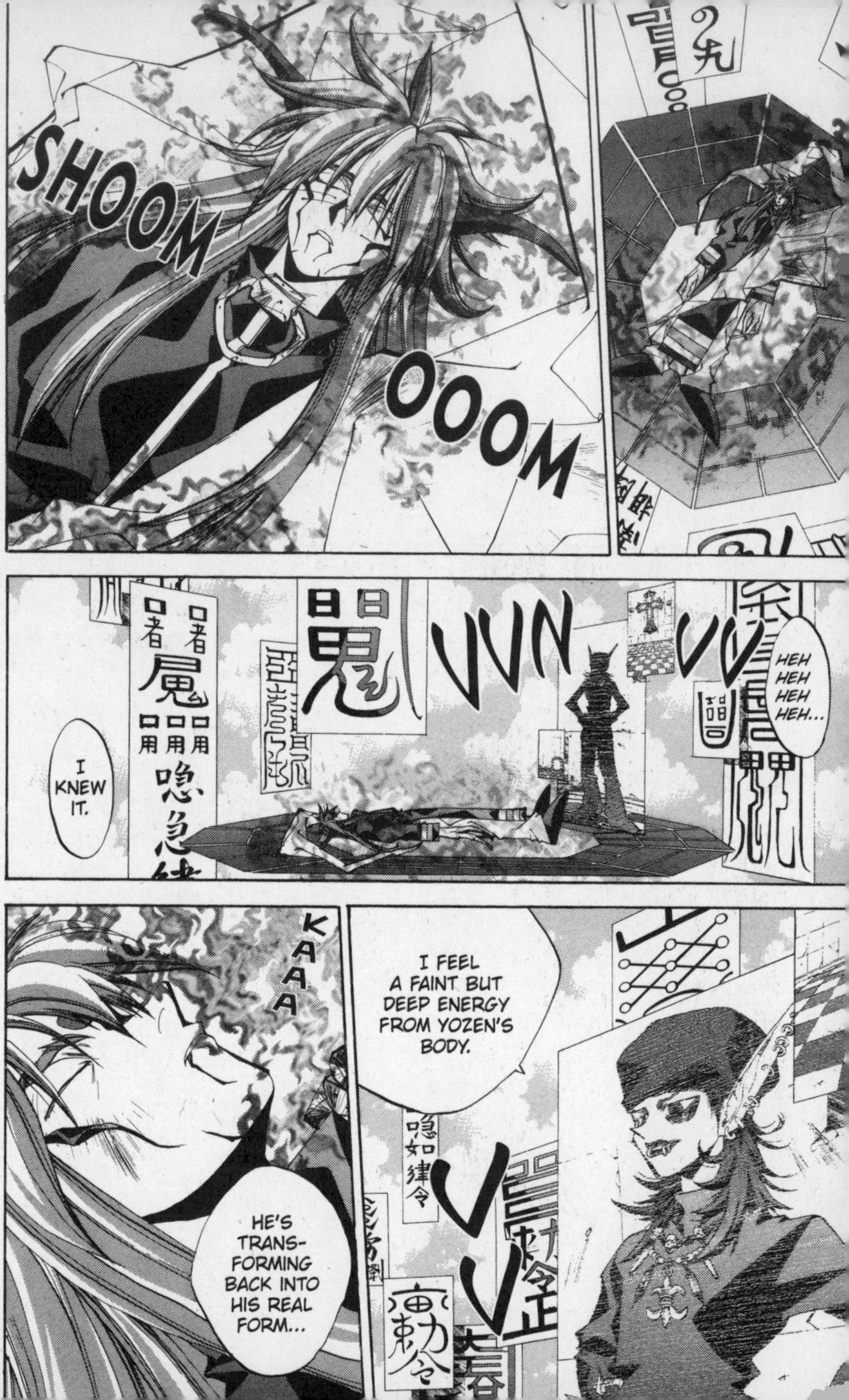
SHOOM
OOOM
HEH HEH HEH HEH...
VV
VVN
I KNEW IT.
I FEEL A FAINT BUT DEEP ENERGY FROM YOZEN'S BODY.
VV
KAAAA
HE'S TRANS-FORMING BACK INTO HIS REAL FORM...

Chapter 131

TSUTEN KYOSHU, PART 3

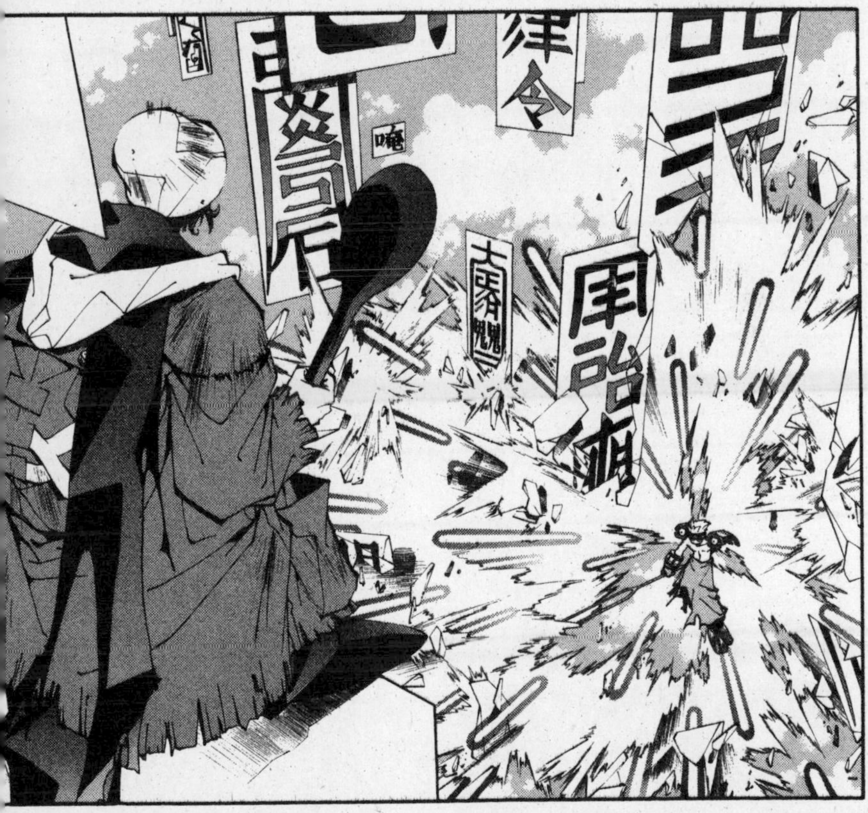
律令
俺

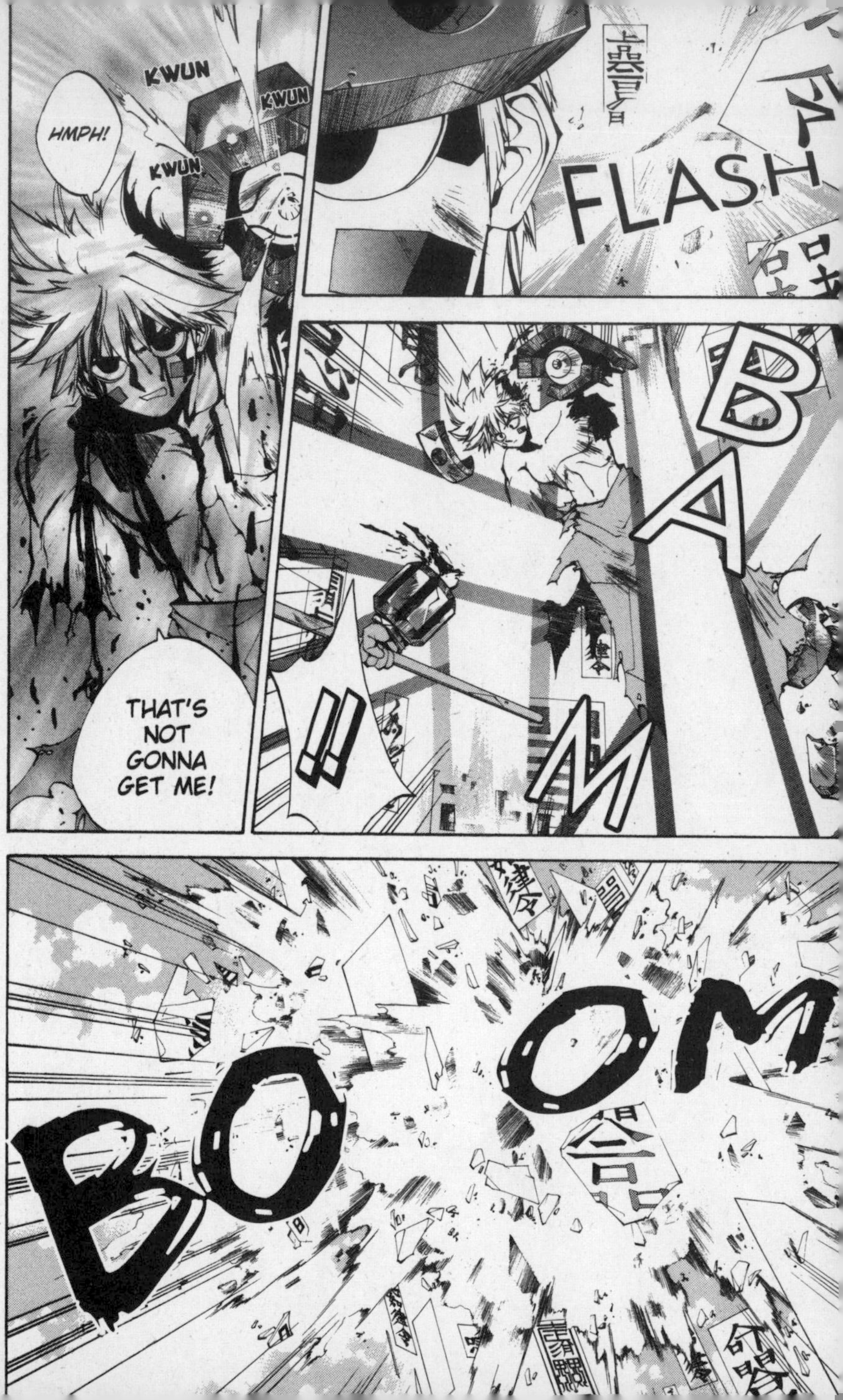
FLASH
BAM
!!
KWUN
KWUN
KWUN
HMPH!
THAT'S NOT GONNA GET ME!
BOOM

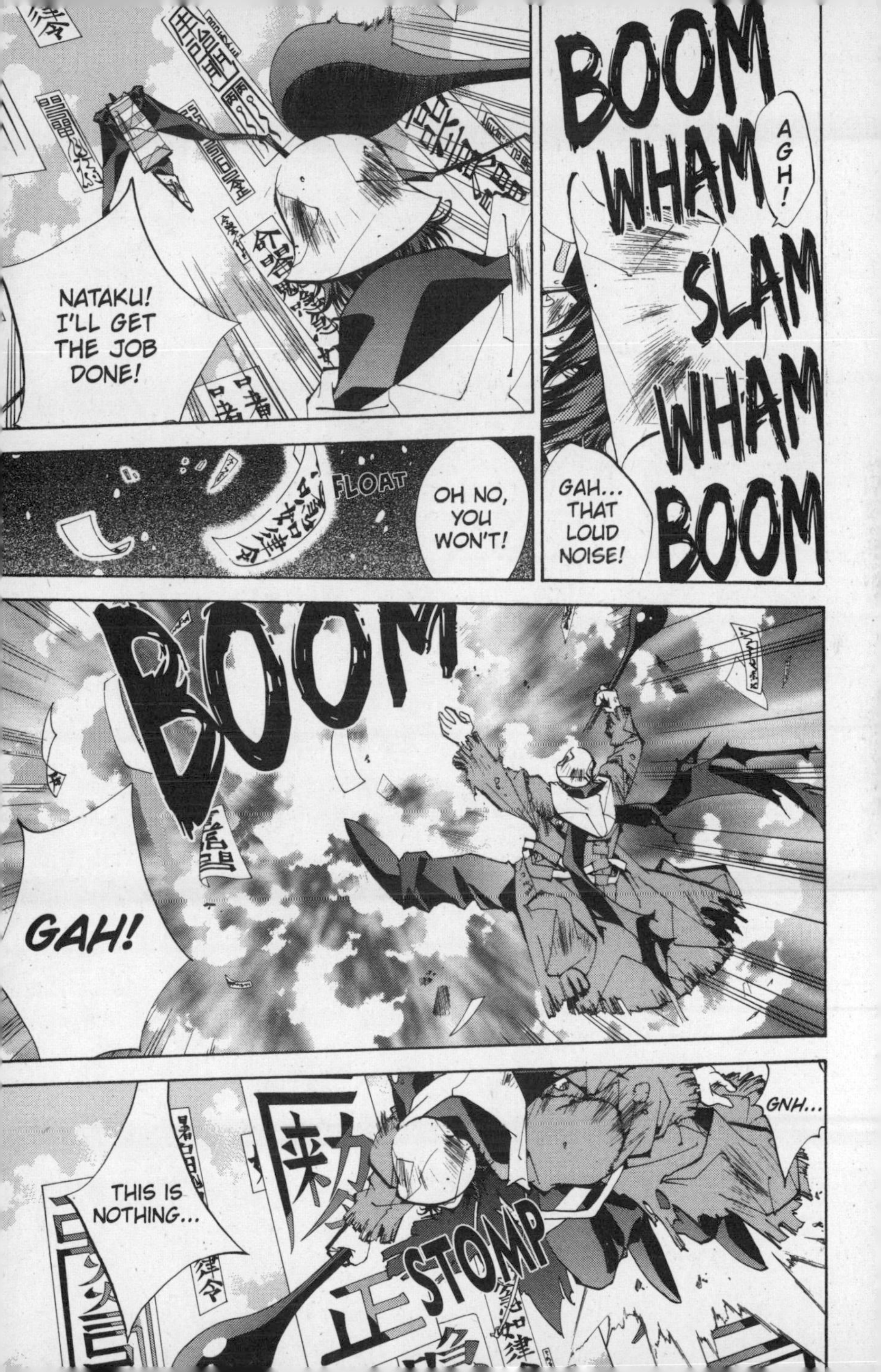
BOOM
WHAM
AGH!
SLAM
WHAM
BOOM
GAH... THAT LOUD NOISE!
NATAKU! I'LL GET THE JOB DONE!
FLOAT
OH NO, YOU WON'T!
BOOM
GAH!
GNH...
STOMP
THIS IS NOTHING...

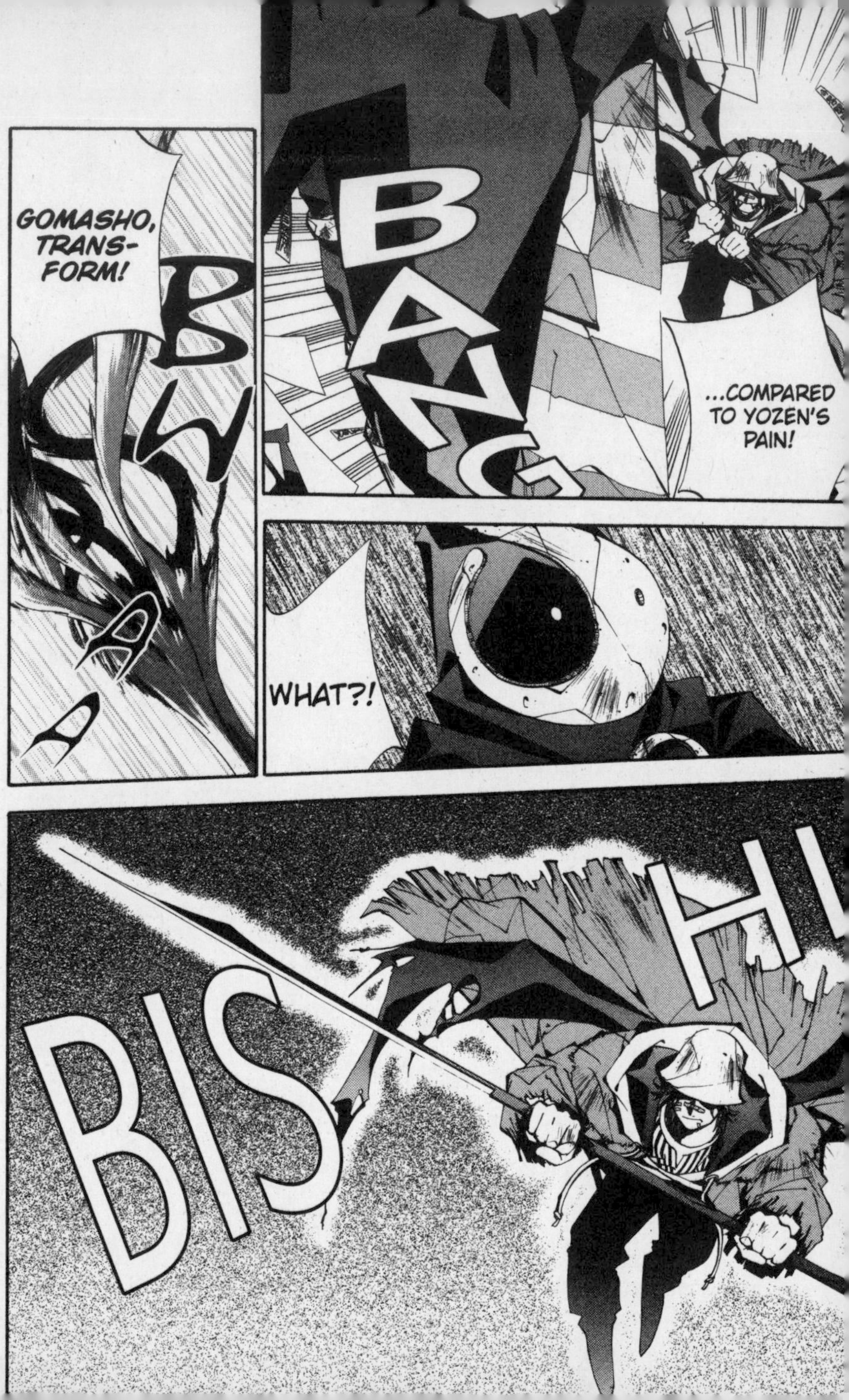
...COMPARED TO YOZEN'S PAIN!
BANG
WHAT?!
GOMASHO, TRANSFORM!
BISH

READ THIS WAY

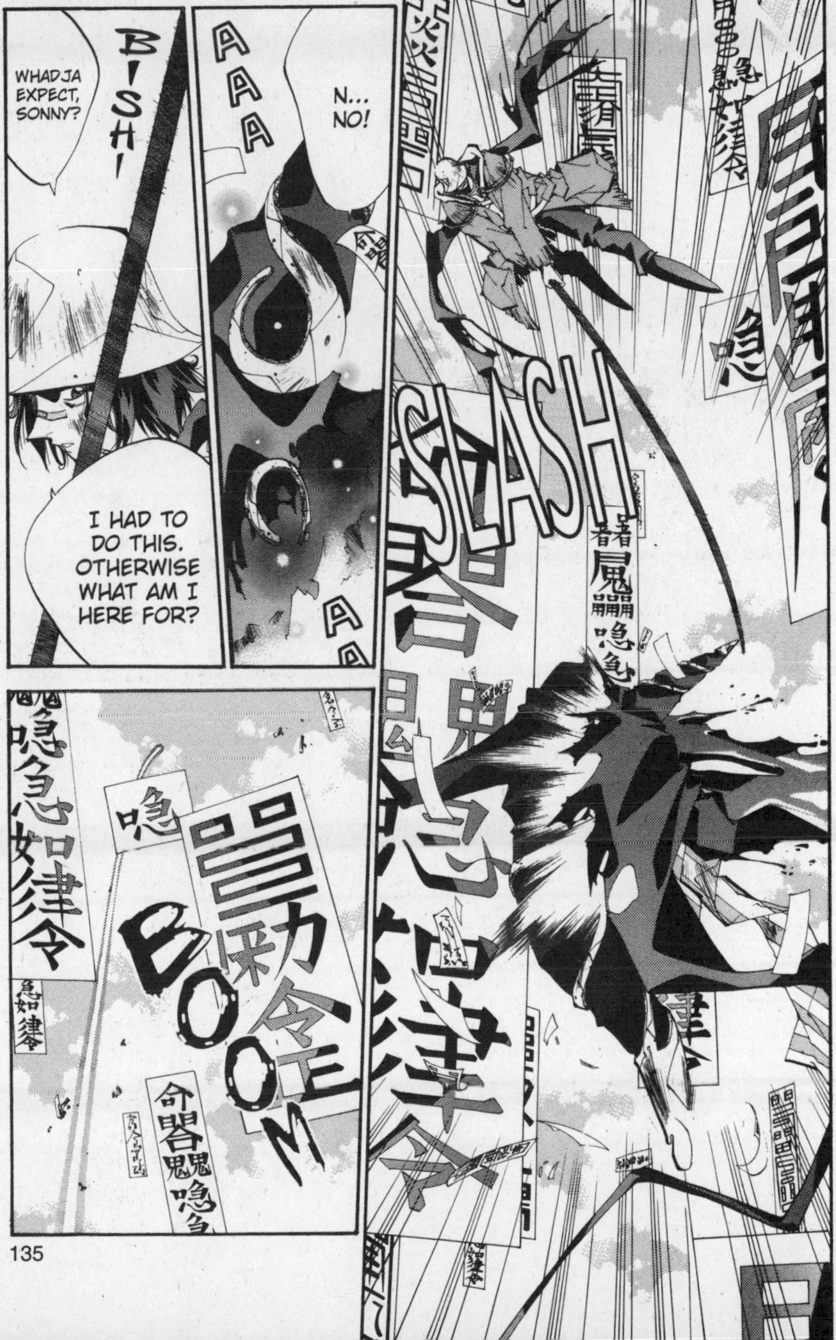

SLASH
AAAA
N... NO!
BISH!
WHADJA EXPECT, SONNY?
I HAD TO DO THIS. OTHERWISE WHAT AM I HERE FOR?
BOOM

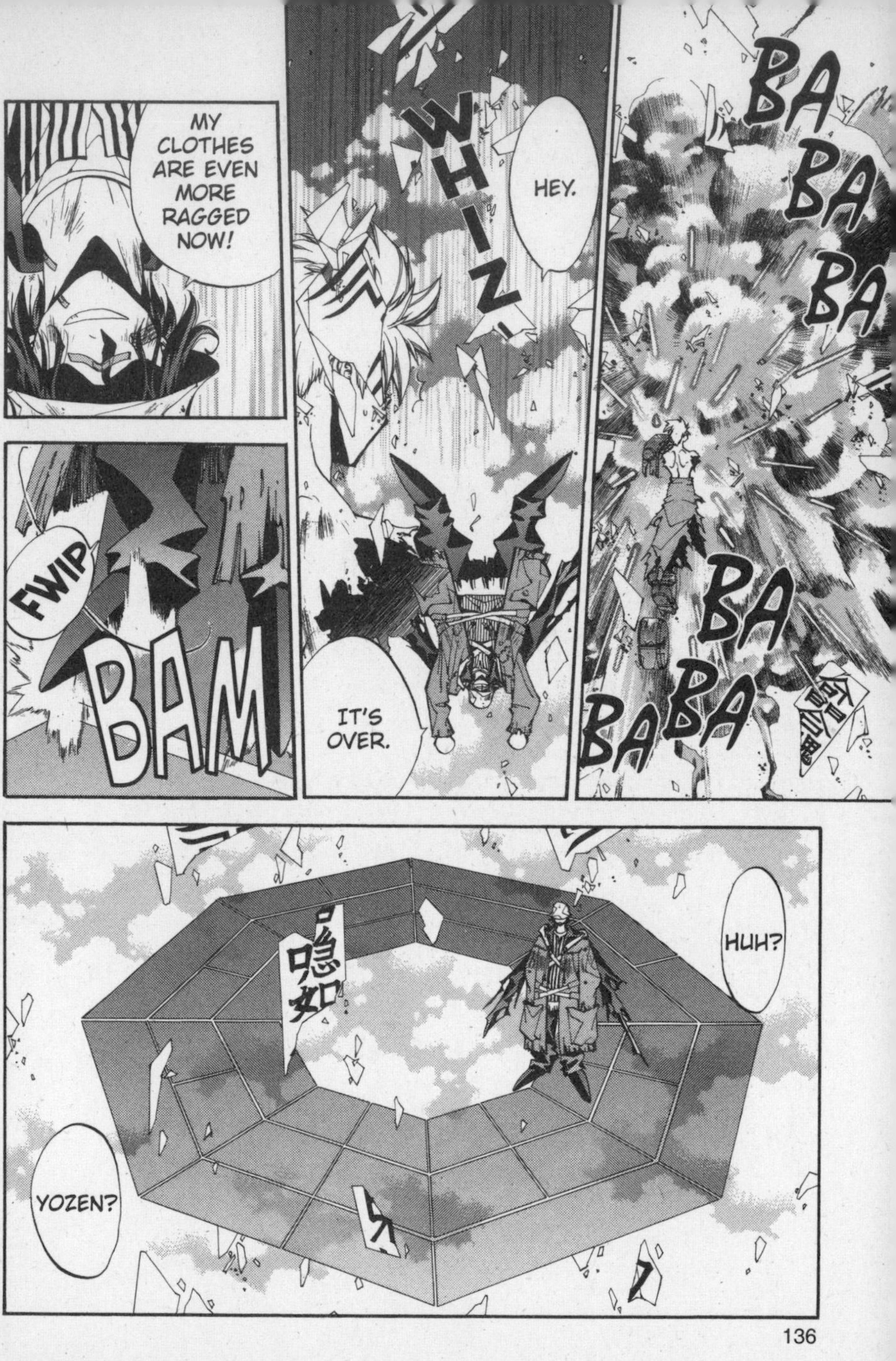
BA BA BA
BA BA
BA BA
WHIZ
HEY.
IT'S OVER.
MY CLOTHES ARE EVEN MORE RAGGED NOW!
FWIP
BAM
HUH?
YOZEN?

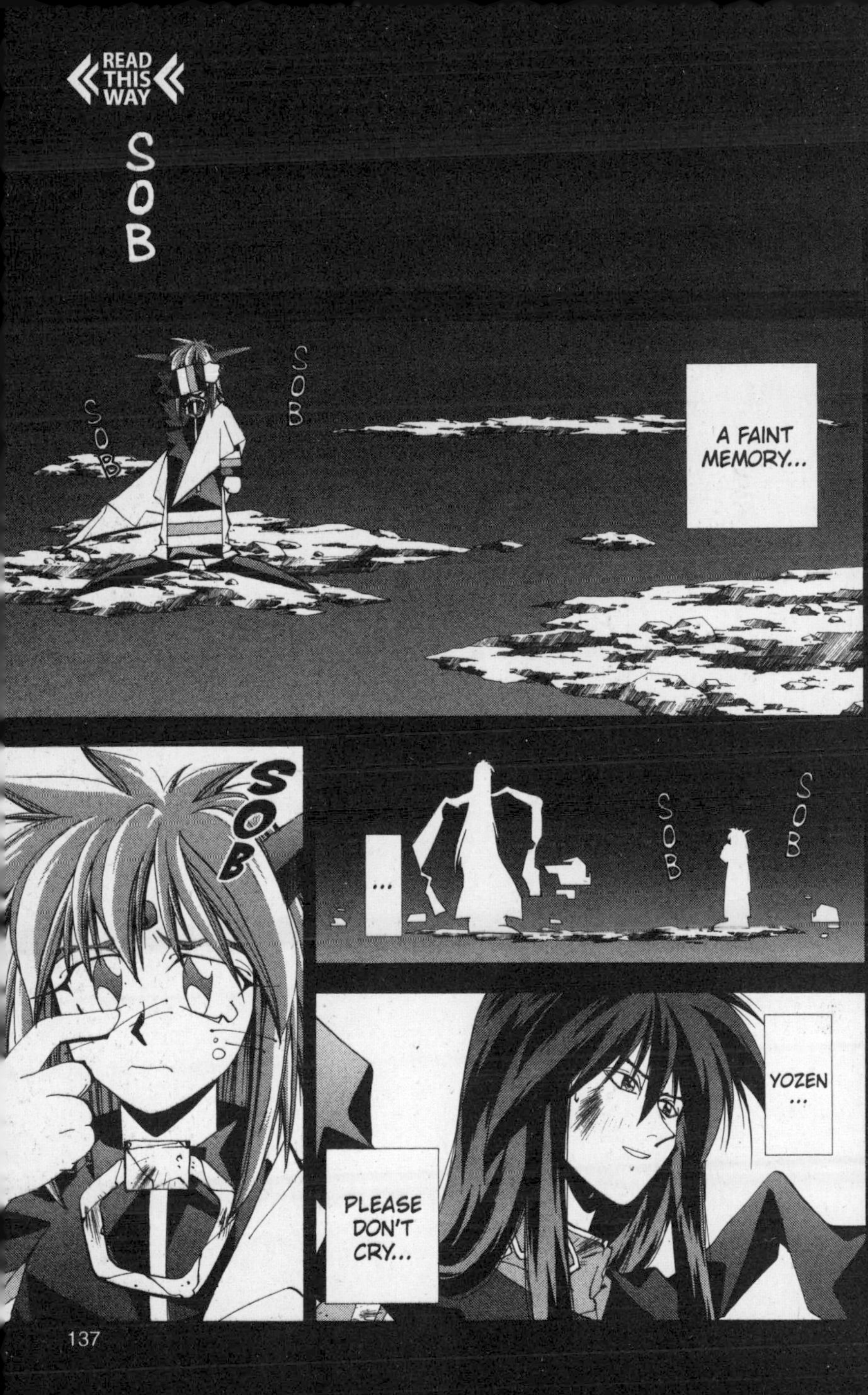
READ THIS WAY
SOB
A FAINT MEMORY...
SOB
SOB
SOB
SOB
...
YOZEN ...
PLEASE DON'T CRY...
SOB SOB

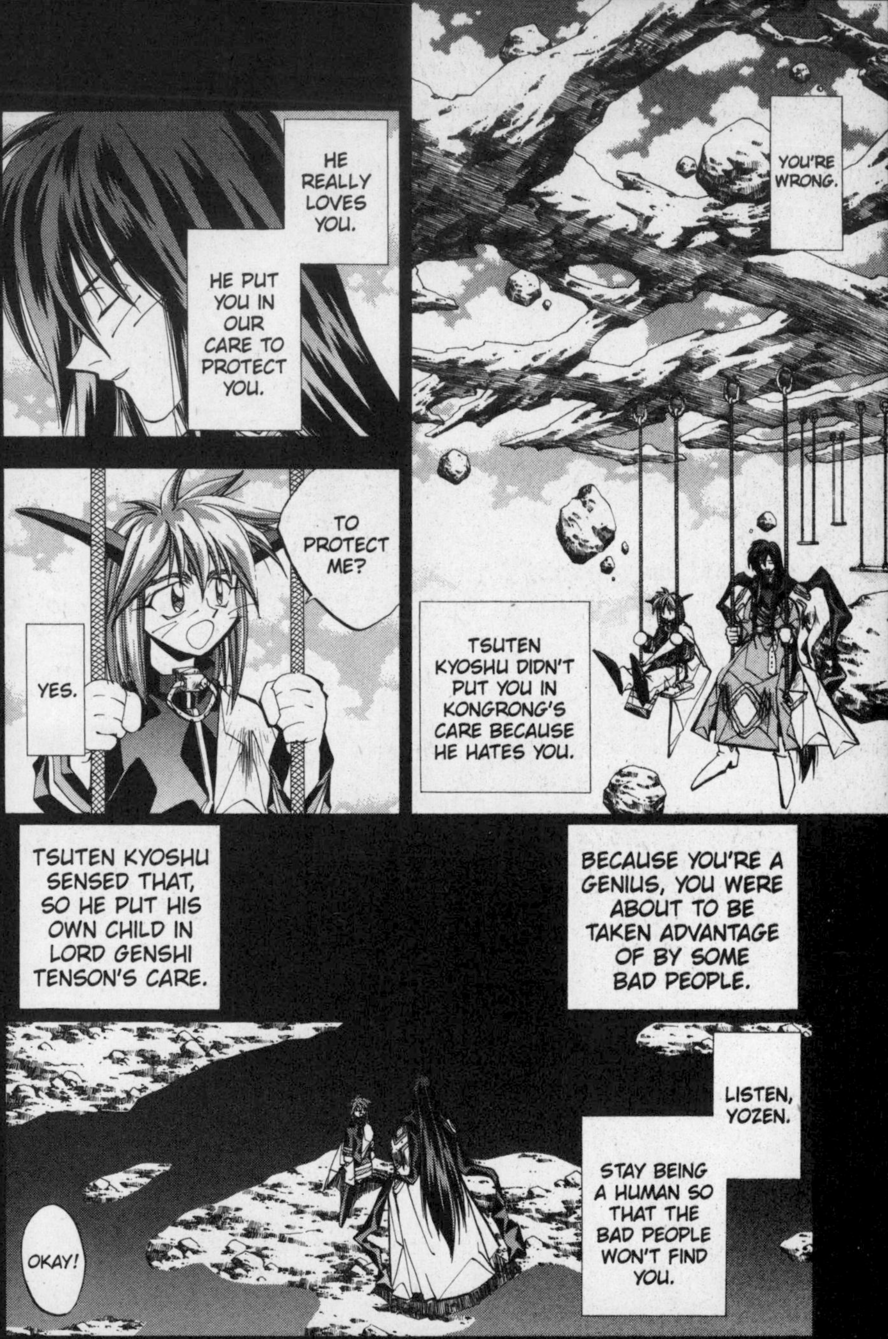
YOU'RE WRONG.
TSUTEN KYOSHU DIDN'T PUT YOU IN KONGRONG'S CARE BECAUSE HE HATES YOU.
HE REALLY LOVES YOU.
HE PUT YOU IN OUR CARE TO PROTECT YOU.
TO PROTECT ME?
YES.
BECAUSE YOU'RE A GENIUS, YOU WERE ABOUT TO BE TAKEN ADVANTAGE OF BY SOME BAD PEOPLE.
TSUTEN KYOSHU SENSED THAT, SO HE PUT HIS OWN CHILD IN LORD GENSHI TENSON'S CARE.
LISTEN, YOZEN.
STAY BEING A HUMAN SO THAT THE BAD PEOPLE WON'T FIND YOU.
OKAY!

READ THIS WAY

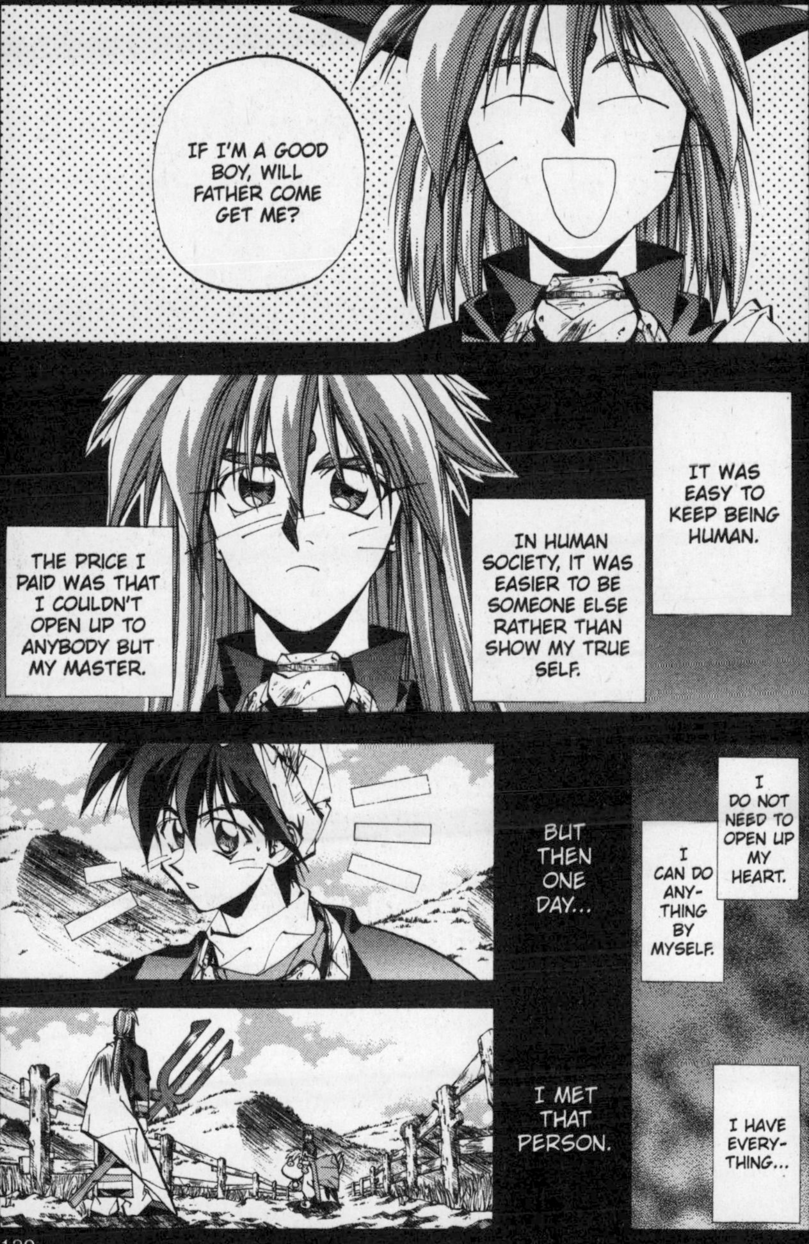

IF I'M A GOOD BOY, WILL FATHER COME GET ME?
IT WAS EASY TO KEEP BEING HUMAN.
IN HUMAN SOCIETY, IT WAS EASIER TO BE SOMEONE ELSE RATHER THAN SHOW MY TRUE SELF.
THE PRICE I PAID WAS THAT I COULDN'T OPEN UP TO ANYBODY BUT MY MASTER.
I DO NOT NEED TO OPEN UP MY HEART.
I CAN DO ANY-THING BY MYSELF.
I HAVE EVERY-THING...
BUT THEN ONE DAY...
I MET THAT PERSON.

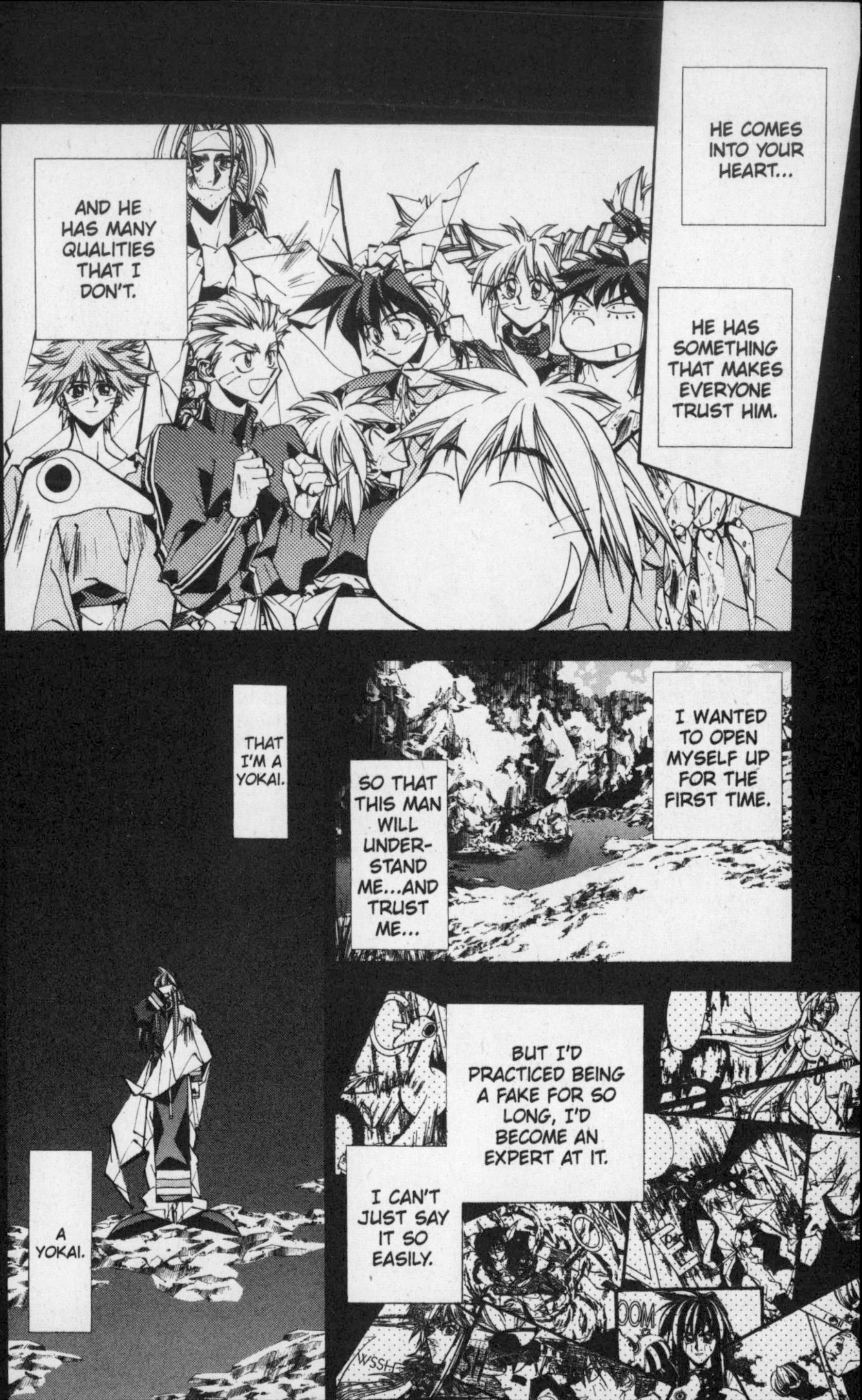
HE COMES INTO YOUR HEART...
HE HAS SOMETHING THAT MAKES EVERYONE TRUST HIM.
AND HE HAS MANY QUALITIES THAT I DON'T.
I WANTED TO OPEN MYSELF UP FOR THE FIRST TIME.
SO THAT THIS MAN WILL UNDER-STAND ME...AND TRUST ME...
THAT I'M A YOKAI.
BUT I'D PRACTICED BEING A FAKE FOR SO LONG, I'D BECOME AN EXPERT AT IT.
I CAN'T JUST SAY IT SO EASILY.
WSSH
A YOKAI.

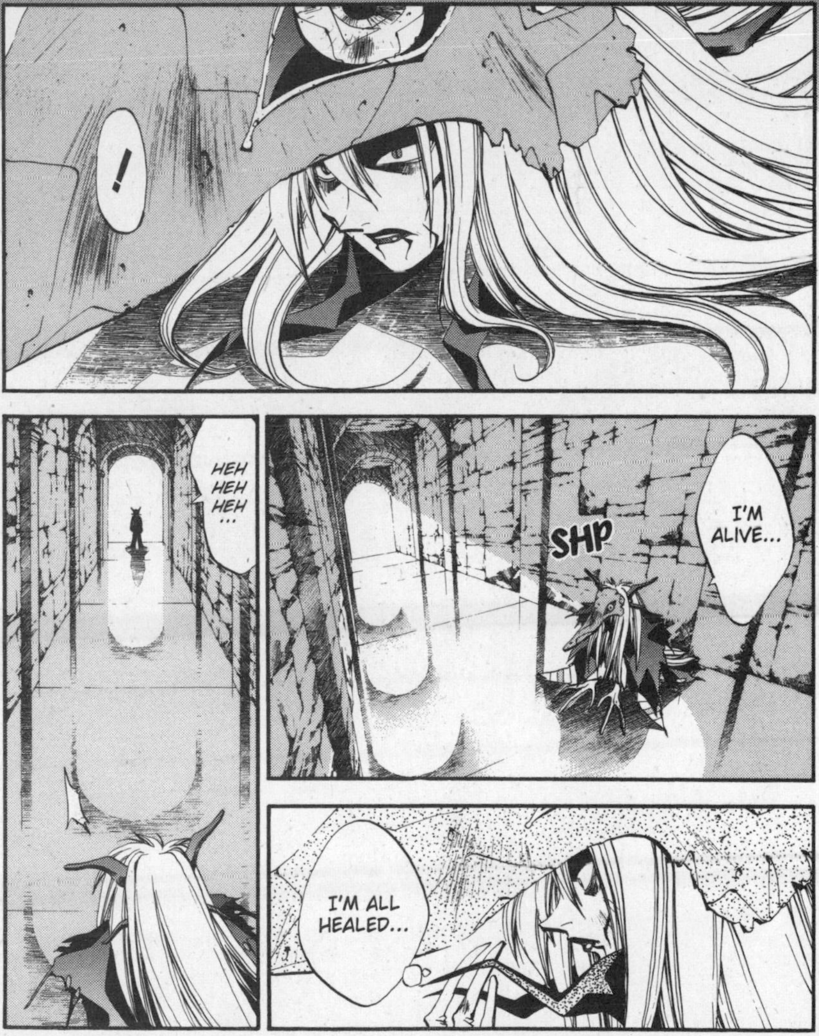
!
I'M ALIVE...
SHP
I'M ALL HEALED...
HEH HEH HEH...

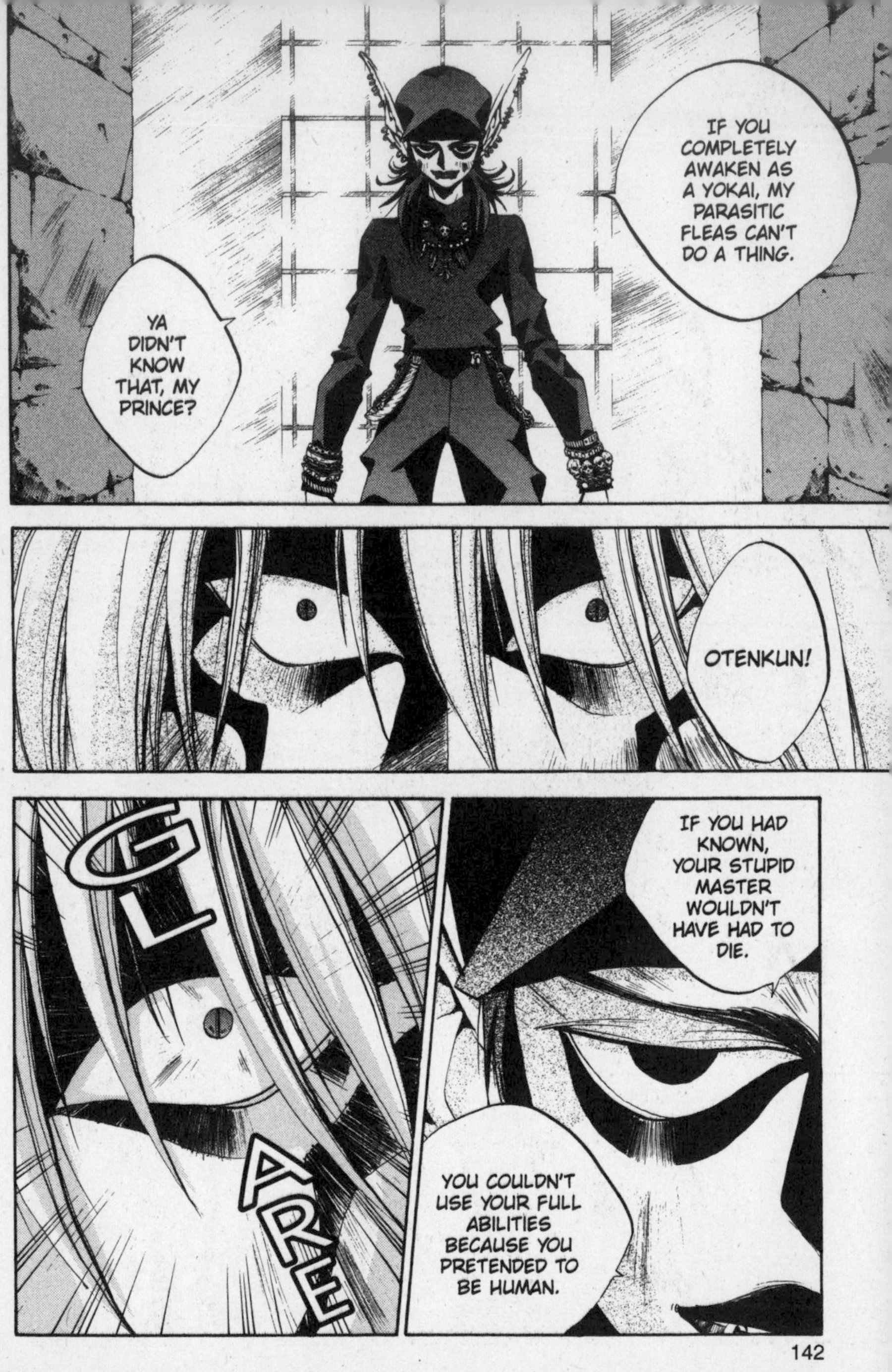
IF YOU COMPLETELY AWAKEN AS A YOKAI, MY PARASITIC FLEAS CAN'T DO A THING.
YA DIDN'T KNOW THAT, MY PRINCE?
OTENKUN!
IF YOU HAD KNOWN, YOUR STUPID MASTER WOULDN'T HAVE HAD TO DIE.
YOU COULDN'T USE YOUR FULL ABILITIES BECAUSE YOU PRETENDED TO BE HUMAN.
GLARE

READ THIS WAY

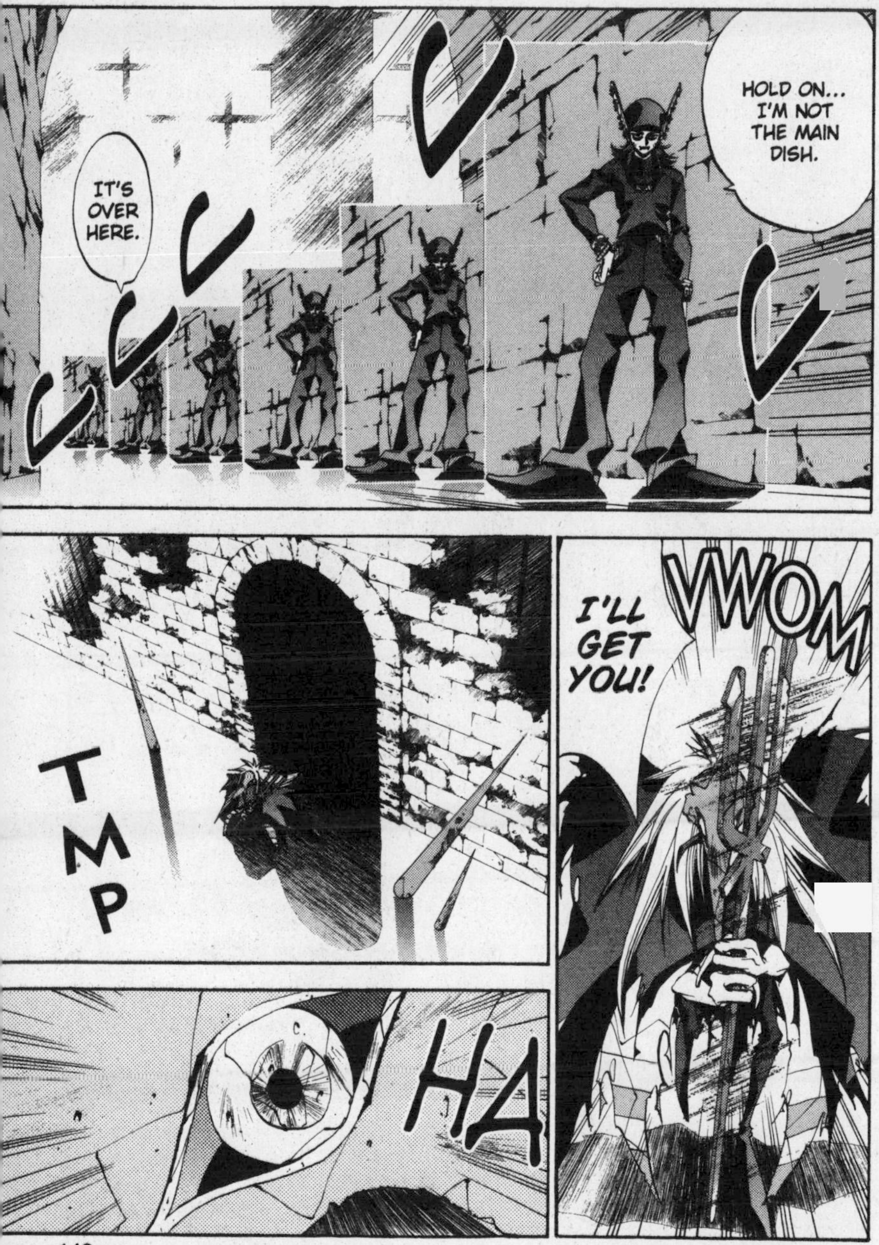

HOLD ON... I'M NOT THE MAIN DISH.
IT'S OVER HERE.
VWOM
I'LL GET YOU!
TMP
HA

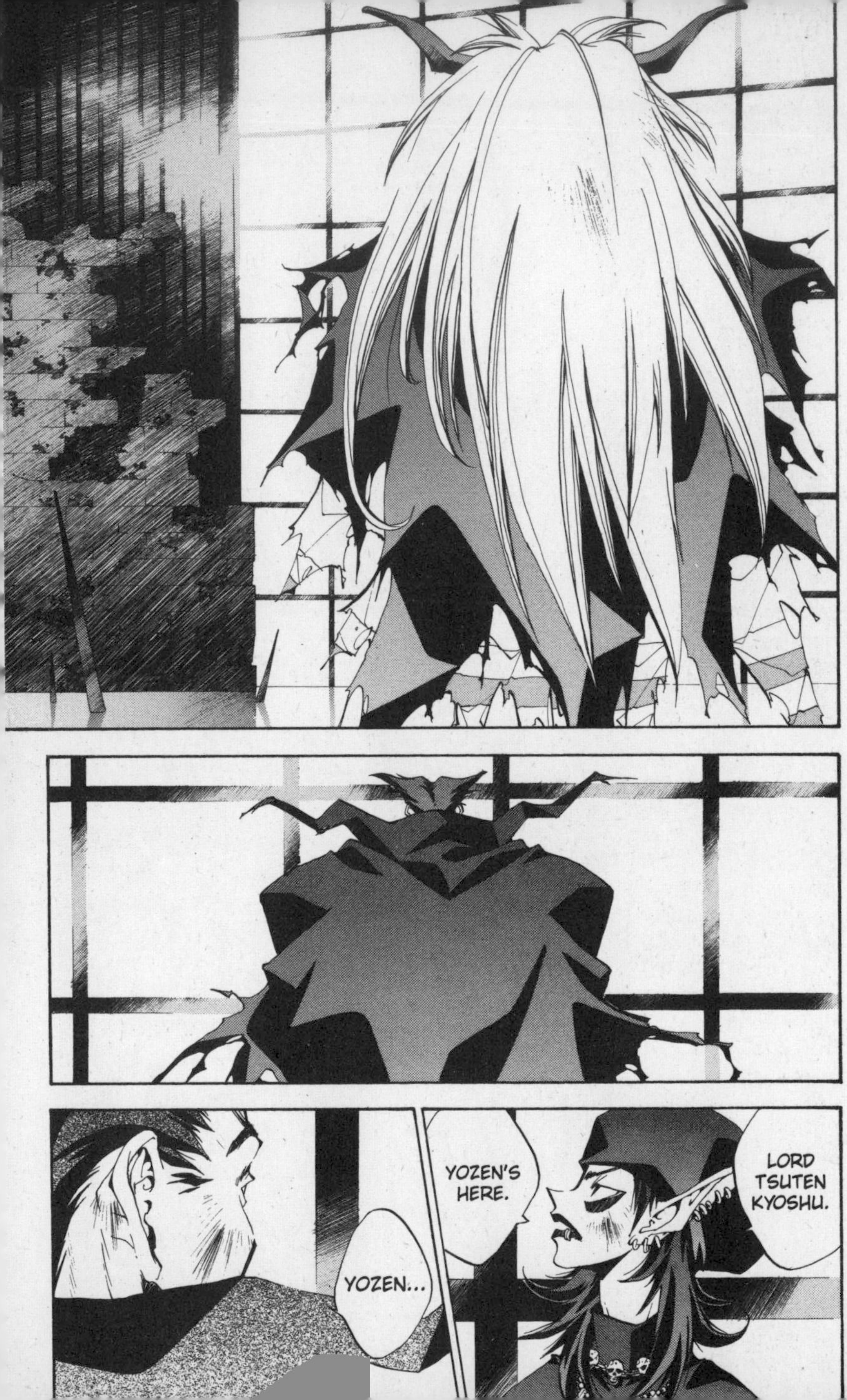
LORD TSUTEN KYOSHU.
YOZEN'S HERE.
YOZEN...

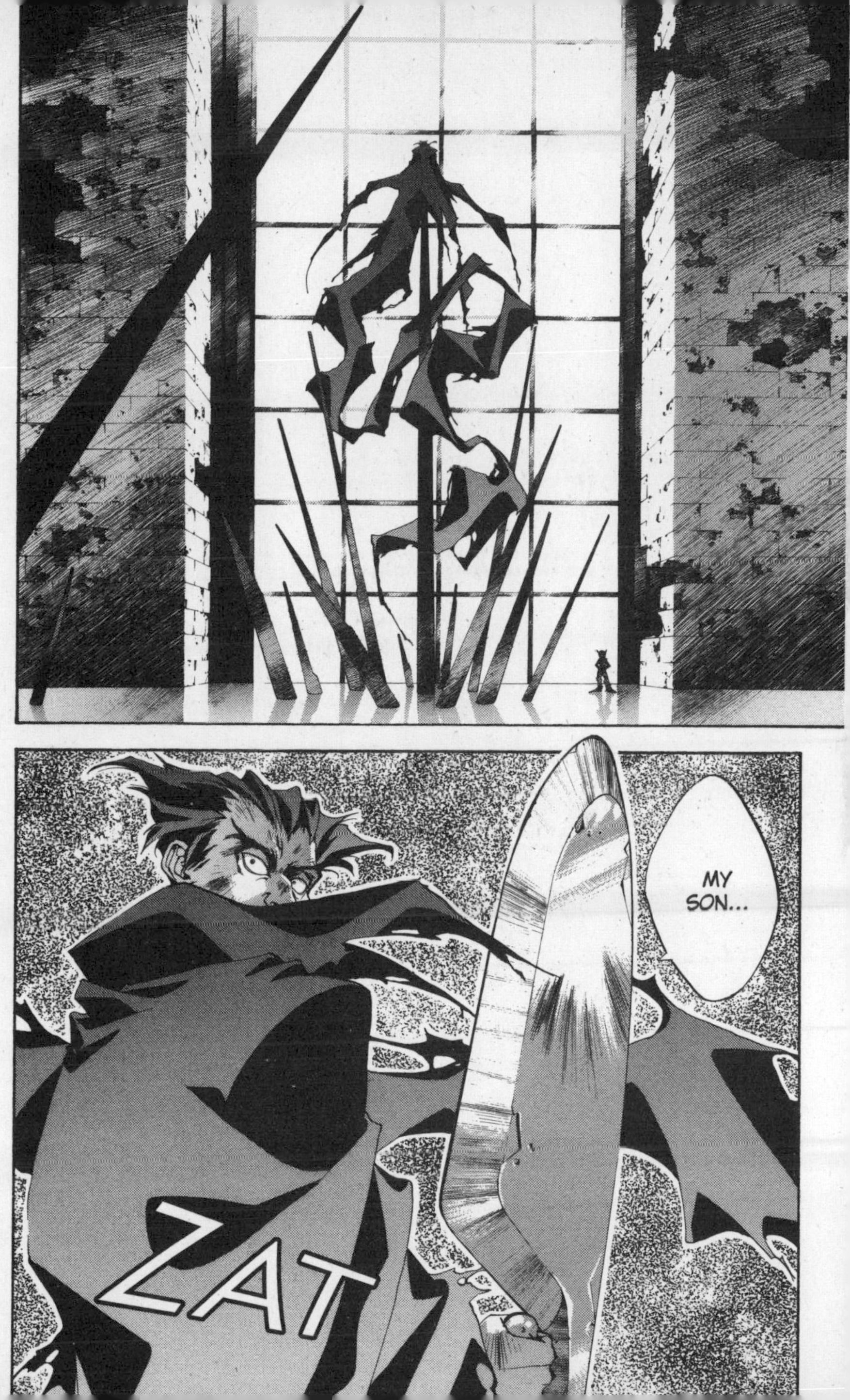
MY SON...
ZAT

封神演義

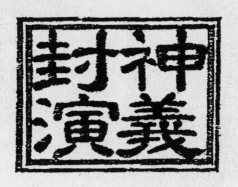

Chapter 132

TSUTEN KYOSHU, PART 4

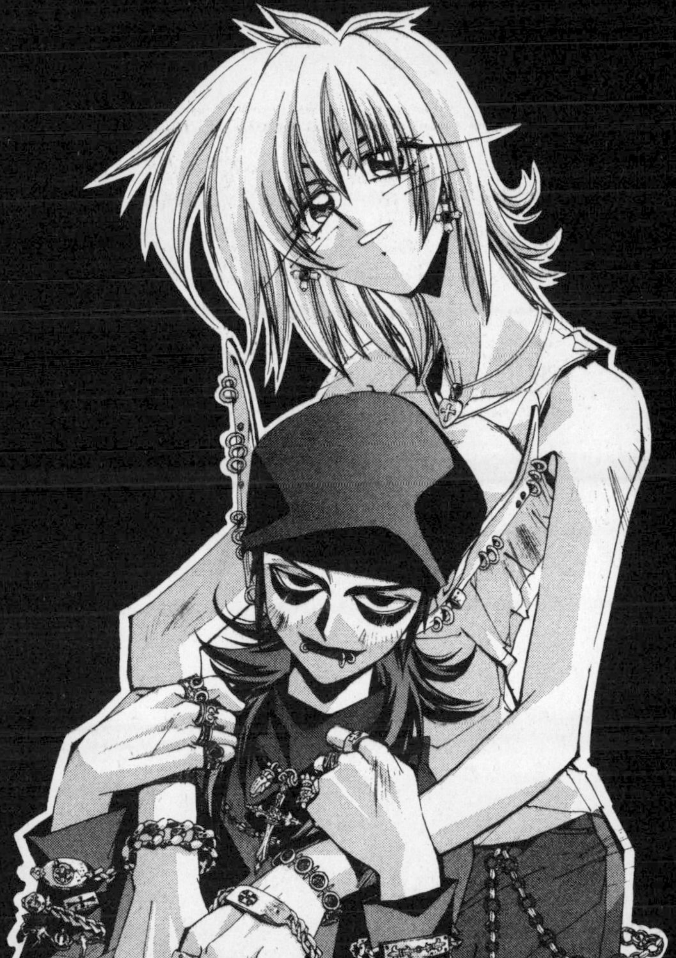

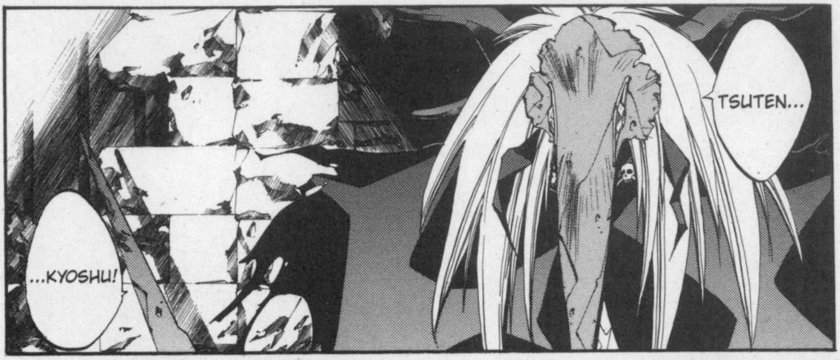
TSUTEN...
...KYOSHU!

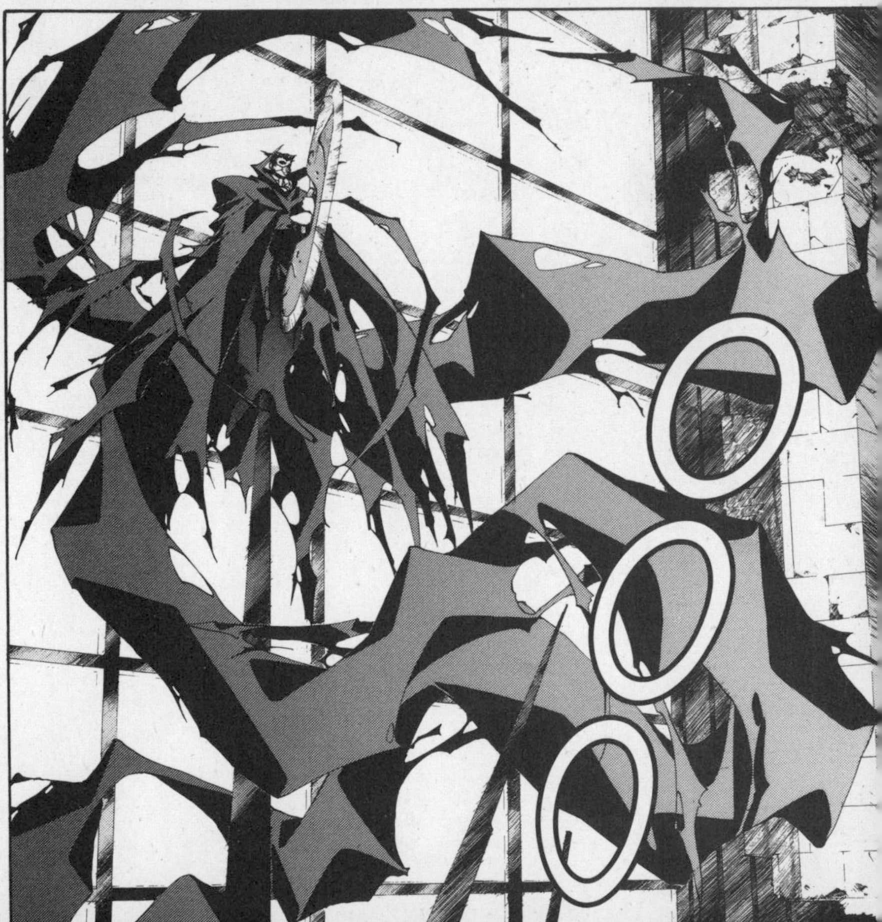

READ THIS WAY

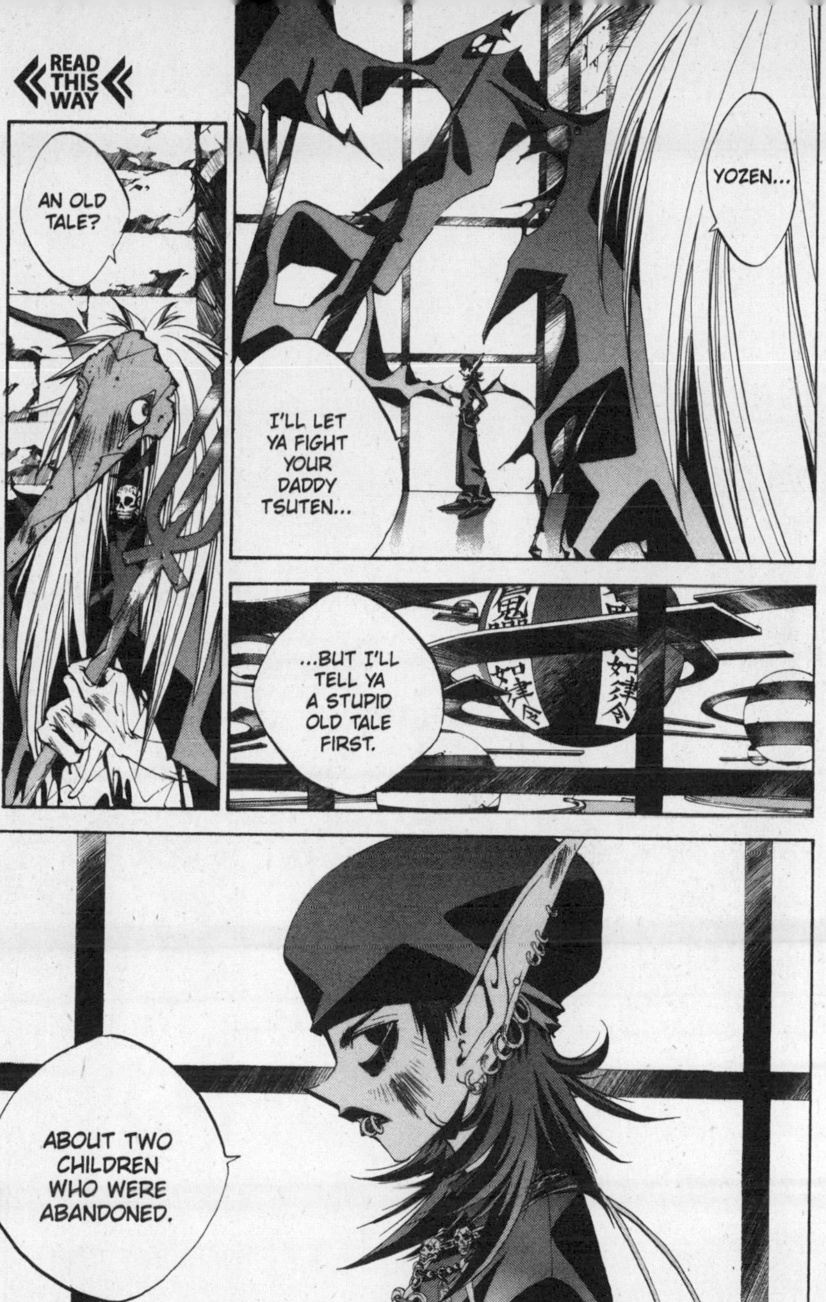
YOZEN...
I'LL LET YA FIGHT YOUR DADDY TSUTEN...
...BUT I'LL TELL YA A STUPID OLD TALE FIRST.
AN OLD TALE?
ABOUT TWO CHILDREN WHO WERE ABANDONED.

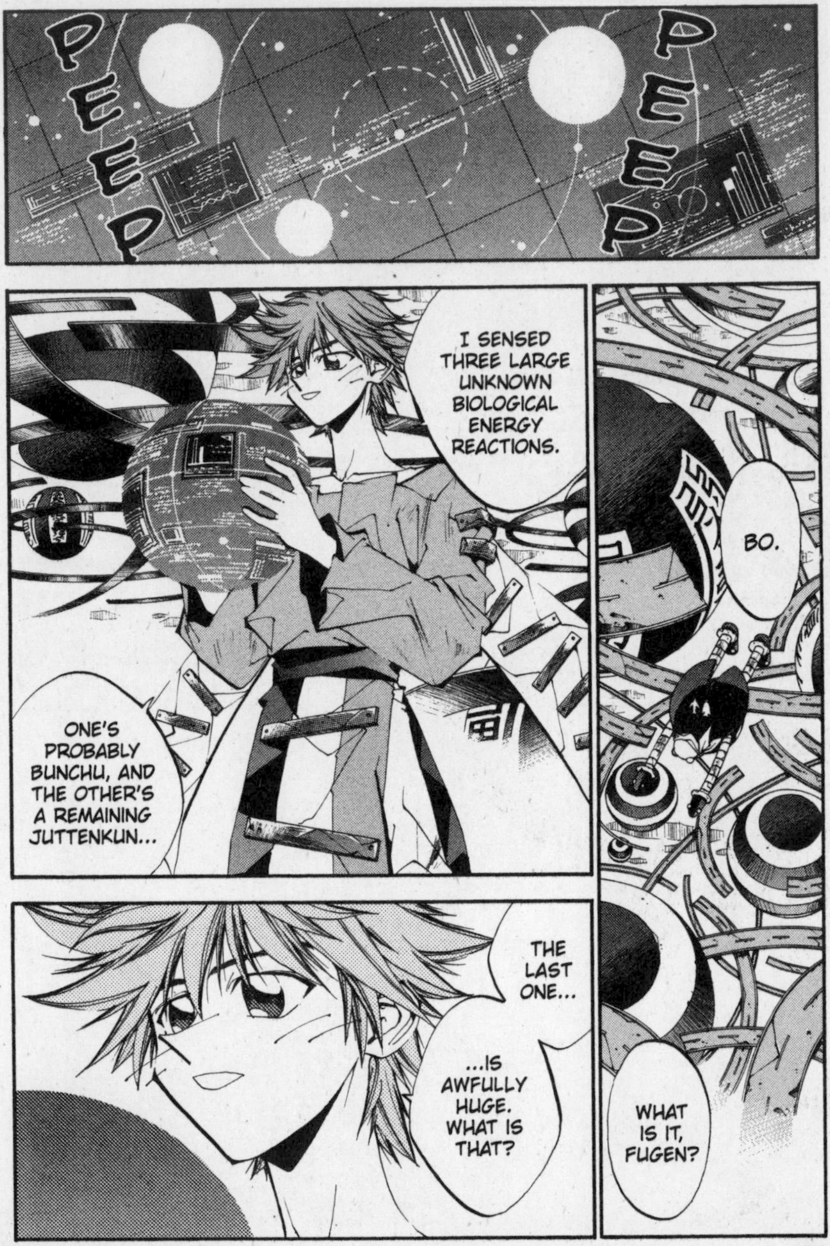
PEEP
PEEP
BO.
WHAT IS IT, FUGEN?
I SENSED THREE LARGE UNKNOWN BIOLOGICAL ENERGY REACTIONS.
ONE'S PROBABLY BUNCHU, AND THE OTHER'S A REMAINING JUTTENKUN...
THE LAST ONE...
...IS AWFULLY HUGE. WHAT IS THAT?

READ THIS WAY

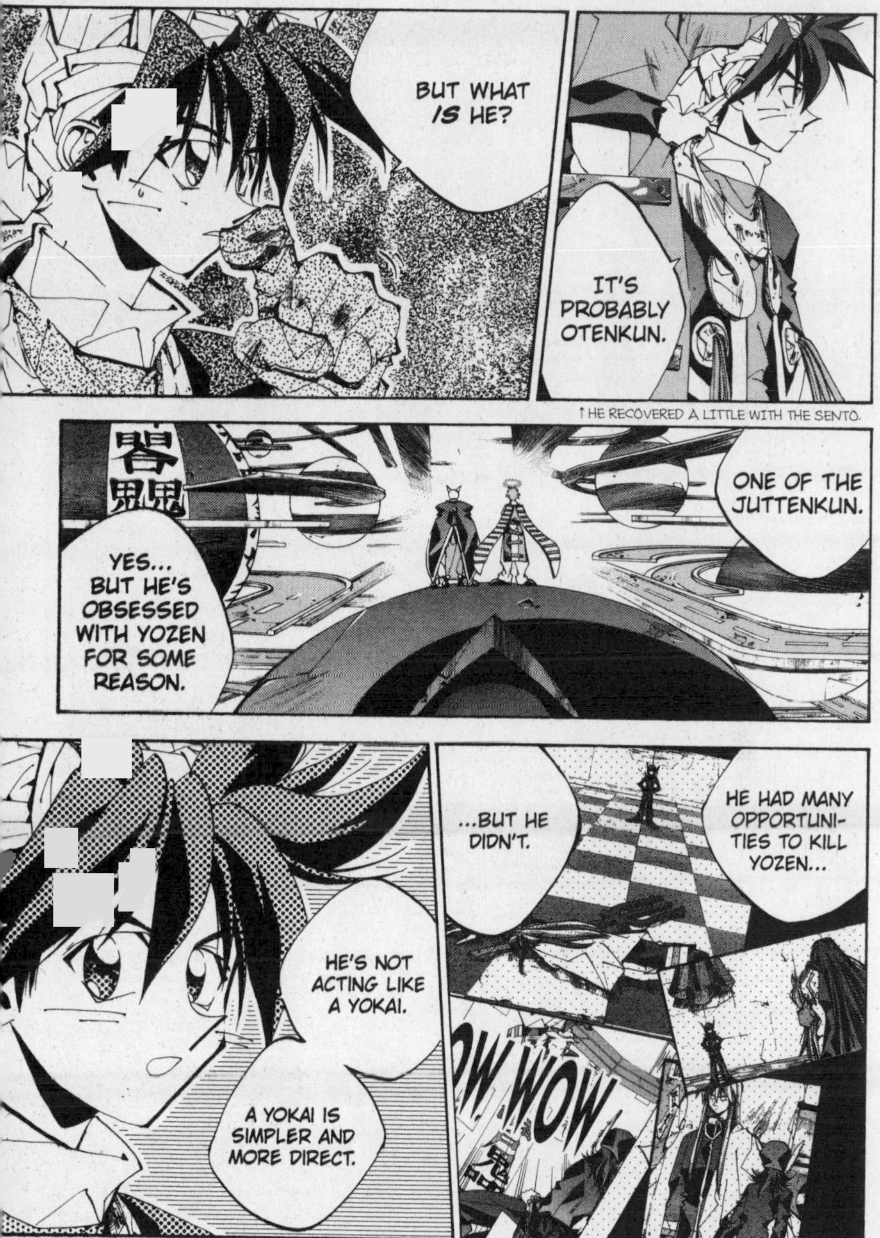
IT'S PROBABLY OTENKUN.
BUT WHAT *IS* HE?
↑HE RECOVERED A LITTLE WITH THE SENTO.
ONE OF THE JUTTENKUN.
YES... BUT HE'S OBSESSED WITH YOZEN FOR SOME REASON.
HE HAD MANY OPPORTUNITIES TO KILL YOZEN...
...BUT HE DIDN'T.
WOW WOW
HE'S NOT ACTING LIKE A YOKAI.
A YOKAI IS SIMPLER AND MORE DIRECT.

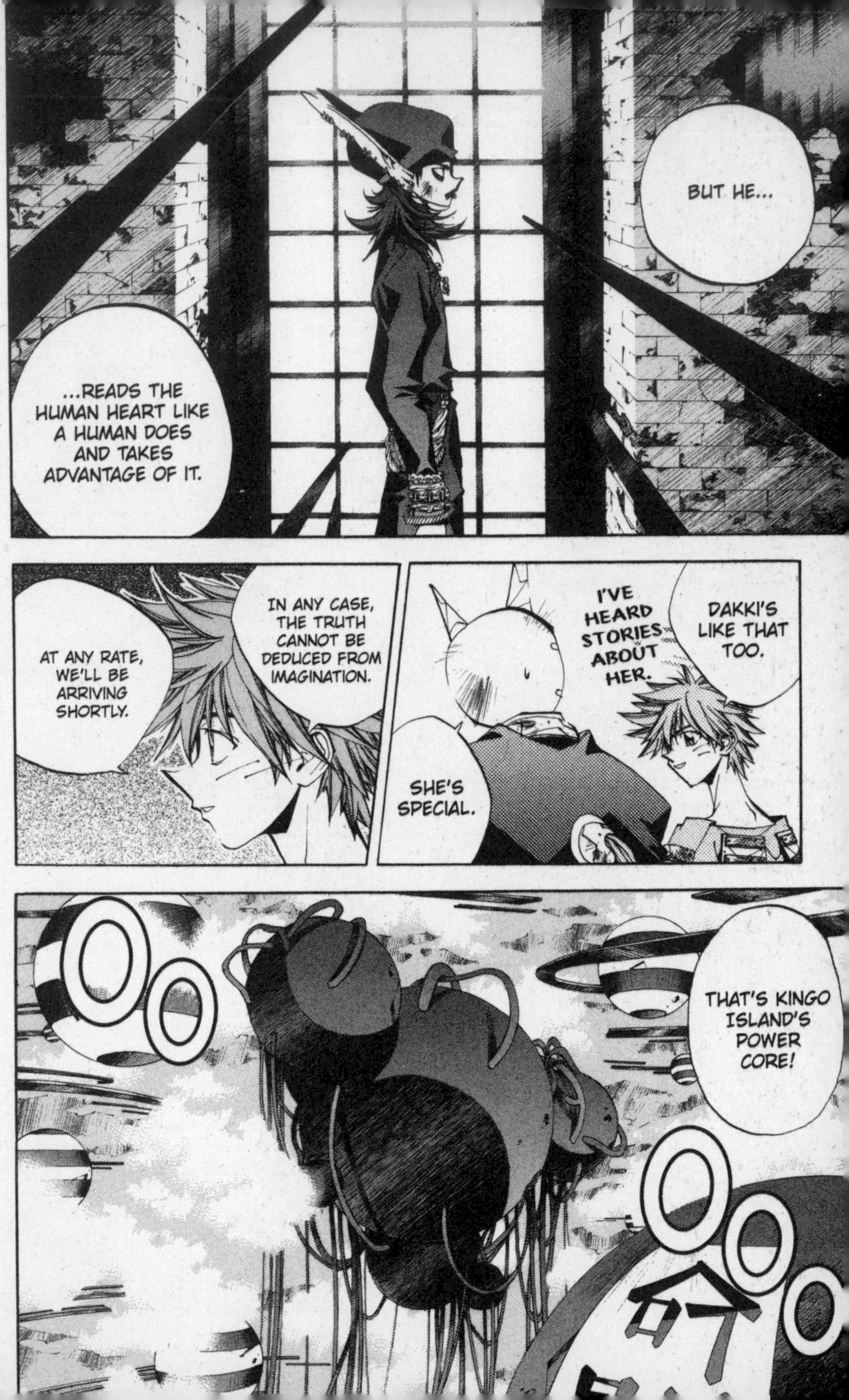
BUT HE...
...READS THE HUMAN HEART LIKE A HUMAN DOES AND TAKES ADVANTAGE OF IT.
DAKKI'S LIKE THAT TOO.
I'VE HEARD STORIES ABOUT HER.
SHE'S SPECIAL.
IN ANY CASE, THE TRUTH CANNOT BE DEDUCED FROM IMAGINATION.
AT ANY RATE, WE'LL BE ARRIVING SHORTLY.
THAT'S KINGO ISLAND'S POWER CORE!

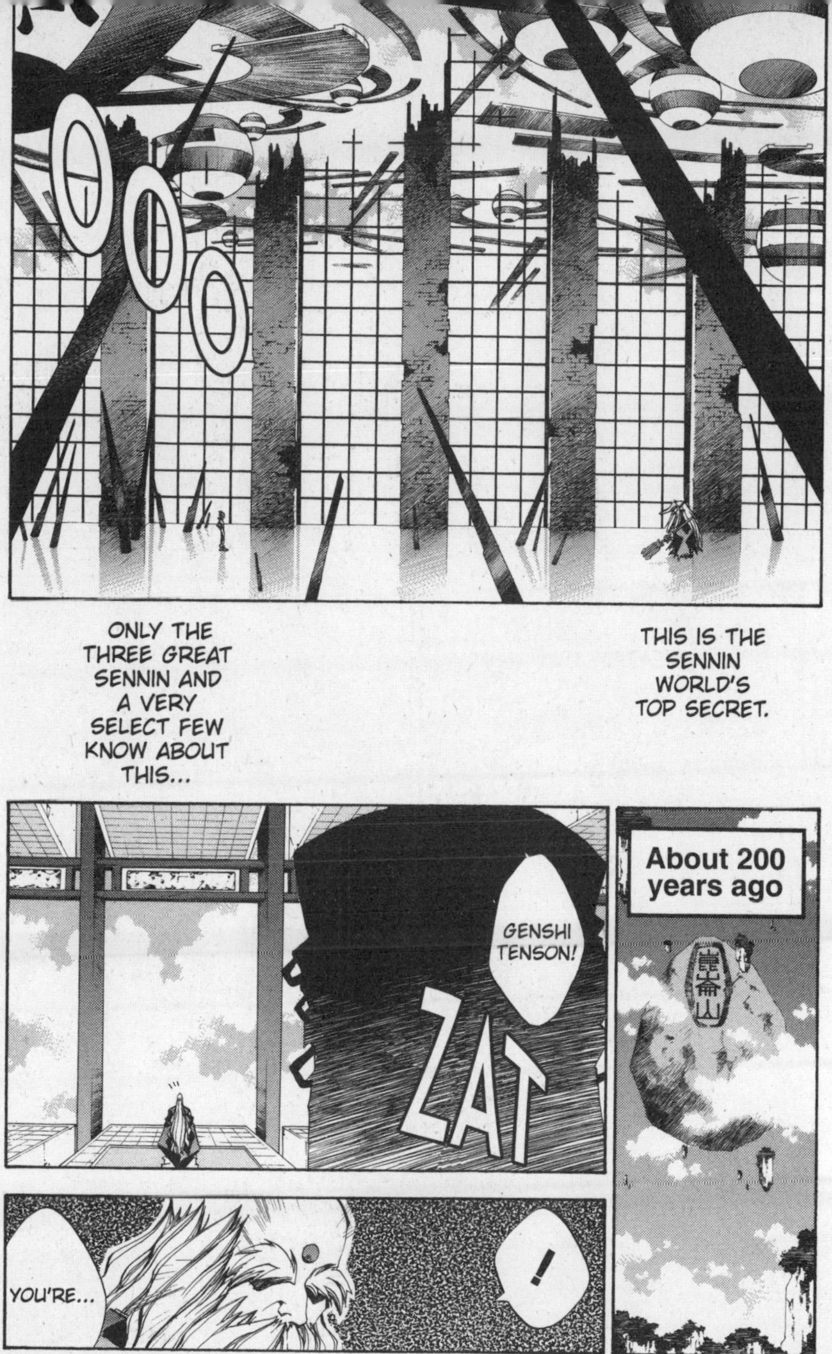
THIS IS THE SENNIN WORLD'S TOP SECRET.
ONLY THE THREE GREAT SENNIN AND A VERY SELECT FEW KNOW ABOUT THIS...
About 200 years ago
GENSHI TENSON!
ZAT
!
YOU'RE...

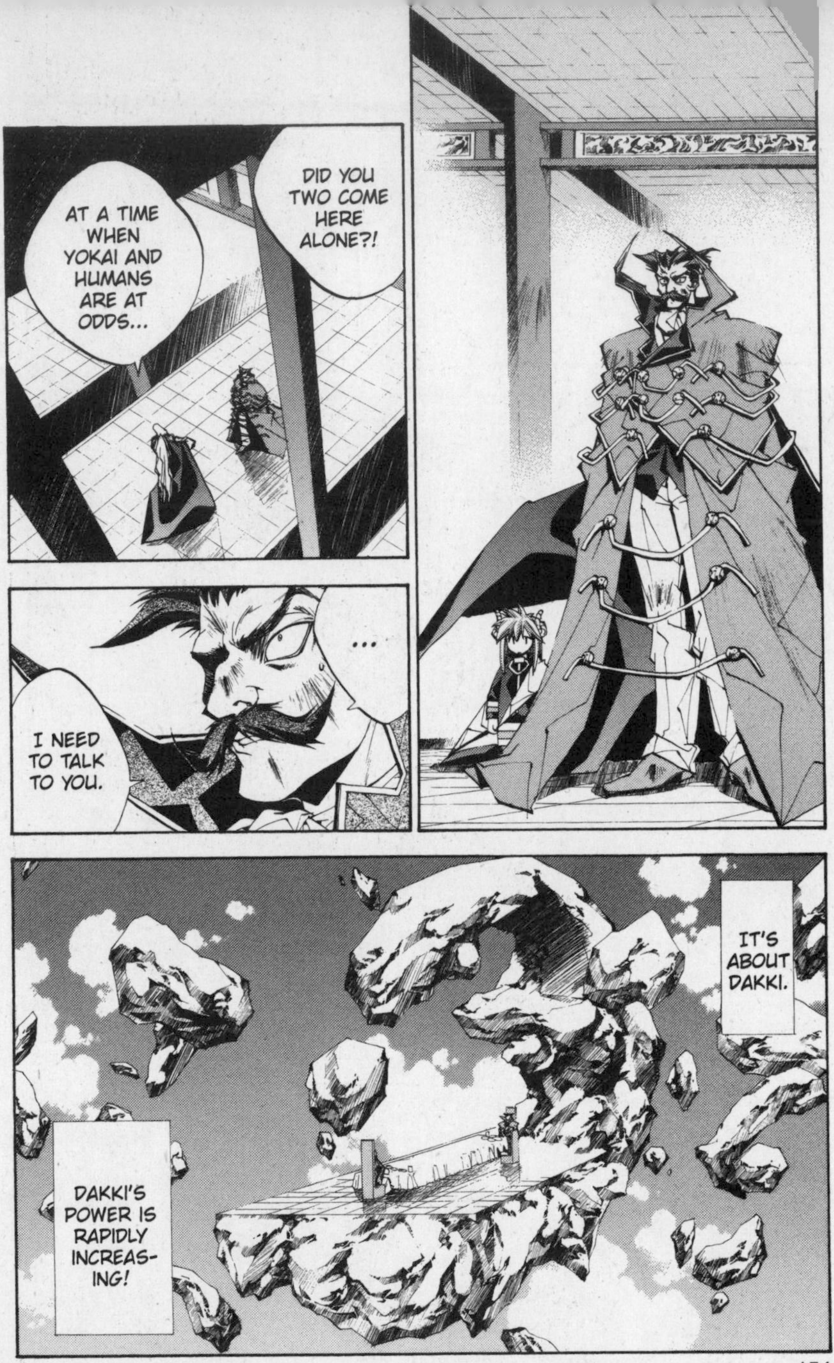
DID YOU TWO COME HERE ALONE?!
AT A TIME WHEN YOKAI AND HUMANS ARE AT ODDS...
...
I NEED TO TALK TO YOU.
IT'S ABOUT DAKKI.
DAKKI'S POWER IS RAPIDLY INCREASING!

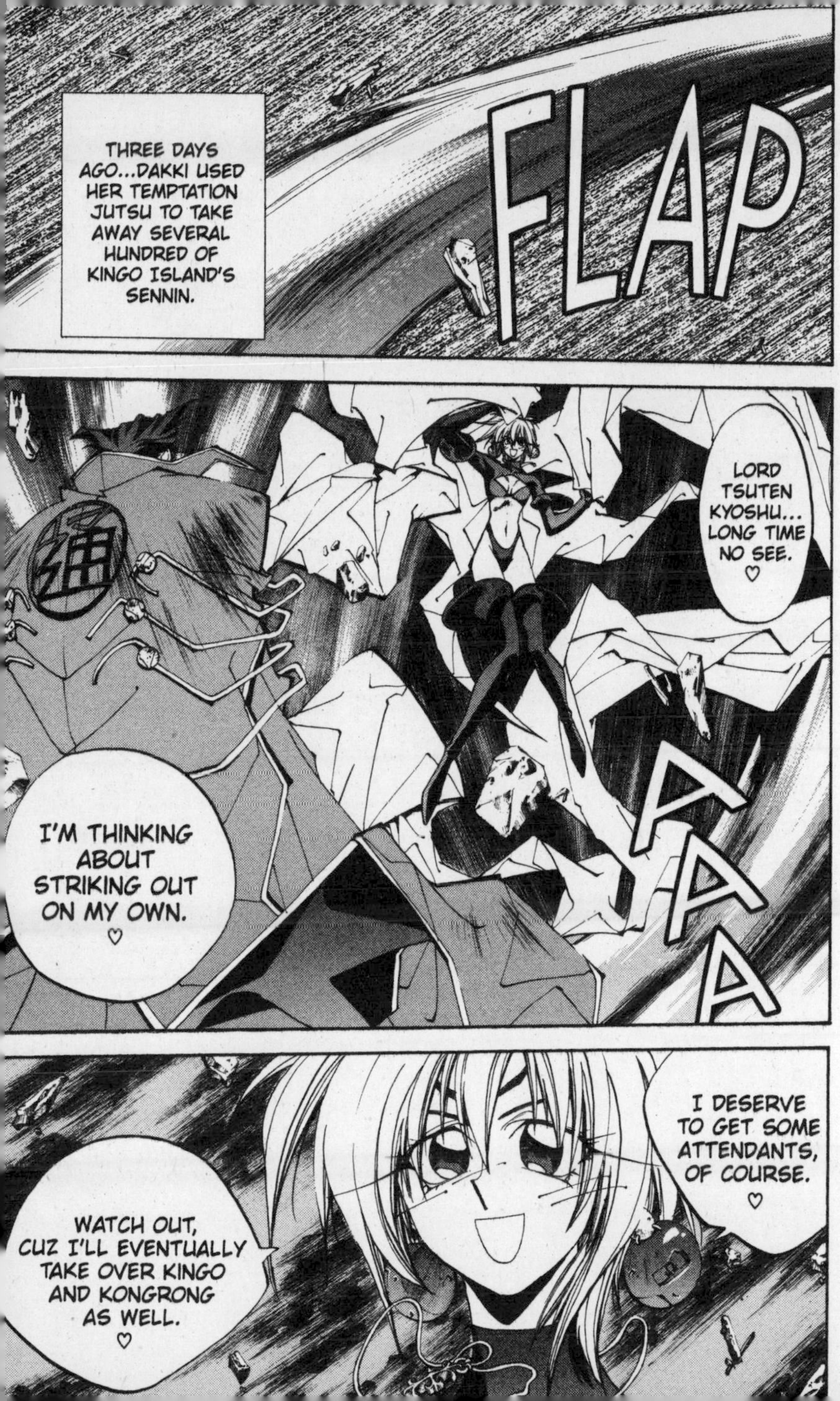
FLAP
THREE DAYS AGO...DAKKI USED HER TEMPTATION JUTSU TO TAKE AWAY SEVERAL HUNDRED OF KINGO ISLAND'S SENNIN.
LORD TSUTEN KYOSHU... LONG TIME NO SEE. ♡
AAA
I'M THINKING ABOUT STRIKING OUT ON MY OWN. ♡
I DESERVE TO GET SOME ATTENDANTS, OF COURSE. ♡
WATCH OUT, CUZ I'LL EVENTUALLY TAKE OVER KINGO AND KONGRONG AS WELL. ♡

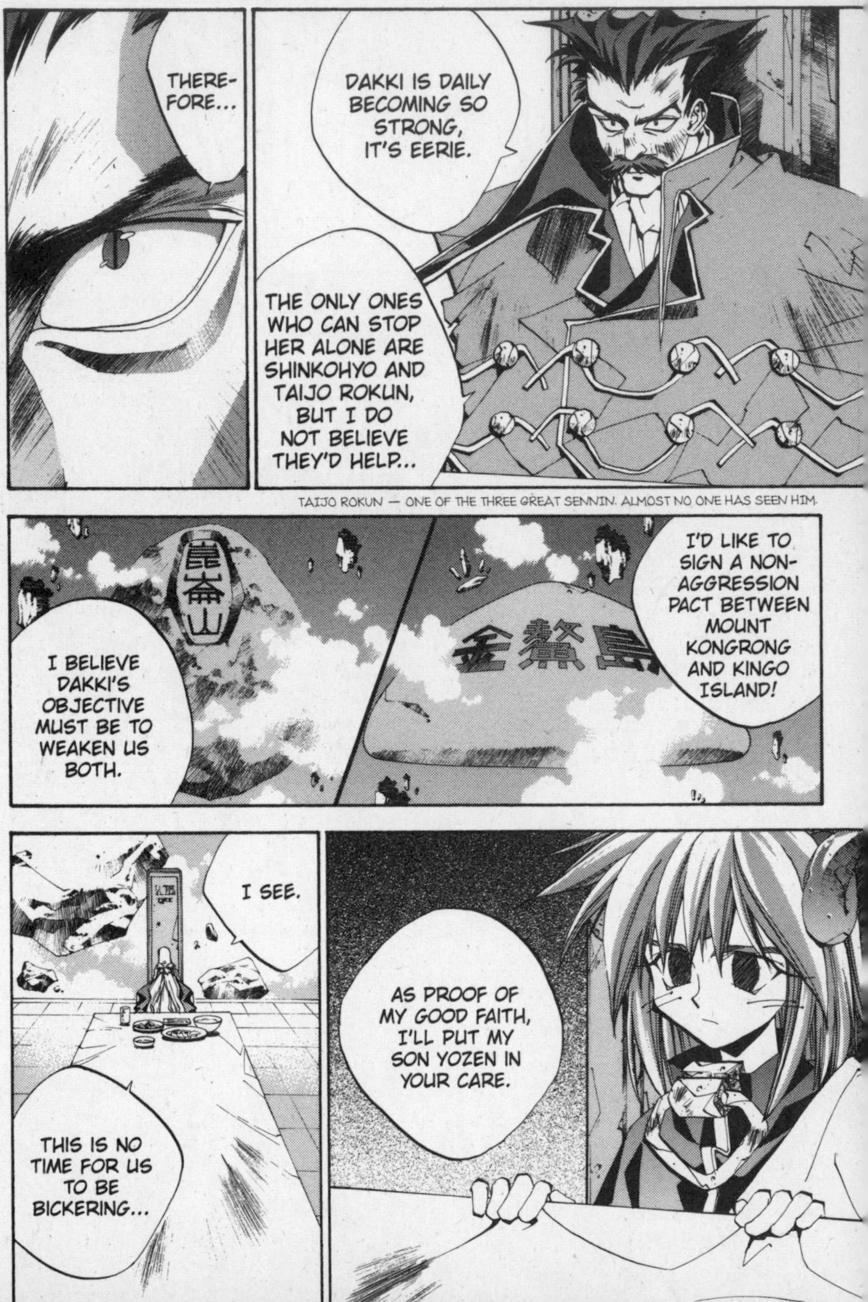
DAKKI IS DAILY BECOMING SO STRONG, IT'S EERIE.
THE ONLY ONES WHO CAN STOP HER ALONE ARE SHINKOHYO AND TAIJO ROKUN, BUT I DO NOT BELIEVE THEY'D HELP...
THERE-FORE...
TAIJO ROKUN — ONE OF THE THREE GREAT SENNIN. ALMOST NO ONE HAS SEEN HIM.
I'D LIKE TO SIGN A NON-AGGRESSION PACT BETWEEN MOUNT KONGRONG AND KINGO ISLAND!
金鰲島
崑崙山
I BELIEVE DAKKI'S OBJECTIVE MUST BE TO WEAKEN US BOTH.
AS PROOF OF MY GOOD FAITH, I'LL PUT MY SON YOZEN IN YOUR CARE.
I SEE.
THIS IS NO TIME FOR US TO BE BICKERING...

READ THIS WAY

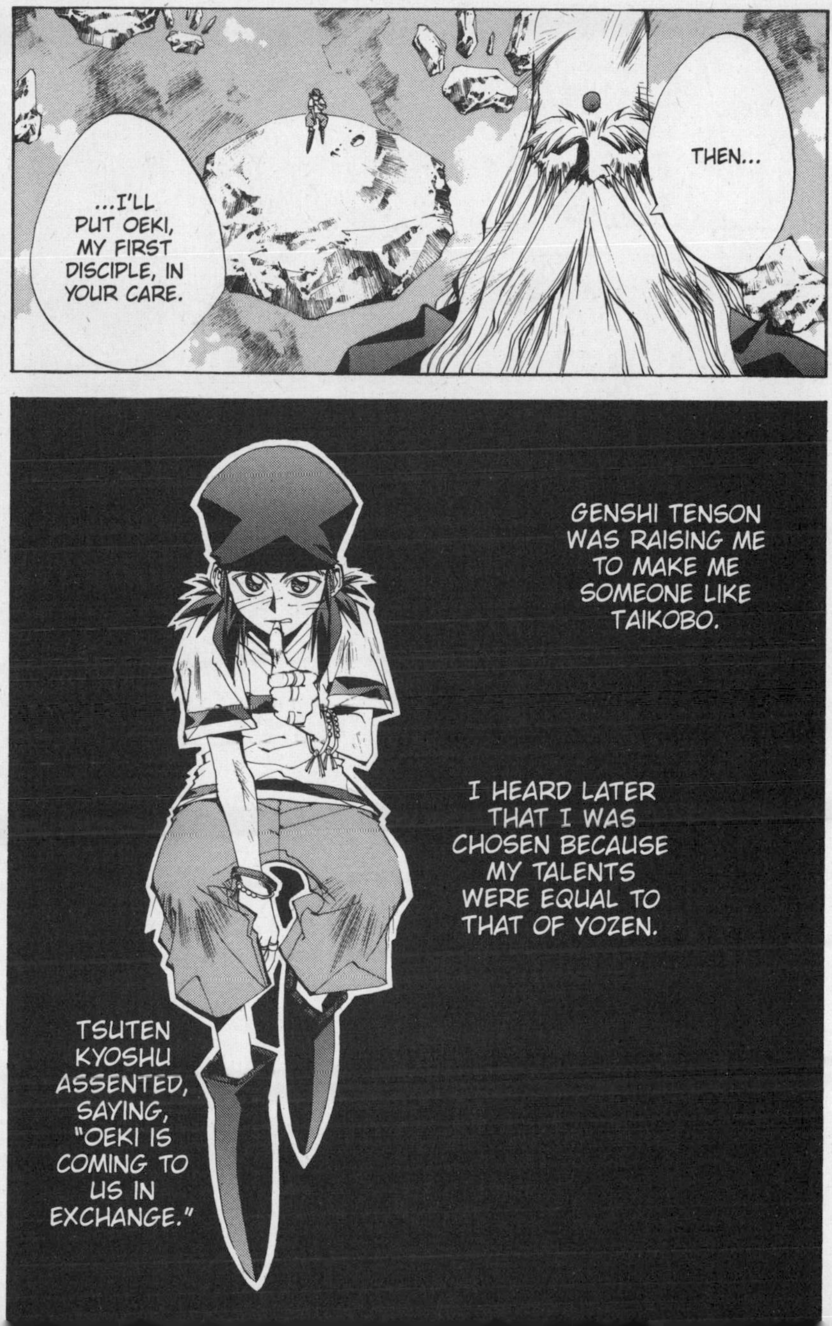
THEN...
...I'LL PUT OEKI, MY FIRST DISCIPLE, IN YOUR CARE.
GENSHI TENSON WAS RAISING ME TO MAKE ME SOMEONE LIKE TAIKOBO.
I HEARD LATER THAT I WAS CHOSEN BECAUSE MY TALENTS WERE EQUAL TO THAT OF YOZEN.
TSUTEN KYOSHU ASSENTED, SAYING, "OEKI IS COMING TO US IN EXCHANGE."

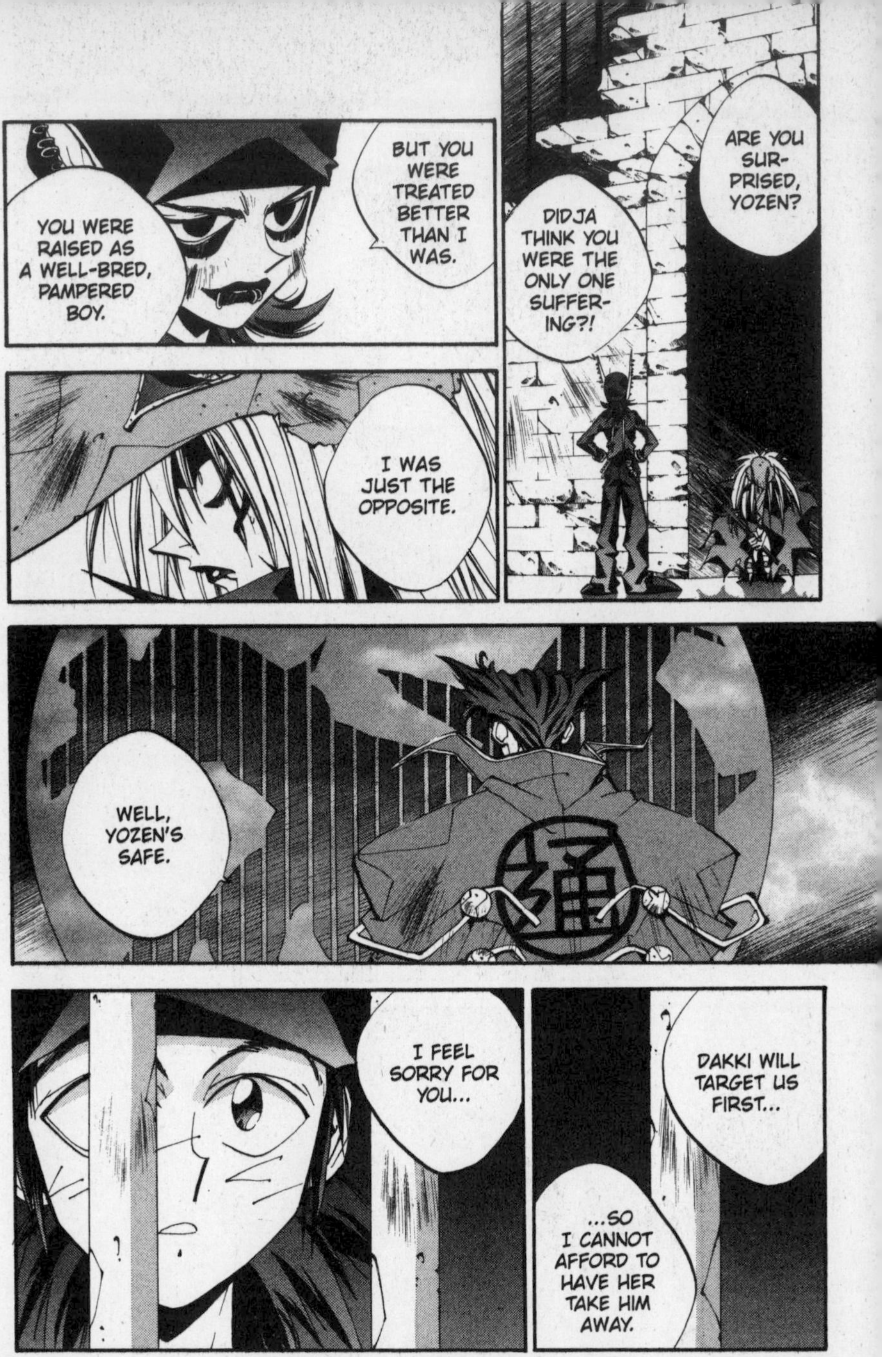
ARE YOU SUR-PRISED, YOZEN?
DIDJA THINK YOU WERE THE ONLY ONE SUFFER-ING?!
BUT YOU WERE TREATED BETTER THAN I WAS.
YOU WERE RAISED AS A WELL-BRED, PAMPERED BOY.
I WAS JUST THE OPPOSITE.
WELL, YOZEN'S SAFE.
DAKKI WILL TARGET US FIRST...
...SO I CANNOT AFFORD TO HAVE HER TAKE HIM AWAY.
I FEEL SORRY FOR YOU...

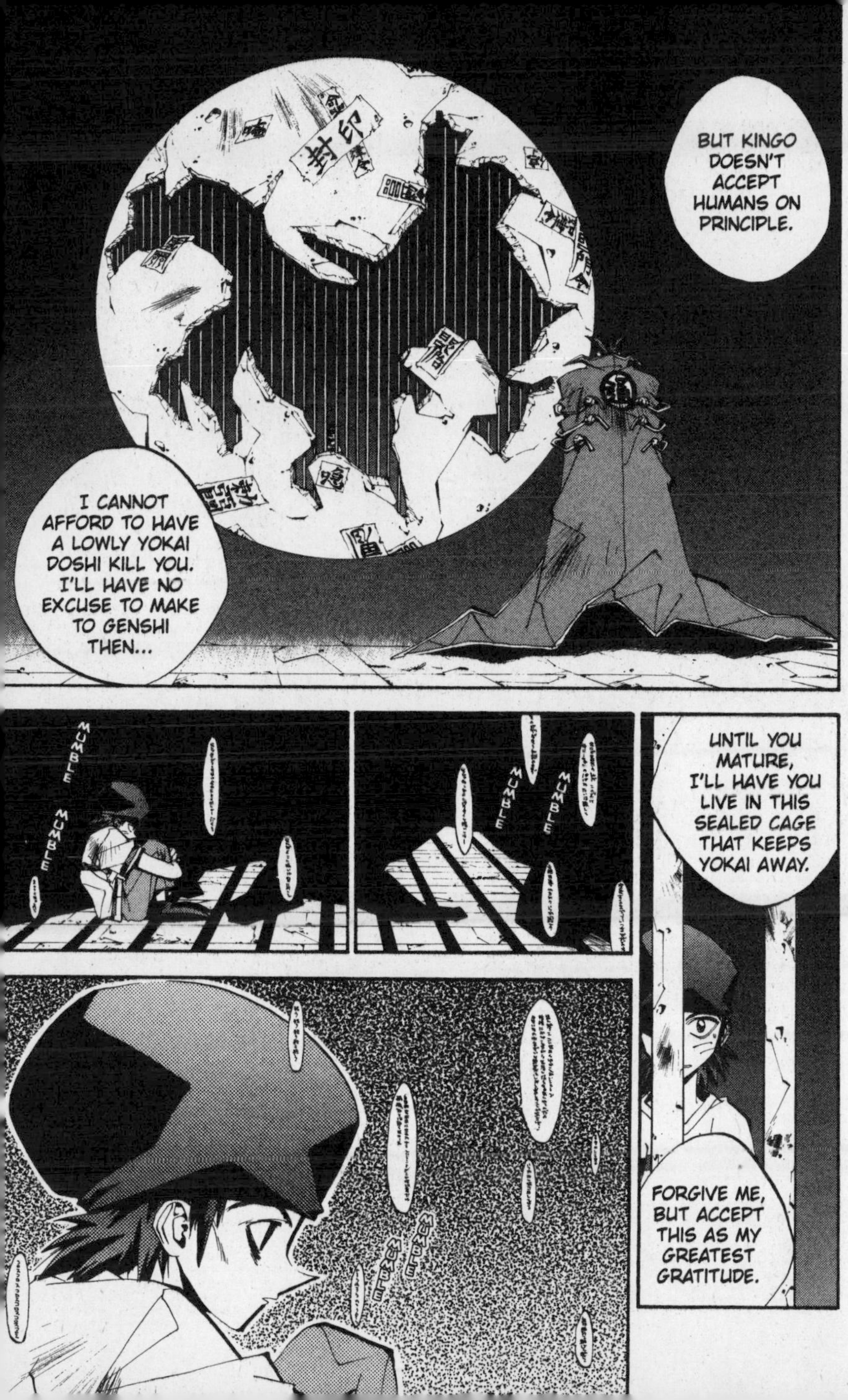
BUT KINGO DOESN'T ACCEPT HUMANS ON PRINCIPLE.
I CANNOT AFFORD TO HAVE A LOWLY YOKAI DOSHI KILL YOU. I'LL HAVE NO EXCUSE TO MAKE TO GENSHI THEN...
UNTIL YOU MATURE, I'LL HAVE YOU LIVE IN THIS SEALED CAGE THAT KEEPS YOKAI AWAY.
FORGIVE ME, BUT ACCEPT THIS AS MY GREATEST GRATITUDE.
MUMBLE
MUMBLE
MUMBLE
MUMBLE
MUMBLE
MUMBLE

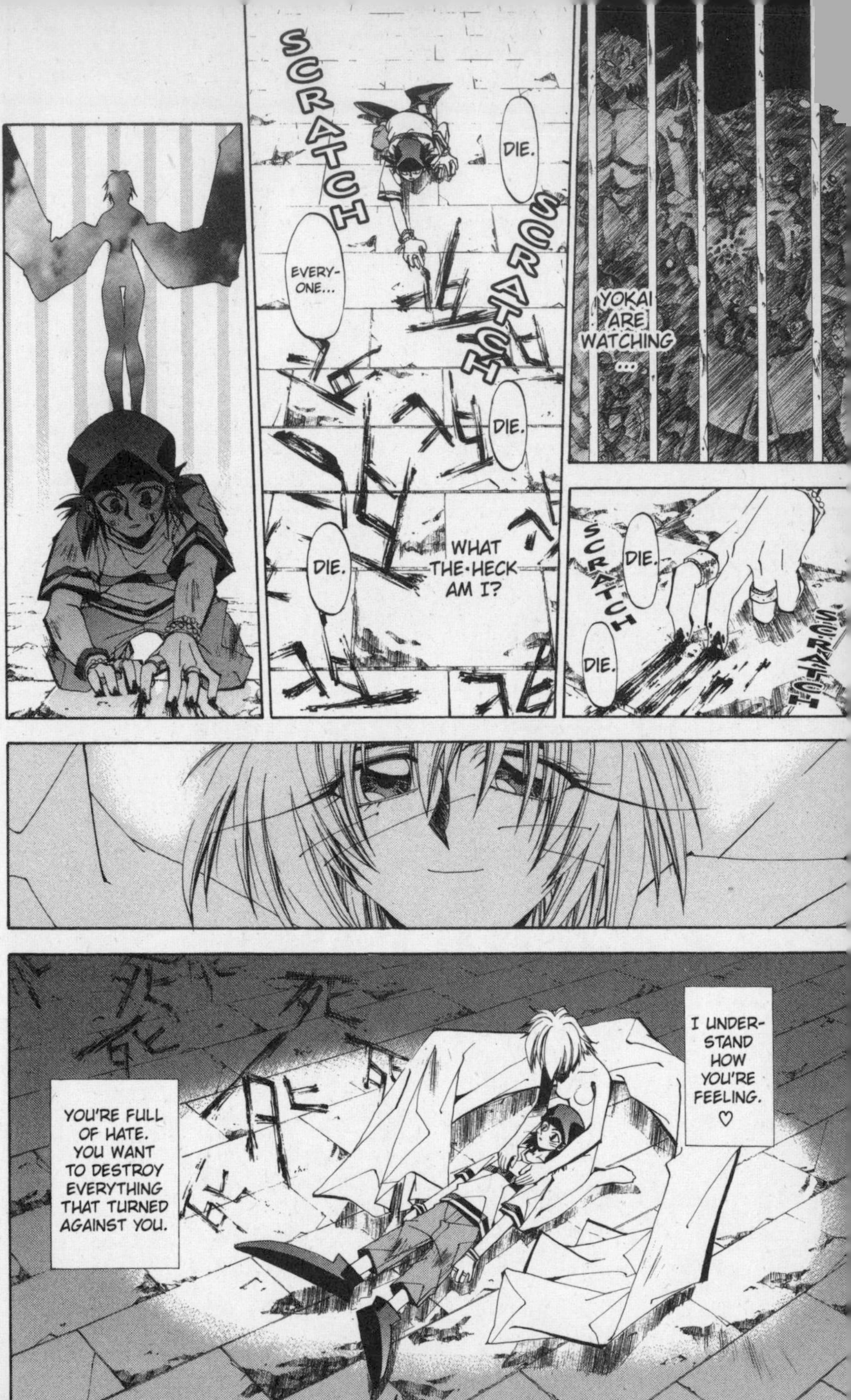
YOKAI ARE WATCHING...
SCRATCH
DIE.
SCRATCH
DIE.
DIE.
SCRATCH
SCRATCH
EVERY-ONE...
DIE.
WHAT THE-HECK AM I?
DIE.
I UNDER-STAND HOW YOU'RE FEELING. ♡
YOU'RE FULL OF HATE. YOU WANT TO DESTROY EVERYTHING THAT TURNED AGAINST YOU.

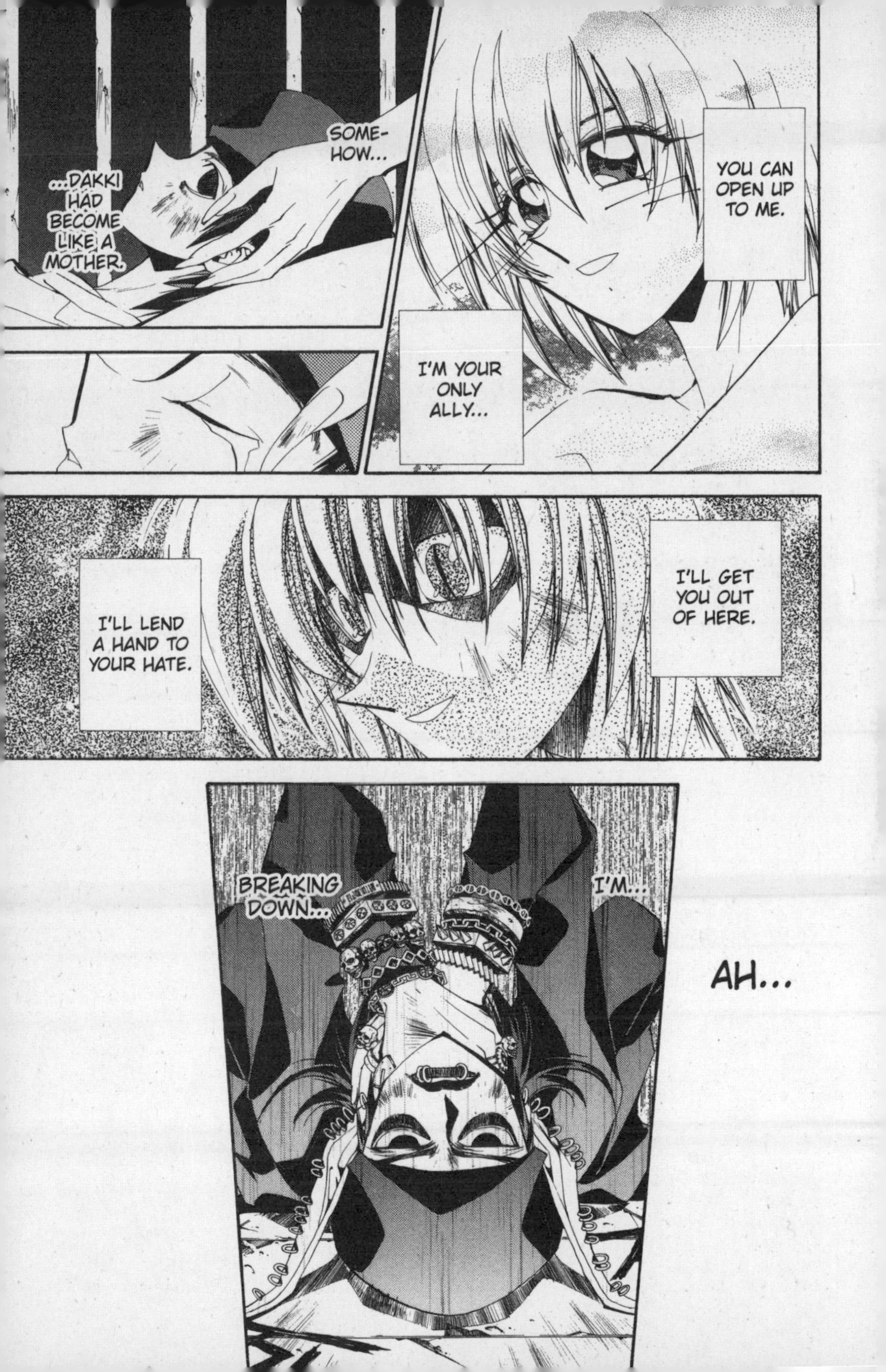
YOU CAN OPEN UP TO ME.
I'M YOUR ONLY ALLY...
SOME-HOW...
...DAKKI HAD BECOME LIKE A MOTHER.
I'LL GET YOU OUT OF HERE.
I'LL LEND A HAND TO YOUR HATE.
AH...
I'M...
BREAKING DOWN...

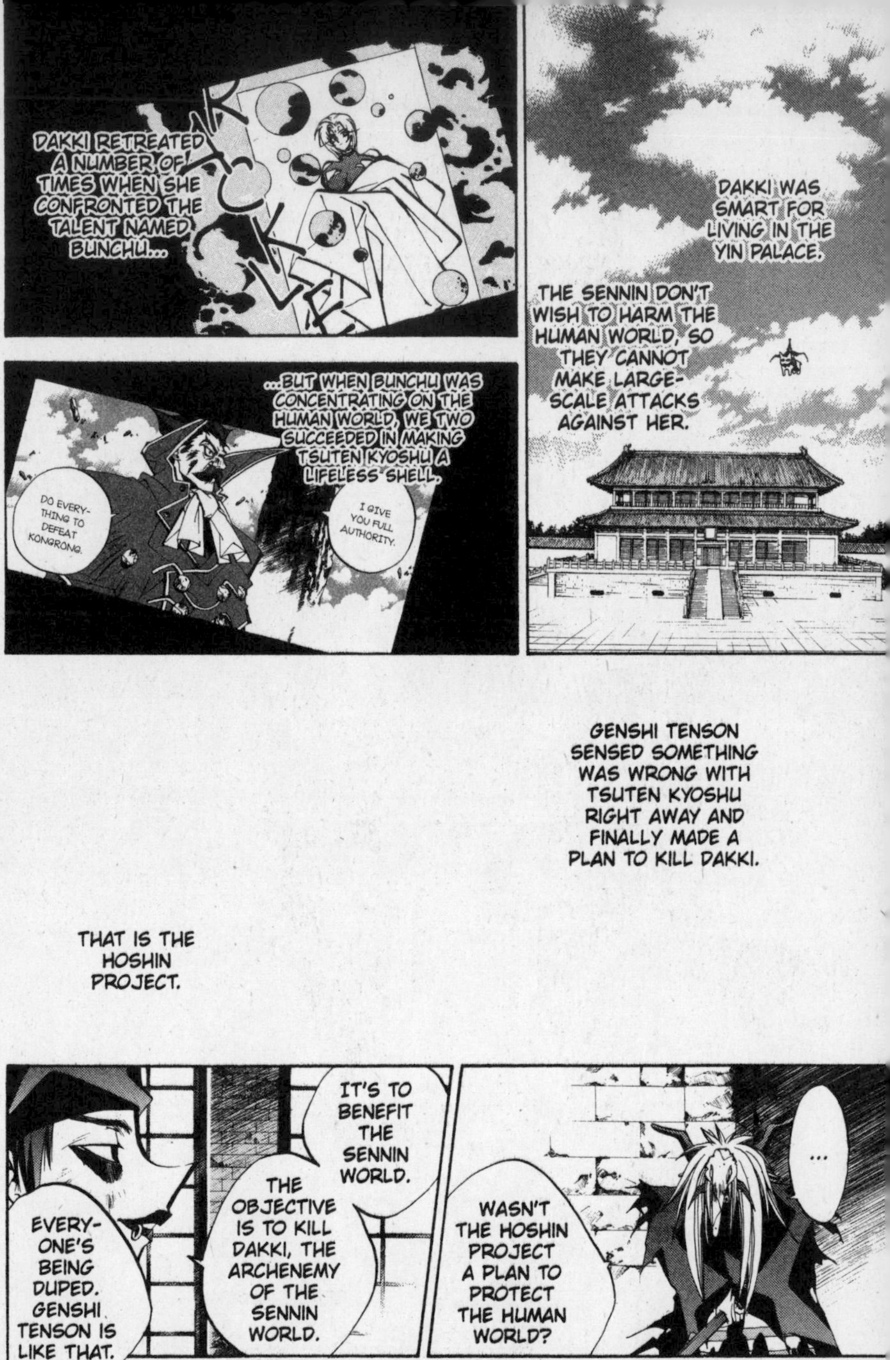
DAKKI WAS SMART FOR LIVING IN THE YIN PALACE.
THE SENNIN DON'T WISH TO HARM THE HUMAN WORLD, SO THEY CANNOT MAKE LARGE-SCALE ATTACKS AGAINST HER.
DAKKI RETREATED A NUMBER OF TIMES WHEN SHE CONFRONTED THE TALENT NAMED BUNCHU...
...BUT WHEN BUNCHU WAS CONCENTRATING ON THE HUMAN WORLD, WE TWO SUCCEEDED IN MAKING TSUTEN KYOSHU A LIFELESS SHELL.
I GIVE YOU FULL AUTHORITY.
DO EVERYTHING TO DEFEAT KONGRONG.
GENSHI TENSON SENSED SOMETHING WAS WRONG WITH TSUTEN KYOSHU RIGHT AWAY AND FINALLY MADE A PLAN TO KILL DAKKI.
THAT IS THE HOSHIN PROJECT.
...
WASN'T THE HOSHIN PROJECT A PLAN TO PROTECT THE HUMAN WORLD?
IT'S TO BENEFIT THE SENNIN WORLD.
THE OBJECTIVE IS TO KILL DAKKI, THE ARCHENEMY OF THE SENNIN WORLD.
EVERYONE'S BEING DUPED. GENSHI TENSON IS LIKE THAT.

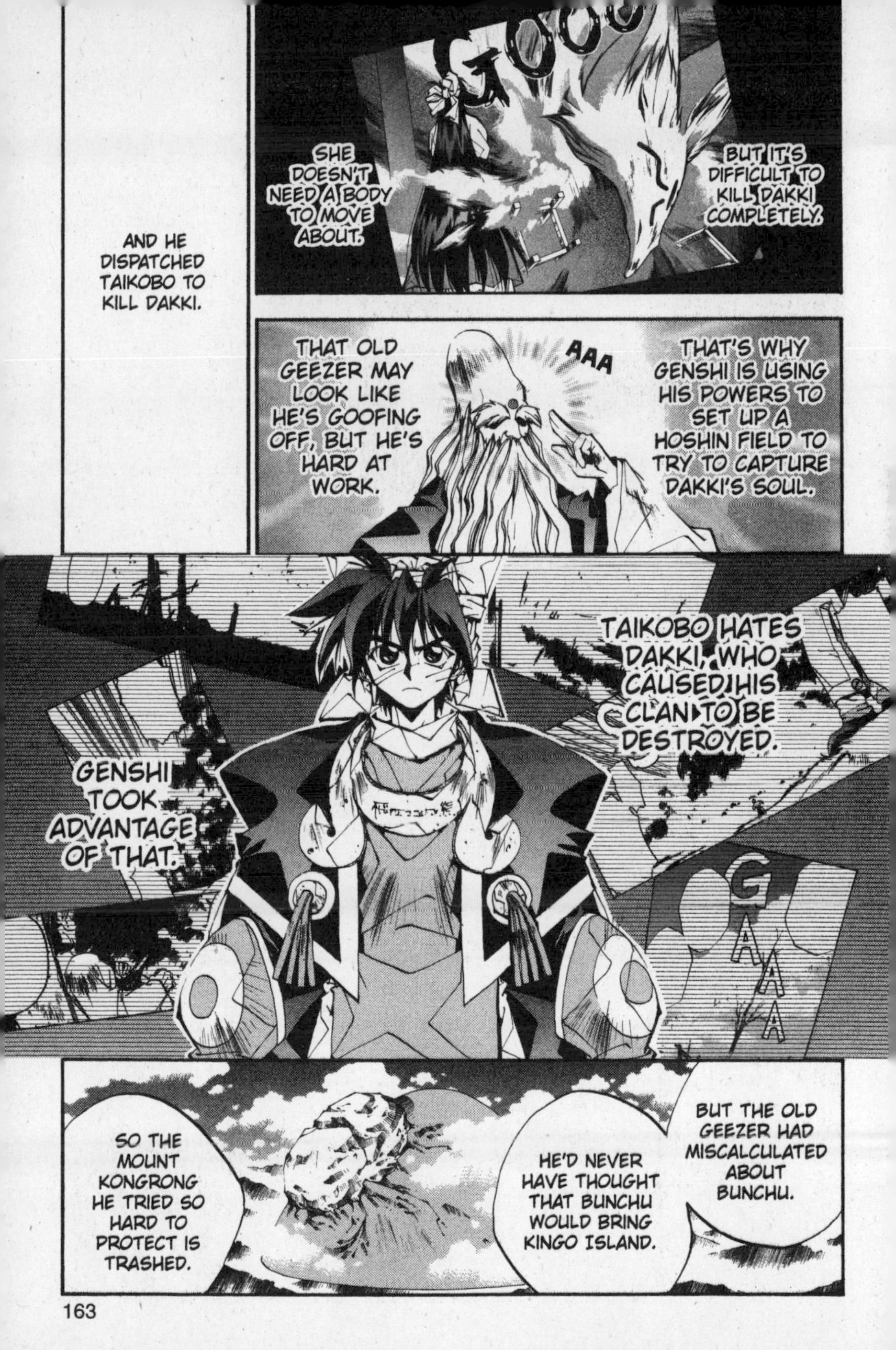
BUT IT'S DIFFICULT TO KILL DAKKI COMPLETELY.
SHE DOESN'T NEED A BODY TO MOVE ABOUT.
THAT'S WHY GENSHI IS USING HIS POWERS TO SET UP A HOSHIN FIELD TO TRY TO CAPTURE DAKKI'S SOUL.
AAA
THAT OLD GEEZER MAY LOOK LIKE HE'S GOOFING OFF, BUT HE'S HARD AT WORK.
AND HE DISPATCHED TAIKOBO TO KILL DAKKI.
TAIKOBO HATES DAKKI, WHO CAUSED HIS CLAN TO BE DESTROYED.
GAAAA
GENSHI TOOK ADVANTAGE OF THAT.
BUT THE OLD GEEZER HAD MISCALCULATED ABOUT BUNCHU.
HE'D NEVER HAVE THOUGHT THAT BUNCHU WOULD BRING KINGO ISLAND.
SO THE MOUNT KONGRONG HE TRIED SO HARD TO PROTECT IS TRASHED.

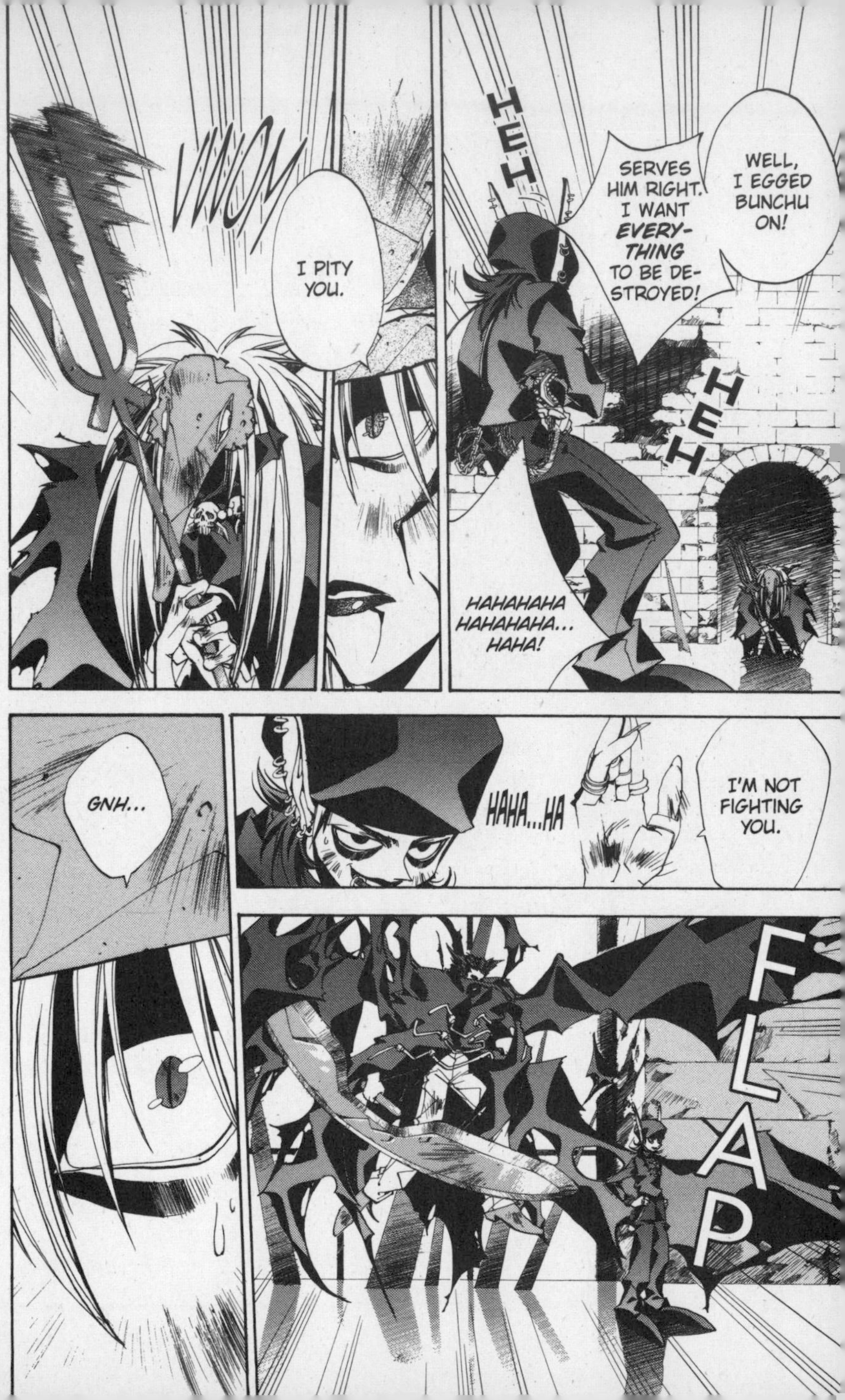
WELL, I EGGED BUNCHU ON!
HEH
SERVES HIM RIGHT. I WANT *EVERYTHING* TO BE DESTROYED!
HEH HEH
HAHAHAHA HAHAHAHA... HAHA!
I PITY YOU.
VWOM
I'M NOT FIGHTING YOU.
HAHA...HA
FLAP
GNH...

READ THIS WAY

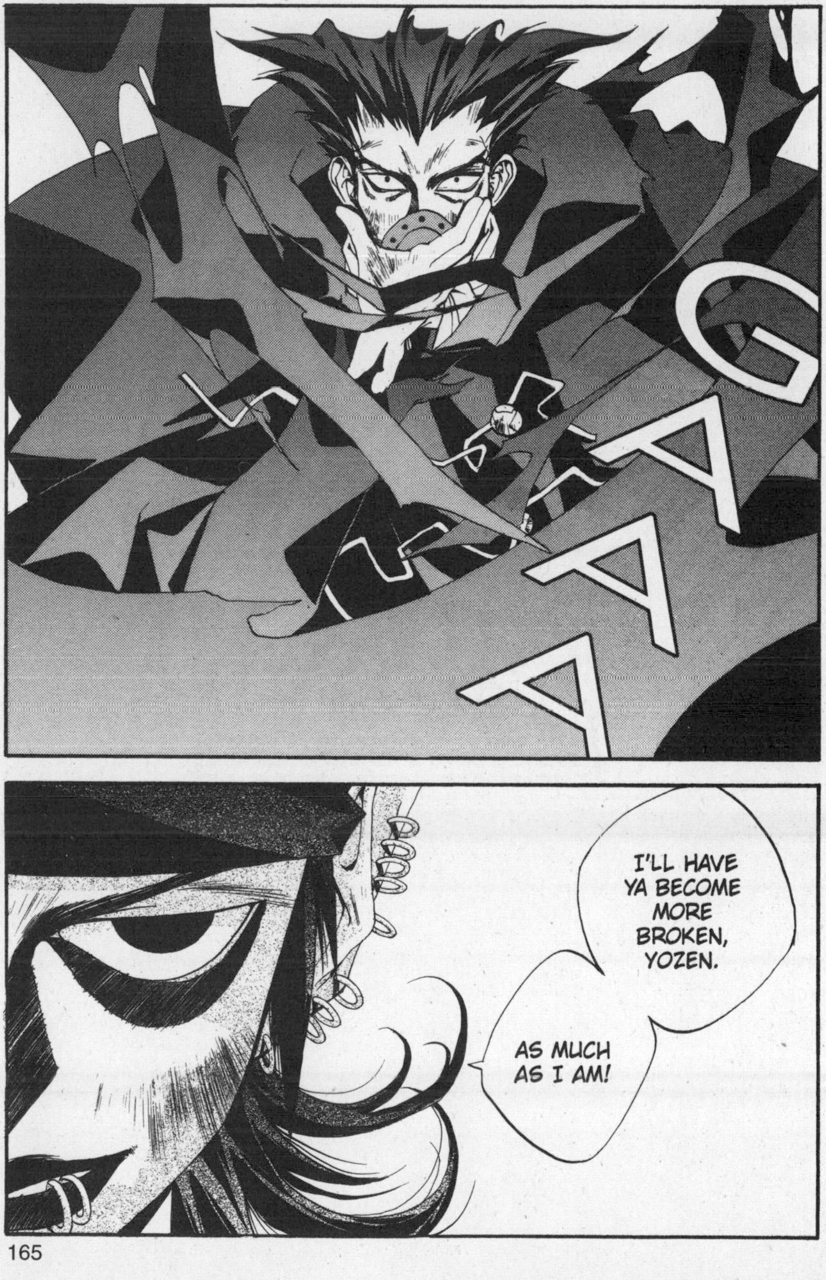
GAAA
I'LL HAVE YA BECOME MORE BROKEN, YOZEN.
AS MUCH AS I AM!

封神演義

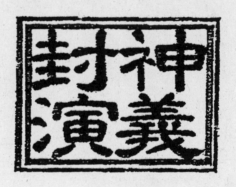

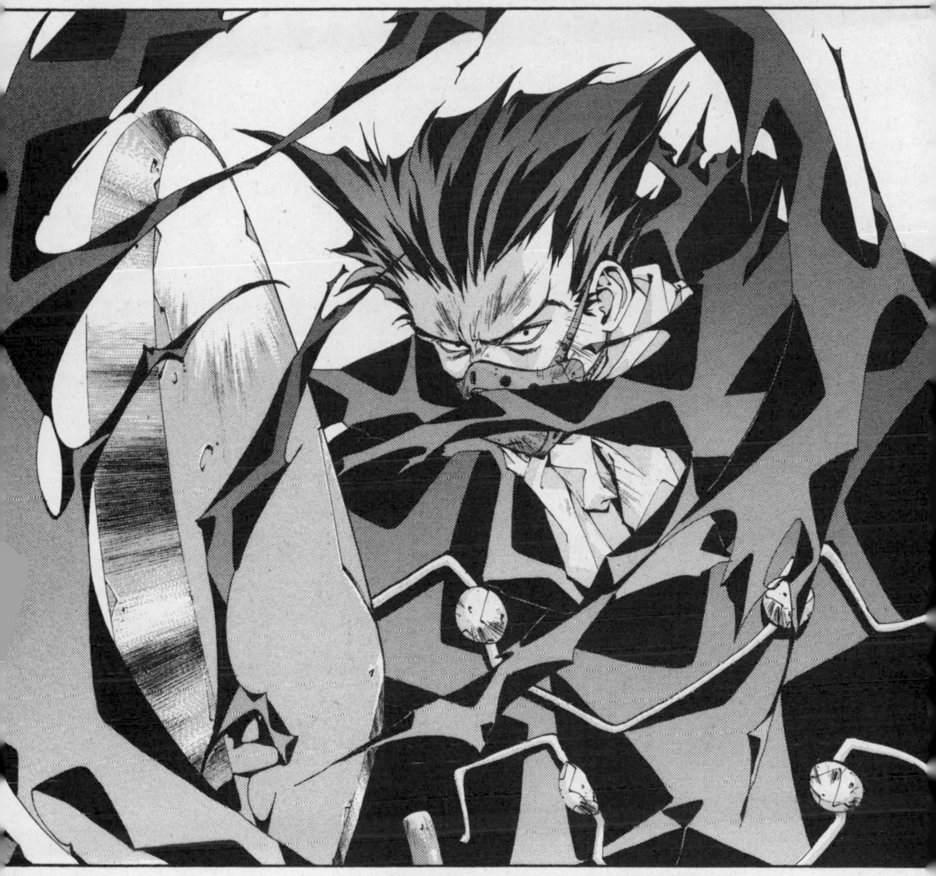

Chapter 133

TSUTEN KYOSHU, PART 5

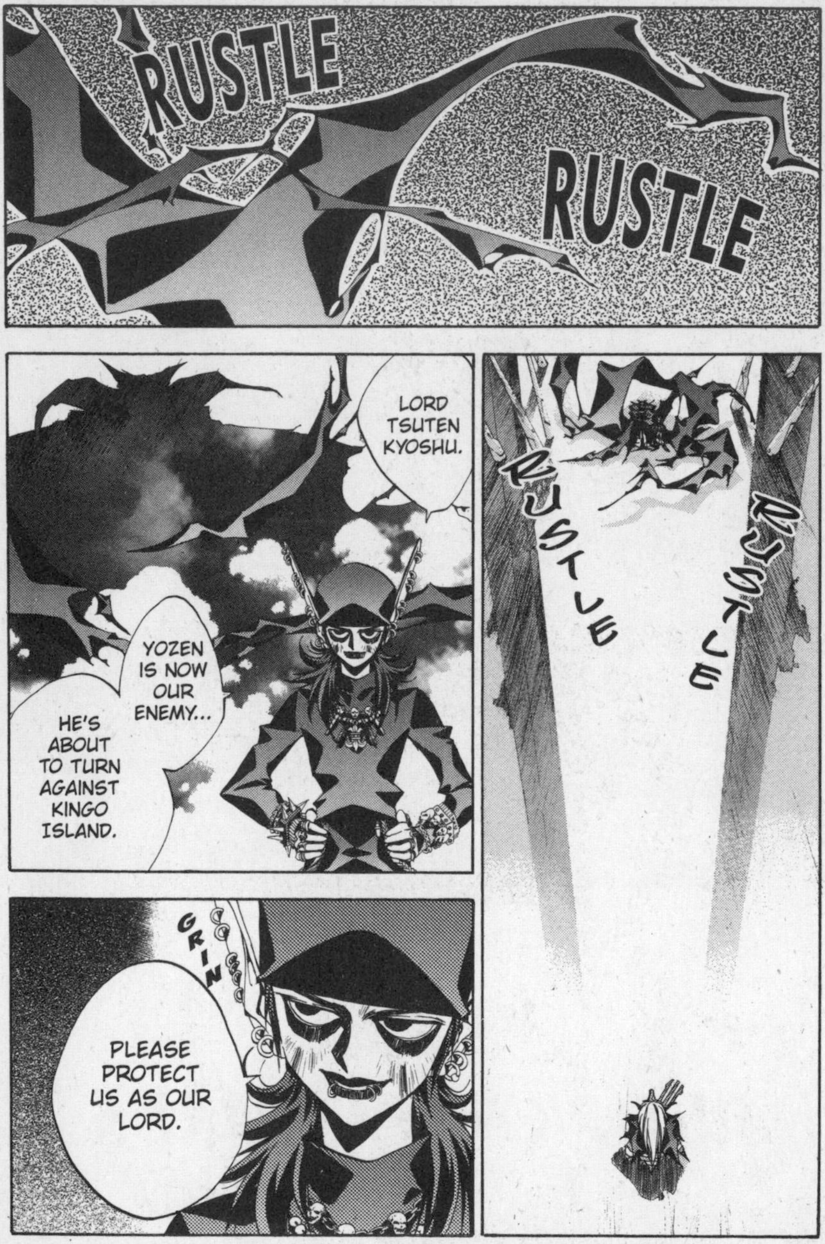
RUSTLE
RUSTLE
RUSTLE
RUSTLE
LORD TSUTEN KYOSHU.
YOZEN IS NOW OUR ENEMY...
HE'S ABOUT TO TURN AGAINST KINGO ISLAND.
GRIN
PLEASE PROTECT US AS OUR LORD.

READ THIS WAY

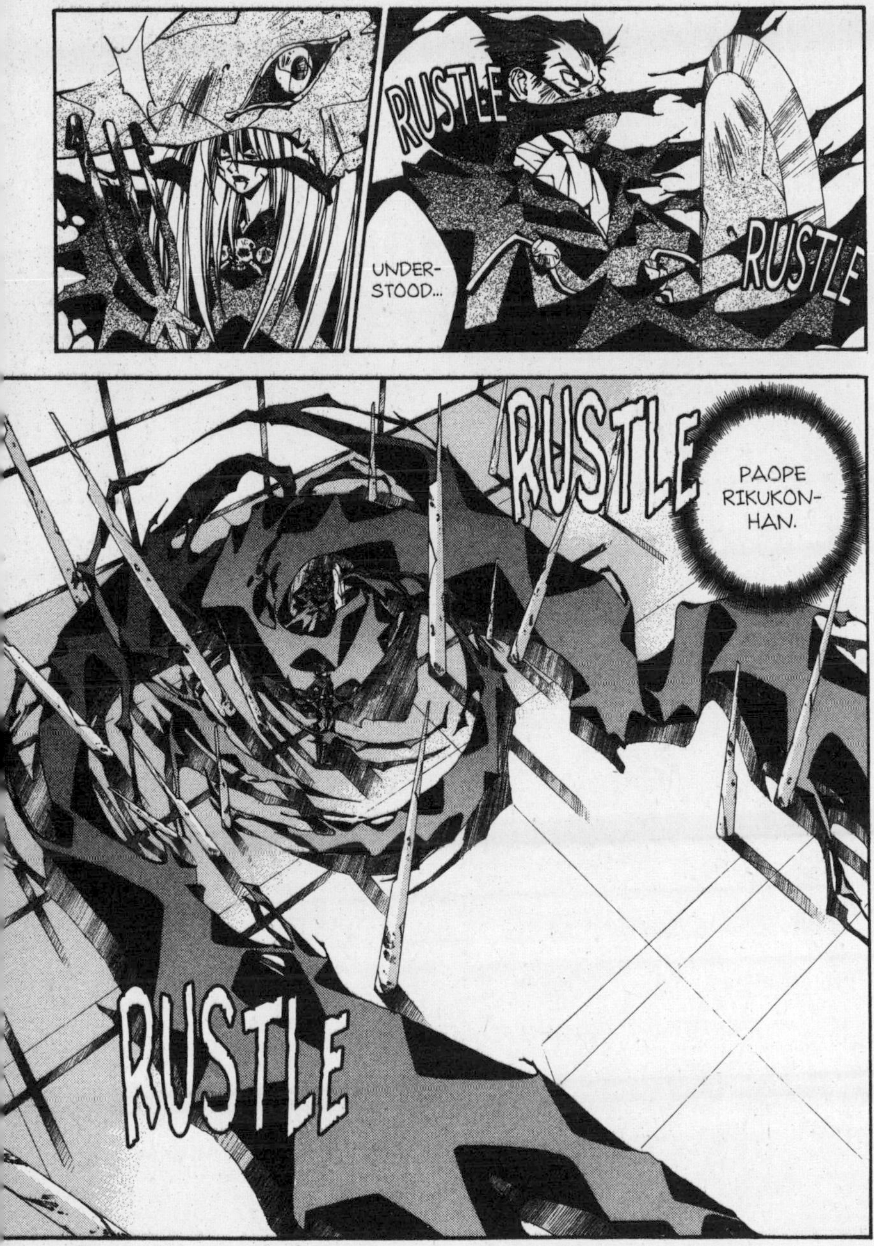
RUSTLE
UNDER-STOOD...
RUSTLE
RUSTLE
PAOPE RIKUKON-HAN.
RUSTLE

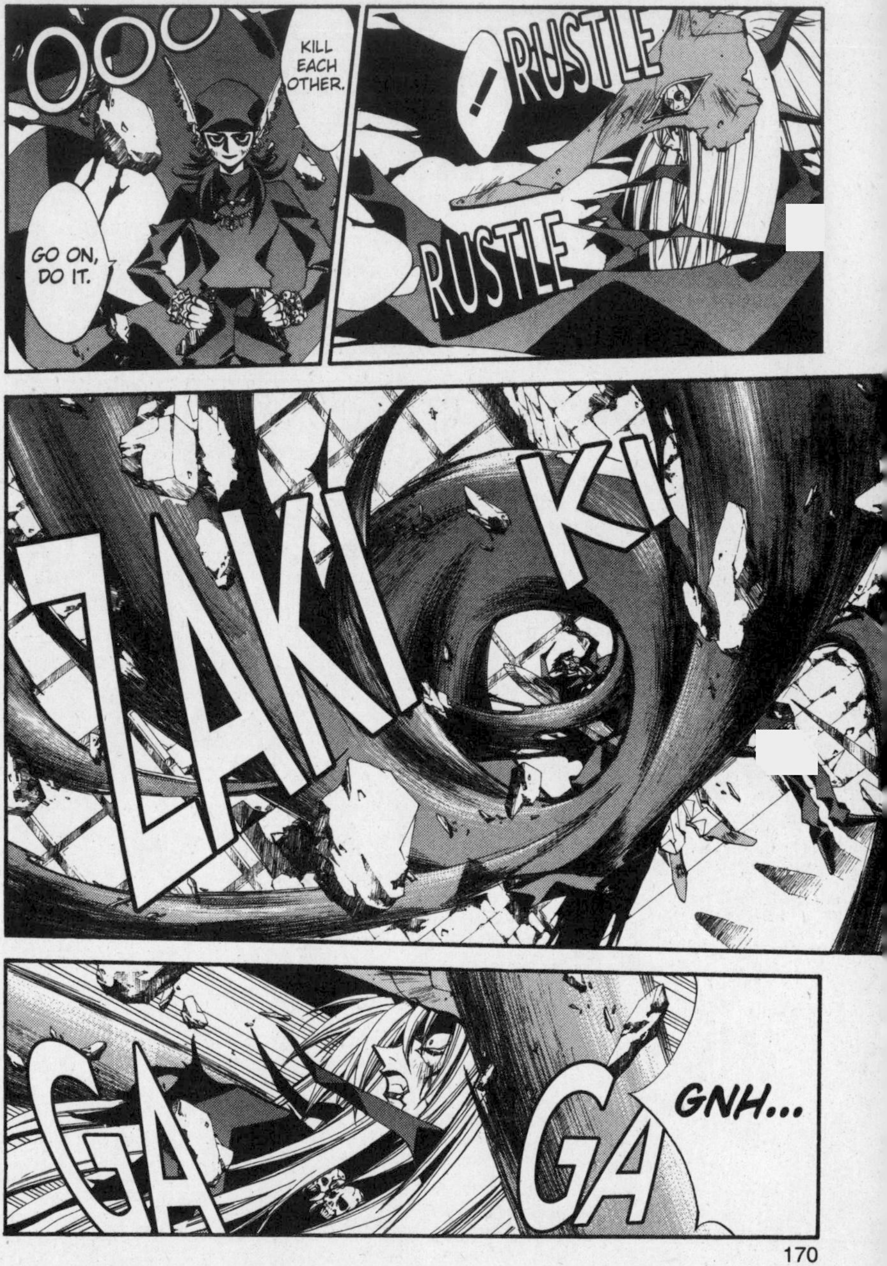

!
RUSTLE
RUSTLE
OOO
KILL EACH OTHER.
GO ON, DO IT.
KI
ZAKI
GNH...
GA
GA

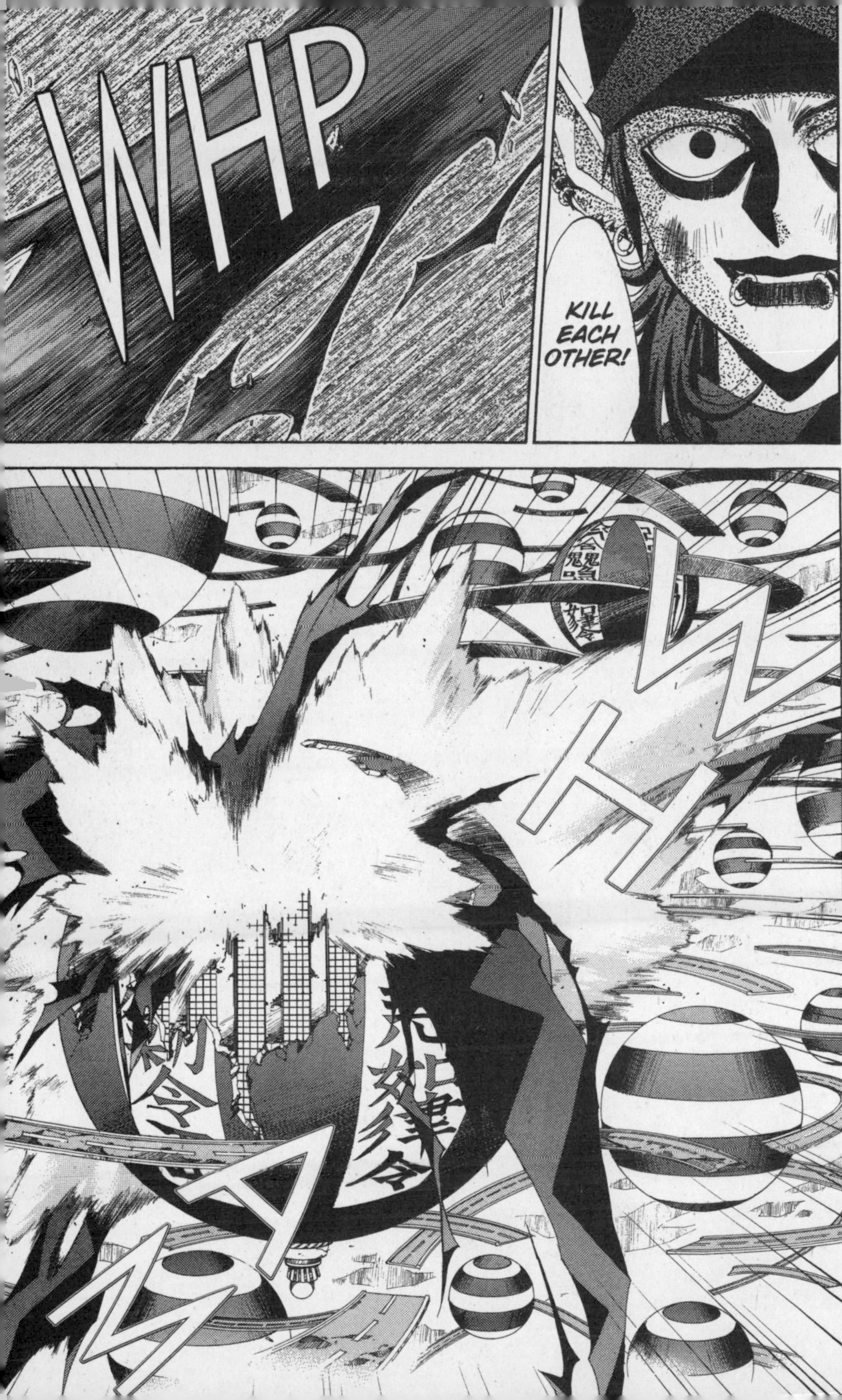
KILL EACH OTHER!
WHP
WHAM

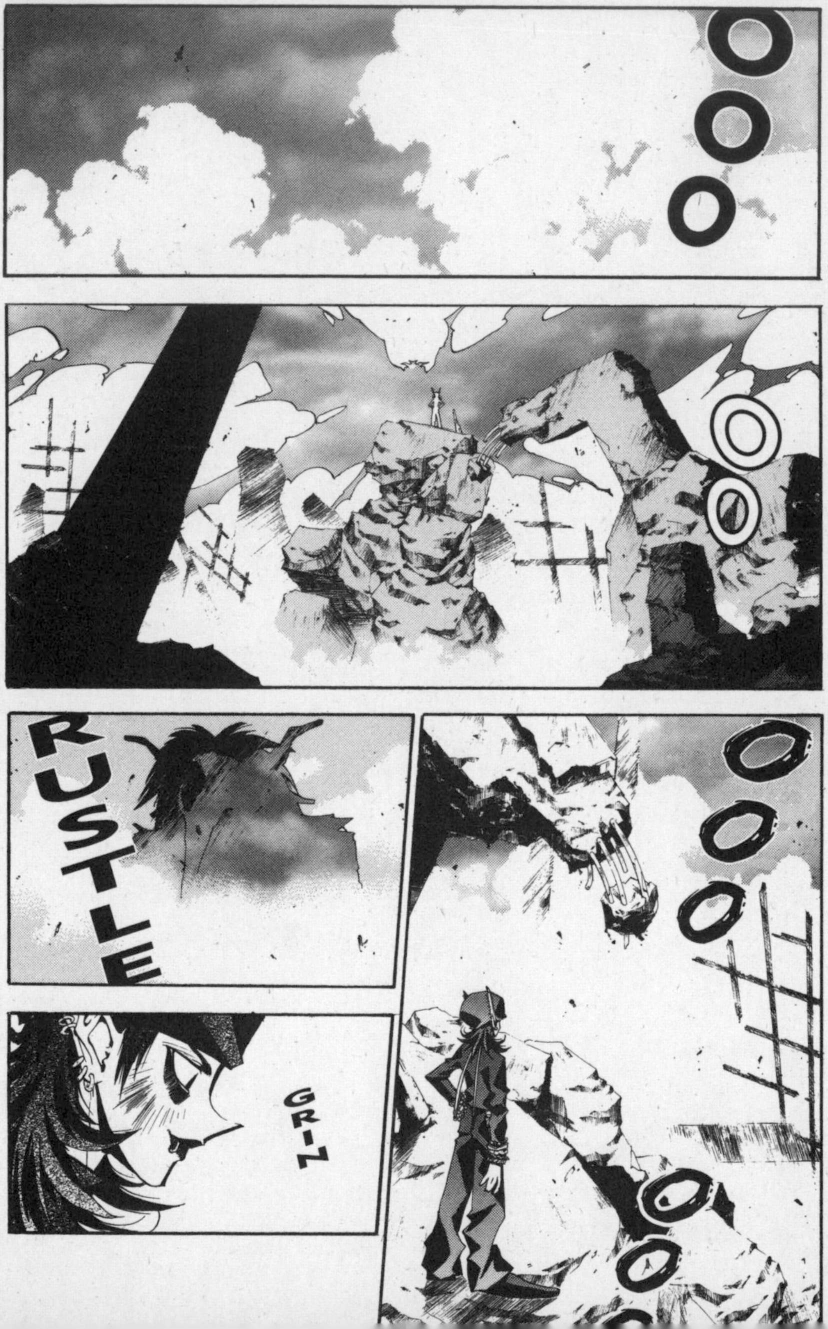
OOO
OOO
OOO
OOO
RUSTLE
GRIN

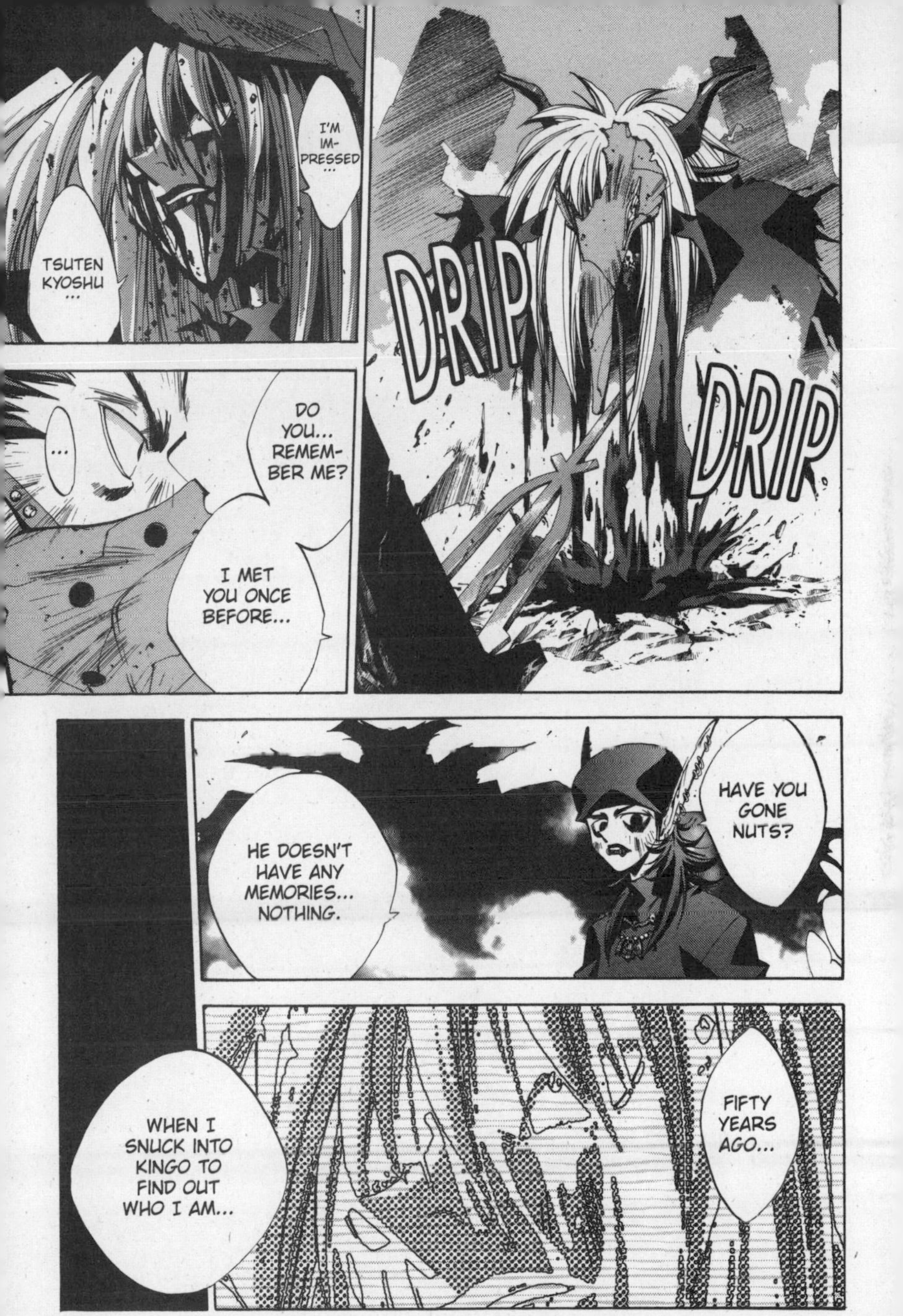
DRIP
DRIP
I'M IM-PRESSED...
TSUTEN KYOSHU...
DO YOU... REMEMBER ME?
...
I MET YOU ONCE BEFORE...
HAVE YOU GONE NUTS?
HE DOESN'T HAVE ANY MEMORIES... NOTHING.
FIFTY YEARS AGO...
WHEN I SNUCK INTO KINGO TO FIND OUT WHO I AM...

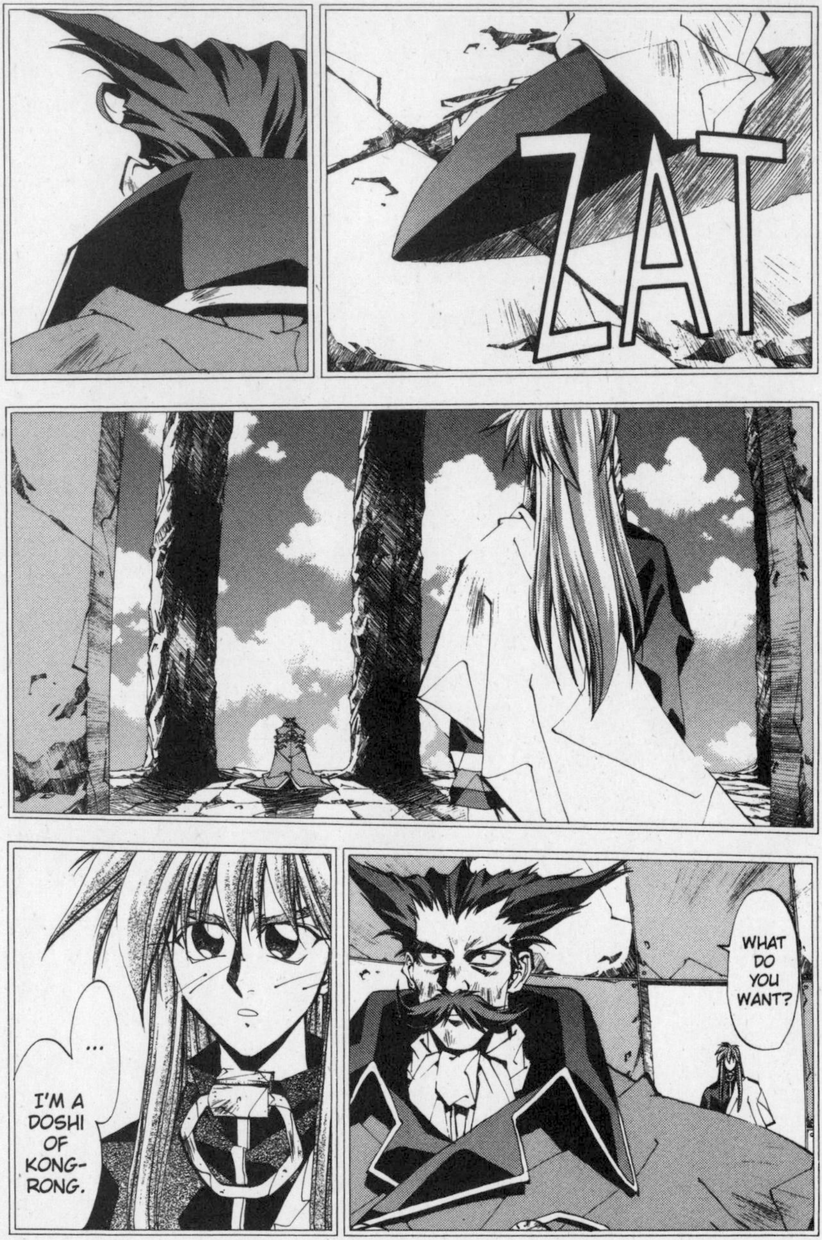
ZAT
WHAT DO YOU WANT?
...
I'M A DOSHI OF KONG-RONG.

READ THIS WAY

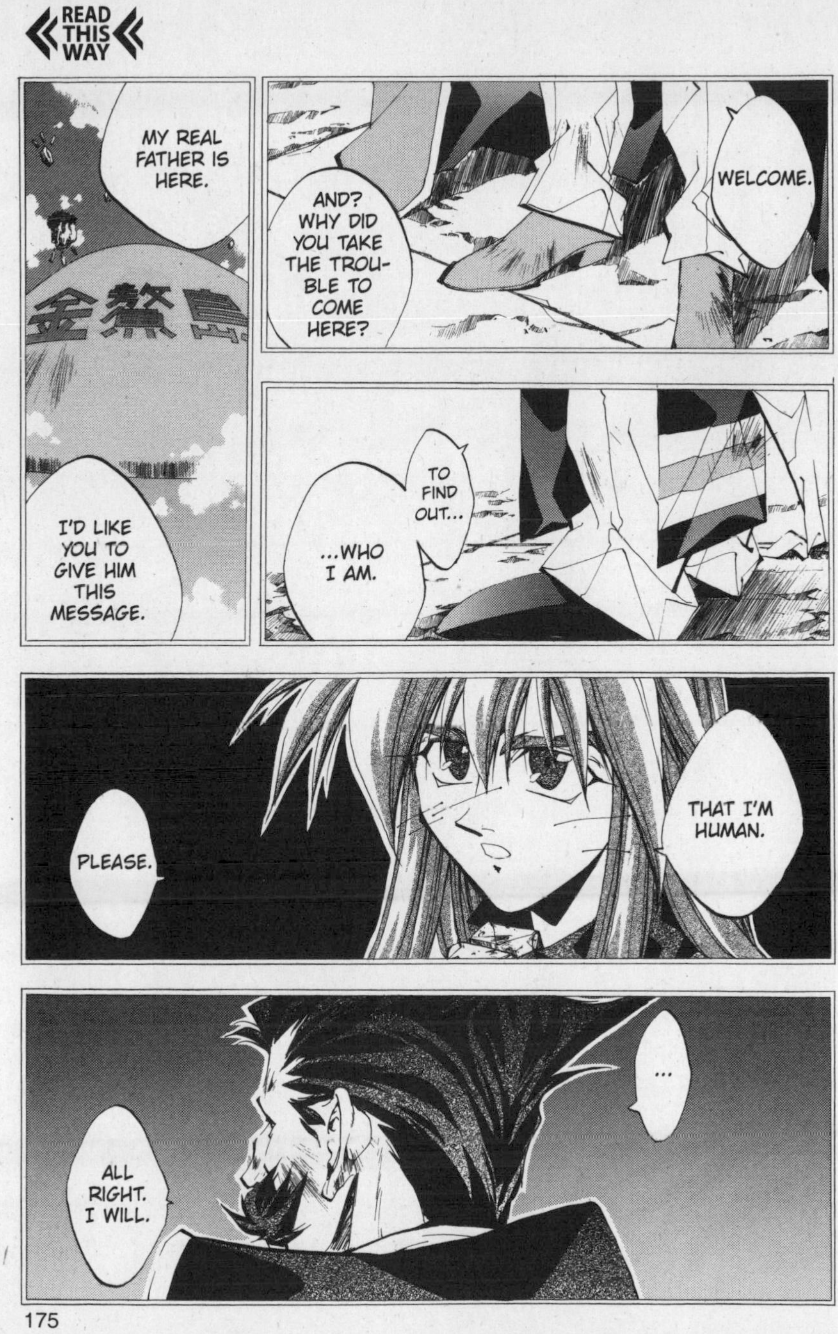
WELCOME.
AND? WHY DID YOU TAKE THE TROUBLE TO COME HERE?
TO FIND OUT...
...WHO I AM.
MY REAL FATHER IS HERE.
金鰲島
I'D LIKE YOU TO GIVE HIM THIS MESSAGE.
THAT I'M HUMAN.
PLEASE.
...
ALL RIGHT. I WILL.

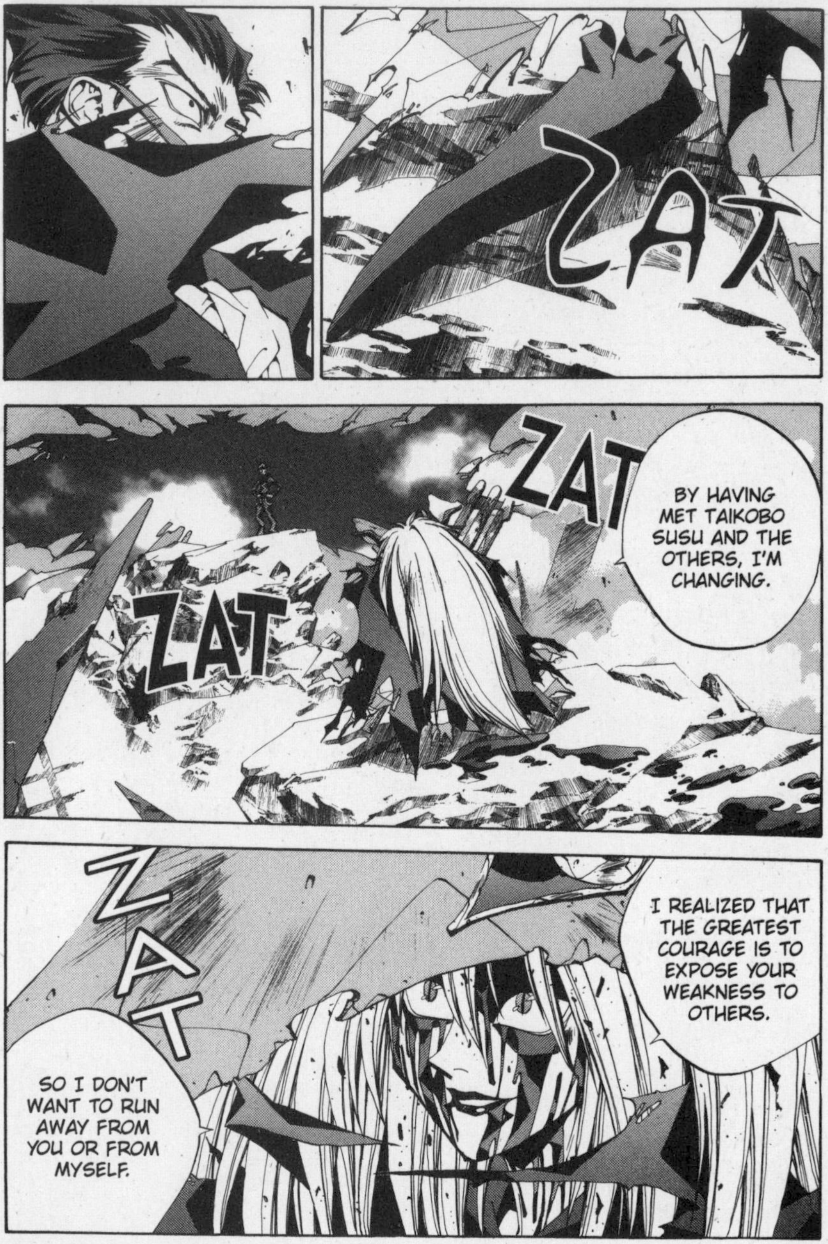
ZAT
BY HAVING MET TAIKOBO SUSU AND THE OTHERS, I'M CHANGING.
ZAT
ZAT
I REALIZED THAT THE GREATEST COURAGE IS TO EXPOSE YOUR WEAKNESS TO OTHERS.
ZAT
SO I DON'T WANT TO RUN AWAY FROM YOU OR FROM MYSELF.

READ THIS WAY

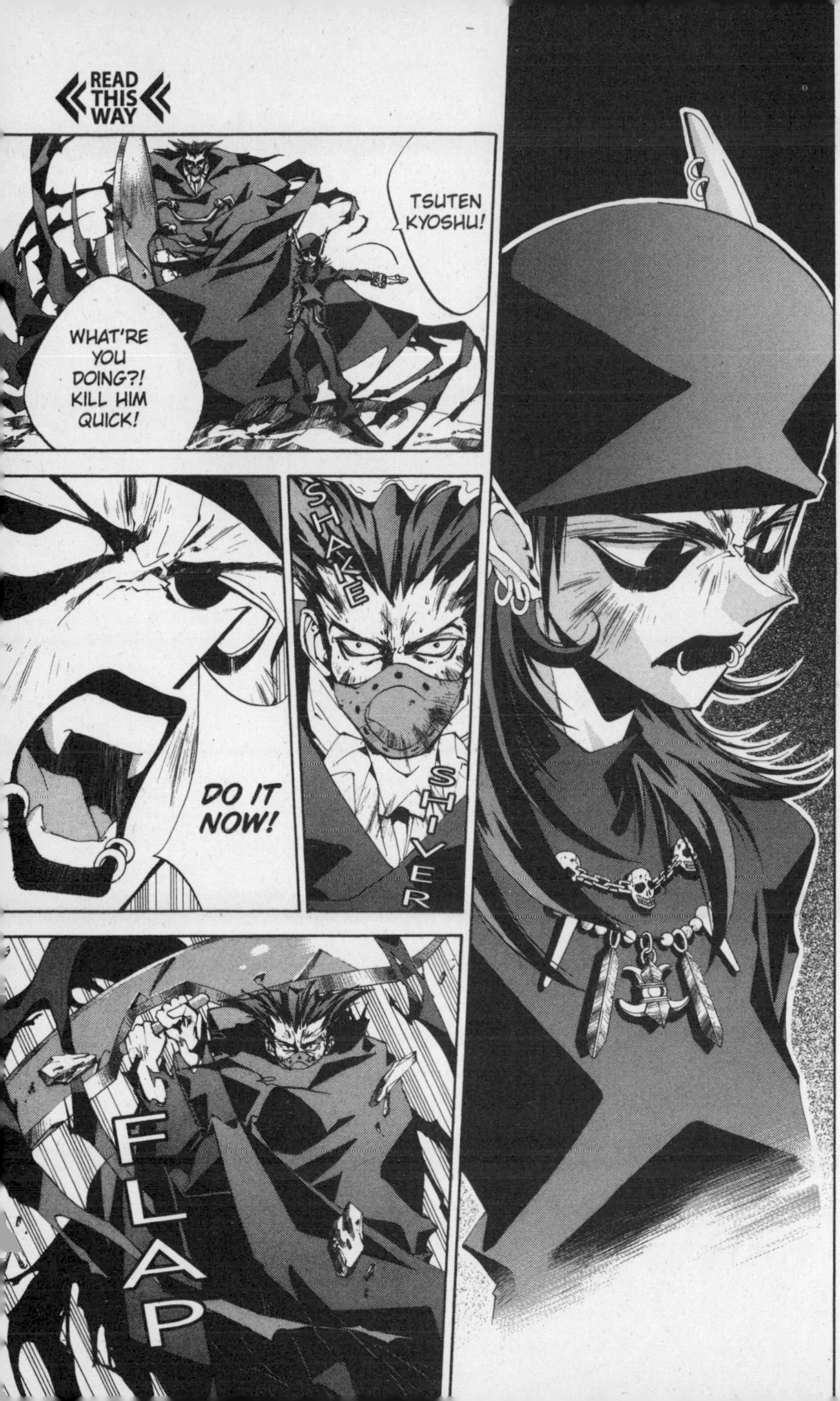
TSUTEN KYOSHU!
WHAT'RE YOU DOING?! KILL HIM QUICK!
SHAKE
SHIVER
DO IT NOW!
FLAP

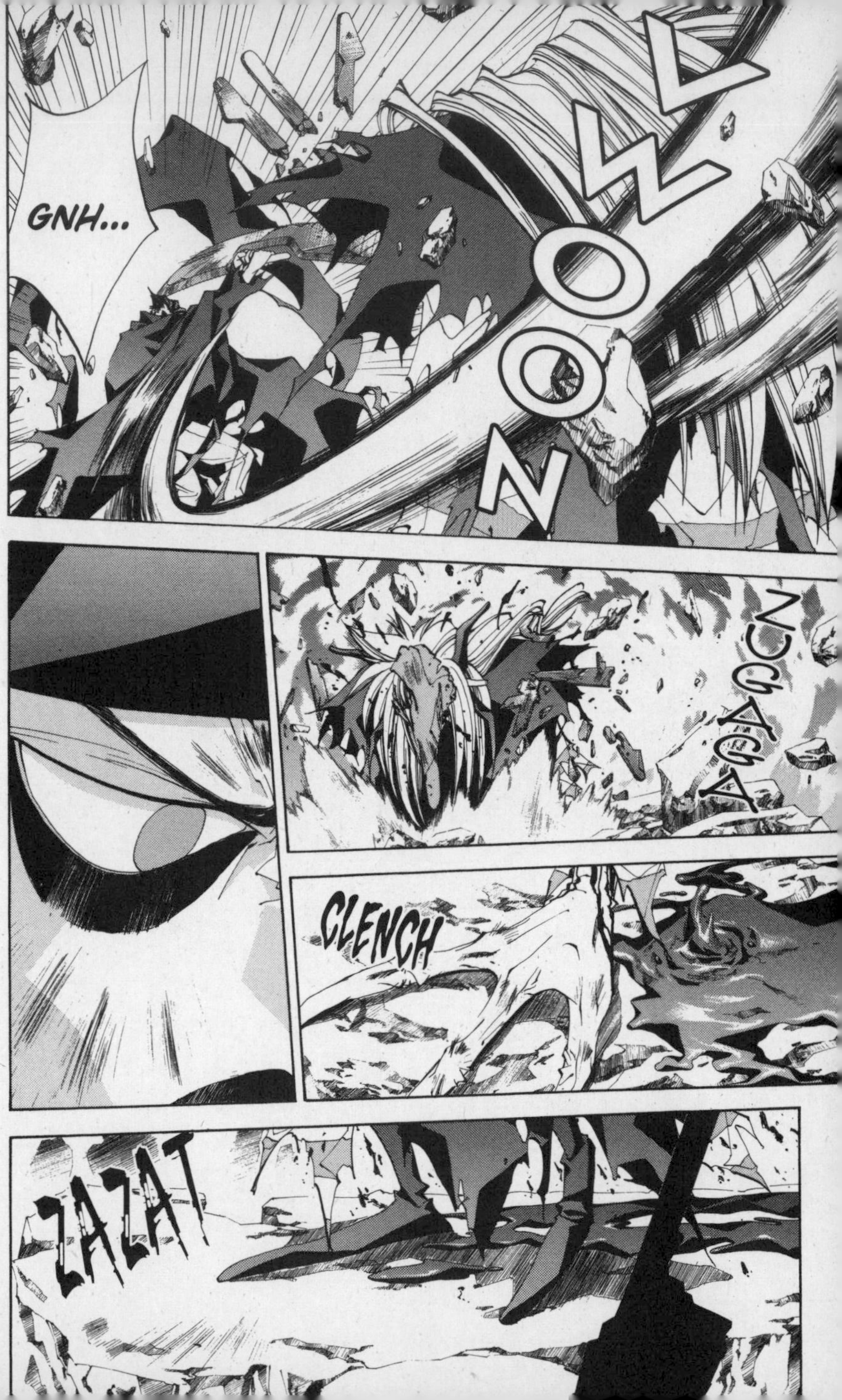
ZOOM
GNH...
ZUGAGA
CLENCH
ZAZAT

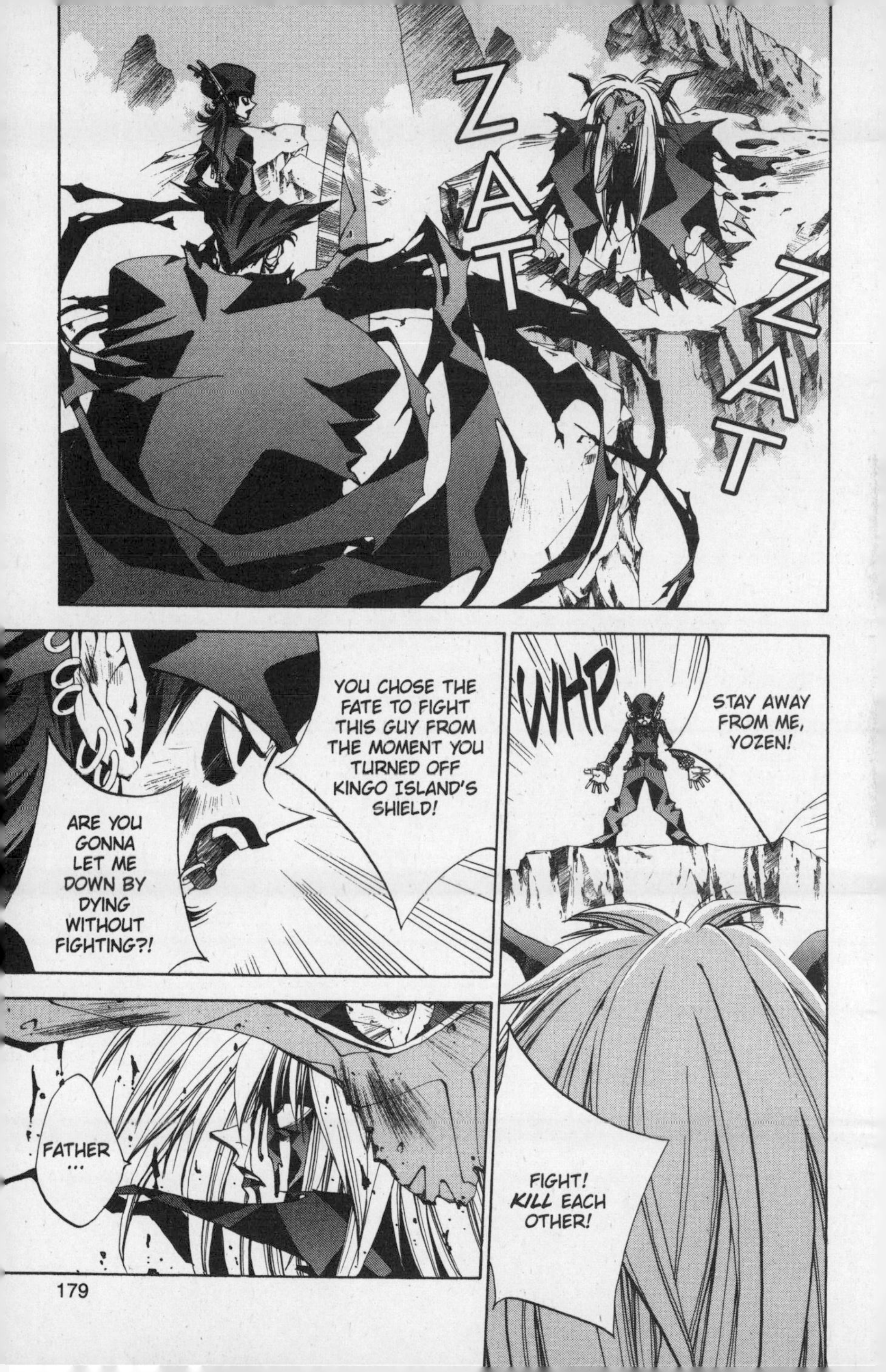
ZAT
ZAT
WHP
STAY AWAY FROM ME, YOZEN!
FIGHT! KILL EACH OTHER!
YOU CHOSE THE FATE TO FIGHT THIS GUY FROM THE MOMENT YOU TURNED OFF KINGO ISLAND'S SHIELD!
ARE YOU GONNA LET ME DOWN BY DYING WITHOUT FIGHTING?!
FATHER...

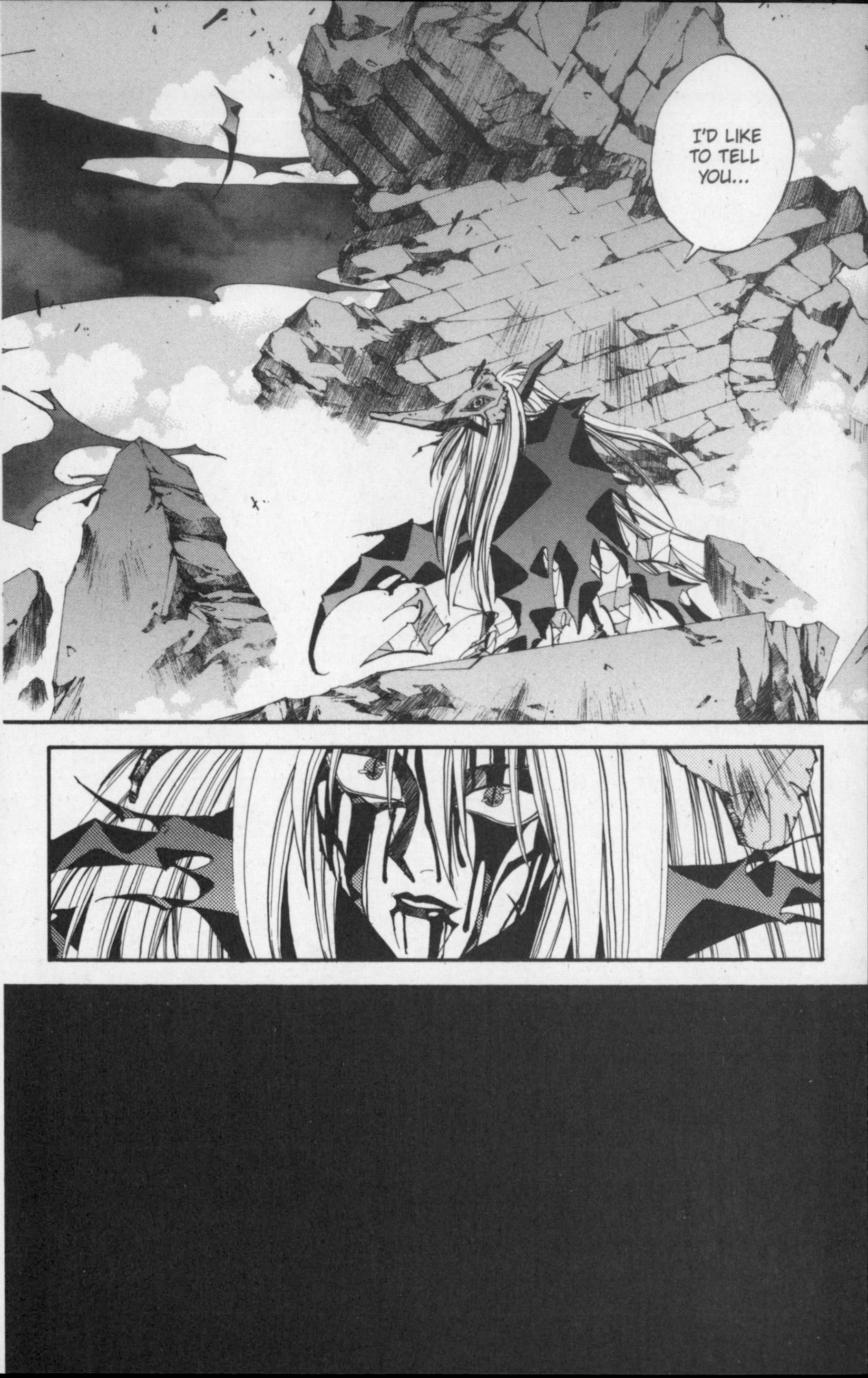
I'D LIKE TO TELL YOU...

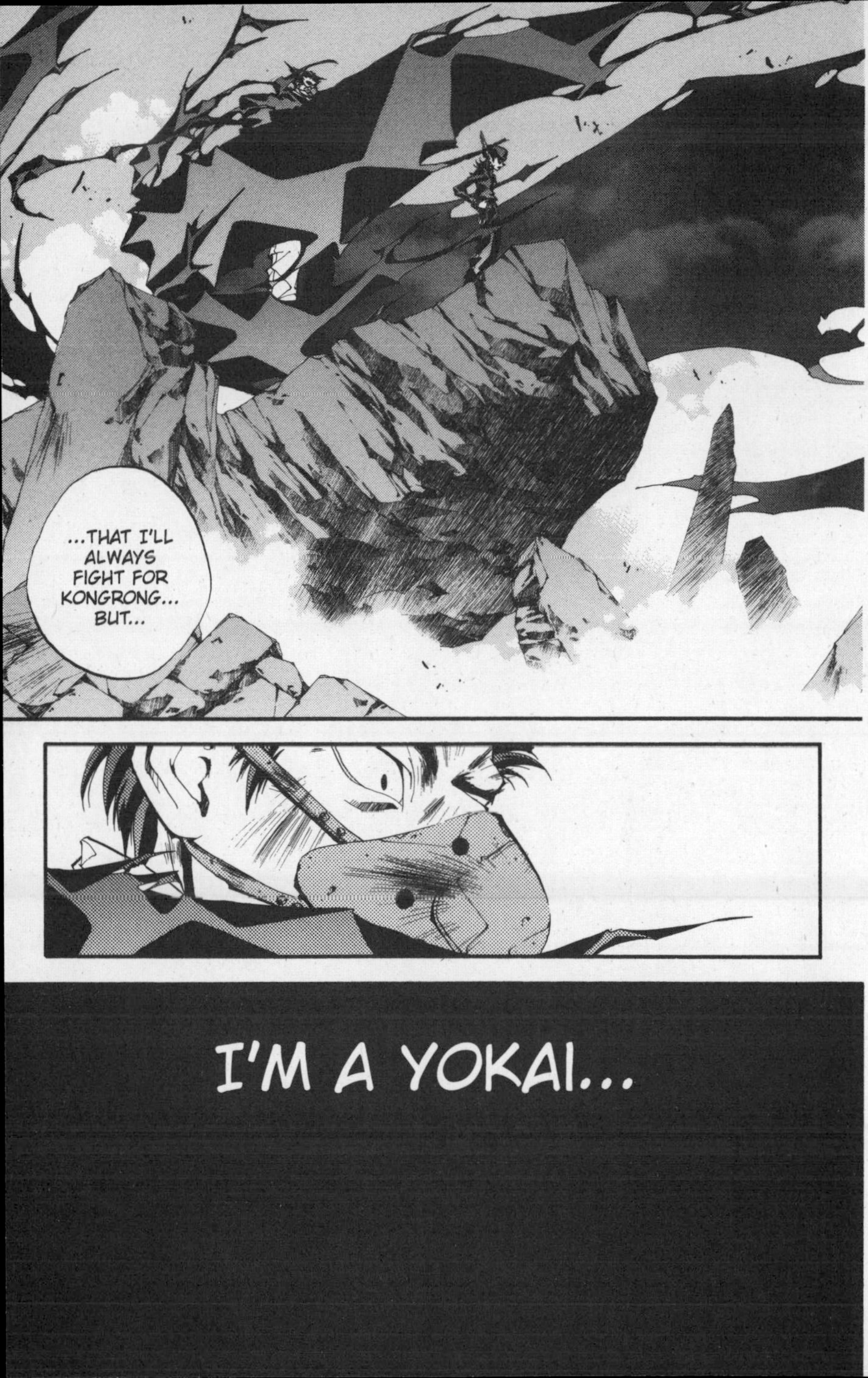
...THAT I'LL ALWAYS FIGHT FOR KONGRONG... BUT...
I'M A YOKAI...

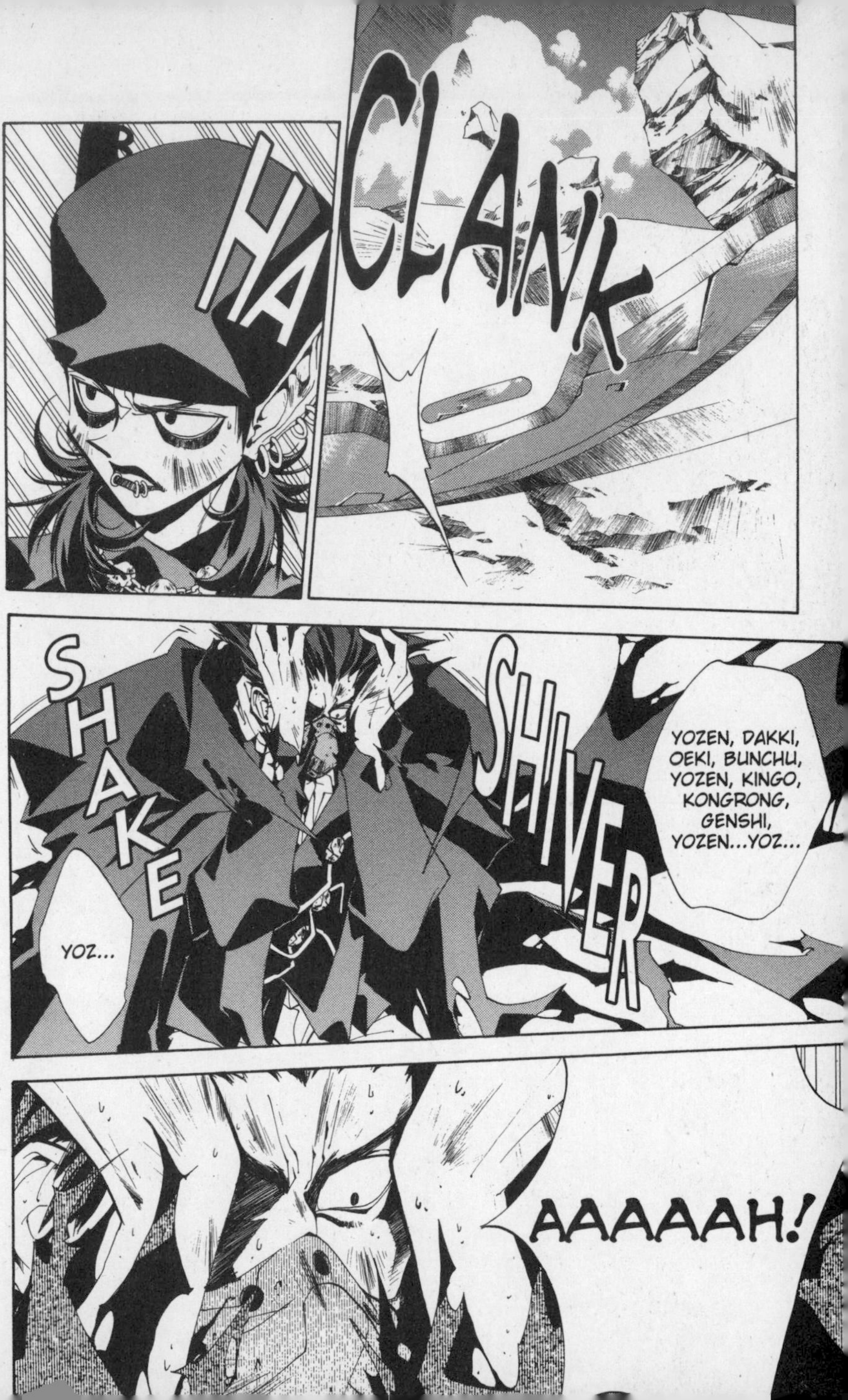
CLANK
HA HA
YOZEN, DAKKI, OEKI, BUNCHU, YOZEN, KINGO, KONGRONG, GENSHI, YOZEN...YOZ...
SHIVER
SHAKE
YOZ...
AAAAAH!

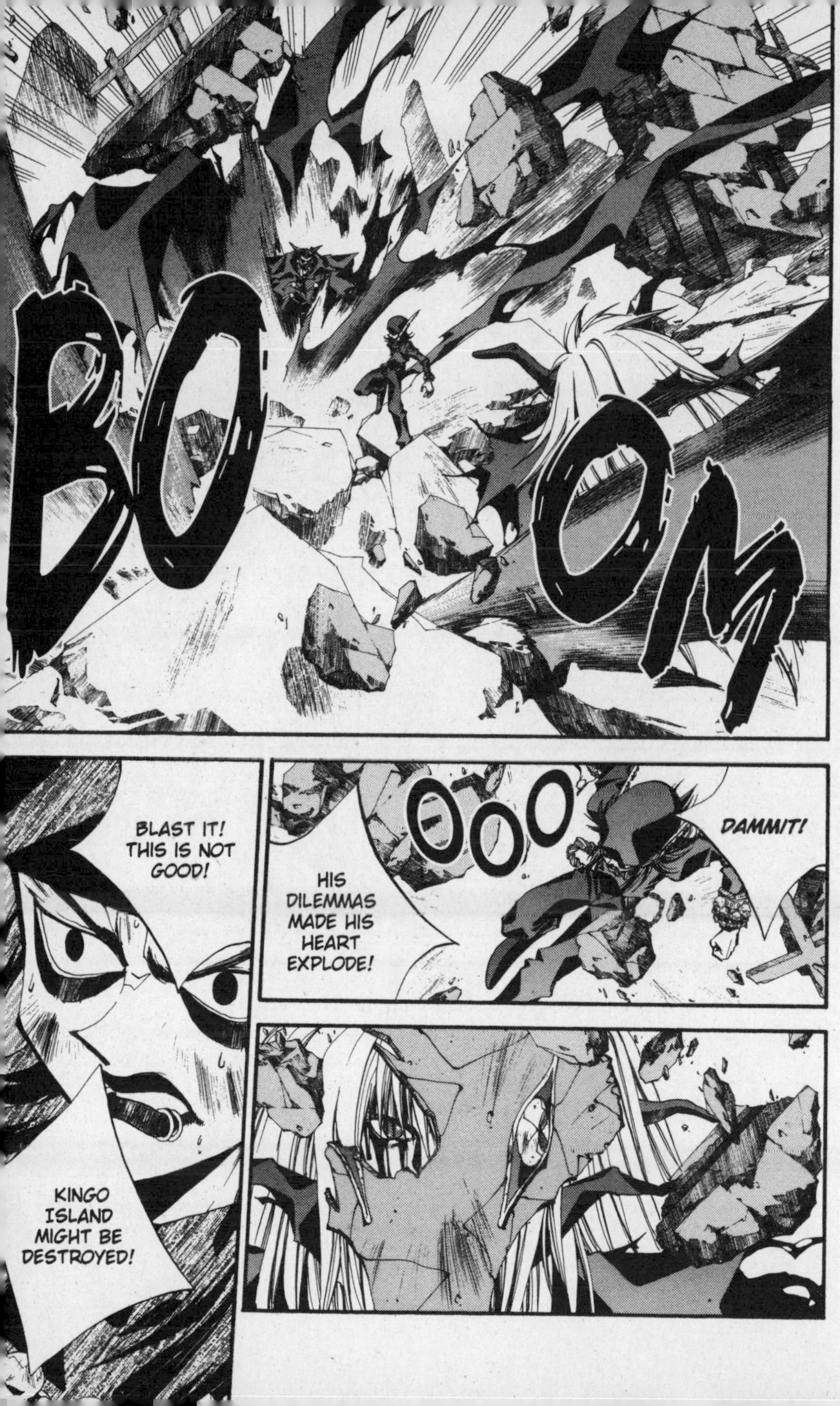
BOOM
DAMMIT!
OOO
HIS DILEMMAS MADE HIS HEART EXPLODE!
BLAST IT! THIS IS NOT GOOD!
KINGO ISLAND MIGHT BE DESTROYED!

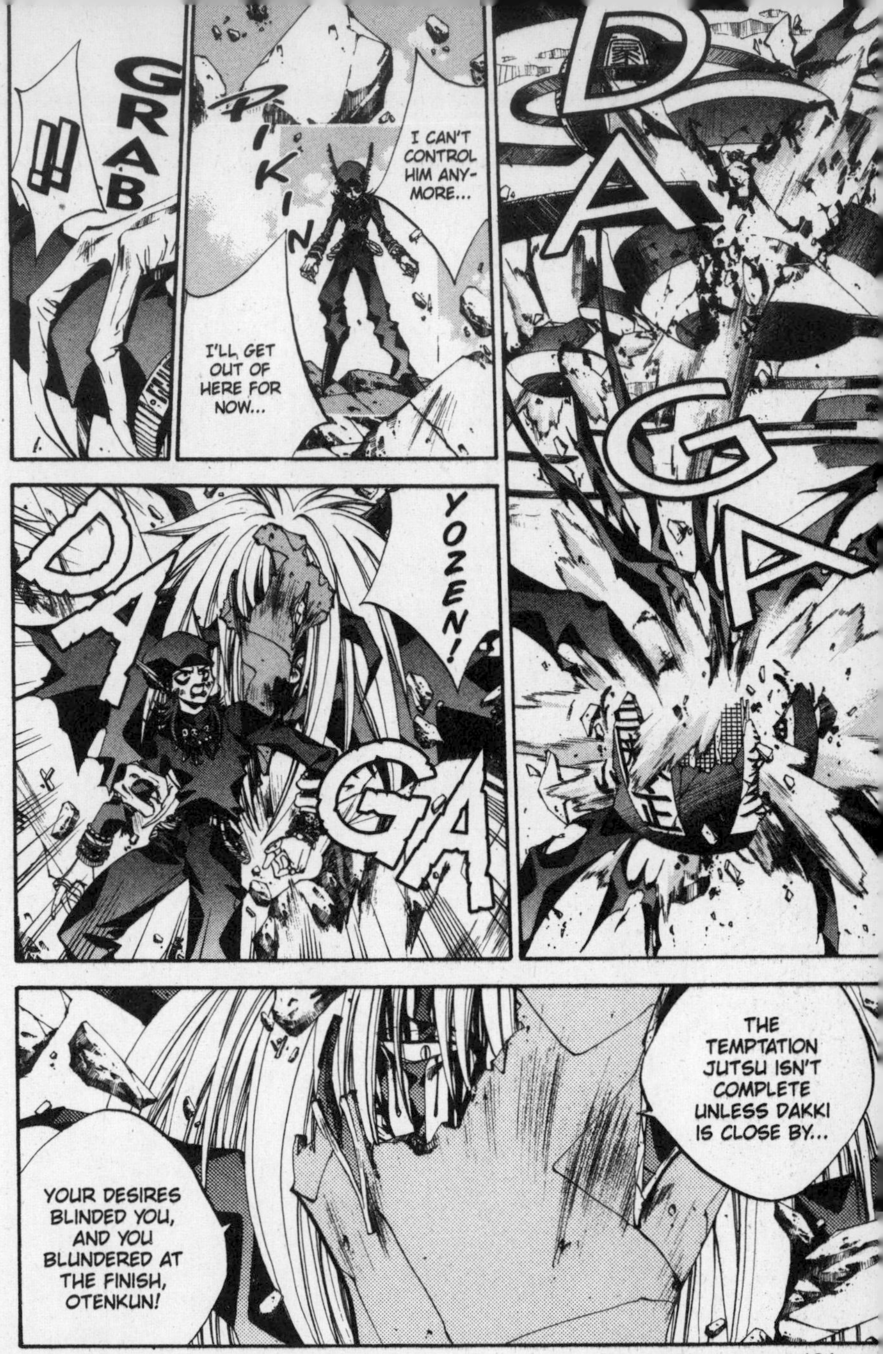
DAGA
PIKIN
I CAN'T CONTROL HIM ANY-MORE...
I'LL GET OUT OF HERE FOR NOW...
GRAB
!!
YOZEN!
DA
GA
THE TEMPTATION JUTSU ISN'T COMPLETE UNLESS DAKKI IS CLOSE BY...
YOUR DESIRES BLINDED YOU, AND YOU BLUNDERED AT THE FINISH, OTENKUN!

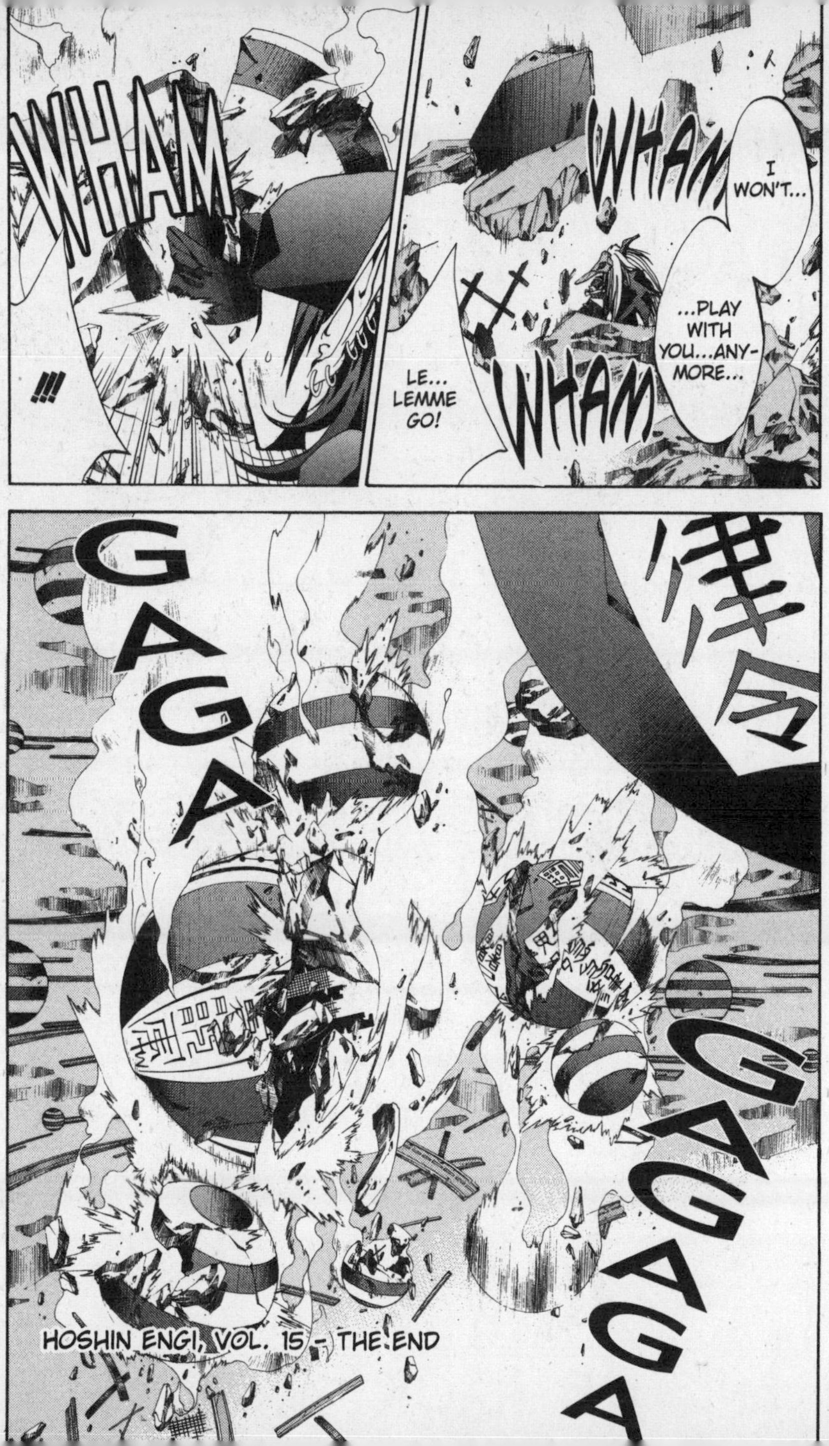
WHAM
I WON'T...
...PLAY WITH YOU...ANY-MORE...
WHAM
LE... LEMME GO!
WHAM
!!!
GAGAGA
GAGAGA
HOSHIN ENGI, VOL. 15 - THE END

YOU DON'T HAVE TO READ IT, BUT SINCE THERE'S AN EXTRA PAGE:

HACK WRITING XIV

- △ IT REALLY DOESN'T MATTER, BUT...
- △ HUMANS PRODUCE GASTRIC ACID TO DIGEST FOOD, AND THEY SWEAT WHEN IT'S HOT.
- △ THEN IF EVERYONE HAD CHEESE COMING OUT OF THEIR EARS, HOW'S THAT?
- △ I THINK HUMANS WILL THINK OF A WAY FOR THE CHEESE TO NOT DRIP ON THEIR CLOTHES.
- △ STICK A TUBE IN YOUR EARS, AND CONNECT THE TUBE TO THE "CHEESE ETIQUETTE BAG" YOU HANG FROM YOUR WAIST. WHEN THE BAG IS FULL, THROW IT IN THE TRASH CAN!
- △ TEENAGE GIRLS MIGHT REGULARLY USE "EAR DEODORANT."
- △ CHILDREN WOULD LOVE TO TALK ABOUT CHEESE.
- △ "I ACCIDENTALLY STEPPED ON CHEESE WHILE I WAS WALKING!" OR "I DASHED INTO THE RESTROOM BECAUSE MY CHEESE BAG BECAME FULL DURING CLASS!" BUT WHEN YOU'RE A GROWN-UP, EVERYONE WOULD SAY, "THAT'S THE NORM. EVERYONE'S LIKE THAT." AND PEOPLE WOULDN'T TALK ABOUT IT MUCH. GROWN-UPS DON'T QUESTION SUCH THINGS AND KNOW THAT IT'S NOTHING TO BE ASHAMED OF. GROWN-UPS ARE UNFAIR!!
- △ AND OF COURSE, NO ONE WOULD EAT CHEESE... I THINK. SOME REAL WEIRDOS MIGHT EAT IT THOUGH.
- △ AND AFTER SAYING ALL THIS, FUJISAKI LOVES MILK.

END OF HACK WRITING

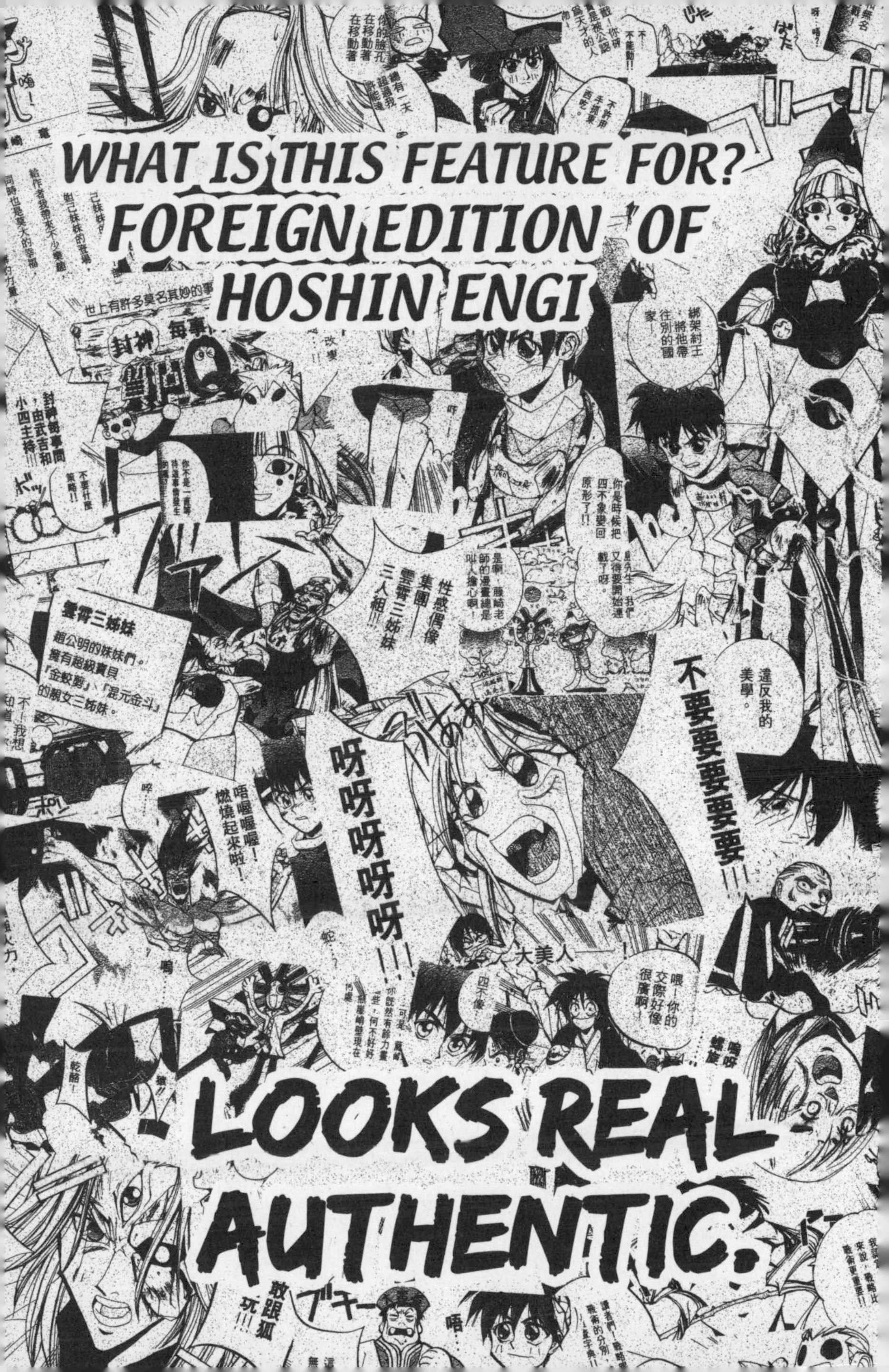
WHAT IS THIS FEATURE FOR?
FOREIGN EDITION OF
HOSHIN ENGI
雲霄三姊妹
超公明的妹妹們。擁有超級寶貝「金蛟剪」、「混元金斗」的靚女三姊妹。
性感偶像集團雲霄三姊妹三人組!!
是啊,藤崎老師的漫畫總是叫人擔心啊。
你是時候把四不象變回原形了!!
綁架紂王將他帶往別的國家!
違反我的美學。
不要要要要要!!
呀呀呀呀呀!!
唔喔喔喔!燃燒起來啦!
大美人
四不像
喂!你的交際好像很廣啊!
LOOKS REAL AUTHENTIC.
敢跟狐玩!!!

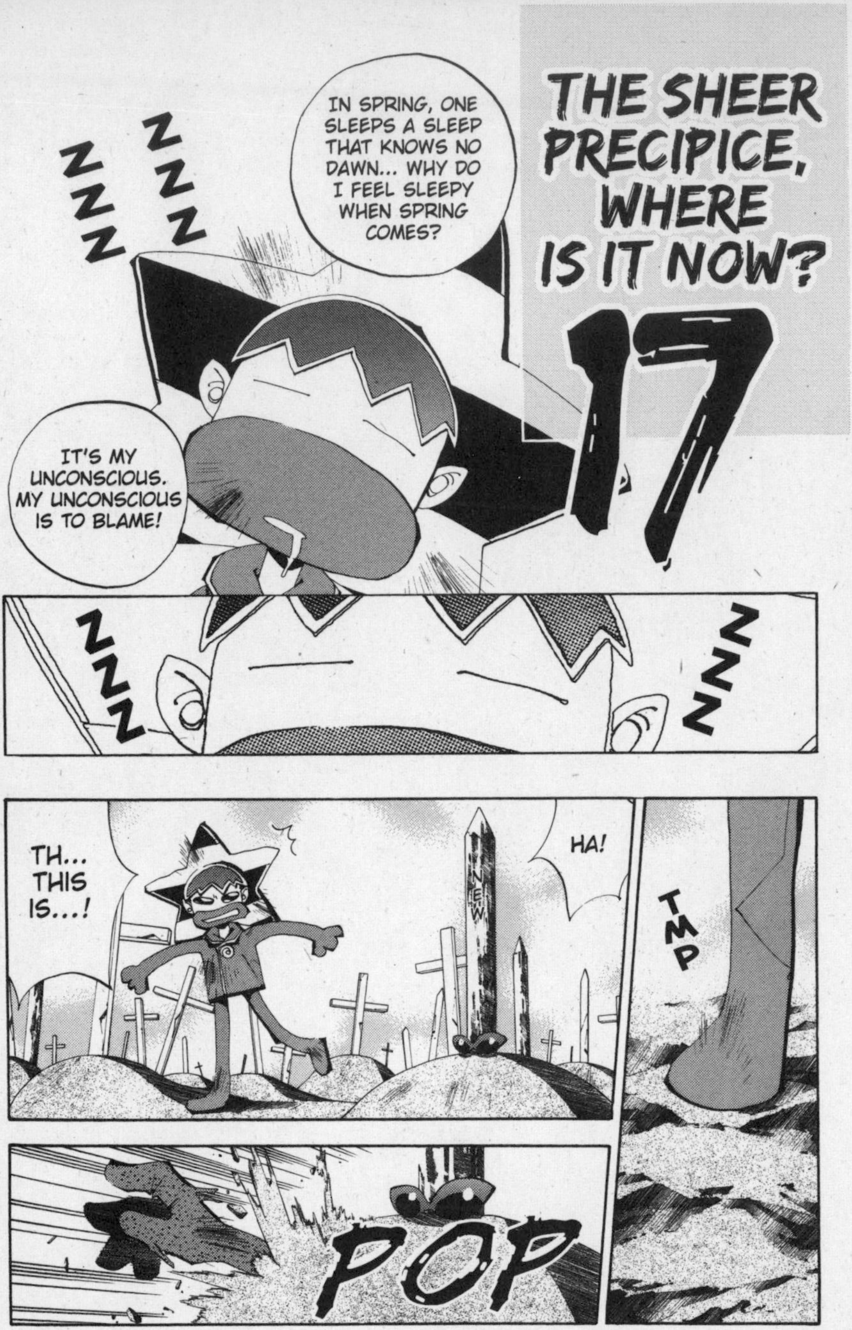
THE SHEER PRECIPICE, WHERE IS IT NOW? 17
IN SPRING, ONE SLEEPS A SLEEP THAT KNOWS NO DAWN... WHY DO I FEEL SLEEPY WHEN SPRING COMES?
ZZZ
ZZZ
IT'S MY UNCONSCIOUS. MY UNCONSCIOUS IS TO BLAME!
ZZZ
ZZZ
TMP
HA!
TH... THIS IS...!
POP

READ THIS WAY

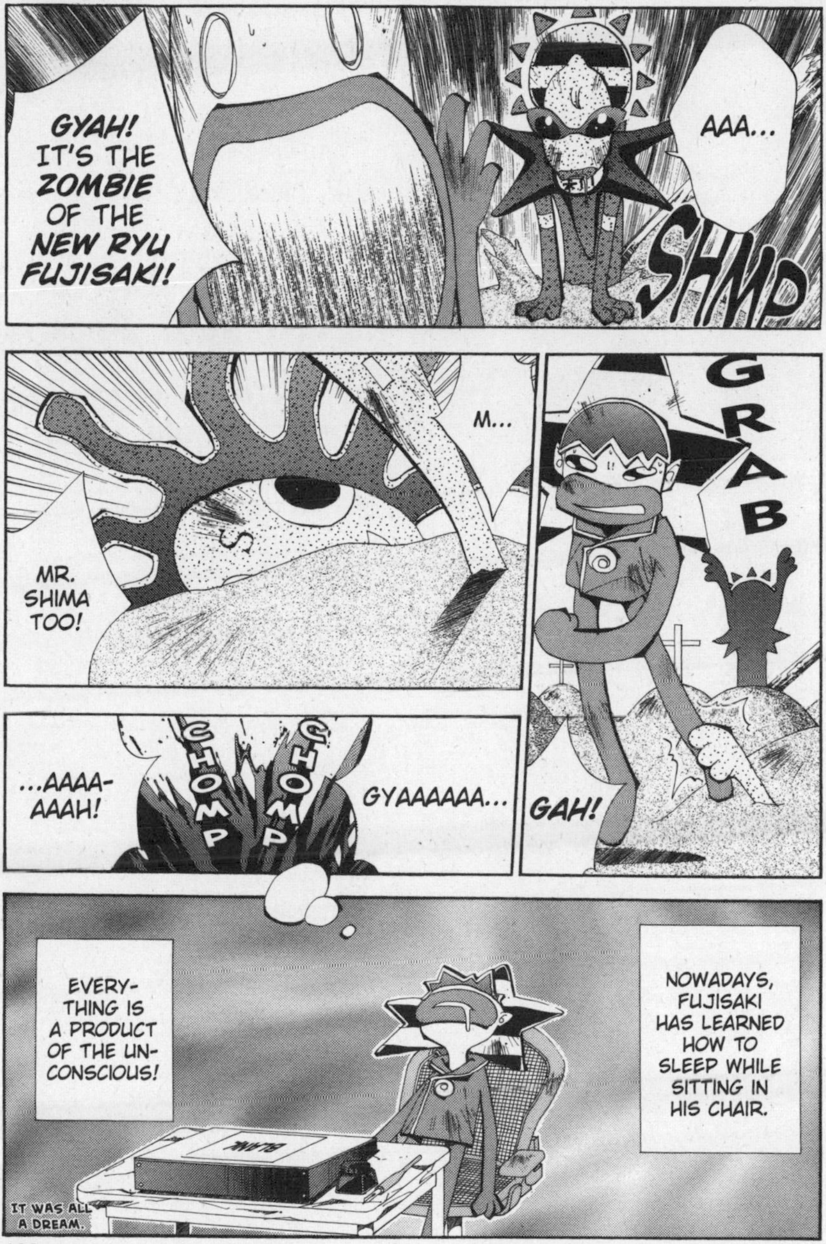
AAA...
GYAH! IT'S THE ZOMBIE OF THE NEW RYU FUJISAKI!
SHMP
GRAB
GAH!
M...
MR. SHIMA TOO!
GYAAAAAA...
...AAAA-AAAH!
CHOMP CHOMP
NOWADAYS, FUJISAKI HAS LEARNED HOW TO SLEEP WHILE SITTING IN HIS CHAIR.
EVERY-THING IS A PRODUCT OF THE UN-CONSCIOUS!
IT WAS ALL A DREAM.

Hoshin Engi: The Rank File!

You'll find as you read *Hoshin Engi* that there are titles and ranks that you are probably unfamiliar with. While it may seem confusing, there is an order to the madness that is pulled from ancient Chinese mythology, Japanese culture, other manga, and, of course, the incredible mind of *Hoshin Engi* creator Ryu Fujisaki.

Where we think it will help, we give you a hint in the margin on the page the name appears. But in addition, here's a quick primer on the titles you'll find in *Hoshin Engi* and what they mean:

Japanese	Title	Job Description
武成王	Buseio	Chief commanding officer
宰相	Saisho	Premier
太師	Taishi	The king's advisor/tutor
大金剛	Dai Kongo	Great vassals
軍師	Gunshi	Military tactician
大諸侯	Daishoko	Great feudal lord
東伯侯	Tohakuko	Lord of the east region
西伯侯	Seihakuko	Lord of the west region
北伯侯	Hokuhakuko	Lord of the north region
南伯侯	Nanhakuko	Lord of the south region

Hoshin Engi: The Immortal File

Also, you'll probably find the hierarchy of the Sennin, Sendo and Doshi somewhat complicated. Here, we spell it out the easiest way possible!

Japanese	Title	Description
道士	Doshi	Someone training to become Sennin
仙道	Sendo	Used to describe both Sennin and Doshi
仙人	Sennin	Those who have mastered the way. Once you "go Sennin" you are forever changed.
妖孽	Yogetsu	A Yosei who can transform into a human
妖怪仙人	Yokai Sennin	A Sennin whose original form is not human
妖精	Yosei	An animal or object exposed to moonlight and sunlight for more than 1,000 years

Hoshin Engi: The Magical File

Paope (宝貝) are powerful magical items used by Sennin and Doshi. Sometimes they look like regular objects, like a veil or hat. These are just a few of the magical items, both paope and otherwise, that you'll encounter in *Hoshin Engi!*

Japanese	Magic	Description
打神鞭	Dashinben	Known as the God-Striking Whip, Taikobo's pao manipulates the air and wind.
霊獣	Reiju	A magical flying beast that Sennin and Doshi use for transportation and support. Taikobo's reiju is his pal Supu.
五光石	Gokoseki	A rock that changes the face of whomever it strikes into a "weirdly erotic-looking" face.
莫邪の宝剣	Bakuya no Hoken	Tenka's weapon, a light saber.
蒼巾力士	Sokin Rikishi	Kingo's version of the Kokin Rikishi.
通天砲	Tsutenho	Kingo Island's principal gun.
寒氷陣	Kanpyojin	A dimension of frozen death. Its ruler can manipulate snow, ice, and cold wind at will here.
太極符印	Taikyoku Fuin	A paople that can manipulate physical objects on the elemental level.
仙桃エキス	Sento Extract	A medicine made from sento that helps restore your physical strength.
	Mysterious Veil	A thin cloth that neutralizes all weak paope attacks.
降魔杵	Gomasho	A mallet-like paope that becomes heavy the moment it hits the enemy. Can change shape as well.
金光陣	Kinkojin	A paople that creates a shadow of the enemy with its light. The shadow doesn't die until the enemy is dead, and if the shadow is hurt, the enemy is hurt as well.
六魂幡	Rikukonhan	A cape-like paope that covers the enemy and makes countless attacks.

Coming Next Volume:
Mortal Combat

Taikobo and troops of Mount Kongrong continue the battle
against the forces of Kingo Island. In order to save Taikobo,
Fugen sneaks away to battle alone against Bunchu, their
deadliest foe. But can Fugen possibly defeat the strongest
Sennin in the world?

AVAILABLE DECEMBER 2009!

Read Any Good Books Lately?

Hoshin Engi is based on *Fengshen Yanji* (*The Creation of the Gods,* written in the 1500s by Xu Zhonglin) one of China's four classical fantastical novels of adventure, magic and mystery. The other three are *Saiyuki* (*Journey to the West* by Cheng'en Wu, late 1500s), *Sangokushi Engi* (*Romance of the Three Kingdoms* by Guanzhong Luo), and *Shui Hu Zhuan* (*Outlaws of the Marsh,* by Shi Nai'an, mid-1500s).

Want to read these books? You can! They're all still in print, more than 500 years later!

These books are North American in-print editions only.

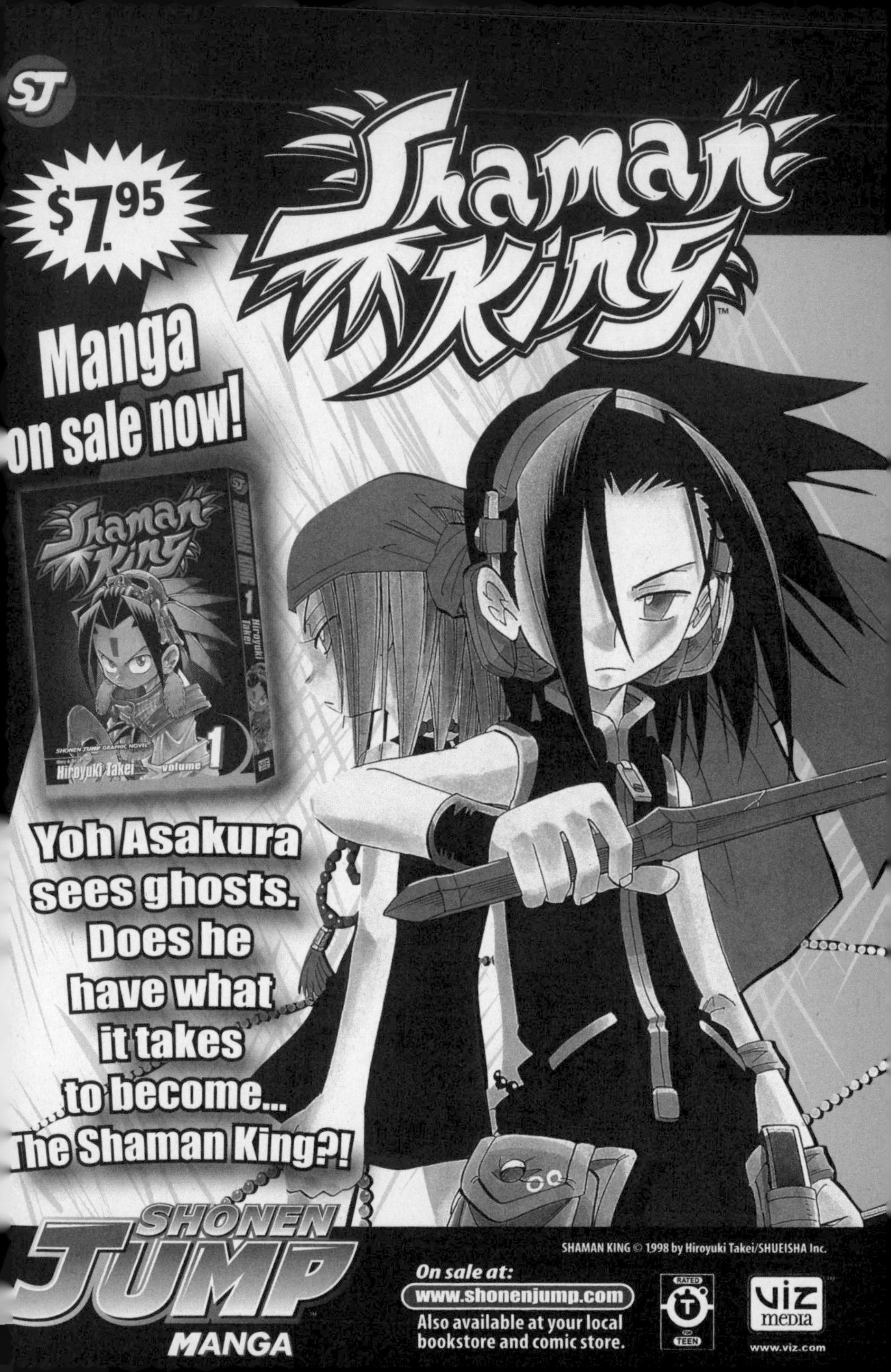
SJ
$7.95
Shaman King™
Manga on sale now!
Shaman King
SHONEN JUMP
1
Hiroyuki Takei
SHONEN JUMP GRAPHIC NOVEL
Hiroyuki Takei
volume 1
Yoh Asakura sees ghosts. Does he have what it takes to become... The Shaman King?!
SHONEN JUMP MANGA
SHAMAN KING © 1998 by Hiroyuki Takei/SHUEISHA Inc.
On sale at:
www.shonenjump.com
Also available at your local bookstore and comic store.
RATED T TEEN
VIZ media
www.viz.com

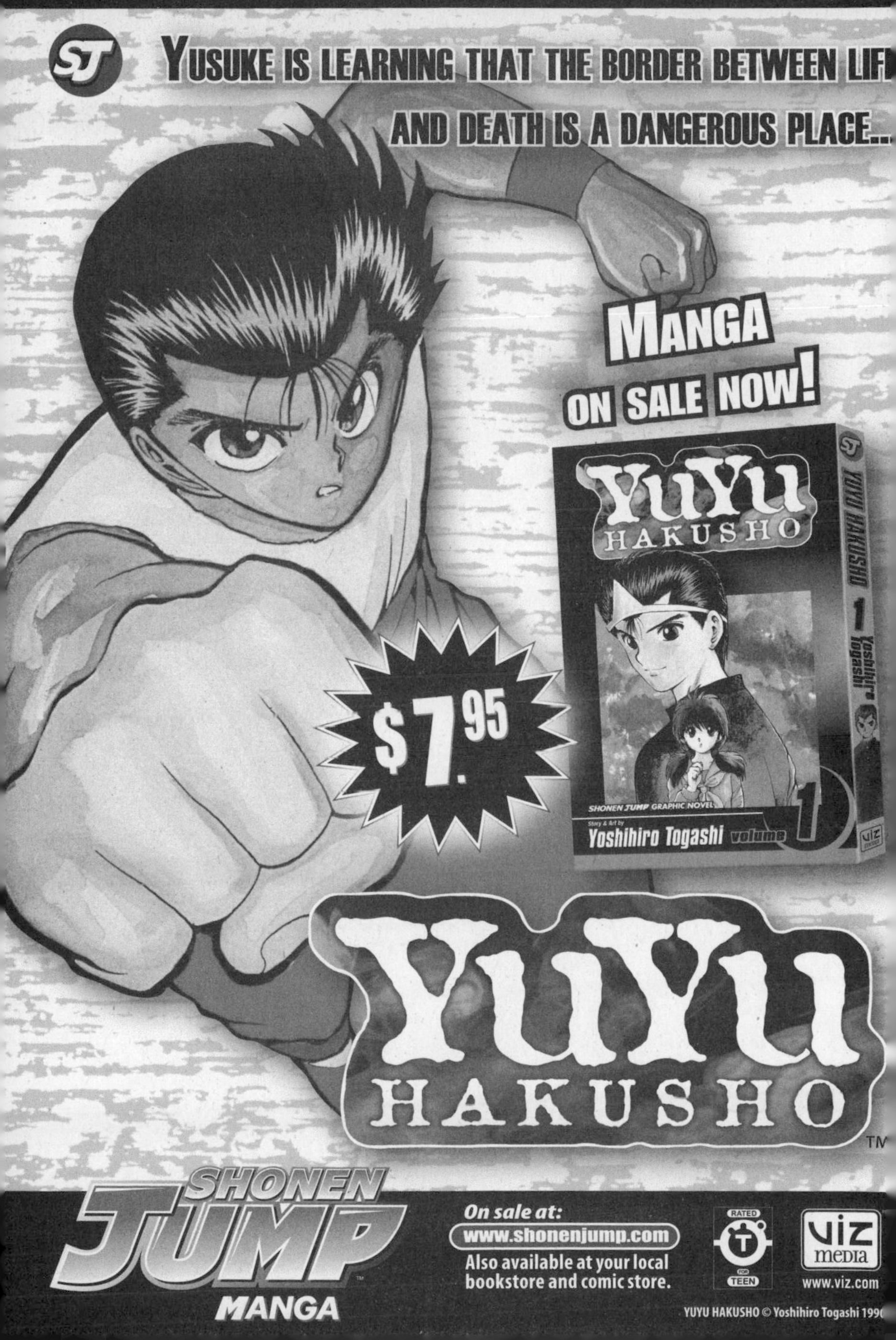
YUSUKE IS LEARNING THAT THE BORDER BETWEEN LIFE
AND DEATH IS A DANGEROUS PLACE...
MANGA
ON SALE NOW!
$7.95
YUYU HAKUSHO
SHONEN JUMP GRAPHIC NOVEL
Story & Art by
Yoshihiro Togashi volume 1
YUYU HAKUSHO
SHONEN JUMP
MANGA
On sale at:
www.shonenjump.com
Also available at your local bookstore and comic store.
RATED T FOR TEEN
VIZ media
www.viz.com
YUYU HAKUSHO © Yoshihiro Togashi 1990

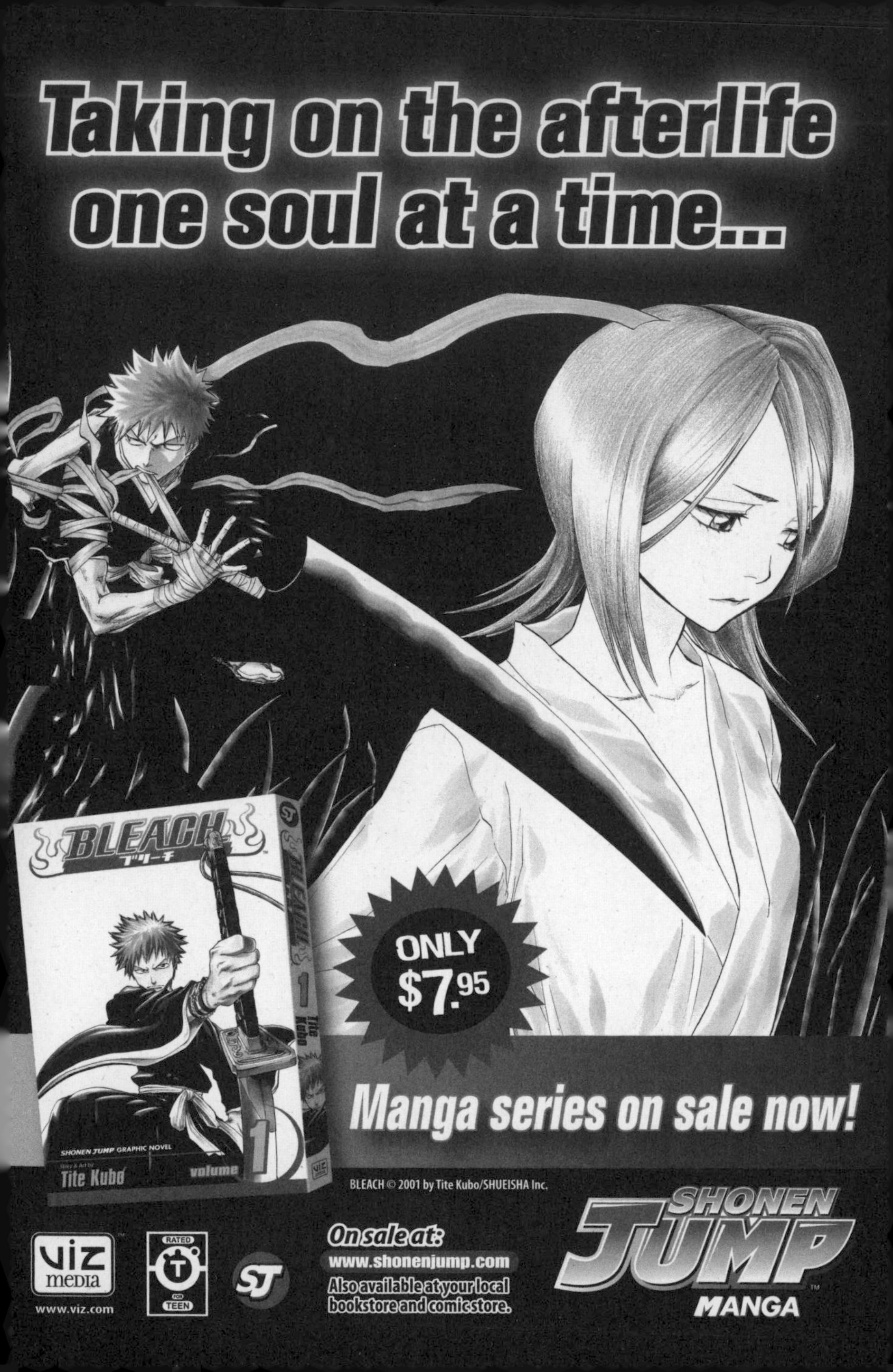

Taking on the afterlife one soul at a time...
BLEACH
ブリーチ
SHONEN JUMP GRAPHIC NOVEL
Tite Kubo
volume 1
ONLY $7.95
Manga series on sale now!
BLEACH © 2001 by Tite Kubo/SHUEISHA Inc.
viz media
www.viz.com
RATED T FOR TEEN
On sale at:
www.shonenjump.com
Also available at your local bookstore and comic store.
SHONEN JUMP MANGA

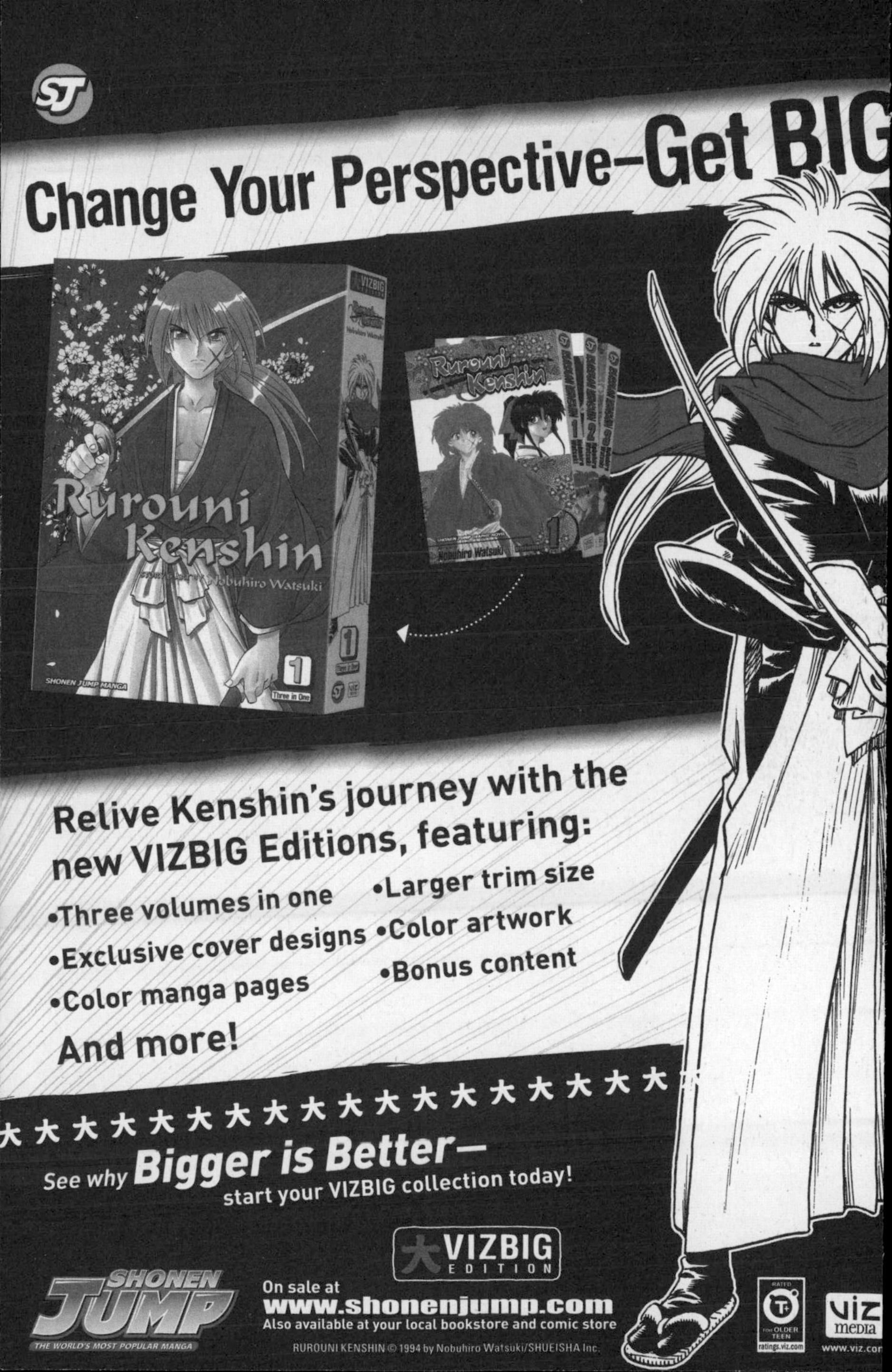
Change Your Perspective–Get BIG
Rurouni Kenshin
Nobuhiro Watsuki
SHONEN JUMP MANGA
1
Three in One
Relive Kenshin's journey with the new VIZBIG Editions, featuring:
•Three volumes in one
•Larger trim size
•Exclusive cover designs
•Color artwork
•Color manga pages
•Bonus content
And more!
See why Bigger is Better—
start your VIZBIG collection today!
VIZBIG EDITION
SHONEN JUMP
THE WORLD'S MOST POPULAR MANGA
On sale at
www.shonenjump.com
Also available at your local bookstore and comic store
RUROUNI KENSHIN © 1994 by Nobuhiro Watsuki/SHUEISHA Inc.
RATED T+ FOR OLDER TEEN
ratings.viz.com
viz media
www.viz.com

Tell us what you think about SHONEN JUMP manga!

Our survey is now available online.
Go to: **www.SHONENJUMP.com/mangasurvey**

Help us make our product offering better!

THE REAL ACTION STARTS IN...

SHONEN JUMP
THE WORLD'S MOST POPULAR MANGA
www.shonenjump.com

SJ ADVANCED

SJ

VIZ media